NEW PLAYWRIGHTS
The Best Plays of 1998

NEW PLAYWRIGHTS

The Best Plays
of 1998

CONTEMPORARY PLAYWRIGHTS
SERIES

SK
A Smith and Kraus Book

A Smith and Kraus Book
Published by Smith and Kraus, Inc.
PO Box 127, Lyme, NH 03768
www.SmithKraus.com

First Edition: March 2000
10 9 8 7 6 5 4 3 2 1

The Library of Congress Cataloging-In-Publication Data

New Playwrights: the best plays of 1998. —1st ed.
p. cm. — (Contemporary playwrights series)
Contents: Introduction/by Romulus Linney—The job/by Shem Bitterman—Nobody dies of Friday/by Robert Brustein—Snakebit/by David Marshall Grant—Killer Joe/by Tracy Letts—The one-eyed man is king/ by Carter W. Lewis—Bobby Supreme/by J.B. Miller—The uneasy chair/by Evan Smith.
ISBN 1-57525-171-X
1. American drama—20th century. I. Series.
PS634.N416 2000
812'.5408—dc21   00-029707

CONTENTS

INTRODUCTION

This substantial and adventurous volume, presented to us by Smith and Kraus, who continue to publish for the theatre where others fear to tread, will take the lover of new plays into uncharted and rewarding territories. Reading a new play, often by a new playwright, is a vigorous business that demands a reader's attention and insight, but the rewards are many, and there are lots of them here.

In *The Job,* by Shem Bitterman, murderous, suicidal, amorous, and treacherous cross-purposes run into each other in brisk, eloquent dialogue. David Marshall Grant's *Snakebit* will take you into the comic squalor of Los Angeles wannabee actors, which then begins to be played out against an emerging, darker, and deeper reality. Constant amazement is the hallmark of *Killer Joe,* for its characters as well as its readers, as the Tracy Letts trailer trash vision of remorseless brutality both horrifies and delights at once. Carter W. Lewis, in *The One-Eyed Man is King,* taken from a story by H.G. Wells, unfolds a sleek fable about the mysteries of the seen and the unseen. *Bobby Supreme* is J.B. Miller's caustic portrait of the performance artist as a modern Pal Joey with a blistering up-to-date vocabulary. In *The Uneasy Chair,* Evan Smith explores odd realities concealed in past customs of marriage and divorce, whose repetitions ,even as we speak, makes an old-fashioned comedy all too modern. And Robert Brustein adds to his many achievements *Nobody Dies on Friday,* seeing Lee Strasberg and his first wife and children not as blighted theatre royalty but as a real family struggling with love, resentment, a terrible lust for fame, and a deeply questionable generosity to a dangerous and helpless giant, Marilyn Monroe.

Energy and originality, the two vital forces of any good new play, await you. Enjoy.

Romulus Linney

THE JOB
by Shem Bitterman

To Cindy

"A picture held us captive, and we could not get outside it, for it lay in our language and language seemed to repeat it to us inexorably."

Ludwig Wittgenstein,
Philosophical Investigations

THE AUTHOR

Shem Bitterman has his M.F.A. from the University of Iowa Playwright's Workshop and is an alumnus of The High School of Performing Arts in New York and The Julliard School, where he studied acting. In November 1998, he directed the world premiere of his play *The Job* (developed at The Midwest Playlabs and winner of the 1997 Stanley Award) for Circus Theatricals at The Hudson Guild in Los Angeles, and in June 1999 at the WPA Theatre in New York. *The Job* won the coveted 1998 Schmitt Award for World Premiere of an Outstanding New Play and was nominated for Best Production and Best Performance by the LA Critics Circle and for Best Play, Best Ensemble, and Best Performance in the LA Weekly Awards. Other produced plays include *A.K.A.; A Beverly Hills Musical Morality Tale,* an adaptation of Wedekind's *Marquis of Keith* for Cornerstone Theatre Company's BH project; *survivors* and *Buffalo Hunters,* both at the Mark Taper Forum's New Works Festival; *Justice* at the Padua Hills Playwrights Festival in Los Angeles; *Ten Below* at the WPA (and developed at Sundance); *Peephole* at GeVa in Rochester, New York (and adapted into a film with Shem directing); *Night-Side* at The Actor's Theatre of Louisville; *The Ramp* at South Coast Rep; *Beijing Legends* at the Taper's New Works Festival and the Pacific Jewish Theatre in Berkeley, California (and winner of the Fund For New American Plays); *Self Storage* (with Tony Spiridakis) at the Taper's New Works Festival and The Odyssey Theatre in Los Angeles (and as the film *Tinseltown*); and *Iowa Boys* at the Actor's Studio in New York. He has won numerous awards, including The California Playwrights Competition, The National Play Award, The White Dove Award, Mixed Blood Versus America and the CBS/FDG New Play Award. He recently completed the screenplay for *Off the Lip,* which shot November, 1999 in Hawaii. Currently Shem is adapting David and Daniel Hayes' *My Old Man and The Sea* for Dreamworks SKG and developing *The Circle,* a play about youth violence, commissioned by the Taper. For the past several years he has taught screenwriting and playwriting in a maximum security prison in California.

ORIGINAL PRODUCTION

The Job was originally produced by Circus Theatricals (Jack Stehlin, Artistic Director/Jeannine Welles, Producing Director) at the Hudson Guild Theater in Los Angeles in November, 1998 with the following cast:

Frank	Barry Cullison
John	Robert Cicchini
Mags	Deborah Offner
Jim	Jack Stehlin
Martin	Daniel Nathan Spector

It was produced in New York City by the WPA Theatre (Kyle Renick, Artistic Director/Lori Sherman, Managing Director) in June, 1999 with the following cast:

Frank	Barry Cullison
John	Robert Cicchini
Mags	Deborah Offner
Jim	Jack Stehlin
Martin	Ron Orbach

Both productions were directed by Shem Bitterman.

ACT I

A stage, all but bare. Fragments of real things are broken and doubled. A clock which spins like a wheel of fortune, a pulpit echoing the bow of a ship, a bed that's also a grave. The dim outline of a huge tent overhead. Calliope music plays. The lights come up. A job agency. Bright but dingy. John at work. Frank seated opposite.

JOHN: Name.

FRANK: Brand.

JOHN: B-R-.

FRANK: A-N-D-.

JOHN: Skills?

FRANK: No.

JOHN: No skills?

FRANK: I'm a quick learner. Whatever I put my mind to. I'm a fast study.

JOHN: Previous employment?

FRANK: Been on the road.

JOHN: No previous employment?

FRANK: Yard work.

JOHN: Yard work?

FRANK: Field work. Yard work.

JOHN: And that's—?

FRANK: Lifting. Hauling.

JOHN: Hauling?

FRANK: And lifting.

JOHN: Boxes?

FRANK: Boxes. Crates. Barrels. Bags.

JOHN: Bags?

FRANK: Of stuff. Junk.

JOHN: Sanitation—

FRANK: Trash. Yeah. Well. That and—

JOHN: Those jobs are—

FRANK: —other things.

JOHN: —hard to come by. And you're—

FRANK: What? I'm—

JOHN: —not young. How old are you anyway?

FRANK: Forty.

JOHN: Forty?

FRANK: Five. I. I really don't remember.

JOHN: Really?

FRANK: I never…really knew.

JOHN: I see.

FRANK: Yes. And—

JOHN: What?

FRANK: My back. I. I'm not really good for that anymore. Lifting. Hauling. That type of…

JOHN: I see. Well, in that case— *(John starts for the door, to show Frank out.) (Frank holds John.)*

FRANK: I just need a chance. I'll do anything.

(Beat.)

JOHN: Your—uh.

FRANK: What?

JOHN: Your hands.

FRANK: Oh. Sorry. *(Frank lets go.)*

JOHN: I couldn't help but notice—

FRANK: I. Was a boxer.

JOHN: Ah.

FRANK: Look, I'm sorry—I'm sorry I—

JOHN: No, no—

FRANK: —wasted your—

JOHN: No. Wait. I—

FRANK: What?

JOHN: I…think I…may be able to help you. *(Pause.)* Sit down. Please. *(Frank sits. John returns to his desk. Slight pause.)*

JOHN: Can you type?

(Frank shakes his head.)

JOHN: Alphabetize?

FRANK: Are you asking, can I read?

JOHN: Can you?

FRANK: Yes.

JOHN: Good. Good.

FRANK: I can read.

JOHN: Good. That's good. What about driving? Can you drive?

FRANK: A car?

JOHN: Yes. A car.

FRANK: I can drive a car.

JOHN: Ride a bike?

FRANK: I can ride a bike too.

JOHN: What about a horse? Can you master a horse?

FRANK: I don't—

JOHN: Never mind. Doesn't matter. As long as you can walk.

FRANK: I can definitely walk.

JOHN: Some people can't, you know.

FRANK: No, I—

JOHN: Some can't. Some WON'T.

FRANK: So you think there may be a—?

JOHN: Some won't do anything. Welfare cases. Just there to waste your time.

FRANK: I want to work.

JOHN: There may be a chance.

FRANK: Really?

JOHN: I don't want to get your hopes up, but there may be. Can you come back tomorrow at this time?

FRANK: Really?

JOHN: You can deliver, right? You can read addresses?

FRANK: Yeah. Yes!

JOHN: All right. Good. That's very, very good. I think we're going to get along fine.

FRANK: Good. Thanks. Thank you. *(Frank stands to go, hesitates, wets his lips.)*

JOHN: What?

FRANK: Do you mind? I'm wondering if—uh.

JOHN: Go on?

FRANK: Nothing. Never mind.

JOHN: Oh. I understand. Here. *(John goes into his pocket. Pulls out a ten. Hands it to Frank.)*

FRANK: That's generous. Thank you.

JOHN: Don't worry about it.

FRANK: I never do this. I'm just.

JOHN: You're hungry.

FRANK: Yes.

JOHN: I know what it's like to be hungry. Not to have work.

FRANK: Can I take your address?

JOHN: That's not necessary.

FRANK: I'll send it back.

JOHN: Bring it in if you really want to. But it really doesn't matter.

FRANK: …you can trust me. *(Beat. Frank turns.)*

JOHN: Wait. Mr. Brand. Take this as well.

> *(Frank holds it up to the light. It dangles at the end of its chain. Frank looks at John.)*

JOHN: I noticed you weren't wearing one.

> *(Frank reaches for the pocket watch. Lights shift. Park Bench. Mags is there. Traffic passes.)*

MAGS: Where you been?

> *(Frank pockets the watch. Starts down towards Mags. He pulls a wrapped sandwich from his jacket pocket. Its enormous. He unwraps it and begins devouring it. Mags laughs.)*

MAGS: You're hungry anyway.

FRANK: Been out hunting up a job.

MAGS: Find one?

FRANK: Got a lead.

MAGS: You did, huh?

FRANK: Yeah. I did.

MAGS: Wanna share?

> *(Frank breaks off a piece. Mags just looks at it.)*

MAGS: I mean the lead.

FRANK: No.

MAGS: Why not? Think I'm gonna take it from you? I'm not gonna take it from you. I don't want your lousy job.

FRANK: You don't, huh?

MAGS: I don't want it. I don't need it. I been working myself.

FRANK: Doin' what?

MAGS: None of your business.

FRANK: That means nothing.

MAGS: No, it doesn't mean nothing. It means what it says. None of your business. *(Off his look.)* What?

FRANK: You never worked a day in your life.

MAGS: Not 'cause I'm not willing. I just don't like schedules. If they came up with a job that didn't involve schedules, I'd be working in a second.

FRANK: I can think of plenty 'a jobs like that.

MAGS: Name one.

FRANK: Fry cook.

MAGS: Fry cook opens up. Closes down. Gotta keep a schedule.

FRANK: Word processing.

MAGS: Deadlines.

FRANK: How about nursing? Good benefits.

MAGS: Long hours.

FRANK: Teacher.

MAGS: Forty minute periods.

FRANK: You don't wanna do a thing. You think you're a Goddamn princess.

MAGS: I'd sell drugs.

FRANK: What!?

MAGS: I could be my own boss at least.

FRANK: Oh, that's great!

MAGS: You got a problem with that?

FRANK: Yeah. Is that what you're doing now?

MAGS: No. Can't break in.

FRANK: All right, so what's the mystery gig?

MAGS: Has to do with personal charms.

FRANK: No, Mags.

MAGS: What?

FRANK: Say no.

MAGS: You don't think I have personal charms?

FRANK: I think. Sadly. No.
    (She hits him.)

MAGS: That's a nice thing to say!

FRANK: I say it with love in my heart.

MAGS: You mean that?

FRANK: In a manner of speaking.
    (She hits him.)

MAGS: You're a brute.

FRANK: *(Smiles.)* Yeah, I guess I am.

MAGS: You comin' by? I'll take the night off.

FRANK: Can't.

MAGS: Why?

FRANK: Don't wanna screw up.

MAGS: Screw up?

FRANK: The job.

MAGS: What's that gotta do with comin' by?

FRANK: Gotta be rested. Top form.

MAGS: You know you got no other place to stay. *(Ties Frank's shoe.)* How come
    you're so proud all the time?

FRANK: I'll come by, okay.

MAGS: Right!

FRANK: I promise. I'll be there.

MAGS: I'll let my hair down for you.

FRANK: I'll take you anyway I can get you.

MAGS: Charmer.

FRANK: You make it easy.

MAGS: Go on, get outta here. And stop being in such a good mood!

FRANK: I love you.

MAGS: You're a kid, Frank. Still.

FRANK: Don't.

MAGS: What?

FRANK: Call me that, okay.

MAGS: A kid?

FRANK: Frank. Nobody around here knows me by that…

MAGS: Sure. Fine. Whatever.

FRANK: I'll see you.

> *(Mags stops him, holds him.)*

MAGS: Don't be a stranger.

> *(Frank goes. Mags looks after him. Lights shift. Pulpit. Frank listens as Jim, dressed as a priest, speaks out.)*

JIM: I saw them rise up and stagger onto the deck. Lost souls! And the fire of a setting sun was terrible against that sky. Hurricanes. Tornadoes. Fish with two heads or five eyes. All of nature and the cosmos was in rebellion against the fateful ebbing of that day. The broken masthead bobbing up and down, and up and down. The waters too rough for the ship to touch the shore. They had to put back out to sea.

> *(Frank starts to leave.)*

JIM: Be not afraid, the angels called unto them. The Lord will comfort you and watch over you. And you will be reawakened. The dawn will come and reawaken you. The sun will rise up again for you. And light will be everywhere. They fell to their knees and prayed. And the waters raged as the storm came. And the ship lost its bearings and crashed against the rocks. And many were lost. And fear was upon them. Their wills were all but spent. And they leaned upon the staff of law and called up to an empty sky from which the hard rain fell. And many died. And many went unanswered. And they forgot the angels, forgot how to kneel, how to pray. They were lost in an unending darkness, without the possibility of light.

> *(Blackout. Lights dim up. Backstage. Jim drinks as he removes his coat. Frank stands in the door.)*

FRANK: I didn't think it was you at first.

JIM: Enjoy yourself?

FRANK: You had me scared there for a minute. You looked real.

JIM: Who says I'm not?

FRANK: What happened to aluminum siding?

JIM: It was a bust. Different times you know.

FRANK: Revival meetings—?

JIM: Got to keep meat on the table.

FRANK: You don't look like you got any complaints, anyway. You're raking it in. I saw 'em shovin' it in the basket. Just from you saying stuff.

JIM: That money was for the Lord.

FRANK: Right.

JIM: I'm serious. Grab a fistful.

(Frank hesitates.)

JIM: Go on.

(Frank does.)

JIM: Now throw it up in the air.

(Frank throws it up. The money flutters down.)

JIM: See. Whatever He grabs He keeps. The rest is mine.

FRANK: Same old Jim.

(Jim pours.)

JIM: Here you go.

FRANK: Thanks. I…uh. I quit.

JIM: You?!

FRANK: Why do you say it like that?

JIM: Sobriety. Just doesn't suit you.

FRANK: Suits me now.

JIM: Yeah. *(Beat.)* It's been a long time, though, hasn't it? Where was it last? Memphis?

FRANK: Kansas City.

JIM: Kansas City! That's right. Running a little scam along the waterfront.

FRANK: I don't do that anymore. I'm goin' straight.

JIM: That so?

FRANK: Yeah. I'm gonna get a job. Tomorrow. I went into one of those agencies.

JIM: Job agencies?

FRANK: Yeah, that's right. And the man said. He said, tomorrow. Maybe.

JIM: I used to run a scam out of an agency.

FRANK: This place is legit.

JIM: Well, congratulations. I'm sure that must make you very proud.

FRANK: It's okay.

> *(Beat.)*

JIM: You see Mags?

FRANK: I see her.

JIM: She's a good woman.

FRANK: Yeah. She is.

> *(Beat.)*

JIM: So how'd you find me?

FRANK: I heard a voice. While I was taking a leak actually. It sounded familiar.

JIM: Did it hypnotize you?

FRANK: Sure. Put me in a trance. Just like it always used to. *(Quotes.)* "Some people are poor and some are ugly—"

JIM: *(Cuts him off.)* "—but *you're both.*" *(Laughing; intones.)* I put my basket in the window of Heaven, at the place of windows where the sky kissed the ground. And I prayed. And when I turned back, my basket was missing, and I said—are there thieves here? *(Gleeful.)* Yes, there are.

FRANK: When I saw you in the outfit, I said…not Jim.

JIM: You were right.

FRANK: Yeah?

JIM: It's Santini now.

FRANK: Santini? Wasn't that a T.V. show?

JIM: Why not? People like something they can relate to. What about you? What're you callin' yourself nowadays?

FRANK: Brand.

> *(Beat.)*

JIM: Just Brand?

FRANK: Mr.

JIM: I'll remember that. Brand. Well, Mr. Brand. I gotta get some shut eye. I got a long day ahead. Exorcisms, Bingo, brownies. Long legged school girls in little plaid skirts…

FRANK: Mind if I, uh. Crash. The shelters all close at ten.

JIM: Shelters, huh? You really are going straight.

FRANK: What do you say?

> *(Beat.)*

JIM: Sure, why not.

FRANK: Thanks.

JIM: Turn around.

FRANK: What?

JIM: *(Waves the money.)* Nothing personal. I still got faith in my fellow man and I kinda wanta to keep it that way.

FRANK: *(Turns; peeks.)* You can trust me, Jim.

JIM: *(Laughs.)* Sure I can. *(Jim hides the money.)* Go on. You can turn back. *(Jim undresses, gets into bed.)* Turn out the light, wouldya.
(Frank crosses to the light.)

FRANK: That stuff you were saying. About the men. In the boat.

JIM: I don't know what I'm sayin' half the time.

FRANK: Sounded like you were talking about me. *(Frank clicks off the light, crosses back to his bed, lays down.)*
(A baby cries. Jim sits up.)

JIM: You hear that?

FRANK: What?

JIM: Some kid…crying. Does that every night. Wanna go out there some day. Find that kid. Tell him to shut the fuck up. *(Jim lays back down.)*

FRANK: You believe in God?

JIM: Sure, why not. Makes the show better. *(Beat.)* Go to sleep.
(Frank takes out the watch, runs it along his sleeve.)

FRANK: I used to have a canary. Crawled up one arm, swung off the hairs of my neck, then crawled down the other…really brightened things up.

JIM: What happened to it?

FRANK: Lost it on a train under a straw hat I forgot to take with me cause I was drunk and illegal.
(Pause.)

JIM: G'night.

FRANK: Yeah. G'night. *(Frank stays awake, staring at the watch.)*
(Blackout. Pause. Lights up. Morning. Jim is gone. Shower noise. Frank spins. Knocks up against a wall. Stops. Listens. Hesitates, then goes for the place where he saw Jim hide the money. Nothing. Toilet flush. Frank runs back to his place. Jim enters, buckling his pants. He sees his mussed stuff, starts to laugh. Frank joins in the laughter. Jim dresses, laughing, then comes and stands before Frank.)

JIM: Time to go, Frank. Nothing personal.

FRANK: I'll come back tomorrow.

JIM: Do us both a favor. Don't.
(Frank looks up at him, ashamed.)

FRANK: I wasn't looking for the money.

JIM: And even if you were…it wasn't there, was it?

FRANK: I could stay with you.

JIM: No room. *(Jim starts out.)*

FRANK: You leaving?

JIM: Close the door behind you.

FRANK: You trust me in your place alone?

> *(Jim is gone. Frank stands alone. Lights shift. Office. John at the desk. Frank is in the door.)*

JOHN: You can pay me back later.

FRANK: Pay you back?

JOHN: My time. My very valuable time.

FRANK: I'm sorry. I don't—

JOHN: You're late. I haven't got all day.

FRANK: I'm sorry. Did you find me something?

JOHN: I did. It's gone now.

FRANK: No!

JOHN: Yes. Coffee?

FRANK: No.

JOHN: No coffee?

FRANK: No.

JOHN: Why?

FRANK: Not thirsty.

JOHN: How come?

FRANK: Don't know.

JOHN: Sit down. Sit.

> *(Frank sits.)*

JOHN: Good.

FRANK: Yes?

JOHN: I've been giving you a lot of thought.

FRANK: Yes? Really?

JOHN: Really. Yes.

FRANK: And—?

JOHN: Your qualities.

FRANK: Yes?

JOHN: Unique.

FRANK: Yes?

JOHN: I like them. I like them a lot. But I'm disappointed.

FRANK: How?

JOHN: Tardiness.

FRANK: I won't let it happen again.

JOHN: Don't.

FRANK: I won't.

JOHN: You can't. Not and work for us. We're exclusive. Very. Very. Exclusive.

FRANK: I appreciate that.

JOHN: Do you? Fully?

FRANK: Yes.

JOHN: Your job is gone.

FRANK: No.

JOHN: Yes. It's gone. But there may be another job. There just may. If—

FRANK: If—?

JOHN: I can depend on you.

FRANK: Depend on me how?

JOHN: Ah.

FRANK: Ah?

JOHN: Ah. Yes. Ah. That's everything.

FRANK: What's everything? I'm not—

JOHN: No?

FRANK: —understanding you. Completely, I mean. I mean. Completely.

JOHN: Do you want me to speak clearer?

FRANK: Yes. I. No. I. That is.

JOHN: Say it. Don't spare my feelings.

FRANK: Yes. Please.

JOHN: Be in your time. If you're out of your time, you're out. Out.

FRANK: *(Hesitates, uncertain.)* All right.

JOHN: Now, this job…

FRANK: Yes! The job. That's what I'm here about. That's what I need.

JOHN: You need it?

FRANK: Yes.

JOHN: How bad?

FRANK: Bad.

JOHN: But how?

FRANK: Very.

JOHN: It's delicate.

FRANK: That's all right.

JOHN: Is it?

FRANK: Yes. Yes.

JOHN: It's hard. Nowadays. I don't have to tell you. I know. You know. It's
    hard. Very. Very. Hard. People are desperate. They want to work. I can't
    accommodate them all. I can't accommodate the whole fucking planet.
    I wish I could. I wish. I could. I can't. I can't. I can't. I wish I could give

them all something to do, but there are too many. Everywhere. Wanting to do. To do something. But no. I can't. I can only help a special few. A very special few. As a precondition for offering assistance in my capacity as a representative for this organization I demand what I consider to be an absolutely minimal, reasonable request.

FRANK: Yes?

JOHN: I demand loyalty. Absolute loyalty.

FRANK: I thought this was an agency.

JOHN: It is. What makes you think it's not an agency?

FRANK: …nothing.

 (Beat.)

JOHN: I can assist you if you'll let me. But if you want to go out on your own, without my assistance, then look. *(Pulls out a thick stack of folders.)* All these people are ahead of you. Most are younger or stronger or more alert. Some have college degrees. Some have Masters, even PHDs. And still no jobs.

FRANK: Times are hard.

JOHN: That's right. Times are hard. And why should one person get a leg up over another?

FRANK: Suitability?

JOHN: Loyalty.

FRANK: What exactly does that mean?

JOHN: It means if I ask you to do something, you'll do it. Even if it seems wrong. You'll trust me. You'll have faith in me.

FRANK: I don't know.

JOHN: You don't want to miss another opportunity. You don't want to lose your place. Be out of your time. Be here now, Mr. Brand. Be here now.

FRANK: I have to think. *(Frank goes.)*

 (Lights shift. Jim stands at the pulpit.)

JIM: The flesh is lost in the perspective of time. The skin grows white and unhealthy. Man loses his way, groping in the darkness for salvation. Where does he turn, but to licentiousness? To crime, to satisfy his needs. To drugs, to mask the truth from himself. He sacrifices morals. Ethics. He loses dignity, self respect. He loses identity. He becomes a victim of events spiraling beyond his control. He has lost his purpose, his place. Time rushes on without him. He can do nothing but apologize—

 (Lights shift. Mags' tiny place. Frank in the door. Mags has been drinking.)

FRANK: I'm sorry.

MAGS: Sorry?

FRANK: Can I sleep a while?

MAGS: Sleep.

FRANK: I meant to call.

MAGS: Call.

FRANK: What's wrong?

MAGS: Wrong?

FRANK: Stop it, okay.

MAGS: Okay.

FRANK: Mags—

MAGS: Mags.

FRANK: Stop.

MAGS: Stop.

FRANK: Stop!

MAGS: Stop!

FRANK: All right. I'll go.

MAGS: Wait.

FRANK: What?

MAGS: Wait. *(She kisses him, reaches for his belt.)*
    (He pulls away.)

FRANK: Don't.

MAGS: Why?

FRANK: Tired.

MAGS: Always.

FRANK: So?

MAGS: So where were you?

FRANK: Out.

MAGS: Job no good?

FRANK: It's okay. I haven't heard yet. Still waiting. Still on hold.

MAGS: I know.

FRANK: How do you know?! What do you know?! You haven't worked a fuck-
    ing day in your life!!

MAGS: I work. *(Beat.)* I just don't work.

FRANK: What the fuck does that mean?!

MAGS: It means what it means. Why you have to be so hard on me? I'm the
    one who waited. I'm the one who got stood up.

FRANK: I'm sorry.

MAGS: You're always sorry.

FRANK: I know.

MAGS: What's wrong with us?

FRANK: I don't know. I wish I did. I don't.

MAGS: It's you. It's not me.

FRANK: I know. It's me. I'm the bad guy.

MAGS: I waited anyway.

FRANK: I know. You waited. I fucked up. I—

MAGS: What?

FRANK: I just didn't want to come back. I wasn't ready. I…

MAGS: We can't keep playing around like we're kids. We're not kids anymore.

FRANK: I know. We're not kids.

MAGS: I wanna get married.

FRANK: Don't. Mags.

MAGS: Why? Why?!

FRANK: Cause how can I when I—

MAGS: What? When you what?!

FRANK: When I haven't got a job. When I haven't got a job, okay. I don't even know who I am. Some days I think I do, then I turn around and everything changes. I think I should be somewhere else. Or somehow else. Or something… *(A moment passes.)* Did you make anything?

MAGS: What am I gonna make, huh? Who's gonna stop for me?

FRANK: I stop.

MAGS: You never stay.

FRANK: I always come back.

MAGS: You never change.

FRANK: I want to. You know I do.

MAGS: Marry me. It's been too many years. Marry me.

FRANK: God.

MAGS: What?

FRANK: I shoulda been the one to ask.

MAGS: It doesn't matter.

FRANK: Let me get something together first. I wanna get you a ring. Buy you a house.

MAGS: That stuff doesn't matter.

FRANK: It matters to me. I want a wife in a house. I want a ring on her finger. That's what I want.

MAGS: Kiss me.

FRANK: I'll stay. This time. I promise.

MAGS: Frank.

FRANK: Shhh.

MAGS: Let's watch T.V.

FRANK: Do we have one?

MAGS: No.

FRANK: So how we gonna watch it then?

MAGS: Close your eyes. I'll show you.

> (*She smiles, seductive. Lights fade to black. Lights dim up. Street. John is waiting. Frank appears.*)

JOHN: Looks who's here. I'd just about given up on you.

FRANK: The job.

JOHN: What job?

FRANK: Don't. You know what I'm talking about. It is still available?

JOHN: As luck would have it. Yes.

FRANK: Good then. I'll take it. Whatever it is.

JOHN: Then you trust me, Mr. Brand?

FRANK: I trust you.

JOHN: You'll do whatever I say?

FRANK: …yeah.

JOHN: Good. Shake my hand on it.

> (*They shake. Frank tries to pull away, but John keeps hold of him.*)

JOHN: That's a pact. That's binding. Like a contract. A verbal contract, but enforceable. It might as well have been written in blood. (*John pulls a slip of paper from his breast pocket, hands it to Frank.*)

JOHN: Here you go.

> (*Frank studies it.*)

JOHN: You said you could read.

FRANK: I'll be there.

JOHN: Be on time. You don't want to lose your place. (*John goes.*)

> (*Frank looks after him, then down at the paper. Lights shift. Mags' apartment. Night. Mags in bed. Frank stands over her. He kisses her back. Butterfly kisses. Starts out. She wakes.*)

MAGS: Frank? (*Sits up.*) Where are you going?

FRANK: Job interview.

MAGS: It's late. Jesus. It must be one.

FRANK: That's when the interview is.

MAGS: A job interview at one A.M.?

FRANK: Yeah.

MAGS: What kind of a job?

FRANK: I don't know.

MAGS: Why don't you know?

FRANK: I don't know.

MAGS: Don't you want to know?

FRANK: That's why I'm going.

MAGS: Where did you find this job?

FRANK: Employment agency.

MAGS: What kind of an employment agency has interviews at one in the morning?

FRANK: I don't know. This one.

MAGS: What's its name?

FRANK: Can't say.

MAGS: Why? Why can't you say?

FRANK: Promised.

MAGS: Who? Who did you promise?

FRANK: I gotta go.

MAGS: Don't, all right.

FRANK: I have to.

MAGS: Why? I'll talk care of you. Why don't you let me take care of you?

FRANK: With what?

MAGS: I can work too.

FRANK: Where?

MAGS: I'll find something.

FRANK: I'm tired.

MAGS: Come to bed.

FRANK: No time.

MAGS: Please, Frank.

FRANK: You said you wanted us to get together. You still feel that way?

MAGS: Yes.

FRANK: Good.

MAGS: You mean—?

FRANK: I'm doing this for us. For the future. (*He takes out his pocket watch, checks the hour.*)

MAGS: Frank? Where'd you get that?

(*He pockets it.*)

FRANK: I love you.

(*He goes. She looks after him. Blackout. Lights fade up. A warehouse. A hanging light. Frank is looking at his watch. Martin and John sit at a table, opposite him. Rhythmic hum of machinery like the ticking of a clock, nearby.*)

JOHN: You have to remember to wind it, Mr. Brand, otherwise this will keep happening.

(Frank winds the watch, pockets it.)

FRANK: Have I missed it? Is the job still available?

JOHN: Oh, yes.

FRANK: Good. *(Beat.)* Who's your friend?

JOHN: Name's Martin.

FRANK: What's he doing here?

JOHN: He wanted to be here.

FRANK: I see.

JOHN: It's not a problem, is it?

FRANK: He the boss?

JOHN: Actually, you'll be accountable to me.

FRANK: What does he do then?

JOHN: It's kind of a sore point.

MARTIN: I used to be an engineer.

FRANK: You don't work anymore?

MARTIN: You see!

JOHN: It's all right, Martin. *(To Frank.)* He's a little skittish. *(To Martin.)* You're all right, Martin?

MARTIN: I'm fine. I'm all right.

JOHN: Good. *(To Frank.)* Let's talk about what you're going to do.

FRANK: With him here?

JOHN: Yeah. With him here. See, he's part of it.

FRANK: Part of it how?

JOHN: Do you want to tell, Martin, or shall I?

MARTIN: You tell. And I'll have that cigarette now, John. What's it matter now, right?

(John and Martin share a laugh. John hands Martin a cigarette. Martin lights up.)

JOHN: This is how it all happened. You see, Martin here came in to see me about a job.

MARTIN: I came to see John about a job. I was desperate.

JOHN: You remember I told you about the desperate people. The desperate people looking for a job.

MARTIN: Employers don't want you if you've been let go. They don't understand. If you were doing a good job, why don't you have it now? Sure, times are tough, companies downsize, but a good worker is always valued, always retained. And the longer you're out of work the less your chances are of ever going back. There's a stigma. People don't like the stigma.

JOHN: I tried with Martin but I couldn't do anything. It isn't always easy. Months passed, and Martin didn't want to go on unemployment.

MARTIN: What good would it do? It's not enough.

JOHN: Now Martin's concerned about his family.

MARTIN: I have two children and a wife. I have a house. A nice house. We bought it when I was making good money. It's supposed to be good to be a home-owner. Security for the future. But now we're trapped.

JOHN: Martin was a proud home-owner. But Martin was out of a job. He had no way to pay the bills. And yet there was one ray of hope.

MARTIN: It's for the kids. I don't want them living in a cardboard box. It's for their future.

JOHN: We need someone with strong hands. Someone who understands what the situation…requires.

FRANK: I don't —

JOHN: I know what happened…Frank.

FRANK: How do you know my name?!

JOHN: I know about your past. I checked your references.

FRANK: I didn't come with any references.

JOHN: You're the man for the job.

FRANK: What job!? What the fuck are you talking about?

JOHN: You see, Martin was thinking he'd like to be murdered.

(Pause.)

FRANK: I. Uh.

JOHN: Are you afraid?

FRANK: I'm not afraid!

JOHN: Then what's the problem?

FRANK: You said something about deliveries!

JOHN: You wanted me to place you, I'm placing you!

(Beat.)

FRANK: I don't want it.

MARTIN: He says he doesn't want it!

JOHN: What are you going to do for money, Frank?

MARTIN: I'd take the job if someone offered it to me!

JOHN: Martin needs to find a man.

MARTIN: I need to find a man.

JOHN: He's looking to hire someone.

MARTIN: I need a man.

JOHN: If not you then some other.

MARTIN: A worker. *(Throws up hands; frustrated.)* It's a mercy killing, for
    Christ's sake.

JOHN: Yes, and poverty's a grind. *(Glances at Martin, then back to Frank.)* No,
    no. I'm sorry, Frank. You did say you trusted me.

FRANK: I did, but—

JOHN: And you agreed to do whatever I asked.

FRANK: Yeah, but—

JOHN: We *shook,* Frank. You can't go back now.
    (Frank looks down at his hand.)

JOHN: *(Reasonably.)* Now, there can't be any connection.

MARTIN: No connection whatsoever.

JOHN: It's got to look random.

MARTIN: They won't pay if it's a suicide.

JOHN: The pay is good.

MARTIN: The price is nonnegotiable.

JOHN: I just take a ten percent commission.

MARTIN: John's been very considerate.

JOHN: The rest goes into your pocket.

MARTIN: But I won't pay more. I need that money. *(Beat; softly.)* You'll do it
    with your bare hands. It's safer. There can be no mistaking it for a sui-
    cide.

JOHN: Have a cigarette, Frank.

FRANK: I don't...smoke.

JOHN: Start. *(John puts a cigarette in Frank's mouth. Lights it.)*
    *(Frank inhales. Blackout. Lights fade up. Mags'. Frank is in the open door.
    Mags is in bed, asleep. Frank squats, watching her.)*

MAGS: Frank?

FRANK: Yeah. It's me.

MAGS: How'd it go?

FRANK: All right.

MAGS: Did you get the job?

FRANK: Yeah. I got the job.

MAGS: That's good. When do you start?

FRANK: Tomorrow night.

MAGS: Is it a night job?

FRANK: Yeah. It's a night job.

MAGS: I'll miss you, Frank.

FRANK: I'll miss you, too.

MAGS: I'm sorry I got angry at you. Before. Sometimes you just hurt me so much. I get so lonely for you.

FRANK: I miss you too.

MAGS: Come into bed, why don't you?

FRANK: I will in a minute. *(Pause.)* You sleeping?

MAGS: *(Murmers.)* Goodnight.

FRANK: G'night. *(He places a blanket over her, starts to leave.)*
(She turns.)

MAGS: Is that cigarette smoke?
(Blackout. Wind blows fiercely. A storm is coming up. Lights fade up on Jim's place. Frank watches Jim sleep. Jim opens his eyes.)

JIM: Frank? *(Jim sits up.)* What are you doing here?

FRANK: I wanted to talk with you.

JIM: What time is it? *(Checks his watch.)* Shit.

FRANK: I want to make a confession.

JIM: I'm no priest.

FRANK: I don't know a real one.

JIM: Well, find one, cause I'm asleep. It's four A.M.

FRANK: It's important.

JIM: I thought I told you to get lost.

FRANK: I brought you something.

JIM: I don't drink after I've already passed out.

FRANK: Please.

JIM: Come back in the morning.

FRANK: It can't wait that long.

JIM: Why?

FRANK: I gotta talk to somebody.

JIM: All right. *Jesus! (He clicks on the light, squints in its glare.)* Christ, you look like shit.

FRANK: I was at Mags'. I couldn't sleep.

JIM: Where's the bottle?
(Frank hands it over.)

JIM: Rot gut.

FRANK: It's the best I can afford.

JIM: You gotta lotta nerve comin' back here after that stunt you pulled.

FRANK: I went on the interview tonight.

JIM: What interview?

FRANK: For the job. Remember. I told you—

JIM: Yeah, yeah.

FRANK: Anyway, I got it, I got the job.

JIM: So congratulations.

FRANK: No, listen. I got the job. But the job is—

JIM: What?

FRANK: The job's no good. For me, I mean. And now there's no way out of it. I had already said I would take it, see. And this guy's holding me to it.

JIM: Did you sign a contact?

FRANK: It's no joke. This guy, he works at this agency. But I'm telling you, this guy means business. I don't know what to do.

JIM: I thought this agency was on the up and up.

FRANK: So did I.

JIM: What's the job?

FRANK: Will you do it for me?

JIM: How'm I gonna say if I'll do something, I don't even know what it is?

FRANK: Just say.

JIM: I can't.

FRANK: For me.

JIM: I don't give a fuck who it's for, I'm not gonna do a job if I don't know what the job is…

FRANK: It's…it's a burglary.

   (Beat.)

JIM: Yeah?

FRANK: That's all.

JIM: So what's the catch?

FRANK: No catch. Guy needs the insurance money. Will you do it?

   (Beat.)

JIM: You woke me up at fucking four in the morning for this! What the hell's the matter with you!

FRANK: I told you I'm trying to go straight. I'll give you my share.

JIM: What's your share?

FRANK: Five gee.

JIM: Five gee? Seems high.

FRANK: Please, I don't want to die forever.

JIM: Who said you're gonna die forever?

FRANK: Isn't that what happens, when you—?

JIM: When you what?

FRANK: Rob a guy?

   (Jim laughs.)

JIM: You're really something, you know that.

FRANK: *(Grabs him.)* Shut up! It's not funny.

JIM: Okay. Sure. It's not funny.

> *(Frank lets go.)*

JIM: God. You're really wound up.

FRANK: *(Near tears.)* Help me.

JIM: Gimmie the details.

FRANK: *(Can't look at Jim.)* Tomorrow night. Mags' place. There's gonna be a package. In the package there's gonna be an address. I'm supposed to break in. The guy won't be there. He's goin' out to dinner with his wife, or—Anyway, that's it.

JIM: Five gee?

FRANK: Nonnegotiable.

JIM: Can I trust this guy?

FRANK: You can trust…me.

> *(A moment.)*

JIM: All right. Sure. Why not. If a guy wants to lose his stuff, who am I to say no.

FRANK: Promise?

JIM: Yeah. I said.

> *(Frank grabs the bottle from Jim, takes a long drink.)*

JIM: Hey, what are you—?

> *(Frank brings the bottle down.)*

FRANK: God. I don't know what's wrong with me.

> *(Frank holds the bottle out to Jim. Jim takes it from him. Frank lowers his head to his hands. Wind comes up. Blackout.)*

JIM: Light.

> *(Pin spot up. Pulpit. Jim in his shirtsleeves.)*

JIM: It's what the angels promise. The angels promise light. That's why man loves the angels.

> *(Lights wide. Mags' place. Traffic. Mags is there, opposite Jim. Frank watches.)*

JIM: Lo, Mags.

FRANK: You remember Jim?

MAGS: Sure I remember him. How you been, Jim?

JIM: Been all right. Only the name's not Jim anymore. It's Santini.

MAGS: Santini, huh. Wasn't that a T.V. show?

> *(Jim shrugs.)*

MAGS: What are you doin' here?

JIM: Frank found me. I was passin' through, Mags.

FRANK: We got anything to drink?

MAGS: I'll look. *(Mags goes.)*

JIM: She's lookin' good.

FRANK: She still cares about you, Jim.

JIM: The way it was between us. You remember?

FRANK: Sure.

JIM: You had all the angles back then. Mags too.

FRANK: That's over now.

JIM: Yeah, I guess. But it's still the same. Things like that don't change.

    (Mags comes in with a bottle and two glasses.)

MAGS: Bourbon.

JIM: Hell, yes! Reminds me of the old days. The three of us, drinking. *(Jim offers to Frank.)* Frank?

FRANK: No. Thanks.

JIM: What's 'a matter, Frank?

MAGS: Frank's quit.

JIM: That so?

    (Frank shifts, uncomfortable. Jim pours for Mags, who drinks. Jim drinks.)

JIM: Know what I heard yesterday? The life of a fly is so short that if you see one hittin' at the window and you don't let it out just then, it'll die hittin' at the window. Imagine that. You ever see 'em after they die? Got their legs all nice and folded together like a perfect star. Like the star of Bethlehem…

FRANK: Jim's preachin' now.

MAGS: You were always a good talker.

JIM: Yeah, I talked. Never said much though. Not that made a difference with you, anyway.

FRANK: Mags' looking for work, too.

MAGS: Yeah, I go out.

JIM: You're not tricking anymore?

    (Slight pause.)

MAGS: I never did that.

JIM: I thought maybe…maybe you did one time. *(Beat.)* You got a nice place anyway. I like it. I like how spacious it is. And the cool air. Has a nice breeze.

MAGS: We do okay.

JIM: That's all. You don't need to make no excuses.

FRANK: Hon, why don't you see if we got something to feed our guest.

JIM: I'm not hungry.

FRANK: Well, I'll have something…if there is.

> *(Mags goes.)*

FRANK: What are you tryin' to do, Jim?

JIM: Nothing, Frank. Just sittin' here. Just passing the time of day.

> *(There's a knock. They share a look. Frank goes. Mags re-enters with a cereal box.)*

MAGS: Who was that?

JIM: Don't know. Frank went for it anyway.

> *(Mags hands Jim the cereal. Jim holds her arm.)*

JIM: Thanks.

> *(She tries to pull her arm away. Jim keeps hold.)*

JIM: I said, thanks.

> *(They stare at one another. Frank comes in with a package. Jim lets Mags go. She's flustered.)*

MAGS: Whatcha got there, Frank?

FRANK: Just…nothin'. I guess we should go now, huh, Jim.

JIM: We got time.

FRANK: I don't think so.

JIM: Yeah. Maybe you're right. *(He stands.)* Sorry, Mags. Don't like to drink and run.

MAGS: What about work?

FRANK: Jim's gonna drop me.

JIM: Why don't I come back after I drop Frank off? We can continue with our little party.

FRANK: C'mon, Jim. I don't wanna be late.

> *(Mags holds Frank.)*

MAGS: Have a good first night, Frankie.

FRANK: I'll be thinking of you. *(Gestures.)* C'mon, Jim. *(Frank goes.)*

> *(Jim stares at Mags for a moment.)*

JIM: G'bye, Mags. *(He kisses her. Goes.)*

> *(Mags looks after him. Lights shift. Street. Jim and Frank stand in the shadows. Jim is in his preacher's outfit.)*

JIM: That the house?

FRANK: Yeah.

JIM: Give me the tools.

FRANK: …with your hands.

JIM: What are you talking about, Frank?

FRANK: Nothin'. Be careful.

(Jim stares at Frank a moment, then goes. Frank watches the house a while. John steps out of the shadows.)

JOHN: 'Lo, Frank.

(Frank jumps, frightened at the sound of his name.)

JOHN: Surprised? Just me. Making sure you got here all right.

FRANK: I'm here.

JOHN: Where are your tools?

FRANK: Hidden in the bushes. *(Beat.)* Wanna see?

JOHN: That's all right. I trust you.

FRANK: I been watching the house. Just making sure everything's clear.

JOHN: You're not dressed right. A burglar should be dressed in black. Like a preacher. He comes forth in the night.

FRANK: I don't have black.

JOHN: That's too bad. I would have included a uniform in the package. To be deducted later of course from your salary.

FRANK: Look. I said I'd do the job and I will!

JOHN: Don't take it personally. I always check up on my employees their first day of work. Just to make sure everything is running smooth.

FRANK: All right. So you checked up on me. So I'm here. So what.

JOHN: You're a little behind schedule.

FRANK: Yeah, well. It took a while to find.

JOHN: You're always running a little late, aren't you, Frank? Day late and a dollar shy.

(John goes. Frank looks after him. Lights fade. A floor lamp comes up. Martin's place. Martin sits in an easy chair, reading. Jim opens the door, stands in the hall light. Martin looks up, frightened.)

MARTIN: …Frank? *(Sees Jim.)* You're not Frank.

JIM: Sub-contractor.

MARTIN: Did the agency arrange for this?

JIM: I don't know anything about any agency. This is a business deal worked out strictly between Frank and me.

MARTIN: All right, then. But I want you to know, I'm not completely comfortable with this.

JIM: You got any complaints you might wanna lodge 'em up your ass.

MARTIN: That's uncalled for.

JIM: Maybe.

(Pause.)

MARTIN: It's a early still. I thought you'd be coming later.

JIM: I'm here now.

MARTIN: Do you mind…uh…waiting a moment?

JIM: What for?

MARTIN: I need to prepare myself.

    (Pause.)

JIM: Sure. All right. Whatever.

    (Martin pulls out a skullcap and a small velvet bag, from which he removes the tephillin. He begins to wrap it round his arm.)

JIM: What's with the get-up?

MARTIN: It's for the prayer. If I'm going to die, I want to be prepared.

    (Beat.)

JIM: Oh.

MARTIN: What?

JIM: Nothing.

MARTIN: What's wrong?

JIM: Nothing.

MARTIN: I want a professional job. I don't want any pain.

JIM: No. No pain.

MARTIN: With the hands, but no pain. That's the understanding.

JIM: With the hands, huh? *(Beat.)* Yeah. Sure. I get it.

    (Martin prays. Jim enters, eyes the room, winds up opposite Martin, facing him.)

MARTIN: "And it shall be as a sign unto Thee upon my hand, and for a memorial between my eyes, that the law of the Lord shall be in my mouth—" *(Beat.)* Would you mind turning around? I didn't know Frank'd be sending a priest.

JIM: I'm not a priest. Didn't want to be seen, that's all. Matter of expediency. And besides, turning around's against my religion.

MARTIN: It makes me feel uncomfortable to have you watching.

JIM: Why don't you turn that off?

MARTIN: Not allowed to.

JIM: I'll turn it off for you.

MARTIN: Wait! Not just yet. Please…

    (Jim stares at him.)

MARTIN: I'm unarmed. Clearly.

    (A pause. Jim turns to face the wall. Martin prays.)

MARTIN: "For with a strong hand hath the Lord brought Thee out of Israel."

    (Jim peeks.)

MARTIN: Would you mind not watching?

JIM: I don't mean anything by it.

(Martin resumes the prayer.)

MARTIN: "And thou shalt tell thy son in that day, saying: It is because of that which the Lord did for me when I came forth out of—"

(Jim goes for a silver tray on the mantle. He pulls out a bag.)

MARTIN: What are you doing?

JIM: Huh?

MARTIN: That isn't yours.

JIM: You want it to look real, don't you? I have to take stuff. Those insurance guys aren't gonna pay off if it doesn't look real.

MARTIN: Can't you make it seem like you got scared and ran off without taking anything?

JIM: Cold blooded killer like me?

MARTIN: It's an heirloom.

JIM: What good is it to you where you're going?

MARTIN: It's just. It's been in the family for generations. Please. There's a stereo downstairs.

JIM: Killing a guy for a stereo?

MARTIN: I've read worse.

JIM: You're right. Okay, let's do it.

MARTIN: Wait! Let me finish. I didn't finish.

(A moment. Jim considers. He turns to face the wall. Martin remains silent.)

JIM: What now?

(Pause.)

MARTIN: I…uh…forgot the prayer for a moment.

(Jim waits.)

MARTIN: I…uh. I've been reading the Messianic texts. Rereading them, actually. According to the Jewish calendar we're in the twilight era of man. We've got another two thousand years before the coming of the Messiah. So where does that leave us, huh? Maybe that's why I feel like I'm out of my time. I imagine many people feel like this. Out of their time. Caught up in the wheel of history. Bound to a fate in opposition to their faith…which should be timeless. For example, I've never felt comfortable with the materialism of my generation, yet I'm sacrificing my life for it—for something I don't even believe in. It's funny. That is, it would be if it weren't so tragic. *(Puts the book aside.)* Look at this. I put the book mark back in The Talmud as if I were going to pick it up again. But of course I won't. I ought to just throw it against the wall or let it drop to the floor. Just open, to the floor. Random. So it looks like I was surprised. I hate to do that to the Talmud. But there. *(Drops the book.)* It's done. We were taught never to treat that book with disrespect. Never to put another book on top of it. Never to burn it. Only to bury it. It's the word of God and the voice of God. Our elders teach us that you can't live without faith. And if you die without faith, they say you die forever. Do you believe that?

(Jim turns on Martin.)

JIM: Let's get this over with. You know the routine.

MARTIN: I do.

JIM: *(Approaches.)* I'm ready to work.

MARTIN: Wait! Just a moment more. Please.

    (Beat.)

MARTIN: Please.

    (Jim walks away, faces the wall.)

MARTIN: What's your name?

JIM: What does it matter?

MARTIN: I want to know.

JIM: You don't need to know my name. You can call me what you want. Call me Santini.

MARTIN: I imagine you've seen your share of hard times, Santini.

JIM: I do all right.

MARTIN: You're lucky. I've never been poor before. I've never had to look at my children and wonder how they'll be able to survive. I never imagined there would come a time when I couldn't provide for my family.

JIM: It happens to the best of us.

MARTIN: *(Beat.)* Santini?

JIM: What?

MARTIN: Turn around. Look at me.

    (Jim turns.)

MARTIN: I don't wanna die.

JIM: Too late. The deal's been struck.

MARTIN: I'm not prepared.

JIM: I just gave you ten minutes.

MARTIN: I've changed my mind.

    (Jim starts forward. Martin circles away.)

MARTIN: Please. I'm not ready. I didn't have time.

JIM: To what? Get away?

MARTIN: To prepare myself.

JIM: Prepare yourself for what? You made a deal.

MARTIN: I want to take it back.

JIM: You can't take it back.

MARTIN: *(Falls to his knees.)* Show mercy. Have pity. I don't want to die for all eternity. I close my eyes I see nothing, forever. I'm frightened for my eternal soul.

JIM: I have a job to do. *(Jim comes forward.)*

MARTIN: Is it about the money? Is that what you're concerned about? Your fee? Because I can pay you. I'll find the money. All fifteen. I'll get it for you. Somehow.

JIM: *(Stops.)* Fifteen?

MARTIN: Fifteen, like we agreed on. Please. Like we agreed on. I'm not trying to shirk my responsibilities. I just don't want to die this way. I close my eyes now and I see nothing. I need a minion. For my salvation.

(Jim begins ransacking the house.)

JIM: *(Vicious.)* Where's the money?!

MARTIN: I'll have it for you! Give me time. I promise. It was a crazy idea. *(Joyous.)* I'm going to live. For my family. For my salvation. I've changed my mind. I've changed my mind!

(Jim eyes him.)

JIM: I made a promise. *(Jim starts towards him, menacing.)*

MARTIN: Oh, God, no. What are you doing?! What are you going to do?! *(He struggles with the tephillin and begins to mouth the prayer as Jim advances.)*

MARTIN: "The Lord is my rock, and my fortress, and my deliverer; In him I take refuge; My Savior, Thou savest me from violence. Praised, I cry, is the Lord, and I am saved from my enemies. For the waves of death compassed me, the floods of Belial assailed me—"

(Jim clicks out the light.)

END ACT I

ACT II

Storm. Lightning. Tent. Frank is drinking. Pacing. Wind. Jim comes in carrying a sack, goes to hide something from it.

FRANK: Jim?

JIM: *(Turns fast.)* Who's there!?

FRANK: It's me. Frank.

JIM: Frank?

FRANK: Yeah. Frank. You know. Frank.

JIM: What are you doin' here, Frank?

FRANK: Waiting.

JIM: Why?

FRANK: I wanted to know…how it all turned out.

 (*Jim comes up for the bottle. Frank flinches. Jim takes the bottle. Drinks deep.*)

JIM: It's done.

FRANK: What do you mean?

JIM: You wanted me to do him, didn't you? So I did him.

FRANK: You—?

JIM: Yeah.

FRANK: How'd he take it?

JIM: He took it.

FRANK: You did it with your hands?

JIM: Yeah. With the hands.

FRANK: Cause it had to be with the hands is all. They don't pay if it's not with the hands.

JIM: Well, thanks for letting me know that beforehand.

FRANK: Jim. You gotta believe me when I say I didn't know.

JIM: How come I have to believe that, Frank?

FRANK: That guy from the agency, he was waiting for me outside the house. Just after you left. And that's when he told me. It was already too late for me to go in and get you.

JIM: Sure, Frank, these things happen.

FRANK: I woulda never done that to you, Jim. Except. Except I knew when he said it, I knew you wouldn't mind.

JIM: You're right, Frank. Why would I mind? It's just a job.

 (*Beat.*)

FRANK: What was it like?

JIM: What was what like?

FRANK: For you? What was it like?

JIM: Like…nothing. I just did it, that's all.

FRANK: Did he fight you?

JIM: Yeah. He fought.

FRANK: He was afraid—?

JIM: No.

FRANK: Didn't act afraid?

JIM: I just told you, no.

FRANK: But you said—you said he fought.

JIM: At first, yeah. Then…

FRANK: Then?

JIM: Who knows, he was prepared.

FRANK: Prepared? How?

JIM: How should I know?! He was religious.

FRANK: Religious?

JIM: Yeah. I don't know. So he was prepared.

FRANK: What kinda religious?

JIM: I don't care. Don't wanna know.

FRANK: How could a guy not fight? Thing like that?

JIM: I gotta get some sleep.

FRANK: Have the strength to just—

JIM: I don't remember inviting you.

FRANK: —accept it?

JIM: Goodnight, Frank. It's been a long night. I'm tired.

FRANK: Did you take stuff?

JIM: Doesn't matter.

FRANK: Sure it does. The insur—

JIM: Yes. I TOOK STUFF! I TOOK STUFF, okay! Now get out! I owe you
    nothing. I took the heat on this. YOU have nothing to SAY.

FRANK: The guy at the agency—

JIM: That guy! Like I care.

FRANK: He's gonna wanna know details.

FRANK: I got a sunrise service. I can't be bothered with this—

FRANK: Jim—

JIM: What? Say it.

FRANK: We been together a long time.

(Jim goes to the hiding place, pulls out the silver platter.)

JIM: Some family thing.

FRANK: You want me to—?

JIM: *(Keeps hold of the platter.)* I'll do it myself.

FRANK: I don't want division between us.

JIM: Who said anything about division?

FRANK: I go. Tomorrow. Ten A.M.

JIM: I'll be waiting.

FRANK: I'm glad you took that anyway. Makes it look more—

JIM: —that's what I thought.

FRANK: For the insurance guys. *(Beat.)* Did you ever...before tonight...did you?

JIM: Sure. You want me to say yes? Sure. Okay?

FRANK: You said it's just a job.

JIM: Are you feeling responsible for me now?

FRANK: I'm just hoping you can cope.

JIM: I can cope...perfectly. Now how 'bout you?

FRANK: I never knew how to pray. I mean. Once maybe. I prayed. It was strange.

JIM: Not premeditated?

FRANK: No.

JIM: They don't fry you if it's not premeditated.

FRANK: I'm not talking about that.

JIM: Level with me, Frank. You knew beforehand. All that talk about being damned forever. For a robbery?

FRANK: All right. I knew.

JIM: *(Punches him.)* Now get the fuck outta my house.

FRANK: I knew you'd be pissed off—

JIM: You're weak. That's pathetic. You're never gonna amount.

FRANK: You didn't always think that, Jim.

JIM: How would you know?

FRANK: So why were we in business together?

JIM: So you could lie to me...set me up.

FRANK: That's not the way it was.

JIM: Get outta here, Frank. Come back with my money. My payment. Then I never want to see you again.

> *(Jim clicks out the light. Frank stands a moment in the dark.)*

FRANK: You sleepin'?

> *(No response from Jim.)*

FRANK: Anyway, the sin's on you.

(Flash of lightning. Frank turns fast. Mags appears in her robe.)

MAGS: You look like you seen a ghost.

FRANK: Leeme be. Go back to sleep.

MAGS: What are you doin' home so soon?

FRANK: Early night.

MAGS: How'd it go?

FRANK: Went.

MAGS: What's wrong?

FRANK: Nothing.

MAGS: Been home long?

FRANK: I don't know. Go back to sleep.

MAGS: All right, you don't have to bite my head off. I just didn't hear the door open. *(She lays down.)*

(Frank stares out the window. Rain is coming down.)

FRANK: Do you believe in the sin of omission?

MAGS: What?

FRANK: It's the sin you commit by not stoppin' somethin' you know's a sin.

MAGS: This is the Bible?

FRANK: Do you believe in the Dead? That they live on somehow? Even after they're dead?

MAGS: What's with you, Frank?

FRANK: I need sleep. I haven't slept since Thursday.

MAGS: So come to bed.

FRANK: I wanted to be in shape. Instead, look at me!

MAGS: Frank—

FRANK: Don't CALL me that! How many times I gotta say!

MAGS: Fine.

FRANK: Mags, no. Forgive me. I don't know what's wrong with me. I'm feelin' not myself. It's like…like I'm trapped somehow. Like I been here before and the same stuff happens and I can't break free…into…

MAGS: Into what?

FRANK: Whatever. Whatever I'm supposed to be next. Straight, I guess. I don't know. *(He comes to her.)* Mags, let's get out.

MAGS: Go where?

FRANK: I don't know. Anywhere. Country.

MAGS: Last time I was out I got lost. Wound up back where I started.

FRANK: That's what I'm saying. This time it can be just you and me. The two of us. Together. Get married. But not here. Not in this city.

MAGS: But you got a job here, Frank.

(Beat.)

FRANK: I was fired, Mags.

MAGS: Fired?

FRANK: Yeah, well, laid off anyway. You know how it is. New guy on. Lack of seniority.

MAGS: But it was your first day! What'd you do, Frank?! Frank, what'd you DO?!

FRANK: I didn't DO anything, okay. It's not my fault! I'm not gonna take the rap for this!

MAGS: For what? What are you talkin' about?

FRANK: Mags, let's go…let's just go.

MAGS: Now I see what this is all about! It's Kansas City all over. You got fired off that job too. Or you scared yourself off.

FRANK: It wasn't like that, Mags, I—

MAGS: Don't tell me! I lived through it. You started talkin' like this, 'bout havin' a family, goin' to the country…And I didn't see you again for years!

FRANK: It's not the same.

MAGS: It's exactly the same!

FRANK: I'm not gonna leave you like that.

MAGS: I've heard all that!

FRANK: Mags, I love you.

MAGS: That's the worst thing you could say. *(Mags heads for the door.)*

FRANK: Wait! Where you goin?!

(Mags is gone. Frank chases her to the door, calls.)

FRANK: Mags! *(Frank turns abruptly into the room, spooked.)* Who's there?!

(Lights shift. Office. John at the desk. Frank in the doorway.)

JOHN: You're late. I was expecting you at ten.

FRANK: Well.

JOHN: Ten's not eleven. It's not twelve fifteen.

FRANK: I'm here, okay.

JOHN: What do you do with your time, Frank? You got a lot of friends? They call you on the telephone? Or is it the booze?

FRANK: I stopped that.

JOHN: Sure you did. But the habit dies hard. Don't take it personally, I'm just trying to understand. You see, my life is very precisely arranged. Every second counts. When I'm not here, something's going on without me. And when I am here, then I'm not somewhere else. Do you understand? Look around you. Read the paper. Do you ever read the paper, Frank?

People are either in ascendancy or they're sinking. Do you know the angle of your trajectory? Are you on a rise, Frank? Or are you falling… fast? The Roman Empire fell in a night. One bad decision on a hill in Thessaly. After a thousand years of world domination. You're a part of that, Frank. Whether you want to be or not. We all are. So be where you are.

FRANK: I'm here now.

JOHN: Are you sure, Frank? Or are you somewhere else? Have you got something on your mind, Frank? Something you wanna tell me? Some little confession?

FRANK: I'm here. I did my job. You don't have a right to ask these kinds of questions. I'm here and I did my job. I did my Goddamned job. I'm late but I'm here. Okay?!

JOHN: You're drunk. You're falling apart.

FRANK: It's none of your business.

JOHN: Your business is my business. I am your representative in the employment field. How you look has a direct bearing on how I'm perceived.

FRANK: I did my job, that's all that matters. I did my job. What I look like, how I dress, what I do on my day off—that's my—affair!

JOHN: Sit down, Frank. You look tired. Are you tired? Did you have a bad night? Did you sleep at all? You didn't, did you? You walked the streets. And maybe in the morning you grubbed a little change and bought yourself a little something. It doesn't matter. You can tell me. I'm your friend. I'm on your side. I want to help.

FRANK: I don't need your help. Just gimmie what's owed me.

JOHN: What's owed you. That's right. It's payday. You're going to get my pocket watch out of hock.

(Frank looks up.)

JOHN: Wondering how I knew? We're not stupid here, Frank.

FRANK: You gave me that watch.

JIM: What happened last night?

FRANK: I told you.

JOHN: Details, Frank. I want the details.

FRANK: I. I did the guy. I did him. He's done.

JOHN: You're talking about…

FRANK: Martin.

JOHN: How'd you do him, Frank? Can you show me how you did him?

(Frank illustrates.)

JOHN: *(Slaps Frank's hand.)* Frank, you can do better than that. Gimmie a real
    show.

FRANK: Lay off!

JOHN: How long did it take, Frank? Took a while, I imagine. For a man to
    die like that.

FRANK: Yeah, took a while.

JOHN: Sure, it did. Took a long while for a man to go like that. And did you
    watch him, Frank? Did you look him in the eye?

FRANK: *(Avoiding John's eye.)* I watched him.

JOHN: But did you look him in the eye? Look me in the eye, Frank. *(Slaps
    Frank's hand.)* Look me in the eye like you looked him in the eye.

FRANK: What do you want from me?!

JOHN: How long did it take, Frank? Before it was done? About? What? A
    minute?

FRANK: Minute. Sure.

JOHN: You sure it wasn't more?

FRANK: Maybe more.

JOHN: You probably didn't check.

FRANK: No.

JOHN: Must of been in a rush. The stink of mortality. All that.

FRANK: Yeah.

JOHN: Did he lose his nerve? At the end? Sometimes they do. Think they
    want a thing, but when it's right there facing them it's a different story.
    That happens.

FRANK: He was…prepared.

JOHN: Prepared? How? How was he prepared?

FRANK: He was…religious, you know.

JOHN: So then he what? Prayed? Is that what he did, Frank?

FRANK: Yeah.

JOHN: How, Frank? How'd he pray? Like this? *(John puts his palms together
    and faces upward in supplication.)*

FRANK: Yeah. Like that. Yes.

    (Beat. John stands, walks away.)

JOHN: Why you lying to me, Frank?

FRANK: I'm not…

JOHN: You're not telling the truth.

FRANK: Sure, I am.

JOHN: You know, the police got a call last night. A concerned neighbor, noises
    in the night, possibility of a break in, you know the type of call I'm talk-

ing about. So they went by to investigate. Calm the neighbor. The front door was open. The house was dark. And what do you think they found on the carpet in the study just in front of the fireplace?

FRANK: Martin's body.

JOHN: Nothing, Frank. Zilch.

FRANK: …what?

JOHN: Oh, there were signs of a break-in—window smashed, silver tray missing, but no body. A mystery, wouldn't you say?

FRANK: I…don't know.

JOHN: Maybe Martin knows. Oh, right. I forgot. Martin's dead. So that leaves only you.

FRANK: I don't know!

JOHN: You have to do better than that.

FRANK: I swear!

JOHN: You look tired, Frank. *(John passes a cup of coffee across to Frank.)* Wake yourself up.

FRANK: I don't want—

JOHN: Drink!

FRANK: Hot.

JOHN: Burn yourself.

FRANK: Please.

JOHN: Burn yourself.

(Frank drinks, scalding his throat.)

FRANK: *(Grabs his throat.)* This…isn't…coffee. *(He drops the cup, sinks to his knees, gasping.)*

JOHN: *(Enjoys this.)* Did you really think you had the courage to cross this organization? Did you think you could buck your fate? You're nothing, a lump of clay…a creature…created by us for no other purpose but to till the land…to make it lush and plentiful…to make it bear fruit…to struggle until you die…or else to be worthless…a groveling wretch…a burden and a drain on the community…Is that what you are, Frank? A defective human being? Do you hear me, Frank? Are you listening? Do the job. Do the job, Frank. Do the job. Don't come back until it's done. Do the job.

FRANK: *(Gasps it out.)* Please…can't…

JOHN: Breathe, Frank?

(John reaches into his pocket, pulls out an inhalator, tosses it to Frank. Frank doesn't know what to do with it.)

JOHN: Stick it in your mouth and squeeze…

(Blackout. Mag's place. Frank in the empty apartment. Turns fast, spooked.)

FRANK: Mags?

(No response.)

FRANK: Mags?!

(Jim comes in from the bedroom. Beat.)

JIM: Lookin' for Mags?

FRANK: What are you doin' here?!

JIM: It got late. I got tired of waitin' for my money.

FRANK: *(Desperate.)* Where is he, Jim?

JIM: Who's that, Frank?

FRANK: You know who I'm talking about.

JIM: I guess I don't.

FRANK: Well, who do you think?

JIM: Well, I don't know.

FRANK: WELL, TAKE A GUESS!

JIM: Gee.

(Frank lunges, grabs Jim by the throat.)

FRANK: Goddamnit! What happened?!

JIM: Let. Go! *(Jim breaks free.)* You shouldn't do that, Frank. You shouldn't choke me like that. You're gonna upset my stomach.

FRANK: Answer me! Where's Martin?

JIM: Martin?

FRANK: Yeah, Martin. Where is he?!

JIM: Martin's where I left him.

FRANK: Not anymore.

JIM: Last I saw.

FRANK: Jim, don't bullshit—

JIM: I take it this means you don't have my money.

FRANK: What?!

JIM: My money, Frank. My money. You remember that?

FRANK: Don't you hear what I'm telling you?!

JIM: No, I don't. Unfortunately no. I don't hear a thing until I get my money.

FRANK: Well hear this. Martin's gone.

JIM: He was where I left him.

FRANK: That's what you say.

JIM: Yeah, that's what I say. You got a problem with that?

FRANK: Just tell me where he is! I'll take care of him! I'll pay you the money!

JIM: What money?

FRANK: Five, like we agreed.

JIM: Like who agreed? You said five. Try more like fifteen.

FRANK: What are you talkin', fifteen? He told me five.

JIM: He who?

FRANK: The agency guy.

JIM: See, this is where misunderstandings arise. I was told from the horse's mouth so to speak it was fifteen.

FRANK: It isn't anything if I don't have the body.

JIM: That's your problem.

FRANK: It'll be your problem too if I tell the agency.

JIM: Oh, yeah. I'm sure they'd love to hear you hired out a subcontractor. That would endear them to you real fast.

FRANK: Look, if it's fifteen, it's fifteen. I don't care about the money.

JIM: Sure you don't. That's how you got yourself in this jam in the first place.

FRANK: Jim. I know these guys. They don't fuck around. Now you gotta level with me.

JIM: Excuse me. I gotta? I don't GOTTA nothing.

FRANK: Jim. We're friends. Kansas City, Jim.

JIM: What the fuck is it with you and Kansas City?! That was another time.

FRANK: Jim, please.

JIM: Please nothing. You already wrinkled the suit—

FRANK: Jim—

JIM: —now you're telling me you don't wanna pay me!

FRANK: Don't you understand, they're gonna kill me if I don't find him.

JIM: Unless I do first. Now stop bullshitting and give me my money.

FRANK: It's not bullshit, there's no money!

JIM: Then someone pulled a fast one on you cause I left a dead guy in that house last night.

FRANK: Who?

JIM: Maybe your friends at the agency. Maybe they wanted to keep all the dough for themselves instead of just most of it. Maybe they let you do the muscle work, then came in for the quick clean up. Whatever the hell happened, I don't really care as long as I get my money.

FRANK: Then do your job. Find the sonofabitch and kill him.

JIM: He's dead.

FRANK: Kill him again. Kill him till he stays dead. I don't know.

JIM: Well, don't ask me.

FRANK: Well, who the hell am I supposed to believe?!

JIM: Well, how the hell should I know?!

FRANK: Jim, if I find out you crossed me—

JIM: What, Frank? What are you gonna do? You gonna hurt me, Frank? Like
    you hurt that guy? You're useless, Frank.
    (Mags has come in, brown bag in hand.)
FRANK: Mags—?
MAGS: …Frankie.
    (Frank reaches for her.)
MAGS: No—! *(Mags dodges him, runs out.)*
FRANK: What's goin' on here?
JIM: Sit down, Frank.
FRANK: Sit, what, in my own house?
JIM: Your house?
FRANK: Yeah, mine.
JIM: You don't pay the bills. Don't live here on a regular basis.
FRANK: Fuck, where you get off—?!
JIM: I'm just asking in what sense is this your house.
FRANK: It's my house 'cause it's Mag's house and I'm with Mags.
JIM: Were.
FRANK: Were?
JIM: With Mags.
FRANK: *(Calls to her.)* Mags!
JIM: She won't come out.
FRANK: Mags!
JIM: She's afraid of you, Frank. Doesn't want you around.
FRANK: Mags!
JIM: It won't do any good calling. Mags and I had a long talk about it this
    morning. Mags has found God.
FRANK: Why you—fake—
    (Frank lunges. The two men grapple. Mags comes in.)
MAGS: Don't! Stop it!
    (The two men part. Both are breathing heavily. Mags runs to Jim.)
MAGS: Did he hurt you?
JIM: You're a sucker, Frank!
FRANK: Mags, they're gonna kill me.
MAGS: I can't…hear that.
JIM: You're an ignorant son of a bitch.
MAGS: Make him shut up.
FRANK: I love you.
MAGS: *(Turns on Frank.)* …I love you. Let your hair down, Baby. Ooo, I can't

wait to get you back in my arms. Then it starts again! Can't you see, I'm sick! I got no way of gettin' free of this…

FRANK: Mags, no!

MAGS: I said, don't be a stranger. *(Cries.)* Shit. Now you got me all. Oh, you love this. You can't do this to me anymore. I am not gonna let you do this to me, Frank.

FRANK: Don't call me that.

(She attacks him.)

MAGS: Motherfucker! What are you trying to do?! Go on. Get outta here. Go. We don't want you here. Don't come back, you hear me. Don't you ever come back. *(Mags runs out.)*

(Beat.)

JIM: She chose the steady earner, Frank. It's as simple as that.

(Frank sinks down. Jim rises, comes up to Frank. Beat.)

JIM: It's just you and me now, Buddy. What're you gonna do?

(A moment. Then Frank slinks out. Jim laughs. Blackout. Lights dim up. Freeway underpass. Night. Roaring of cars above. Frank drinking. A slouching figure enters. The man slumps past, finds shelter under a pillar. Frank rises.)

FRANK: Mister? Help a guy out? I'll work for food. Could you spare a little somethin'?

MAN: *(Glances up, then back down fast.)* I don't think so.

FRANK: *(Eyes lighting up.)* Sure, you can. You can spare a little something. After I spared you.

MAN: *(Gruff.)* What are you talkin' about? Fuck off.

FRANK: C'mon, Martin. You know me.

MAN: *(Crawling away.)* You got the wrong guy. There's no one here named Martin.

FRANK: Sure, there isn't. And Frank's not my name either. But what are we gonna do, huh? We didn't make this world, we just crawl around in it. *(Frank flips the crawling man over. Martin is revealed. He stares at Frank, terrified.)*

MARTIN: How'd you find me?

FRANK: Dumb luck. I wasn't even looking 'cause I figured you were dead. *(Beat; studies him.)* How'd you come to be here, Martin? This isn't the kind of place for a guy like you.

MARTIN: I tried to get your friend the money, but I couldn't. I don't know how to go home now. I'm scared for my wife and kids. I wanna sell the house but the time's not right. I'll lose my investment and then some.

FRANK: So he made a deal on the side, old Jim.

MARTIN: He turned out the light. Made me give him everything I had. Twenty five hundred, cash. I was saving it for my wife. And a silver tray. Been in my family for generations. He said he'd give it back after I brought the rest of the money. Then he told me to get lost.

(Frank laughs, can't stop.)

FRANK: You got off…cheap.

MARTIN: (Relieved.) You're not gonna kill me. I'm right, aren't I? You're a good man. (Laughs along with Frank.) That's why you sent that other man in your place. Cause you just couldn't face it. The other one. He was a killer. But not you.

FRANK: (Stops laughing abruptly.) You're wrong, Martin.

MARTIN: (Backs up.) Please.

FRANK: I killed a man.

MARTIN: (Covers ears.) Don't tell me this.

FRANK: I gotta tell someone and I can't find a priest.

MARTIN: I'm no priest.

FRANK: I know you're no priest, Martin.

MARTIN: So don't tell me. I don't wanna know. This has nothing to do with me.

FRANK: This was Kansas city. This job. You like Calliope?

MARTIN: Calliope?

FRANK: Music. They play it on the merry-go-round…at the county fair. This is at the county fair in Kansas City. I'm so drunk I'm fallin' off the horse. We break in at night and get it runnin' just for us. Just for us, the horses goin' round. We're drunk. We're high. We feel GREAT! And the horses. You know. The horses! They lift you up when you're a kid, lift you up and put you on the horses…you go round…round…round. (Spins, stops.) It's not good if you're drunk. You fall off. And this man, he's—I'm supposed to. You know. On the horses. But the music is so. Light. Like childhood. That I. I let him go. I let him go and I run…I disappear.

MARTIN: I thought you said—

FRANK: Me. I'm the dead man. I'm the man I killed.

(Martin kneels, frightened, fishes through his wallet.)

MARTIN: I'll give you what I have. It's not much, but maybe it's enough. Twenty. Twenty-two dollars. What do you say? (Holds out money.) Please.

(Frank kneels as well. They are face-to-face.)

FRANK: Don't do that. Don't crawl on the floor. We're brothers, you and me.

MARTIN: I'll give you anything you want.

FRANK: You a religious man, Martin?

MARTIN: I don't know. I'm weak. I don't know. Some say the universe is a machine, like a clock, endlessly ticking. And God lives in the machine. Others say there's no need of God. The machine runs by itself. With no hope for us of Grace. I don't know what I believe. I only know that without God we're living in a hollow world, dispensable except in how we serve the machine…fate. And that our lives have no greater meaning or possibility. I can't accept the loneliness of that. I thought I could. I'm not strong enough.

(Martin falls into Frank's arms. Begins to cry. Frank holds him close.)

FRANK: The only thing I want is peace. I only want to stop running, Martin. *(Frank takes Martin's neck in his hands and begins to squeeze. Martin remains motionless, gagging, staring into Frank's eyes. Frank is powerful. He squeezes for a long time, looking Martin right in the eye. Then Frank looks upward. After a beat he releases Martin. Martin collapses back, gasping in air. Frank rises, looks down at Martin.)*

FRANK: *(Quietly.)* Go home, Martin. Go home.

(Martin runs. Frank watches. Then he stares down at his hands, amazed. Blackout. Lights dim up. Seedy apartment. Bed like a grave. Frank, in the shadows, looks at a sleeping form. The sleeper sits up, fast. It's John.)

JOHN: Who's that? Who's there?!

(Beat.)

FRANK: I brought you back your money.

JOHN: Who are you?

FRANK: The money you loaned me. I brought it back. Ten bucks. It's not all here. I had a sandwich.

JOHN: Frank?

FRANK: This is your place, huh.

JOHN: What are you doing here?

FRANK: I thought you woulda had a bigger place. More air.

JOHN: How'd you find me?

FRANK: A fancy place with nice stuff on the walls. And a real nice carpet on the floor. But this place is like a coffin. Everything's cheap. And you don't even get any fresh air.

JOHN: *(Beat.)* Did you do it?

FRANK: I wanna go back to square one. But I can't go back to square one cause I already had a sandwich. So I owe you three bucks and change.

JOHN: Did you kill him?

(Pause.)

FRANK: Yeah. Sure. It was a beautiful murder. You shoulda seen him die.

JOHN: You brought the body to the house?

FRANK: I brought it to the house. I put it out back in the bushes. I watered it up real good.

(Pause.)

JOHN: Turn around. *(Beat.)* Turn around! I gotta get up outta bed.

FRANK: What are you afraid of?

JOHN: Turn around, you stupid son of a bitch!

FRANK: *(Simply.)* I looked it up. From the Bible. This merchant leads a wise man to the place where the sky kisses the land. And there are hundreds of windows there. More windows then you ever saw. And the merchant puts his basket of goods in the window of Heaven. And he turns around to pray. And when he turns back the basket is gone. And he asks. Are there thieves here? But there aren't any thieves. It's the Heavens turning around. Reincarnation. That means you get another chance.

(John stands, pulls on his pants.)

FRANK: Why are you embarrassed, John?

JOHN: What's your problem, huh? What the fuck is your problem?!

FRANK: I brought you back your money. I'll bring the rest tomorrow.

JOHN: Don't come back here!

FRANK: And here's your watch. I got it out of hock. I think something happened to it, cause it's not running right anymore. Doesn't keep time at all. *(He tosses it to John, turns to go. John lunges for him. They struggle in the middle of the room then separate, with no clear victor. Both breathe, Frank on the floor, John against the bed.)*

FRANK: John? Is that really your name?

JOHN: No.

FRANK: What is it then?

JOHN: It doesn't matter.

FRANK: Then it's what I thought.

JOHN: Nobody does this, Frank. Nobody does what you're doing.

(Frank stands.)

JOHN: Where are you going?

FRANK: You know where to find me. I'm not running anymore. Never again.

(Frank starts out.)

JOHN: *(Blocks his way.)* They're gonna come for you with a package. You're gonna unwrap the package. In the package there's gonna be a gun with a silver bullet. You're gonna stick that gun into your mouth and squeeze that trigger—and if you CAN'T—if you lack the REQUISITE WILL—

then one big man's gonna hold you and the other big man's gonna grind that muzzle in deep till you taste it with the back of your throat and choke on it till you can't plead and wish you never saw my face or came into my office or WASTED MY TIME! WHO DO YOU THINK YOU ARE?! WHERE DO YOU THINK YOU LIVE?! We're connected, you selfish prick! I checked your references! I recommended you! We're in this together!

FRANK: I don't wanna die.

JOHN: Yeah, well, you're dead! YOU'RE DEAD! You hear me? YOU'RE DEAD!

FRANK: I don't wanna die forever.

(Frank walks out. John thrashes in the empty, dark room. Blackout. Lights dim up. From the pulpit, Jim speaks.)

JIM: Two thousand years of darkness and it was dawn. The sun rose again just like the Angels had promised. It was the brightest sun that ever shone upon the face of the earth. And the waters receded. And the men, pale and blinking, like moles, like ferrets, walked out upon the face of the green land. And the land sprung up beneath their feet. And the sun caressed their faces. It had rimmed round the world and was so beautiful. Was it the last sunrise, or the first? Had the sky cracked open, and would it close again forever? Or was this only the beginning of a light without end? One by one the men fell upon their knees and raised their faces up to the sky in thanksgiving for deliverance from the darkness. And though the light stung their eyes, yet they forced them open. And they were blinded by the sunlight for its radiance was too intense. They had lost their faith in light and so when it came they were unprepared. *(Lights shift. Tent. Jim counts money. Turns, spooked. Frank comes out of the shadows.)*

JIM: Christ!

FRANK: What's the word, Jim?

JIM: What are you doing here?

FRANK: What's the word on the street?

JIM: Mags'll be out any second.

FRANK: Just tell me the word. You know what I'm talking about.

(Beat.)

JIM: Thirty.

FRANK: Thirty, huh? Never figured my life'd be worth that much.

JIM: You musta done something to really piss 'em off.

FRANK: Imagine that.

JIM: You been drinking?

FRANK: I'm straight, Jim. For good.

JIM: So what's that got to do with me?

FRANK: Kansas City. *(Beat.)* I let you go. *(Beat.)* Now let her go.

JIM: It's not up to me.

FRANK: You don't love her.

JIM: Who says?

FRANK: I'll let them know you're still alive. I promise you. I've got nothin' to lose now.

JIM: Think you can scare me?

> *(Jim approaches, is close. Frank stands his ground.)*

FRANK: Got the guts, Jim? Thirty gee. It's a lot of money.

> *(A beat.)*

JIM: They won't let you get away with this. You know that.

FRANK: *(Quietly.)* I'm…prepared.

> *(Beat.)*

JIM: You're a sucker, Frank. You always have been. And this…changes nothing.

> *(Jim walks. Frank watches. Sunrise slowly to bright dawn. Mags' place. Sound of birds. Mags passed out in sunlight. Frank standing over. She wakes.)*

FRANK: Morning.

MAGS: Frank?

FRANK: Got you something.

MAGS: Oh…God.

FRANK: It's out of a cracker jack box. But still. Fit?

MAGS: Frank….

FRANK: Try it on.

> *(She does. It fits.)*

FRANK: So?

> *(She cries.)*

FRANK: Shhh. *(He stands her up.)*

MAGS: I'm sorry, Frank. I'm so sorry.

FRANK: *(Holds her.)* No more apologies. Never again. Not for me either.

MAGS: *(Through her tears.)* What happened?

FRANK: Don't you know? It's Sunday. Got the day off.

MAGS: How 'bout Monday?

FRANK: I'll be off then too.

MAGS: Tuesday?

FRANK: All week.

MAGS: Next week?

FRANK: Next week, next month, next year. Gonna be a long vacation.

MAGS: Yeah?

FRANK: Long as you're with me, gonna be a holiday all the time…

MAGS: I got a choice?

FRANK: In this life?

MAGS: Guess I'll have to say yes, then, huh?

FRANK: Yes.

> *(Beat.)*

MAGS: *(Fights back joy.)* Then…yes. Yes, Frank. Yes.

FRANK: *(Kisses her.)* Care to dance?

MAGS: No radio.

FRANK: I hear somethin'. In some room…some room nearby, but far off. You hear it too?

MAGS: Yeah. Yeah, I do.

> *(He dances in circles with her in the silent room.)*

MAGS: *(As she turns.)* Frank? You with me for good?

FRANK: *(As he turns.)* I'm here now, Mags. I'm here now.

> *(Calliope music comes up gently. Lights fade to black.)*

END OF PLAY

NOBODY DIES ON FRIDAY

by Robert Brustein

THE AUTHOR

As founding director of the Yale Repertory and American Repertory Theatres, Mr. Brustein has supervised well over two hundred productions, acting in eight and directing twelve, including his own adaptations of *The Father, Ghosts, The Changeling,* and the trilogy of Pirandello works: *Six Characters in Search of an Author, Right You Are (If You Think You Are),* and *Tonight We Improvise.* He has written eleven adaptations for the A.R.T. (most recently *Shlemiel the First, The Wild Duck,* and *The Master Builder*) and is the author of twelve books on theatre and society, including *Reimagining American Theatre; The Theatre of Revolt; Dumbocracy in America; Making Scenes,* a memoir of his Yale years when he was Dean of the Drama School; and *Who Needs Theatre,* a collection of reviews and essays for which he received his second George Jean Nathan Award for dramatic criticism. His latest book, *Cultural Calisthenics,* was released last year. Mr. Brustein is also Director of the Loeb Drama Center, Professor of English at Harvard, and drama critic for the New Republic. He is a recipient of the George Polk Award in journalism, the Elliot Norton Award for professional excellence in Boston theatre, the New England Theatre Conference's 1985 Annual Award "for outstanding creative achievement in the American theatre," the 1995 American Academy of Arts and Letters Award for Distinguished Service to the Arts, the Pirandello Medal, and a medal from the Egyptian Government for his contribution to world theatre. His *Six Characters in Search of an Author* won the Boston Theatre Award for Best Production of 1996. His play *Demons,* which was broadcast on WGBH radio in 1993, had its stage world premiere as part of *A.R.T. New Stages.* His new play *Nobody Dies on Friday* was given its world premiere last spring in the same series and presented at the Singapore Festival of Arts last summer, and his short play, *Poker Face,* was presented by The Boston Playwrights Theatre this spring. He is currently working on a new play called *The Face-Lift.* Mr. Brustein is a member of the American Academy of Arts and Letters and the American Academy of Arts and Sciences.

Nobody Dies On Friday is a play about celebrity in America, inspired by reflections on the death of Marilyn Monroe and on the career of Lee Strasberg. I'd been reading Susan Strasberg's *Marilyn and Me.* I'd also been writing about her father for many years, though I had never met him. I was curious to know what it was about his Method that made most of his actors abandon the stage for the movie, why he ended up in the movies himself, starting with *The Godfather,* and how symbolic it was that he died after dancing in a celebrity chorus line of a TV program called "Night of a Thousand Stars."

Strasberg interested me as a peculiarly American character, one who as a youth absorbed the high ideals of the Group Theatre, but who was gradually swallowed up by his own ambition and competitiveness. Under Strasberg, the Studio became a celebrity factory, a symbol for me of how people abandon their calling to seek fame in the movies, for Strasberg's technique was essentially something designed for movies, not for the stage.

His greatest contribution to American theatre was his introduction of proletarian naturalism, a style best represented by the acting in plays like *A Hatful of Rain* and movies like *On the Waterfront,* along with a number of other things from the period that nobody remembers. But the performers in them are remembered because of their capacity to create a believable personalized reality. Some of the people he took credit for had little to do with the Actors Studio—Marlon Brando, for example, and James Dean. But others, like Paul Newman, Ben Gazzara, and Shelly Winters owe a lot to Strasberg's teachings.

Nobody Dies on Friday, though, is essentially a family play, about the stresses a famous man puts on the people he loves. It takes place in one day, it observes the Aristotelean unities: time, place, and action. It also takes some liberties with history—not with what events happened, but with when they happened (like Arthur Miller's breakup with Monroe which occurred a few months later than New Year's Eve, 1959). I've tried to make this family play a microcosm of an important time in American society, when values were shifting and people were suffering as a result.

Nobody Dies on Friday premiered at A.R.T. New Stages, Hasty Pudding Theatre, Cambridge, Massachusetts, on April 16, 1998. It was directed by David Wheeler with the following cast:

Lee Strasberg . . . . Alvin Epstein
Paula Strasberg . . . . Annette Miller
Susan Strasberg. . . . . Emma Roberts
John Strasberg. . . . . Robert Kropf
Marilyn Monroe . . . . Rachael Warren

CHARACTERS

LEE STRASBERG: head of the Actors Studio
PAULA STRASBERG: née Miller, his wife, an acting coach
SUSAN STRASBERG: his daughter, an actress of twenty-one
JOHN STRASBERG: his son, a young man of eighteen
THE VOICE OF MARILYN MONROE: an actress

NOTE

Although partly based on the memoirs of Susan and John Strasberg, this play is a work of fiction and should not therefore be regarded as documentary fact.

ACT I

It is New Year's Day, 1960, eleven o'clock on Friday morning. The living room of the Strasberg home—a spacious West Side apartment in the mid-eighties overlooking Central Park. The kitchen is upstage left, a hallway leading to the front door stage right, bedrooms up center. The bedroom area is reached by another hall, which should be lit in a non-realistic manner. It is an area pervaded by the spirit of the woman who inhabits it throughout the play, and therefore characterized by a spectral glow, which may change to a shimmer whenever she speaks from the bedroom.

The room also contains an ample bar. The walls are lined with books and record albums. Signed framed photos of Marlon Brando, James Dean, Eli Wallach, Kim Stanley, Montgomery Clift, Shelly Winters, and other Actors Studio-related movie stars decorate whatever walls aren't monopolized by the books and records. There is also a photograph of the Strasberg family at the beach, which sits prominently on a table near the couch.

The room is in serious disarray. The remains of a raucous New Year's Eve party are strewn everywhere. Bottles and glasses are on every table and counter. Articles of clothing. Half-finished sandwiches. Party hats and confetti. At rise, Paula, in a stained housecoat, is trying her best to clean up the mess.

Paula is a dumpy woman in her late forties, whose fallen features retain some vestige of beauty modified by an air of resignation. She has bad feet, which she rubs a lot. She stops to straighten the pictures, some of which have been knocked akilter. Seeing Dean's photo, she takes it off the wall, shakes her head sadly, dusts it, and returns it to its mount. John, an intense and precocious young man of eighteen, is asleep on the couch in his clothes. Even in sleep, he seems to have a permanent scowl etched into his features. When his mother accidentally clatters an ashtray, he abruptly jerks into a sitting position, rubbing his eyes. His hair is mussed and he's dressed in a pair of slept-in jeans and tee shirt, no shoes.

JOHN: *(Looking around him wearily and shaking his head.)* What a rat fuck.
PAULA: Happy New Year to you, too, crankpot.
    (He goes into the kitchen where we hear him rooting through the refrigerator.)
JOHN: *(Calling from the kitchen.)* Any breakfast?

PAULA: Fix it yourself, if you can't wait till people get up. There's some Cheerios in the cabinet.

JOHN: I need something hot.

PAULA: Boil an egg.

JOHN: A-ha!

PAULA: What have you got?

JOHN: Last night's coffee.

PAULA: *(Ready to go in the kitchen.)* You're not going to drink stale coffee. I thought you said hot. Wait, I'll fix you something.

JOHN: Never mind. *(He comes out of the kitchen with the coffee and a Cheerios box, sits down on the couch and gloomily munches.)*

PAULA: You didn't sleep well?

JOHN: On this lumpy sofa?

PAULA: Big deal. She used your room.

JOHN: *Again!*

PAULA: She's very needy.

JOHN: Everyone's needy.

PAULA: Not like her.

    (John picks up a woman's slipper off the couch.)

PAULA: What's that doing here?

JOHN: She staggered in here at four in the morning. In her bathrobe…nothing underneath.

PAULA: What did she want from you?

JOHN: *(Insinuatingly, touching his nose.)* Ahhh.

PAULA: Don't be silly. You're still a virgin. *(Uncertainly.)* Aren't you?

JOHN: *(Not heeding.)* She couldn't sleep. Nobody sleeps.

PAULA: Did she say anything?

JOHN: About what?

PAULA: Never mind. *(Pause.)* Why didn't she wake Dad and me?

JOHN: You tell me.

PAULA: How did she seem to you?

JOHN: Real spacey. Her speech was slurred. Her skin smelled funny.

PAULA: What do you mean funny? *(As if she just heard.)* You were smelling her skin?

JOHN: Kind of acid. Too much drink and pills.

PAULA: Well, she has a lot of things on her mind. She was awake for hours after everybody left.

JOHN: Of course you stayed up with her.

PAULA: I gave her a massage, Daddy held her in his arms. Finally she fell off.
    I thought she'd sleep for weeks.

JOHN: I don't think she slept an hour.

PAULA: How long was she with you?

JOHN: Till about six.

PAULA: So…?

JOHN: *(Finger to his nose.)* Ahh…

PAULA: What would Marilyn want with a kid like you?

JOHN: She likes me. She sleeps in my bed.

PAULA: Not when you're in it.

JOHN: When am I in it?

PAULA: She couldn't go home last night.

JOHN: Another scrap with Arthur?

PAULA: A bad one.

JOHN: How did such a brainy guy hitch up with such a bimbo?

PAULA: Her simple background.

JOHN: *(Scornfully.)* Ma!

PAULA: You know how much he believes in the common man—

JOHN: So who did he think he was shtupping, Willy Loman?

PAULA: Marilyn has a great talent.

JOHN: For wiggling her ass.

PAULA: Wash your mouth out, bubby. You sound just like one of those
    Hollywood types.

JOHN: At least they're not hypocrites.

PAULA: *(Stung.)* You calling me a hypocrite?

JOHN: *(Quickly.)* No, Ma, not you. But you have to admit she's a weird choice
    for Pops.

PAULA: Lee says she's an unopened flower waiting to be watered.

JOHN: With whose hose?

PAULA: Show some respect for your father.

JOHN: Why else does he give her private acting lessons? In our own home. For
    free.

PAULA: *(Suspicious.)* What are you saying?

JOHN: *(Laughing.)* She must be putting out something instead of tuition.

PAULA: *(Her voice rising.)* Your father is only interested in her talent.

JOHN: Which talent?

PAULA: He thinks Marilyn is worth his time, and so do I.

JOHN: *(Hastily, getting up.)* Any of those margaritas left?

PAULA: You're not going to brush your teeth first?

JOHN: *(Going to the bar and ladling himself a glass of margarita out of a tureen, then rolling it around in his mouth, like mouthwash.)* This oughta kill any germs.

PAULA: You had enough to drink last night. Take some orange juice. You need the vitamins.

JOHN: For Chrissake, Mama, by now it's mostly melted ice and fruit juice anyway.

PAULA: It was strong enough to make you pass out last night. In front of everyone.

JOHN: I didn't pass out. I fell asleep.

PAULA: From too many margaritas.

JOHN: I'm old enough to know when I've had enough.

PAULA: At eighteen?

JOHN: At eighteen Susan had the cover of *Life.*

PAULA: What's that got to do with drugs and drinking? You need to learn control.

JOHN: *(Hurt.)* Stop it, Mama.

PAULA: Don't forget Wisconsin.

JOHN: Mom, I've been home—how long now? Three weeks? And all you talk about is Wisconsin. Say something new. It's a new year.

PAULA: Take it easy on Marilyn. She's very vulnerable right now.

JOHN: *(Half to himself.)* Who isn't.

> *(Enter Susan, known as "Blintzes" to her family, a bright pretty girl of twenty-one, carrying a script. Usually dark-haired, she's now a blonde. She's dressed in a tight fitting sweater and pants and looks as if she's had a rugged night.)*

PAULA: Happy New Year, Susie.

SUSAN: Same to you, Mommy. Happy New Year, Johnny. *(Kisses them.)*

JOHN: *(Acknowledging her kiss glumly.)* 'New Year, Blintzes.

SUSAN: Why such a sour face?

> *(John shrugs.)*

SUSAN: Forget I asked. Daddy up yet?

PAULA: I thought I'd let him sleep a little later today. He didn't get to bed till three-thirty.

JOHN: *(Muttering.)* Him you let sleep.

SUSAN: Give me a sip of that coffee, will you, Johnny? I got a roaring headache.

JOHN: It's cold.

SUSAN: I don't mind. *(Sips.)*

PAULA: Take an aspirin with it. *(She hands her some pills from her pocketbook.)*

SUSAN: Thanks, I don't need any. *(Susan furtively reaches into her pants pocket and downs some pills.)*

PAULA: What's that?

SUSAN: Nothing, Mama.

PAULA: I saw you put something in your mouth.

SUSAN: Just some downers.

PAULA: Downers. Uppers. What are you? An elevator?

SUSAN: They're just Placidyls. Perfectly harmless. Best thing for a hangover.

PAULA: You also drank too much last night?

SUSAN: It was New Year's Eve. And I was celebrating.

PAULA: It's definite then, the Italian movie?

SUSAN: Don't start packing my bags yet. I'd much rather do *Peyton Place* and stay home with you.

JOHN: I'd go to Italy in a second.

SUSAN: *Peyton Place* would be a great showcase for me.

JOHN: Playing the town tramp in Grade B *shmutz?*

SUSAN: It's a starring role in a major motion picture.

PAULA: But Susie…

SUSAN: Anyway, I haven't cleared it with Dad yet. *(Looking at the rumpled bedclothes on the sofa.)* So Marilyn stayed over again.

JOHN: How can you tell? My bloodshot eyes?

SUSAN: I knew she wouldn't make it home She was guzzling champagne like soda water.

JOHN: And popping pills like Goobers.

PAULA: Where's your compassion? That woman has been betrayed.

JOHN: Which abomination are we talking about now?

SUSAN: She *has* had a terrible history, Johnny.

PAULA: Yeah. All those men.

SUSAN: She's not the first to rise to stardom that way.

JOHN: You didn't.

SUSAN: I'm not a star. *(Pause.)* Yet. Just because I made a few movies.

JOHN: Movies where you had a chance to act, not boop-boop-a-doop.

SUSAN: She doesn't choose those parts. She hates them.

PAULA: No other star has put herself on the line like Marilyn.

JOHN: On the chorus line.

SUSAN: No, Johnny. She's got something.

JOHN: What?

SUSAN: A totally innocent sensuality.

PAULA: That's the gift of a great actress.

JOHN: Then why does every character come out Marilyn?

PAULA: Lee says acting is about playing yourself. Being private in public.

JOHN: No. Acting is about playing someone else, becoming another character. That's beyond her.

SUSAN: She does play a character role. Marilyn Monroe.

PAULA: *(Interested.)* What do you mean?

SUSAN: Well, the other day we were walking to class together. She had on her dark glasses and that scarf she wears in public. We were talking about acting, as usual, and she said, "Do you want to see me be *her?*" *(Imitating her.)* She whipped off her scarf, shook out her blonde hair, and started sashaying down the street. Doing a Marilyn Monroe.

JOHN: So Marilyn Monroe is her comic creation? Like Chaplin's tramp? But he was a professional. He showed up on time. With her it's like waiting for Godot.

PAULA: So she's late a lot. But think of all she has to worry about—makeup, costume, learning the lines, working up the courage to appear in public.

JOHN: I wish you'd make excuses for me like that.

PAULA: I make excuses for you every day.

JOHN: What is that supposed to mean?

PAULA: Wisconsin. That's what it means.

JOHN: There you go again.

PAULA: Just get off Marilyn. She's had a hard life. Marrying people who don't understand her.

SUSAN: Marilyn has no luck with men.

PAULA: Who does?

JOHN: Don't blame it on the men. She's hardly been a model of fidelity.

SUSAN: When did things go wrong? She and Arthur were so good together.

PAULA: Please, they were never good together.

SUSAN: Sure they were. She was crazy about him. Why else would she change her religion, risk her career when Arthur was being investigated by that House Committee? She once told me he was the smartest man she ever met.

PAULA: That's what she said about Daddy. That Lee was the most brilliant man who ever lived.

JOHN: *(Batting some left-over popcorn with his sneaker.)* Goodbye Einstein. Goodbye Freud.

PAULA: *(Ignoring him and whispering.)* Do you know what she told me last night?

SUSAN: What?

PAULA: *(Conspiratorial.)* Last night she told me Arthur was ashamed of her.

JOHN: *(Batting another piece of popcorn.)* Goodbye marriage.

SUSAN: Why ashamed?

JOHN: Maybe he hates the shitty movies she makes.

PAULA: More likely he resents she's so much more famous than he is. She's a bigger star than Jesus Christ.

JOHN: She certainly grosses more.

PAULA: This isn't a joke! *(Pause.)* The marriage is *kaput.* He's dumped her.

SUSAN: *(Astonished.)* Dumped Marilyn Monroe?

JOHN: That's a first!

PAULA: Last night he told her…Do you promise to keep what I say absolutely confidential between these four walls?

(Together.)

SUSAN: Of course.

JOHN: Sure.

PAULA: He told her she was interfering with his writing…

SUSAN: How awful for her.

PAULA: …and that he wasn't going to play nursemaid any more to a neurotic woman.

JOHN: *(Bitterly.)* I guess that's your job now.

PAULA: Lee and I can care for her a lot better than Arthur did.

JOHN: Arthur did the best he could. He just never figured on marrying an emotional cripple.

PAULA: Selfish man.

JOHN: You and Pops can't say a good word about him.

SUSAN: Arthur's not too wild about our family either.

JOHN: I can't imagine why.

PAULA: Because Marilyn respects your father so much. He knows what's best for her career.

JOHN: What's best for his own.

PAULA: Stop that!

JOHN: Sniffing around the backsides of celebrities.

(Together.)

PAULA: I said stop!

SUSAN: Johnny, go easy.

JOHN: *(To Susan.)* I hate it when she makes excuses for him. *(To Paula.)* You once had a career yourself, I hear.

PAULA: You know what happened to my career. Kazan named names.

JOHN: The blacklist is history. Why aren't you acting now?

PAULA: Because I took the time to act a mother. Making your bed, baking your brownies.

JOHN: When's the last time you baked me brownies? You're always on an airplane going somewhere.

PAULA: Am I taking vacations? Am I flying to Miami Beach? I'm coaching Marilyn, that's what I'm doing.

JOHN: That's no reason to give up acting.

PAULA: When you got a *yeshivabuche* in the house, somebody's got to make money for groceries. Who do you think pays for this apartment? And those books? *(Pointing to the books.)*

SUSAN: I contribute half the rent. And Dad makes money from his private classes.

PAULA: He makes *bupkis.* And he doesn't earn a red cent from the Studio. On his income we'd be lucky to have a flophouse on the Lower East Side.

JOHN: Why doesn't Marilyn pay rent? She uses my room more than I do.

PAULA: She pays me plenty for my coaching. By the hour.

SUSAN: And everything she owns goes to Mom and Dad when she dies.

PAULA: Not everything. But we are in the will.

JOHN: So *that's* why you don't act anymore.

PAULA: One actress in the family is enough.

SUSAN: Don't put it on me, Mom. The theatre can always use a good character woman.

PAULA: I'd like to go back to acting, but a lot of people need me.

JOHN: "The big wet tit."

PAULA: *(Slaps his face.)* Don't you dare talk to your mother like that!

JOHN: Ma!

SUSAN: You had that coming, Johnny.

JOHN: *(Nursing his red cheek.)* It's what everybody calls her.

PAULA: Not you. *(Insistently.)* Marilyn needs me.

JOHN: Tell that to Olivier. To him you were a total pain in the ass.

PAULA: *(Heated.)* He resented I could get a performance out of her, and he couldn't.

JOHN: Anyone can give a performance doing a hundred takes for each shot.

PAULA: She's a perfectionist.

JOHN: Mom, she can't remember lines!

PAULA: She's got to get it right.

SUSAN: Shhhh!

PAULA: And it paid off, didn't it? *She* got the Crystal Star Award for *The Prince and the Showgirl,* not Olivier. That was my doing. Paula Strasberg.

JOHN: Okay, you had to hold her hand. But why did Pop have to hold the other one?

PAULA: Olivier shook her confidence. Marilyn was on the overseas phone with Lee for hours, begging him to come.

JOHN: Pop went for the usual reason, to take credit for her career. *(Imitating Lee at a news conference.)* "Ladies and gentlemen of the press, may I present my newest creation—Marilyn Monroe."

PAULA: Stop knocking your father. *(Pause.)* Anyway, Marilyn is *my* creation. She can't say a line without my help.

JOHN: Tell that to Pops.

PAULA: *(Insistently.)* Marilyn is my creation! *(Having second thoughts.)* But your father has created a lot of great stars! Marlon…

JOHN: …Brando was Stella's student. He couldn't stand Pop.

PAULA: …Jimmy Dean, Paul Newman…

JOHN: Actors Studio Propaganda. Jimmy only spent a few weeks in the Studio. After Pop criticized his acting, he never came back.

PAULA: Your father is the greatest acting teacher in the world. And don't you forget it, bubby. I'm tired of arguing. You hungry yet? I'm going to make you both a nice, hot breakfast. *(As she goes into the kitchen.)* How do you like your eggs softboiled?

SUSAN: Three minutes.

JOHN: Five.

PAULA: Coming right up.

(Lee Strasberg enters from the bedroom, left, carrying the New York Times in one hand, and a book in the other. He is a short, sour-faced man, grey-haired and balding, wearing horn-rimmed glasses, who sniffs a lot on his sentences. He has a Lower East Side accent and a sinus condition which makes his throat click before he speaks. He always carries a handkerchief in his hand to staunch nosebleeds that recur whenever he's upset. Which is often. He's in bathrobe and slippers, and not in a very good mood.)

LEE: Paula, did you take the obituary page?

PAULA: *(From the kitchen.)* No, dear, I haven't seen the paper yet. I'm fixing breakfast.

LEE: *(To Susan.)* Happy New Year, Princess Blintzes.

SUSAN: *(Gives him a warm embrace and kiss.)* Happy New Year, Daddy.

LEE: *(Less warmly.)* Happy New Year, John.

(John is silent.)

LEE: The Terrible-Tempered Mr. Bang. *(Hands John the book he's holding.)* Here. A New Year's present. *(Taking the book back.)* Let me sign it.

JOHN: *(Pleased in spite of himself.)* What is it, Pop?

LEE: An advance copy of a new book on the Actor's Studio. Basically a long interview with your father. *(He scratches a few lines on the flyleaf, then hands it back to John. Takes Johnny's music off and puts a record on the turntable. Caruso singing "Una Furtiva Lagrima." He sings along a few bars from time to time.)*

JOHN: Thanks. *(Reading.)* "To my son John, who will, I hope, one day go further. Lee Strasberg." *(Irate.)* Lee Strasberg?

LEE: What's the matter?

JOHN: What's this for? Your archives?

LEE: *(To Susan.)* Do you know what he's talking about?

JOHN: You sign a book to your son "Lee Strasberg?"

LEE: What should I sign it?

JOHN: "Love, Dad" would have been nice.

LEE: I offer a present, he bites my hand.

JOHN: I'm sorry. Thanks.

LEE: Don't start tummeling me the first day of the new year.

JOHN: *(Muttering.)* I'll save it for Rosh Hashanah.

LEE: *(Sitting on the couch with the papers.)* You're going to give me a nosebleed.

JOHN: *(Backing off.)* Sorry, Dad.

LEE: *(Reaching into the couch and hauling out some coins and bills.)* Is this your cash?

JOHN: *(Feeling his pockets.)* Yes.

LEE: *(Puts it in his bathrobe.)* Not any more.

(John shrugs helplessly. Lee sits back and riffles through the Times.)

LEE: Where's that obituary page?

PAULA: *(Coming in from the kitchen with a breakfast tray.)* It's usually at the back of the B section. I'll find it for you. You finished with the Theatre page already?

LEE: I read it in bed. *(Sniffs.)*

PAULA: Want some breakfast?

SUSAN: *(Rising to help.)* I'll get it for him.

LEE: It can wait.

JOHN: How come you're always so interested in the obituaries? Checking out the competition?

LEE: After my father brought us here from the old country, first thing in the morning he would always look at the obituary page. Now I do. If my name isn't in it, I get dressed and go to work.

(Paula and Susan laugh. John is amused against his will. Susan eats her eggs and drinks some coffee and juice. John toys with his food. Lee reads.)

LEE: Why are the obits always so thin on Saturday? Only three writeups, and I never heard of any of them.

JOHN: Today's Friday.

LEE: It is? Funny. I thought it was Saturday.

PAULA: Maybe because it's a holiday.

LEE: Yeah. But that doesn't explain why the Saturday obituary page is always so thin. Nobody famous ever dies on Friday.

JOHN: Jesus died on Friday.

LEE: I don't count him.

JOHN: Why? Because he didn't make the *Times?*

LEE: I ask a simple question and he gives me Jesus.

JOHN: Famous people wait to make the Sunday paper. Nobody dies on Friday because nobody reads the *Times* on Saturday.

LEE: I do.

SUSAN: Dead people. Obituaries. Is that a subject for the first day of the year? This is a time for happy thoughts.

LEE: Like what?

SUSAN: Well, like the party. Everybody said it was our best ever.

LEE: Darling, people always rave about New Year's Eve at the Strasbergs. It's the social event of the New York season. But, I don't know, I haven't enjoyed these things much since Jimmy died.

JOHN: I never enjoy them. I'm always tripping over bloated egos.

PAULA: *(To Lee.)* You didn't enjoy the party?

LEE: The guests had a good time, Paula.

SUSAN: Your food was a big hit.

PAULA: It doesn't take much to make an actor happy—some chopped liver, a bowl of margaritas. But how do you cheer up an unhappy husband?

LEE: Nonsense, Paula, I'm fine.

PAULA: I saw you moping in the corner with Cheryl Crawford.

LEE: Moping?! She wants me to direct the new Williams play.

SUSAN: That's fabulous!

PAULA: With such an offer, you mope?

LEE: Don't congratulate me yet. Some of the backers have their own ideas.

JOHN: Of course, they want Kazan.

LEE: *(Shaking his head.)* Kazan has too many movies.

PAULA: So they'll offer it to you.

LEE: It's a possibility. They're supposed to let me know today.

PAULA: Of course they'll offer it to you. You're the best director in the business.

LEE: They haven't given me anything on Broadway since *Peer Gynt.* People don't respect me as a director any more. Only as a teacher.

PAULA: You're a great teacher.

LEE: I'm a great director, too. But what does Kazan want me to do in this Lincoln Center of his? The training program. I should be directing half the plays.

JOHN: When are you going to start your own theatre?

PAULA: You could have any actor in America. I would love to be directed by you.

SUSAN: *(Putting her head on his shoulder.)* Me too.

LEE: That's for the future. It'll have to wait.

JOHN: Why?

LEE: Some of my actors still have bad habits. Look at Sandy. With her adenoids, she sounds like she's suffering from permanent nasal drip. And don't give me that song and dance about how the Actor's Studio needs a speech teacher.

JOHN: It does.

LEE: Voice training makes actors artificial. I hate that fake British accent. *(Imitating Olivier in Hamlet.)* "Oh that this too, too solid flesh would melt…" Why give up your own natural accent in order to sound like an English aristocrat?

JOHN: You can't do Shakespeare with your own natural accent.

LEE: Who does Shakespeare any more?

PAULA: Voice work helps actors project.

LEE: It makes them indicate. Between truth and projection, I'll take truth. That's the advantage of the movies. The camera's not interested in projection. It cares only about behavior, about what's going on *inside.*

JOHN: Even in the movies Marilyn could use some voice work. Her acting is mostly heavy breathing.

LEE: That's a psychological problem. When she's depressed, her voice gets small and breathy.

JOHN: Is she depressed on every take?

LEE: She is. I just worry she'll go the same way as Jimmy.

SUSAN: Jimmy was years ago, Daddy. Time to move on.

LEE: Such a waste of talent. I saw *Giant* again the other night on the television and I cried. *(Tears come into his eyes.)* Such a truthful actor. The waste, the waste. All the talent and hard work that goes into getting it right. And then what the hell happens? That strange behavior that ruins so many of our people.

PAULA: They're not all like that.

LEE: Most of them. *(Looking intently at John.)* As soon as they reach a certain place, there it goes, the drugs, the drunkenness, the rest of it. You can tell somebody, Go to a psychiatrist, get help. But do they listen?

JOHN: Are you talking about Jimmy Dean or me?

LEE: Figure it out for yourself.

JOHN: I listened. I went to the shrink.

LEE: For two months.

JOHN: That was enough.

LEE: So what did you accomplish?

JOHN: Nothing. He slept and I lied.

LEE: A waste of money.

SUSAN: You got Marilyn to go to Dr. Kris.

LEE: Yeah, only because I wouldn't work with her unless she got some help.

JOHN: Marilyn can't stand her.

LEE: There's always a period in psychoanalysis when you get to hate your analyst.

JOHN: I never got past it.

LEE: That doesn't surprise me.

JOHN: How come you're always recommending therapy for everyone else but you never went yourself?

LEE: *(Joking.)* Maybe I'm afraid of what I might find out. *(More serious.)* Therapy helps unlock an actor's hidden resources. Without it, all you get is free-floating neurosis. *(Changing the record to the second movement of Beethoven's Seventh.)*

JOHN: How do you know you're not mistaking neurosis for talent with Marilyn?

LEE: *(With certainty.)* I know, that's how. *(Pause.)* She's always very close to the edge. Acting is the only thing that can save her.

SUSAN: I thought we were going to talk about happy things.

LEE: Beethoven makes me happy. This is a funeral march, but it makes me happy. Listen to the texture of that orchestration. It's like great acting.

SUSAN: I feel happy.

LEE: Well, you have a lot to be happy about. But Marilyn has had nothing but *tsoros* all her life. Poor thing, she couldn't fall asleep last night. I had to hold her in my arms and sing her lullabies.

JOHN: She didn't stay asleep long. She kept me up till after six.

LEE: *(Startled.)* Kept who up? You?! Why?

JOHN: How should I know?

LEE: Why didn't she wake me?

PAULA: She's got a thing for Johnny.

SUSAN: Yes, she really likes him. She gave him her Thunderbird.

LEE: Shut up, Susan. You didn't touch her or anything, did you?
   (John stays silent.)

LEE: Did you?

JOHN: *(Reluctantly.)* No.

LEE: I should hope not. She's in a highly vulnerable state.
   (Pause.)

JOHN: I just held her in my arms and sang her lullabies.

LEE: Don't be a smartass. *(Pause.)* Why didn't she come to me?

PAULA: She doesn't like to bother you.

LEE: Nonsense. Just last week, in the middle of the night, she came scratching at my door in that pitiful way of hers. On all fours.

SUSAN: That got your attention.

LEE: It's true psychologically delicate people have more access to their inner feelings.

JOHN: They certainly have more access to you.
   (Lee glares at him.)

PAULA: *(Trying to avoid the row.)* Your father is right. There's no such thing as a happy artist.

SUSAN: I guess I'm not neurotic enough to be a great actress.

LEE: You're a very good actress. After all, you're a Strasberg. You've had the finest training.

PAULA: From your mother.

LEE: From your father. But you're not there yet. Don't forget *Time Remembered*. That wasn't a production, it was a funeral service. You're not ready. You can't compare yourself yet to Kim or Geraldine.

SUSAN: Or to Marilyn?

LEE: There's no comparison.

JOHN: Blintzes is ten times the actress Marilyn is.

LEE: She's a fine actress. I said so, didn't I? But Marilyn is a Somebody. She's a great star.

PAULA: Darling, some day you'll be a great star, too.

JOHN: What are we talking about—talent or celebrity?

LEE: Talent. Marilyn's instrument may be a little rough right now. When she's uncertain, she freezes…

JOHN: That's a great actress?

LEE: *(Ignoring him.)* …but she acts with great instinctual truth.

JOHN: She can't act her way out of her bra.

LEE: *(Continuing to ignore him.)* With my help she could be another Eleanora Duse. Another Jeanne Eagels. In fact, that's one of the parts I'm going to direct her in—Sadie Thompson in *Rain*.

PAULA: So ABC called back about that?

LEE: *(Shaking his head.)* Not yet. But they know I go with the package. No Lee Strasberg, no Marilyn Monroe.

JOHN: Sadie Thompson should be no stretch. She does great hookers. Especially with her skirt blowing over her head.

SUSAN: Shut up, John!

LEE: *(Fiercely.)* Those *Seven Year Itch* parts are unworthy of her. She's the greatest raw talent since Marlon. Maybe she doesn't exactly know how to act yet, but with the right training, this girl could play all the great tragic roles—Lady Macbeth…

JOHN: …with sequins

LEE: …Grushenka…

JOHN: …with spangles.

LEE: I will not have her spoken of with disrespect in this house!

JOHN: Sorry.

LEE: You got a real vicious streak in you, John.

SUSAN: Why do you dish Marilyn so much, Johnny? I know you like her.

JOHN: What I think of her personally is not the point.

LEE: What is the point? You don't think she has great acting talent?

JOHN: She can play comedy. And wounded people. I liked her Blanche in *Streetcar*.

LEE: You liked it? Her Blanche was fantastic. Why do you think everybody at the Studio gave her a standing ovation.

JOHN: Because you did.

LEE: Because she was a sensation.

JOHN: I was in that scene, too. Maybe you don't remember—the newspaper boy?

LEE: You I didn't believe.

JOHN: Then why didn't you help me? You spent enough time on Marilyn.

LEE: She needs the time. Properly handled, there's nowhere she can't go.

(The tinkle of a dinner bell, followed by a voice from the bedroom.)

VOICE: Lee! Are you talking about me in there?

LEE: No, Marilyn, we're discussing the party. *(To the others.)* She's up.

VOICE: I don't like you talking about me there unless I'm there.

LEE: We're not, Marilyn.

VOICE: Where is everybody?

PAULA: We're all here, waiting for you, darling.

VOICE: I don't feel like putting any clothes on yet. And there's something I
  need to speak to Lee about.

PAULA: Do you want me, too, baby?

VOICE: Just Lee right now, Paula. Can you come to my bedroom. Please, Lee?

LEE: I'll be right there, Marilyn.

PAULA: *(Calling.)* I'll bring you in some breakfast.

VOICE: Is there any champagne left? The Veuve Cliquot I brought last night?
  (She pronounces this "Voove Clickquat.") I don't care if it's flat.

PAULA: *(Picking up the bottle of champagne.)* I'll bring it.

LEE: *I'll* bring it. *(He takes the bottle from her.)* She wants me.

JOHN: Ask her when she plans to vacate my room.

  (Lee glares at him and leaves.)

JOHN: He's like a doctor. On twenty-four hour call.

PAULA: Why do you want to upset your father, Johnny?

JOHN: The man is so self-centered.

PAULA: He loves you a lot.

JOHN: Don't crap a crapper.

PAULA: When you were a kid, he couldn't get enough of you. You were always
  on his lap, playing bouncey bouncey.

JOHN: And now?

PAULA: He's just not very demonstrative.

JOHN: *(Throws the book on the table and puts on his shoes.)* I don't know why
  I stay here.

PAULA: This is your home.

JOHN: Yeah, my home.

PAULA: *(Firmly.)* It will always be your home. *(Looking at his plate.)* You didn't
  finish your eggs.

JOHN: I'll just finish these margaritas. *(Refills his glass.)*

PAULA: I've got a son who drinks his meals. *(She exits with the dishes.)*

SUSAN: You're not going anywhere, Johnny. I need you here.

JOHN: You're going to Italy.

SUSAN: That's not certain.

JOHN: Then why didn't you talk to Pops about *Peyton Place?*

SUSAN: I will. At the right time.

JOHN: Something eating you? What?

SUSAN: Every time I think about leaving home I get butterflies in my stomach.

JOHN: Why?

SUSAN: I don't trust my acting away from Mom and Dad.

JOHN: You can act just fine on your own.

SUSAN: They helped me a lot with Anne Frank.

JOHN: They were protecting the Strasberg name. During Anne Frank, you were famous. Let's face it, Pops only loves famous people, beautiful women, and psychotics. In that order.

SUSAN: *(Giggling.)* Marilyn's all three.

JOHN: *(In a hushed voice.)* Is he screwing her?

SUSAN: Definitely not.

JOHN: How do you know? She's always throwing herself around. *(Pause.)* She came on to me last night.

SUSAN: You're kidding!

JOHN: I was lying here asleep, and she climbed onto the couch with me. Right under the blanket. I thought sure I was going to lose my cherry.

SUSAN: Did you?

JOHN: *(Nodding No.)* Too smashed. And it didn't help she kept running on about Pops, what a great man he is. Dammit! My big opportunity.

SUSAN: So nothing happened?

JOHN: She stroked my hair. And told me I was a nice boy.

SUSAN: Poor John. The last virgin. *(Sympathetic, her hand on his arm.)* Anyway, don't worry about Dad. His relationship with Marilyn is strictly professional.

JOHN: He's always had the hots for beautiful actresses—Jennifer Jones?

SUSAN: She was so gorgeous, I was in love with her myself. You know, I darkened my hair and eyebrows to look like her.

JOHN: You're doing the same with Marilyn.

SUSAN: What do you mean?

JOHN: You've gone blonde. You chew a lot of sleeping pills. And that sweater you're busting out of. You could be Marilyn in *Some Like It Hot.*

SUSAN: I like the way she looks, that's all.

JOHN: You want to look like a hooker?

SUSAN: No, I'm talking about her softness and vulnerability. And she has the most wonderful skin, don't you think? Like an elastic powder puff.

JOHN: She's the only woman in the world who looks naked with her clothes on.

SUSAN: That's what I mean.

JOHN: *(Groucho accent, pretending to flick a cigar.)* You want to look naked with your clothes on?

SUSAN: I could use a little of what she's got. Remember that summer we were all on Fire Island? I saw her standing in the nude, looking out a window. And when I told her I wished I had such a beautiful body, she said, "Why? I'm just a joke."

JOHN: I don't get you. One minute you're playing Daddy's girl. The next you're ready to pose for nudie calendars.

SUSAN: I only wish that Dad would look at me the way he looks at her.

JOHN: Listen, Blintzes, don't try to compete with Pop's bimbos.

SUSAN: *(Defensive.)* I'm not competing. I'm just trying to be friends with her.

JOHN: You don't resent Marilyn?

SUSAN: No. I don't mind his interest in famous actresses. But I think it stinks he's fooling around with his students.

JOHN: Last night, Sophia tried to give him an innocent goodbye kiss. You know what he said? *{Imitating Lee.)* "I don't believe it. Embrace me with your whole body." Like he was giving her an acting lesson.

SUSAN: Did Mom see it?

JOHN: I don't know. She was in the room.

SUSAN: She's always surrounded by these gorgeous hunks who adore her. She should be having affairs herself.

JOHN: Oscar Wilde said, "Faithfulness is laziness."

VOICE: *(The bell tinkles.)* Johnny! Can you be a nice boy and give me a hand?

JOHN: *(To Susan.)* Why does she remind me of a gigantic suction machine?

VOICE: *(Ringing the bell again.)* Johnny? Are you in there?

JOHN: What is it Marilyn?

VOICE: I can't get this toilet to flush. It's all stopped up.

JOHN: Isn't Dad with you?

VOICE: No, he's getting dressed.

JOHN: Okay, Marilyn, I'll be right in. *(To Susan.)* Another job for Plungerman. *(Picks up the toilet plunger from inside the kitchen and wields it like a weapon.)*

JOHN: By day, a modest college dropout from Wisconsin. By night, the caped crusader from Central Park! Faster than a leaky faucet! Stronger than a stopped-up toilet. Plungerman!
(Paula enters, passing him as he leaves.)

PAULA: Where's that one going?

SUSAN: To fix Marilyn's toilet. *(Pause.)* Mom—Johnny thinks I should take that Italian film.

PAULA: I do, too. You'll have a chance to test your wings.

SUSAN: I could test my wings right here with *Peyton Place.*

PAULA: Time to get away from Daddy.

SUSAN: I'd go to Italy if you came and coached me.

PAULA: I'm always there for you.

SUSAN: Even if Marilyn needs you?

PAULA: Susie, try to understand. I promised to coach her in *The Misfits.* I can't afford to lose her now. She's our bread and butter.

SUSAN: I'm your flesh and blood!

PAULA: *(Puts her arms around her.)* You can always call. It's not like you're going to China. *(She begins to choke up.)* My little girl. Leaving home. *(Wipes her eyes and arranges her hair.)* I'll go finish up in the kitchen. Oy, my toes feel like sausages. *(Limps into the kitchen.)*
(Lee enters. He's dressed now in slacks and a monastic collarless shirt, without coat or tie.)

LEE: Where's Johnny?

SUSAN: With Marilyn.

LEE: *(Suspicious.)* What?

SUSAN: The toilet's stopped up.

LEE: Oh.

SUSAN: *(Pause, as she pores over her script.)* Daddy…

LEE: What?

SUSAN: I need your help.

LEE: This can't wait?

SUSAN: I have this scene scheduled for tomorrow, and I can't make any sense out of it.

LEE: *(Putting his book down.)* All right, darling. What's giving you the trouble?

SUSAN: The whole character. Here's a woman been a spinster all her life. And she falls for this doctor who's not interested in her.

LEE: *Summer and Smoke.* So what's so difficult?

SUSAN: I have no idea how a dried-up spinster expresses love.

LEE: Like anyone else. Look inside. There are things in yourself you have to explore.

SUSAN: Like what?

LEE: Your feelings for Richard Burton.

SUSAN: *(In real pain.)* Daddy, I'm trying to forget him.

LEE: Pain is the beginning of art. You must be willing to invade any part of yourself for your acting. When you go on stage, you give your life to this character. What did you feel when he dropped you?

SUSAN: I felt numb.

LEE: But underneath the numb, what? Rage? Sorrow? Despair?

SUSAN: I still feel it.

LEE: Then use it.

SUSAN: *(Beginning to cry.)* I can't.

LEE: *(Gently.)* It means you're not over this affair yet.

SUSAN: I try not to think about him any more. The whole thing was hopeless from the start. He sleeps with all his leading ladies. That's how he rehearses his parts.

LEE: An actor prepares.

SUSAN: I should have known he would never leave his wife and kids, no matter what he promised when he was drunk.

LEE: Well, he's a great star. You have to make allowances.

SUSAN: I made all the allowances.

LEE: You learned nothing from this affair?

SUSAN: When he left me… *(Starts to cry.)*

LEE: *(Takes her in his arms.)* Blintzes. Be grateful you have the passion…Some of us don't.

SUSAN: Thank you, Daddy.

LEE: *(Triumphant.) Now* you're ready to play *Summer and Smoke.*

SUSAN: You are so good with actors.

LEE: That's my profession. I was always fascinated with actors, even as a kid. I used to sell candy in the Yiddish theatre—just to get into the shows. I saw all the greats—Boris Thomashefsky, Jacob Adler, David Kessler. Kessler especially. He *was* the Method! You haven't seen *King Lear* or *The Merchant of Venice* if you didn't see Kessler do them in Yiddish. Plays about ungrateful children. That's what Jewish audiences loved best.

SUSAN: An actor was something in those days.

LEE: A God. When Thomashefsky died, they laid out his body on the stage of the Yiddish National Theatre on Houston Street where he played, and there were lines down Second Avenue from Fourteenth Street just to pay their respects.

SUSAN: Today, an actor can't even get an apartment. Unless he's a star.

LEE: Without a big name in this country, you're a nobody.

SUSAN: *(Sits up and puts her arm on his.)* Daddy. *(Pause, while she works up her courage on this difficult subject.)* Daddy, I got the offer on that Italian movie.

LEE: Take it, Blintzes. You need to get away from your Mother. *(Sniffs.)* She means well, but you have to start taking responsibility for your own life.

SUSAN: Then come with me to Rome. One of you has to help me.

LEE: Impossible. I can't leave the Studio.

SUSAN: *(Rebelling.)* Then I'll stay here and do *Peyton Place.*

LEE: *Peyton Place* you will absolutely turn down.

SUSAN: It could make me a somebody in Hollywood.

LEE: I won't have another *Time Remembered* on my hands.

SUSAN: Why does everything always come back to *Time Remembered?*

LEE: *(Heatedly.)* You were a disgrace in that piece of dreck! How could you do that to me?

SUSAN: Dad, it was a classic.

LEE: A classic is a classic only when it is alive and not a corpse. Better classics should die than be butchered like that.

SUSAN: I got no help from the director.

LEE: You'll get no help on *Peyton Place* either. Another hack.

SUSAN: It's my chance to have my name above the title.

LEE: Is that all you want? To see your name above the title?

JOHN: *(Entering during this last speech with the plunger.)* Since when does Lee Strasberg object to stars having their names above the title?

LEE: I won't have my daughter playing trash.

JOHN: That doesn't bother you at the Studio.

LEE: Stick to things you know. Like toilets. Susan, Italy will be good for you. You're too dependent on your mother.

JOHN: That gets her out of the house. How do you propose to get rid of me?

LEE: Take up a decent profession.

JOHN: I could always become a plumber.

LEE: This is serious.

JOHN: What do you have in mind?

LEE: I thought *you* had something in mind. Weren't you once planning to go into medicine?

JOHN: The only doctor this family needs is a head shrinker.

(The phone rings.)

JOHN: In residence.

(The phone rings again. Lee picks it up.)

LEE: Yeah, who is it? *(His face brightens.)* Geraldine, how good to hear from you. It was a fine party, wasn't it? *(Pause.)* I'm sorry you're feeling so low.

Well, don't worry so much about that scene. It'll come, just give it a little time. Remember, Olga is the oldest of the three sisters and the most solitary. She has this unrequited love for Vershinin. I don't care what they say; why else does she live on dreams of the past? Have you connected with any memories yet? Well, for example, you know that beat where Olya says Natasha makes her sick? Make that more immediate. Think of someone who once made you sick. She did? Your mother made you puke? How often? Well, use it. Use everything. You're welcome. Call any time. *(He hangs up.)*

JOHN: *(To Susan.)* See what I mean? Free analysis.

LEE: That's the whole meaning of emotional memory.

JOHN: What's your emotional memory for playing a loving father?

LEE: Say that line again with more conviction. I didn't believe you!

JOHN: *(Shouting.)* WHAT'S YOUR EMOTIONAL MEMORY FOR PLAYING A LOVING FATHER!!!

LEE: Better. Your anger at least I believe. What's cheap and phoney is your sarcasm. All right, shall we start again? What do you intend to do with your life?

JOHN: I dream every day about starting my own theatre.

LEE: Dream a little less, do a little more.

JOHN: You're not interested in my problems.

LEE: Your problems I've heard before. I'm interested in your solutions.

JOHN: Right now I'm trying to become an actor. Maybe you'll have more time for me when I'm famous.

LEE: I won't hold my breath. *(Lee holds a book in front of his face.)*

JOHN: Do you read those books? Or just hide behind them?

LEE: I read *all* of them—some twice. I love great books.

JOHN: Then why don't you love great plays?

LEE: I worship great plays.

JOHN: How do you explain what's coming out of the Studio? *Hatful of Rain?* Who does Shakespeare? Or even O'Neill?

LEE: The Studio isn't about dramatic literature. It's about acting. I teach actors how to be truthful. *Truthful.* No matter how fake the material. Even the television garbage. It's the actor who creates the reality of a scene, not the playwright.

JOHN: And you say you love great literature.

LEE: Literature is my life! When's the last time you read a book?

JOHN: You don't care what I read.

LEE: *(To Susan.)* How do you talk to this boy?

SUSAN: Help him, Daddy. He just needs a little of your time.

LEE: *(Flaring.)* Goddamn it, what do they want from me? Everybody, everywhere—at the Studio, in my house. Chewing off pieces of my flesh. Do you know how many people come to me for attention? And advice? About their sex lives? About their neuroses? About how to be a star? Hundreds!

SUSAN: But Daddy, we're your children.

LEE: I give you twenty-four hours a day. Just because we have a girl in the house—a person of stupendous gifts—aching for love, doesn't mean I don't give you too. You're all my children.

SUSAN: *(Aside to John.)* Isn't that an Arthur Miller play?

LEE: *(Not hearing her.)* I don't play favorites.

JOHN: *(To Susan.)* No, it's a daily soap. *(Louder.)* Pop provides the suds.

LEE: Smartass, you're the rotten actor, not me.

JOHN: I'm out of here. *(Makes for the door and his coat.)*

SUSAN: Johnny!

LEE: You can't even act your resentment truthfully.

SUSAN: *(Trying to stop him.)* Stay. Daddy didn't mean anything. Tell him you didn't mean anything, Daddy.

LEE: Let him go.

PAULA: *(Coming in from the kitchen.)* Where are you off to?

LEE: Our son has decided to pull a Khrushchev and take a walk.

PAULA: He ain't walking nowhere. You stay right here, John. You and your father have got to stop this nonsense.

LEE: You're suggesting it's my fault?

JOHN: No, it's all my fault. Everybody knows Pop is the plaster saint of the American theatre.

LEE: The reading is lousy, but the line I believe.

SUSAN: *(Hastily, to avoid further quarrel.)* Come on, John. We'll both go for a walk.

JOHN: Let's make it a drink.

PAULA: John!

SUSAN: We'll go to Tip Toe Inn for a turkey sandwich.

PAULA: *(To Susan.)* First put on some makeup. You can't be seen like that. You're not a nobody.

SUSAN: Who will see me?

PAULA: Well, wear something on your head at least. And if you're going to Tip Toe, bring back a quart of sauerkraut and some dill pickles. We'll have it with the boiled beef flanken.

SUSAN: Okay, Mom. Bye Daddy. *(She grabs a shawl and starts to go out with John.)*

JOHN: *(Guiltily.)* Wait, Blintzes. I'm broke. Pop grabbed all my cash.

LEE: *(Reaching in his pocket for a few bills.)* Here, big shot. Next time you stage a rebellion, make sure you can afford it.

(John, humiliated, mutters a reluctant thank you, as he and Susan exit.)

PAULA: *(Pause.)* Nu? What's up with Marilyn?

LEE: She's in bad shape, Paula. She wants to go back to Arthur, beg his forgiveness, but I was firm. She'll suffer for a while, but it'll pass. There can be no reconciliation if she wants to work with me.

PAULA: Where is she going to live? In their apartment? Or the Connecticut house?

LEE: Neither place. She can't go back. The break must be complete. It's the only way she can grow as an artist.

PAULA: But where will she stay?

LEE: Here with us.

PAULA: *(Quickly.)* No.

LEE: Why not?. We could put her up for a while. Susan will be in Italy. It's just that kid.

PAULA: Johnny can't sleep on the sofa every night.

LEE: Only until she's settled. Finds another apartment. And in a month she'll be on location in Nevada with this piece of crap! *(Tosses away a script of* The Misfits *he had been reading.)*

PAULA: She's still doing Arthur's movie?

LEE: She has to. She signed a contract. But her part is an insult. Even the horses have bigger roles. She's upstaged by stallions.

PAULA: For Arthur, writing movies is slumming.

LEE: No, you're wrong. He never learned to write parts for women.

PAULA: I'd play Linda Loman in a minute.

LEE: I never believed her. Patience on a monument.

PAULA: And how would you describe me?

LEE: Stop it, Paula. Arthur doesn't understand women—and he certainly doesn't understand her. I'm the one who knows how to dredge up the buried treasure. That girl will become one of the really great actresses of the stage when I teach her to use the pain of this divorce.

PAULA: Do you think that's healthy, Lee? Interfering in her personal life? With someone more balanced, yes. But with a girl in Marilyn's condition, it could be dangerous.

LEE: Stick to coaching. You know nothing about therapy. If she's going to make it as a serious artist, she has to be totally truthful with me about her psychological condition.

PAULA: Sometimes I think…Now don't get mad.

LEE: *(Impatiently.)* What?

PAULA: Sometimes I think the children are right. You give all your time to your actors and nothing to them.

LEE: You, too, on this subject? I give Susan lots of attention. Who was responsible for Anne Frank?

PAULA: I was, that's who—

LEE: You!

PAULA: I coached her every line of that part—

LEE: Some coaching!

PAULA: The same thing with *Time Remembered.*

LEE: *Time Remembered* is nothing to remember.

PAULA: She got great reviews.

LEE: I'm not talking reviews. It was a bad experience for her. She's still mourning that affair with Burton.

PAULA: You blame me for that?

LEE: Of course. Who told Burton to break in your little girl so she could have an experience with a great lover?

PAULA: I wanted her first time to be memorable.

LEE: This is a mother talking?

PAULA: Something to look back on with fond feelings.

LEE: I hope you hear yourself.

PAULA: Better him than some cheap jerk-off from the Studio.

LEE: No one in the whole Studio was worthy of her?

PAULA: Have you any idea what goes on in that pig sty of yours? You got guys like Steve McQueen standing in the doorway asking each girl, "You wanna? You wanna?" Until one of them says yes.

LEE: You tell me not to meddle in Marilyn's personal life, but you can meddle in Susan's.

PAULA: She's my child.

LEE: She's our child.

PAULA: Then treat her that way.

LEE: What do you mean? I spend hours working on her acting.

PAULA: She doesn't want from you acting. She wants from you love. Why don't you take her out sometimes? Maybe to the museum to see the Egyptian collection, like when she was a kid?

LEE: She's not a kid any more.

PAULA: She's more of a kid than you think.

LEE: She doesn't ask me.

PAULA: Marilyn doesn't have to ask.

LEE: I don't take Marilyn to museums. I talk to her about the work.

PAULA: The work, the work. It's always the work.

LEE: *(Passionately.)* There is nothing more important in my life than the work. It is the work I will be remembered for. *(Sniffs.)* Long after all of us are dead, people will say, Lee Strasberg created great actors.

PAULA: And a miserable family.

LEE: If it wasn't for Marilyn in there, I'd walk right out of this goddamn house. This minute.

PAULA: That's all your home means to you? A place to put up Marilyn? Are you fucking her too?

LEE: *(In a rage.)* Just for the sake of argument, will you kindly shut your mouth?!! You're giving me another nosebleed.
(The phone rings.)

LEE: Answer it.

PAULA: Hello? Oh, Cheryl. Yes, it was, wasn't it? Yes, he's right here. *(To Lee, nervously.)* Lee, it's Cheryl Crawford.

LEE: *(Taking the phone.)* Yes, Cheryl. Yes, yes. I understand. No, I didn't expect they would. Yes, I know you did everything you could. Don't worry. Yes, I'm fine, I'm fine. Happy New Year to you too. *(He remains still, absentmindedly tapping the phone.)*

PAULA: So what's the story?

LEE: They're taking Alan Schneider.

PAULA: I can't believe it! You could direct that play with your eyes closed. Doesn't Tennessee have any say in the matter?

LEE: Apparently he doesn't want me either. There's always the new boy on the block. *Goddamn* it!

PAULA: *(Trying to calm him.)* Lee, this too shall pass. Something else will come along. Who knows? Maybe ABC will offer you *Rain.*

LEE: Stop mothering me! I'm not your baby.

PAULA: So what *am* I good for? To powder Marilyn's tushie so you can take the credit?

VOICE: *(Ringing the bell.)* Lee, what's going on in there? Are you arguing about me? Please don't!

LEE: No, darling. Just a little family discussion.

VOICE: Well, then could you come back in here, please? Just for a second? We haven't finished our talk yet.

LEE: I'll be with you in a minute, Marilyn. *(To Paula, handkerchief to his bleeding nose.)* You see how she needs me? Try to pull yourself together.
VOICE: *(The bell rings.)* Lee, are you coming?
LEE: I'm coming, Marilyn. My darling. *(He exits.)*
PAULA: *(To herself, bitterly.)* And he talks about truth.
(Blackout.)

END OF ACT I

ACT II
SCENE I

It is five o'clock in the evening of the same day. The sun is setting. The morning debris in the living room has been thoroughly cleaned up. Paula is sitting on the couch, working on an astrological chart. An old scrapbook lies open on the table. Susan and John enter from the foyer. Susan has a deli package in her hand.

PAULA: Thank God you're back. What time is it?

SUSAN: About five. Where's Daddy?

PAULA: Where do you think?

JOHN: Again?

PAULA: Still. He's been in there since noon.
(*Susan and John exchange glances.*)

SUSAN: Here's your pickles and sauerkraut. What are you working on, Mom?

PAULA: Marilyn's astrological chart. Saturn's in the ascendant. Not a good month for Geminis. (*Closing the chart and taking the packages.*) Nu, what took you so long? You didn't stop at a bar, Johnny?
(*John winces.*)

SUSAN: (*Quickly.*) We went to see *East of Eden* at the Yorktown.

PAULA: (*Returning to the living room.*) Is it still good?

SUSAN: Better. Jimmy really had it. But what a mumbler!

PAULA: That child dearly loved to mumble.

SUSAN: (*Looking towards the audience, as if through a window.*) God, the park is magical this time of year. When the days get short and the lights start to flicker in the mist, it breaks my heart.

PAULA: (*Rises to join her, with her arm around her.*) I love the pond when it's frozen over. Taking this apartment was the best thing we ever did.

JOHN: I don't care if I ever see it again. (*He puts a Jazz record on the turntable.*)

PAULA: You'll change your mind in a few more years.

JOHN: Think I'll have my room back in a few more years?

SUSAN: (*Picking up the scrapbook.*) What's this, Mom?

PAULA: An old scrapbook I found in the bureau. I was looking through it while you were gone.

SUSAN: What a pretty woman you were.

PAULA: I was gorgeous. You can't tell from what I look like now. (*Goes to the table and begins to turn the pages.*) This is me in *Waiting for Lefty.*

(Paula, John, and Susan sit on the couch and examine the scrapbook.)

PAULA: Every man in the Group Theatre was crazy about Paula Miller. Not just your father. When he stole me away, there was such a commotion.

JOHN: Pops stole you away from your first husband?

PAULA: Right out of his arms. *(Turning another page.)* That one, there. The grump. He made such a scene. Shouting, screaming. He threatened to tear Lee apart.

JOHN: Why didn't he?

PAULA: He couldn't catch him. Your father I couldn't resist. Look at him, the firebrand. *(Turning to another snapshot.)* So passionate, so determined.

JOHN: *(Turning the pages.)* Who's this?

PAULA: Stella Adler in *Awake and Sing.* Before she bobbed her nose. I was prettier, don't you think? With my own nose?

JOHN: *(Continuing to turn pages.)* What giants! Stella and Luther Adler. Harold Clurman. Odets. John Garfield.

PAULA: And your father.

JOHN: And my father. But there must have been some reason why they always wanted to kick him out.

PAULA: Jealousy.

JOHN: Jealousy?

PAULA: *(Putting the scrapbook away.)* Well, after Stella met Stanislavsky in Paris, she claimed he disapproved of Lee's emphasis on private moments and emotional memory.

SUSAN: Was that true?

PAULA: *(Shrugs.)* Who cares? Your father was creating a technique for Americans. Not Russians.

JOHN: You mean a technique for American movie stars.

SUSAN: What's wrong with the movies?

JOHN: It's not an actor's medium.

SUSAN: Whose medium is it?

JOHN: Directors. And pretty faces.

SUSAN: Should I take that as a compliment?

PAULA: Don't let him make you feel guilty about Hollywood. The whole Group Theatre ended up there.

JOHN: That may be. But they had a permanent acting company, where people could work together and trust each other. Pop never had Clurman's commitment to a Group ideal.

PAULA: Your father will have his own company when the moment comes.

(Lee enters, looking haggard and distraught. Seeing him, John goes to the bar

to pour himself a stiff drink from the Scotch bottle. Lee takes John's record off the turntable and puts on some Schubert—the Fantasia for Four Hands.)

PAULA: Finally. Do you know how long you've been in there?

LEE: Don't, Paula. Let me listen to some decent music. *(Pause.)* She's more depressed than I've ever seen her.

PAULA: Poor thing.

LEE: She claims you and I don't pay her enough attention. That it all goes to the kids.

JOHN: *(At the bar.)* Ha!

LEE: She's convinced we're always talking about her in here, always watching her. You know what she said? "I can't even have a nervous breakdown in private."

PAULA: What made her say such a thing?

LEE: She feels bad about taking John's room. *(With a look at John.)* She heard him complaining.

JOHN: *(Whispering.)* Is she eavesdropping on us?

LEE: Move away from her door. Come over here.

(They all move away from Marilyn's room.)

LEE: I'm too nervous to enjoy this. *(Taking the needle off the record.)* We got to stop talking about her in here.

PAULA: She needs Dr. Kris.

LEE: I offered to call Dr. Kris. She yanked the receiver out of my hand and smashed it down on the cradle. Broke the plastic.

PAULA: She's scared Dr. Kris will put her in the hospital again.

JOHN: She's a classic paranoid schizophrenic. She ought to be hospitalized.

PAULA: Like her mother? That scares her silly.

LEE: I'm afraid to leave her alone.

PAULA: Did you take away the pills?

LEE: How could I? She's suspicious enough as it is.

PAULA: Those pills are lethal. Especially with champagne.

SUSAN: Don't worry. She's an expert on drugs. Once she showed me how to puncture a sleeping pill with a needle to make it work faster.

LEE: Are you still taking that stuff?

SUSAN: *(Sheepish.)* Not often.

LEE: Don't, it's poison.

PAULA: You think she'll overdose again?

SUSAN: When did she overdose?

PAULA: Last year, when she lost the baby.

SUSAN: Miscarriages and abortions. The great sex goddess and nothing works down there.

PAULA: She scares me. Yesterday she said, "I know I have to die, but do I have to grow old and sick?"

LEE: John's right. For once. She is getting a little *meshuga.* Now she believes we're all plotting against her. She said something about a sweater Blintzes told her she'd give her and then didn't. What was that about?

SUSAN: My God, did that set her off?

(Together.)

PAULA: What did you do?

LEE: What happened?

SUSAN: Well, you know she's always borrowing my clothes. Last night at the party I was wearing my hand-knit Italian sweater. The one I love so much? She said it was her color, it was the style she liked, and asked to try it on.

LEE: Of course, you let her.

SUSAN: Yes, but I told her it wouldn't fit, that she might stretch it out of shape.

JOHN: *(Refilling his glass.)* That's an understatement.

SUSAN: Of course, it did fit. Perfectly. But it was my favorite sweater. So I said, "It's too tight, otherwise you could have it."

PAULA: Susie, that wasn't generous.

JOHN: She has to give Marilyn the clothes off her back?

SUSAN: This morning when I woke up, I found this note under my door. *(She takes a small note out of her pocket and reads it.)* "Thanks for your first impulse. Maybe you could buy me one in Rome. I'd pay you back."

PAULA: Learn to be more generous.

SUSAN: I resent how she's always taking my things.

LEE: That was mean-spirited of you.

SUSAN: Are you telling me I have to give away my clothes to keep Marilyn from committing suicide?

LEE: With a woman in such a condition, you have to humor her.

JOHN: Like you humored me when I had my nervous breakdown.

LEE: You call that a nervous breakdown? Drinking? Skipping classes? Dropping out of school?

JOHN: If it was anyone else you'd call it a nervous breakdown.

LEE: You're a Strasberg. You're supposed to have breakthroughs, not breakdowns.

JOHN: I'm not allowed to have problems?

LEE: You have to be stronger than other people.

JOHN: Oh! That's why I ended up in the hospital! Because I was weak!

LEE: You ended up in a hospital because you jumped out a window.

SUSAN: Daddy!

LEE: It's no secret. He jumped out a window.

JOHN: Only the second floor.

LEE: What's the difference the floor? It was enough to put you in a psycho ward.

JOHN: The psychiatric wing of the university hospital.

LEE: What's the difference the wing? Since when does a Strasberg act like a drunken goy?

JOHN: And you're the soul of Jewish virtue?

LEE: I don't take drugs. I don't get drunk. I don't get thrown out of school.

JOHN: *(Meaningfully.)* There are worse sins.

LEE: For instance?

JOHN: Being a lousy parent.

LEE: Oh, I see. It's my fault.

JOHN: Other fathers visit their sons. Not you. I was in a strange college in Wisconsin for four months, thousands of miles from home, and I never saw you once.

LEE: I hate to fly.

JOHN: To Hollywood you fly. To Marilyn you fly. You could have called me.

LEE: I called you.

JOHN: Once.

LEE: Long distance is expensive.

JOHN: Bullshit.

LEE: Shut your foul mouth. A father should get some respect from his children. In his own house.

JOHN: Sorry.

LEE: In the old days, in Jewish households, what the father said was law. Nowadays the children rule.

JOHN: I say I'm sorry and he gives me a lecture on Jewish history.

LEE: Why, in the Studio, do people keep quiet when I speak? Here the head of the family is a nobody.

JOHN: *(Shouting.)* How many times do I have to say I'm sorry?

LEE: Enough to mean it.

JOHN: *(Going to him and holding his arms in a strong embrace.)* Dad, Dad.

LEE: What are you doing?

JOHN: Help me. Help me!

LEE: Stop holding me so tight! *(Pushes John away so roughly he falls to the floor.)*

PAULA: Lee! John!

LEE: Be careful how you touch people. I've told you before. You're too rough. They don't like it.

JOHN: *(Rising from the floor, red with anger.)* What did I do?

LEE: *(Backs away, cowering.)* Don't let him hit me.

JOHN: *(Pinning his arms to his sides and backing him against the wall.)* You scared of me? Scared of your own son? Well, at least that's some kind of feeling.

LEE: *(Terror-stricken, screaming, trying to wriggle out of his grasp.)* Let go of me! Let go of me! Who do you think I am? Your mother?

JOHN: *(Lets go of him, laughing sardonically.)* What does that mean?

LEE: Get out of here.

JOHN: You teach actors how to feel, but you feel nothing for your family.

LEE: *(To Paula.)* Are you listening to your son?

JOHN: You know why you're such a lousy director? You can't relate to people. That's why *Peer Gynt* flopped.

LEE: *(Irate.)* *Peer Gynt* flopped because of the set.

JOHN: It wasn't the set, it was you. You didn't know how to communicate with the designer. Or anyone else.

LEE: I don't have to hear this.

JOHN: *(Slightly hysterical.)* You talk about Truth, but can you face the truth? Everyone at the Studio thinks you're King Shit. You don't know fuck-all about working with actors on a play. I could outdirect you any day!

LEE: You couldn't direct traffic on Flatbush Avenue.

JOHN: I know how to talk to people. I don't blame them for my failures.

LEE: You're a nobody!

JOHN: You can't even pay the rent on your own apartment.

LEE: I'm not listening to this.

JOHN: You can't even pass a driving test.

LEE: Who needs to drive? I am a great stage director! I take the subway.

JOHN: You're nuts. Do you know that? Absolutely nuts.

VOICE: *(Bell tinkles.)* Can you stop shouting in there? I'm trying to sleep?

LEE: Sorry, Marilyn. We're just having a little family disagreement. We'll be more quiet. *(Whispering to John.)* See, you woke Marilyn.

JOHN: Big deal!

PAULA: *(Moving in to separate them.)* John, that's enough. Apologize to your father.

JOHN: He started it.

PAULA: You refusing?

JOHN: Yes.

PAULA: Then go to your room.

> (*John makes a sardonic gesture.*)

PAULA: Then go to Susie's room. Just get out of here.

SUSAN: Mom's right. Come to my room. You wanted to watch the Rose Bowl, didn't you? Okay?

> (*John hesitates for a moment, then leaves the room with Susan.*)

LEE: You know who your son is now. No control. The little *pisher.*

PAULA: He has a bad temper. Just like you.

LEE: Am I so quick to accuse?

PAULA: Your actors can all act crazy. But the slightest fit from Johnny gives you *spilkes.*

LEE: If he had their talent…

PAULA: Talent excuses everything?

LEE: Of course it does.

PAULA: (*Placating.*) All I mean is you should relate like father and son.

LEE: I can relate to Susan. But I can't get through to Johnny. (*Sniffs.*) It was the same with my father. When he came home from work, he'd look at me and I'd look at him. And nothing would pass between us. All he wanted when he got old was to listen to his radio.

PAULA: Why didn't you sit and listen with him?

LEE: What? *Fibber McGee and Molly? Amos and Andy?*

PAULA: What did it matter what? You could have sat on a couch together, put your arm around him.

LEE: The man was uneducated. His only reading was the Talmud. I asked him once for money to buy a book. You know what he said? "For what you need a book, you already got a book."

PAULA: With all your learning, you're still not close to your son. Or to me. One thing Johnny was right about, the touching. How long has it been since you touched me?

LEE: Back on that subject again?

PAULA: Your dogs you pet, but not your wife.

LEE: Listen, we've been married twenty-five years. You want me to behave like Romeo?

PAULA: I never once stopped feeling like your Juliet.

LEE: Then lose some weight. You're getting fat as a pig.

PAULA: It's Johnny's fault. He kicked out my stomach when he was born.

LEE: That was eighteen years ago! Go on a diet!

PAULA: You see? Once I was your sex goddess. Now I'm your fat wife. *(Pressing on.)* And I sacrificed my career for you.

LEE: Be honest. You weren't that hot an actress.

PAULA: I could have been a damned good actress if I'd gone on with my career. And if you had given me just a taste of what you give Marilyn.

LEE: What are you telling me? *(Imitating Brando in* On The Waterfront.*)* That you could have been a "somebody?" You could have been a "contender?"

PAULA: I had talent. But you can't be an actress if you don't act. It's all shriveled up, but I had talent. All I got left is the desire, like a bubble rattling round in my chest, giving me heartburn.

LEE: Take a bromo.

PAULA: Fuck you. John is right. You were born with no *rachmonos.*

LEE: *Rachmonos* was for millionaires. Not greenhorns fresh off the boat.

PAULA: Your life wasn't that hard.

LEE: No? I worked my way up from zero. Who was supposed to be my role model, a Jewish pants presser who dovened all day and never learned good English?

PAULA: Your parents provided you with a loving home.

LEE: A tenement with no running water? Nothing to eat—the cockroaches were fatter than we were. The only toilet was an outhouse on the ground floor, and we were five floors up. *(Pause.)* And you think it was any easier at the Group? Holding classes for all those self-centered Yids? I was the sparkplug of that place, not Harold. He just made pretty speeches.

PAULA: He was a great inspiration.

LEE: He was a great inspiration, but I did the hard work. Without me the Studio would have closed down like the Group. I'm the one who made it what it is today. I'm the one who made the Method famous.

PAULA: Yes, you did. *(Sighs.)*

LEE: Nothing came easy for me.

PAULA: My life wasn't easy either.

LEE: We all had it hard. That's how we learned to work. Not like John. His own car at eighteen. The most expensive schools. Out of which he gets kicked out of.

PAULA: He'll straighten out.

LEE: Drinking. What kind of thing is that for a Jewish kid? A little schnapps now and then, yes. But he's turning into an alcoholic.

PAULA: It's hard for him, being the son of such a famous man.

LEE: He doesn't know the meaning of work. I don't ask he should be an actor, God forbid. Just that he devote himself to something fully.

PAULA: Tell him that, Lee.

LEE: How do you talk to him? He's always flying off the handle.

PAULA: That he gets honestly, too.

LEE: You're trying to make me fly off the handle? *(Getting up and going.)* What is it today, everybody taking potshots at me? What am I—a clay pigeon?

PAULA: It all goes back to you. Me. Me. Me. I'm talking about Johnny. You give him nothing. That's why he fights with you.

LEE: Johnny fights with me because it's his character action to fight with me. You remember when he was a baby, when we had his crib in our bedroom? I'm taking a nap, and I feel something hit my cheek. You know what it is. Johnny reaching into his diaper and throwing his shit at me. He's still throwing it.

PAULA: All right, but how does that explain Susan? She's a girl. She needs a father. She needs your love.

LEE: Is that what you say to her? That I don't give her love?

PAULA: I never say anything of the sort. I'm always apologizing for you.

LEE: Nobody has to apologize for me to my own children.

PAULA: Your children? They're my children, not yours.

LEE: I made them, they're mine.

PAULA: You made them?!! You had nothing to do with it. I did it all. I practically put it in for you.

LEE: You dare speak to me that way?

PAULA: I don't complain about your women. That's your business. But don't hurt my children.

LEE: I don't know what you're talking about!

PAULA: You know what I'm talking about! Everyone knows you fool around with your students.

LEE: What?

PAULA: I saw you with that girl last night.

LEE: What girl?

PAULA: That girl!

LEE: You saw me give her a goodbye kiss.

PAULA: Some kiss. With your knee up her crotch.

LEE: I'm not allowed to say goodbye to my students?

PAULA: I don't care about your students. What I care about is your family.

LEE: Enough already. You're starting another argument. I've had plenty of nosebleeds for one day.

(He leaves, obviously headed for Marilyn's room. Paula bursts into tears. John enters and puts his arms around his mother.)

JOHN: That's all right, Mom, that's all right.

PAULA: *(Pulling herself together.)* It's nothing. I was just thinking about my parents; they should rest in peace on this New Year's day.

JOHN: I heard everything. The selfish son of a bitch…

PAULA: It doesn't help when you talk about him that way.

JOHN: I don't know how you've managed to live with him all these years.

PAULA: I've asked you not to say bad things about your father.

JOHN: I've got a right to tell the truth. It's a privilege that goes with my condition.

PAULA: What condition?

JOHN: The condition of being the only flop in the family.

PAULA: Your time will come.

JOHN: Your time never came.

PAULA: *(Bitterly.)* No.

JOHN: *(Impulsively.)* Mom, in a few years I'm going to start my own theatre. Not just talk about it like Pop. And you'll be the leading lady.

PAULA: *(Patting him.)* That'll be nice, Johnny. You're a good boy. *(Starts to leave.)* Just one thing, Johnny. Don't argue any more with your father. One day he'll get a nosebleed he won't be able to stop. *(She starts out to the kitchen.)*

JOHN: Mom.

PAULA: *(Wearily.)* What?

JOHN: *(Pause.)* I don't remember Dad ever bouncing me on his knee.

(She looks at him steadily, shakes her head with resignation, and goes into the kitchen. John goes to pour himself another drink from the Scotch bottle. By now he's consumed a lot and is beginning to feel it. He sits unsteadily on the sofa, and with his mother's scissors, cuts his image out of the family photograph on the table.)

JOHN: Out of the picture…That's me. *(He burns the photo in the ashtray. To himself, watching the fire burn.)* Out of the picture.

(Blackout.)

SCENE 2

Eight o'clock at night on the same day. Susan is alone on stage, with a mug of coffee, reading from her script. Lee enters from the kitchen with a coffee mug, stretches, and sits down. He puts on a Vivaldi concerto and picks a book out of the bookcase.

LEE: *(After a pause to Susan.)* I love this piece.
SUSAN: Me, too. *(Mimes brushing her teeth to the music.)*
LEE: What's that supposed to mean?
SUSAN: Great music to brush your teeth with.
LEE: Don't be silly, darling. This is great art.
SUSAN: Just trying to make you smile.
LEE: What's to smile?
    (Paula enters from the bedroom area with a tray. Lee bounds up.)
PAULA: She didn't eat a thing. I made the mistake of giving her a chicken leg. She can't chew it, she tells me, because it looks like a bird. Who once had a mother. *(She shrugs.)*
SUSAN: I cooked her a lamb chop once, and she wouldn't eat a bite until I disguised it as a roast potato.
PAULA: I'll fix her a little salad and tea.
LEE: No, her stomach is probably upset. How's she doing now?
PAULA: She's far away. The pills don't help her sleep, they just put her in a daze. I picked up the tray, she was putting on her makeup. Like it was morning and she was getting ready to go out. It was smeared all over her face—the lipstick and the mascara. She looked like a clown in the circus.
SUSAN: She keeps taking stronger stuff, as if she's becoming immune. She calls herself "a war veteran of the night."
LEE: She's got the blues.
PAULA: She said the strangest thing to me.
LEE: What?
PAULA: She said, "I hear sounds in my head. I have to hit myself on the forehead to make them stop." I told her we all hear a voice in our heads. And she said "What if I hear more than one?"
LEE: Jung says we're inhabited by many personae—male and female, anima and animus.
PAULA: With her it's a mob scene.
LEE: Did she ask for me?

PAULA: *(Shaking her head.)* She was too busy hitting her head.

> *(The phone rings. Lee starts for Marilyn's room.)*

PAULA: Lee, it'll be for you.

SUSAN: I'll finish the washing up. *(Exits to kitchen.)*

LEE: *(Picks up the phone brusquely.)* Yeah. Who is it? Oh, Gadge. Yes, Happy New Year to you, too. Yes, wasn't it? What? What? Now, hold on a minute, hold on! Don't tell me that. So who's going to run the program? What does Bobby know about actor training? Yes, I'm sure you are… No, I don't want you to call me back. This is the second time you betrayed my family. Fucker! Who do you think you are? *Momser! (Slams down the phone.)* Son of a bitch!

PAULA: Lee, Lee, control yourself.

LEE: Bastard!

PAULA: Don't tell me Kazan has dropped you from Lincoln Center.

LEE: I'm out. They're taking Bobby Lewis.

PAULA: Why?

LEE: I'm too invasive, he says, I make sick actors, he says. Sick actors! Who created all his movie stars, for Christ sake?

PAULA: He's jealous. He knows you're more respected than he is.

LEE: It's only the first day of the year and already it's the worst year of my life. First I lose the Williams, now it's Lincoln Center.

PAULA: This too shall pass. Try to appreciate what you've got.

LEE: What I've got is shit.

> *(Phone rings.)*

LEE: Answer it. I've had enough bad news.

PAULA: Hello? Oh, Arthur. Yes, Happy New Year to you, too. No, I'm not sure she wants to talk to you. Of course, I'll ask her. No. Well, all I can do is ask her. *(Calling.)* Marilyn? *(No answer.)* It's Arthur on the phone. Do you want to speak to him? *(No answer.)* Marilyn? *(No answer.)* Arthur, I think she's asleep. Yes, of course I'll tell her. When she wakes up. *(Hangs up. Then to Lee.)* Thank God. She's finally asleep.

LEE: *(With a sigh.)* I'd better go in.

PAULA: Let her sleep.

LEE: I'll just sit by her bed a while. It will comfort her.

> *(Exits into the bedroom area. Paula goes towards the kitchen with the tray, meeting Susan and John on their way out. He's carrying the remains of his coffee, and a little unsteady from drink.)*

PAULA: *(To John.)* I'm going to fix Marilyn some tea and a tossed salad for when she wakes up. She didn't eat her dinner. *(Exits to kitchen.)*

JOHN: Special meals in this hotel.

SUSAN: Not everyone likes boiled beef flanken.

JOHN: I don't either. But I have to eat it.

SUSAN: Since when you don't like flanken? It's been Friday dinner all our lives.

JOHN: Things change. *(Laughs.)* I'm thinking of turning veggie.

SUSAN: And I thought you'd done all the trends. Acid, booze, dropping out. Orgone boxes. What next?

JOHN: *(Shrugs.)* I haven't tried Jesus yet. *(Puts on a Jazz record on the turntable.)*

SUSAN: Ask Jesus to keep your hand from shaking.

JOHN: You think this is bad? In Wisconsin I had the shakes so fierce I couldn't hold a cup of coffee. The only thing that saved me were my "trends."

SUSAN: "Saved" you? You jumped out a window!

JOHN: I did. I did. *(Giggling.)* I took a tab of acid and thought I could fly.

SUSAN: And now you want to live on cauliflower and booze the rest of your life?

JOHN: So what *do* you do, Blintzes, to keep from falling apart?

SUSAN: I act.

JOHN: That's not a drug?

SUSAN: Sure it is.

　　(Pause. They sit holding each other's hands.)

JOHN: You going to Italy then?

SUSAN: It's what Mom and Dad want.

JOHN: What do you want?

SUSAN: I don't know any more.

JOHN: Go. Get as far away from here as possible. You need a life.

SUSAN: What's wrong with my life? I'm only twenty-one, and I've done four movies and three Broadway plays.

JOHN: I'm talking about your life, not your career.

SUSAN: I'm hardly celibate.

JOHN: That's what I hear around the neighborhood.

SUSAN: *(Disturbed.)* What do they say?

JOHN: What do you care what they say? Just find a guy who'll treat you decent. Not ones who reject you.

SUSAN: Those types do seem to attract me.

JOHN: Do you think that has anything to do with Pops?

SUSAN: You're wrong about Daddy. He was very comforting to me this morning.

JOHN: Him? Comforting?

SUSAN: Yes. It was one of the few times I've felt like his child. Most of the time I feel adopted.

JOHN: You're lucky. Most of the time I feel abandoned.

SUSAN: And yet, sometimes I think you and Daddy are closer in your way than anybody in the family.

JOHN: *(Interested in spite of himself.)* How?

SUSAN: You fight. That's a form of contact, isn't it? Somewhere down deep, you really love him.

JOHN: I do love him. *(Pause.)* I just wish to hell I liked him.

(Susan presses his arm sympathetically.)

JOHN: The worst thing, Blintzes, is that I'm afraid I'm becoming him. Every day, I feel his frozen blood creeping through my veins.

SUSAN: *(Hugging him.)* Oh, Johnny.

JOHN: I wish I was never born a Strasberg.

SUSAN: *(A little shocked.)* Don't say that.

JOHN: We're all such depressos. Even you, who always pretends to be happy.

SUSAN: Everyone in the business is unhappy. Even the big stars like Marilyn. They'd all rather be actresses.

JOHN: And all the actresses would rather be movie stars.

(A roar from the bedroom, like a lion in pain, startles both John and Susan.)

LEE: Paula!! Where are you! *(He enters, wringing his hands.)* I need you! This minute!

PAULA: *(Entering from the kitchen.)* What's the matter, Lee?

LEE: She's taken an overdose.

PAULA: My God!

(She starts to go to Marilyn's room, and Susan follows.)

PAULA: *(To Susan.)* Stay here. *(Paula exits to the bedroom.)*

JOHN: What happened, Pop?

LEE: I was sitting by her bedside, holding her hand, watching her sleep. But her breathing got so heavy and she started snoring in a funny way. Then it stopped.

SUSAN: What stopped?

LEE: Her snoring!! She started turning blue! I tried to wake her, but I couldn't. *(Panicking.)* My God, you think she's dead!?

PAULA: *(Entering from Marilyn's room.)* Calm down, Lee. People don't die that easy. Stay here with the children and let me take care of this. She needs a cold shower. And some oxygen. Thank God we keep a tank for John's asthma.

SUSAN: Shouldn't we call an ambulance? Or Arthur?

PAULA: *(Exiting to the bedroom.)* Don't call anybody. First let me try to revive her.

LEE: My God, what if she's dead? This could be the end of me.

JOHN: Take it easy, Pop! Mom's taking care of things.

(Lee sits on the sofa. He has another nosebleed. There is a long silence.)

JOHN: Maybe it's for the best. She can go to a detox and get some decent treatment.

LEE: She can't be dead. She can't be dead.

JOHN: That's true—it's Friday.

LEE: What are you talking about?

JOHN: Celebrities don't die on Friday, you said it yourself.

LEE: Do you know what he's talking about?

JOHN: You said it.

LEE: Get out of here.

SUSAN: Poor Marilyn. Just like a butterfly—beautiful and brief.

LEE: She brought us so much hope.

JOHN: "Hype," you mean.

LEE: My poor golden girl.

SUSAN: She means that much to you?

LEE: Yes. No. Not to me. To my work. My work.

SUSAN: Your work is the Actors Studio.

LEE: Susan, try to understand. I was creating a miracle. I was making a sex queen into a great actress. Can't you appreciate the wonder of that? To turn Marilyn Monroe into Eleanora Duse?

SUSAN: *(Quietly.)* You used to call me your golden girl.

LEE: Susan, don't say such things. You'll always be my golden girl. But Marilyn may be dying in that room. You're not. Susan get me another handkerchief. I've bled right through this one.

(Susan starts to go out. Lee stops her.)

LEE: No, stay here. Don't leave me alone with that one.

JOHN: Don't worry, I won't hassle you while you're sitting *shiva*.

LEE: The whole world will sit *shiva* for Marilyn. Her name will live as long as anyone in our profession. She created a myth of what a poor girl…

JOHN: Wait till she's dead before you deliver your memorial speech.

(The kettle begins to whistle in the kitchen.)

SUSAN: I'd better get the tea.

LEE: Stay here! I need you!

SUSAN: *(Bitterly, with emphasis.)* No! You don't need me.

LEE: Susan, stay. *(In desperation.)* Stay!!! I'll go to Italy with you!

SUSAN: *(Enjoys a moment of triumph.)* I'll just get the tea.

> *(Goes into the kitchen. The whistling of the tea kettle stops. Silence while Lee and John glare at each other.)*

LEE: Why is Paula taking so long? I can't stand all this stress. *(He starts to weep again.)*

JOHN: *(Softening in spite of himself.)* Dad, she'll be all right.

LEE: I know you never liked her being here. I know she put you out of your room. But can't you feel some pity for the poor girl? *(Begins to wipe his eyes with his bloody handkerchief, smearing blood over his face.)*

JOHN: You're getting blood all over your face. Take some tissues. *(Hands him some Kleenex from the table.)*

LEE: Thanks.

> *(A nervous pause.)*

JOHN: Why do you think you get these nosebleeds?

LEE: You're the doctor. You tell me.

JOHN: They always happen when you're upset

LEE: *(Nodding.)* The first nosebleed I can remember was when I was upset. I was a little kid. On Clinton Street. The gangs used to come over from the Italian neighborhood to look for a Jew to beat up.

JOHN: You were alone?

LEE: Usually I had some friends around for protection, but this time I was alone. This one guy, a real gorilla, saw me playing ball against a stoop and I heard him say, "There's a kike mockie. Let's go straighten out his hooked nose." One of them held my arms, and the big guy drew back his fist…

JOHN: And punched you in the nose?

LEE: No, that's the funny part. My nose began to bleed before he hit me. Great streams pouring down my face. Those guys got so scared I was dying they all ran away.

> *(Lee laughs, and John laughs too.)*

LEE: I vowed then I would become such a somebody that no one would ever shake his fist at me again.

JOHN: *(Pause.)* You don't talk enough about your childhood.

LEE: *(Getting up.)* What's to talk about? It was grim. At the age of seven, I was driving a horse-cart. It's my worst memory, the time I was going over the Third Avenue bridge in winter, and the horse slipped on the ice and fell over. All the goods were ruined. I sat down on the ice and cried. My nose bled then, too. I remember thinking it looked like roses in the snow.

JOHN: I didn't realize you had it so tough.

LEE: In those days, you had to harden yourself to stay alive. *(Starts to weep.)* I guess I never got strong enough.

JOHN: *(Trying to comfort him.)* Dad, Dad, that's all right. Everything will be all right.

LEE: *(With new resolve.)* I know what I have to do. I have to form my acting company.

JOHN: You really mean it?

LEE: It was always the idea behind the Studio. To make a great American acting company. Why did I put it off so long?.

JOHN: You had distractions.

LEE: I'll start with *Three Sisters.* For months I've been working scenes with Kim and Geraldine. Then an O'Neill, a Williams, maybe even a Shakespeare. That'll show Kazan. The whole world will see what American actors can do.

JOHN: Let me help. Sweep the floors. Clean the toilets.

LEE: *(Tears in his eyes again.)* Marilyn would have been the perfect Natasha.

JOHN: *(Hugging him, he pulls Lee onto his lap and puts his head against his back.)* Dad, it's all right. It's all right
(Lee allows himself to sit on John's lap in silence. John begins ever so gently to bounce him on his knee, like a child, hugging him and crooning softly.)

LEE: How did I ever let that idea slip away from me?

LEE: *(As if suddenly realizing what John is doing, gets abruptly off his lap.)* Stop that! Get your hands off me! You're drunk!
(John reacts as if he's been slapped in the face.)

SUSAN: *(Enters from the kitchen.)* Here's your tea.
(Lee takes a cup from the tray, and sits silently, sipping tea. A moment later, Paula enters the room from the bedroom area, wiping her hands on a towel.)

PAULA: She's going to be all right.

LEE: *(Leaping to his feet.)* She's alive? Thank God.

PAULA: She's conscious and breathing normally. I told you I'd take care of things.

LEE: Is she asking for me?

PAULA: *(Nodding No.)* Give her a little time to recover.

LEE: You didn't tell her Arthur called?

PAULA: What am I, crazy?

LEE: What did she say?

PAULA: She's very sheepish.

LEE: So she did it on purpose.

PAULA: Who knows? With someone in her condition, who can say what's an accident and what's on purpose. One of these days, she's going to take one pill too many, and nobody will be able to bring her back.

LEE: *(Back in command, folding his handkerchief and putting it in his pocket.)* Well, well, that's the end of it. Paula, thank you. I'll take charge now. She'll stay here, of course, until she's fully recovered. Someone will have to speak to Arthur and have him send her things over. We'll need lawyers. Divorce proceedings must begin as soon as possible.

PAULA: Of course.

LEE: First thing in the morning I'll call ABC. If they want Marilyn in *Rain*, it will have to be this season.

JOHN: And your acting company?

LEE: Marilyn Monroe is my acting company. No one is to say a word about what happened here tonight, you understand? No one! If this were to get in the papers it would be a disaster.

JOHN: For Marilyn or you?

LEE: What does that mean?

JOHN: You'd get a shitload of publicity.

PAULA: John!

JOHN: That's what he lives on, isn't it? He'd be more famous than Elia Kazan.

LEE: I've had just about enough of your sarcasm. I've tried to bring you up right but somehow I failed.

JOHN: *(Sadly.)* We both failed.

LEE: The prodigal son.

JOHN: No, father Abraham, the son you sacrificed.

LEE: What sacrifice! We supported you all your life. We sent you to the most expensive schools. You always had more money than you needed.

JOHN: That's true.

LEE: I don't ask for gratitude. That would be too much. But maybe a little respect?

JOHN: Respect you have to earn.

LEE: Like you earn your allowance?

JOHN: Like you earn yours? Letting women pay your rent?

LEE: And who pays yours?

JOHN: *(Reaching in his pocket for some bills and loose change and throwing the money on the floor.)* Here, take your goddamn allowance.

LEE: Fine. Support yourself. You won't get a red penny more from us.

JOHN: Cut me off. I dare you to cut me off. At last I'll be free of your fucking hypocrisy.
(Lee raises his fist threateningly.)

PAULA: Lee, John. Please. Stop it already.

A SMALL VOICE FROM THE BEDROOM: *(Tinkling the bell.)* Lee, I want you to promise not to call Dr. Kris. Okay? I'm fine now. Everything's fine. Promise me, Lee.

LEE: I promise. No need to call her, darling. You're doing fine.

VOICE: Thank you, Lee. I'm feeling ever so much better now. Can you come into my room with some more champagne? I need to talk about this whole thing. Before I forget what happened.

LEE: I'm coming Marilyn poor sweetheart. You know I'm always here for you. *(To John.)* We'll finish this later, young man. *(He leaves with a champagne bottle.)*

JOHN: *(To himself.)* No, we won't.

PAULA: I hope I never have to go through something like that again. She vomited all over the bed.

JOHN: Mom, I'm leaving.

PAULA: Because she threw up on your bed? I changed the sheets.

JOHN: She can have the bed. She can have the room. I'm leaving. *(Gets his coat from the hall and drapes it over the couch.)*

SUSAN: No, Johnny.

JOHN: *(To Susan.)* And if you know what's good for you, you'll leave too.

PAULA: Your father didn't mean anything. He hasn't had such a good day.

JOHN: I can't stay here…

SUSAN: Please, Johnny.

JOHN: I know it now.

PAULA: *(With a sigh.)* Well, maybe it's for the best.

SUSAN: Mom, don't let him go.

PAULA: They don't get along. Maybe a little distance will help. *(Sheepishly.)* And Marilyn does need the bed right now.

JOHN: *(Ironically.)* See? It's all for the best.

THE VOICE FROM THE BEDROOM: *(Tinkling the bell.)* Paula, can you come, too? And Susie? John? I would really like all of you in my room. Now.

PAULA: I'm coming, Marilyn.

VOICE: And Paula, bring *The Misfits* script. I'm ready to start work on it now—with you.

PAULA: *(Looking sadly at the children.)* What can I do? She needs me. *(She goes toward the bedroom with* The Misfits.*)* Susan, you coming? She wants you, too.

SUSAN: In a minute. *(To John.)* Don't go, Johnny. I'll fall to pieces without you.

JOHN: You got what you want. He said he's going to Italy with you.

SUSAN: What I want is you here.

JOHN: *(Pouring himself another drink.)* I'll be around. I can find myself a cheap place here on the West Side. Wait tables, make rounds as an actor. The Strasberg name should count for something.

SUSAN: Promise me something. A New Year resolution.

JOHN: What?

SUSAN: Cut out the booze.

JOHN: The booze. Ah yes, the booze. The booze is what I do in place of being a son.

SUSAN: *(Moved.)* Hold me a second.

(They embrace, quietly.)

VOICE: *(The bell tinkles.)* Susie!!! John!!!

SUSAN: Why is it so hard to ignore that voice?

JOHN: You don't ignore the summons of a goddess.

(Susan squares her shoulders and goes off towards Marilyn's bedroom. John puts Schubert's Fantasia for Four Hands on the phonograph. Carrying his drink, he walks downstage and looks out the window towards the audience for a period of time. The bell in the other room begins to ring.)

VOICE: Johnny, are you coming? We're all here waiting for you, Johnny. Johnny?

(John downs his drink and becomes perfectly still, looking out over the park. He goes to the table and puts down his glass, upside down, facing upstage. He then grabs his overcoat and heads into the hall. The slamming of the front door. The bell continues to ring.)

VOICE: Johnny?

(The lights fade to black.)

END OF PLAY

SNAKEBIT
by David Marshall Grant

For Tom Slaughter, who has given so much to this, in so
many ways, and for so many times.
And for Jessie Nelson and Charley Lang.

"Haven't seen a snake yet, but I haven't been across to the
rock pile and lifted a rock."

E.B. White

AUTHOR'S NOTE
Snakebit is about being stuck. It's about when the game plan doesn't work anymore. It's about the shifting ground on which we lay our assumptions and conceits. It's about that moment in life when one decides to be courageous. Or not. Mostly, it's about two men and a woman who love each other very much.

ORIGINAL PRODUCTION

Snakebit was originally produced by The Remains Theatre Company (Larry Sloan, Artistic Director; R.P. Sekon Producing Director; Neel Keller, Associate Director) in Chicago, on January 29, 1993. It was directed by Campbell Scott; the set design was by Jeff Bauer; the costume design was by Laura Cunningham; the lighting design was by Kevin Snow; the sound design was by Christian Petersen; and the production stage manager was Mary McAuliffe. The cast was as follows:

Michael	John Benjamin Hickey
Jenifer	Talia Balsam
Jonathan	D.W. Moffett
(Gary) Young Man	Harry Hutchinson

Snakebit was subsequently produced by The Powerhouse Theatre at Vassar (Dixie Sheridan, Executive Producer; Beth Fargis-Lancater, Producing Director) and New York Stage and Film (Mark Linn-Baker, Max Mayer, Leslie Urdang, Producing Directors; Peter J. Manning, Producer) in association with Jay S. Harris, Ron Kastner and Randy Finch in Poughkeepsie, New York on July 20, 1994. It was directed by Joe Mantello; the set design was by Donald Eastman; the costume design was by Laura Cunningham; the lighting design was by Brian MacDevitt; the sound design was by Darren Clark; and the production stage manager was William H. Lang. The cast was as follows:

Michael	John Benjamin Hickey
Jenifer	Cordelia Richards
Jonathan	Jon Tenney
(Gary) Young Man	Matt McGrath

Snakebit was produced in New York City at the Century Theatre by Hal Luftig, Daryl Roth, and Ted Snowdon, in association with Roy Gabay, who presented the production by Naked Angels (Julianne Hoffenberg, Producer Director; Sherri Kotimsky, Managing Director) on March 1, 1999. It was directed by Jace Alexander; the set design was by Dean Taucher; the costume design was by Elizabeth Roles; the lighting design was by Renee Molina; the sound design was by Raymond D. Schilke; and the production stage manager was Kimberley Berdy. The cast was as follows:

Michael. . . . . Geoffrey Nauffts
Jenifer . . . . Jodie Markell
Jonathan . . . . David Alan Basche
(Gary) Young Man . . . . Michael Weston

CHARACTERS

MICHAEL

JENIFER

JONATHAN

YOUNG MAN (GARY)

PLACE

Los Angeles

TIME

Act I: Monday afternoon
Act II Scene One: Wednesday afternoon
Act II Scene Two: Thursday morning

ACT I

The living room of a Spanish style house in Los Angeles. It's a little after twelve on a Monday in August. The sun is young and tireless, pouring in through large windows. Everything is everywhere: stacks of books, pots from the kitchen, clothes, a CD player. Cardboard boxes, some filled, some not, lay sprawled on the floor. A few pieces of furniture are bubble-wrapped. The built-in bookcases are mostly empty. A hallway leads off to the bedrooms. Another one to the kitchen. Michael sits, looking at the mess. After a while he speaks.

MICHAEL: I can't move. I'm not sleeping. Well, I sleep, but in fits and starts. I have dreams of anxiety: I can't find a place to live. I can't get the packing tape unstuck from the roll. They taught us in school moving is the most traumatic event you can go through. Second only to the loss of a loved one. I never understood that. I mean, really, don't you think, I don't know, kidnapping would be more traumatic than moving to Glendale? I had this client once who contracted Polio three months before they came to his elementary school with the vaccine. He watched as his entire class was inoculated with tiny pin pricks of brand new magic serum. Three months. How do you live with that? How do I live with that? They also taught us you should never get emotionally involved in the work.

JENIFER: *(Offstage.)* I can't hear a word you're saying.

MICHAEL: Forget it.

JENIFER: *(Offstage.)* What?

MICHAEL: Nothing.

(The phone rings.)

MICHAEL: I got it.

(Michael stares at the phone, but doesn't move. It rings again.)

JENIFER: *(Offstage.)* I think the phone's ringing.

MICHAEL: I got it.

(The phone rings again. Michael shuts the door to the hallway. The phone rings again.)

PHONE MACHINE: Hello, you have reached Michael. If you want to leave a message please do so at the sound of the beep.

A GIRLS VOICE: Michael it's Mariama. What's up? I'm basically so pissed right

now because I think one of the nurses stole my Entertainment Weekly. That is so shady, right. So, like why won't you call me at least?
(Michael stands there frozen.)

A GIRLS VOICE: I get out of here in a few days. Did you tape Dawson's Creek? Okay, like I would kill for a cheeseburger so if you…So, um…Okay… Um…
(Michael seems to want to pick up, but doesn't.)

A GIRLS VOICE: Hospital food sucks. Okay, um…Bye. Maybe you moved already. Okay, um…Bye.
(The machine clicks off. Michael unplugs the phone machine and wraps the cord around it, and puts it in one of the boxes. He sits down. Jenifer enters from the hallway. She's wearing a bathing suit.)

JENIFER: Oh, my God, it is so bright out here. You can see every…Why does it have to be so bright out here? Oh, my God. I am so old. I look horrible. Why can't I be thirty again?

MICHAEL: When you were thirty you wanted to be twenty-five. In a few years you're going to want to look exactly like you do now.

JENIFER: I look skinny. But with this wrapping of fat. I'm like a skinny fat person.

MICHAEL: I really don't think I should go to the beach.

JENIFER: Then why am I standing here in a bikini???

MICHAEL: You look great. The last time I saw you in a—

JENIFER: Stop.

MICHAEL: Was Montauk. You look great.
(The sound of a loud motor starting up. They shout over the noise.)

JENIFER: What is that?

MICHAEL: It's the Nelson's gardener.

JENIFER: That's a gardener?

MICHAEL: It's a leaf blower.

JENIFER: Well, can't you tell him to stop?

MICHAEL: He's a Mexican man with a family of about twenty-eight hungry children. You tell him to stop.
(The machine stops.)

JENIFER: I have to settle down for a second. Who was on the phone?

MICHAEL: Mariama.

JENIFER: Where is she?

MICHAEL: What? At friends.

JENIFER: She should have stayed here. We would have slept on the couch. What time is it in New York?

MICHAEL: The same time it was ten minutes ago.

JENIFER: *(Looking around.)* Michael. You haven't done anything.

MICHAEL: I can't move.

JENIFER: You have to move.

MICHAEL: No.

JENIFER: You're not going to the beach until you make some progress. The beach is a reward.

MICHAEL: I don't want to go to the beach. You want to go to the beach.

JENIFER: I want to relax. Come on, I'm going to help you. It's very hard, I know. They say moving is one of the most traumatic events you can go through.

MICHAEL: Second only to the loss of a loved one.

JENIFER: Get up.

MICHAEL: Alright. Alright. *(Michael slowly gets up.)*

JENIFER: *(Holding something up.)* What is this?

MICHAEL: That? It's a wet suit.

JENIFER: What's it for?

MICHAEL: Scuba diving.

JENIFER: You *scuba dived?*

MICHAEL: It's Gary's.

JENIFER: Gary scuba dived?

MICHAEL: He snorkeled. Once. He bought it in Hawaii. We came home; he never touched it again in three and a half years. It just sat in the closet terrorizing my raincoat.

JENIFER: Is he going to come get it?

MICHAEL: No.

JENIFER: Then throw it out. *(She starts to stuff it in a garbage bag.)*

MICHAEL: Wait. Wait. Don't. *(Saving it from the garbage.)* It's a reminder of something.

JENIFER: Of what? His attention span? What are you going to do with it?

MICHAEL: I don't know. I could wear it if I ever have sex again. I could fold it up and carry it around in my wallet.

JENIFER: People shouldn't be having sex anymore. Throw it out.

MICHAEL: I don't want to have sex, believe me. I haven't combed my hair in three months.

> *(The leaf blower starts up again.)*

JENIFER: This is the most un-relaxing place I've ever been in my life. How did you live here?

MICHAEL: You get used to it.

(The noise stops.)

MICHAEL: It's broken again. They don't pay the poor guy enough money to afford a decent one.

JENIFER: No wonder you broke up.

MICHAEL: We didn't break up. He did.

JENIFER: He's having a fling. It's stupid. You wouldn't be going out and having a fling.

MICHAEL: Don't throw out the coat hangers. I recycle them.

JENIFER: Of course you wouldn't.

MICHAEL: Would you remind me to walk the neighbor's dog.

JENIFER: I just asked you a question.

MICHAEL: I thought you were telling me. No, I would not have gone out and had a fling.

JENIFER: Do you consider yourself a top or a bottom?

MICHAEL: Jenifer!

JENIFER: What. Isn't that the terminology?

MICHAEL: Yes, it's just incredibly private, that's all. And simplistic. God.

JENIFER: Why do you always get like this? You are always so uncomfortable talking about sex with me. If I just say a guy is cute, you're like… *(She makes a face.)*

MICHAEL: Because it makes me feel like one of your girlfriends when you do that.

JENIFER: Well…

MICHAEL: *(Pointing.)* Boy. Girl. There's a relationship men have with women. And I don't want to lose that with you. You're a beautiful woman. And when we talk about sex that way, it limits us. It reduces me.

JENIFER: Was I the last woman you slept with?

MICHAEL: Yes.

JENIFER: God, I don't know if I should be proud of that.

MICHAEL: What are you talking about? You spoiled me for life. I had to go to a whole other chromosome mix.

JENIFER: How many boys were there then? Who was I competing with? Who was that guy? Bobby or Billy?

MICHAEL: Brendon. That lasted a minute. He was a long, blond, high pitched shriek. It was like dating a test from the Emergency Broadcast System.

JENIFER: What's he doing now?

MICHAEL: He's probably still blow drying his hair.

JENIFER: He's a dancer, right?

MICHAEL: Was. He quit. I think he sells exercise equipment now.

JENIFER: Why? What happened?

MICHAEL: He got old.

JENIFER: How old could he be?

MICHAEL: Dancers don't have the same life expectancy as normal people. It's like dog years.

JENIFER: But he's alright and everything.

MICHAEL: I'm sure he's fine.

JENIFER: Well, that's good. I thought I read about him.

MICHAEL: Where?

JENIFER: I read about dancers. Because of you. I follow dance.

MICHAEL: Because of me?

JENIFER: Balanchine came to your house, Michael. Balanchine.

MICHAEL: His assistant did. Twenty-six years ago. You guys have the worst habit of romanticizing this. I was a boy, and I had great feet. The combination slays them.

JENIFER: You were brilliant—

MICHAEL: Who cares. Ballet is nothing but a technical obsession ruled by hopelessly self-involved fascists.

JENIFER: I'm sorry, but I cried when I saw "Swan Lake."

MICHAEL: Why?

JENIFER: They drown in the lake.

MICHAEL: They float off into heaven. Dry. That's not what happens when people drown.

JENIFER: Alright, what's the one with the rich guy and the peasant girl?

MICHAEL: All of them.

JENIFER: She has a bad heart.

MICHAEL: "Giselle."

JENIFER: "Giselle." It's horrible.

MICHAEL: It romanticizes the betrayal of a working class girl by a nobleman.

JENIFER: Maybe I should start acting again.

MICHAEL: Oh, no. What?!!! Stop it! No! That's out of the question.

JENIFER: Now, wait. Just listen to me.

MICHAEL: Jenifer, you'd be catatonic in three days.

JENIFER: I'll be catatonic if I don't. I'm more mature now. I could handle it.

MICHAEL: In certain areas you are more mature, but not in ways germane to acting.

JENIFER: You're wrong, I've changed. I haven't said one self-deprecating thing since I've been here.

MICHAEL: I'm like a skinny fat person?

JENIFER: Well, what am I supposed to do with my life? Being a mother is such a…I know you want to be a parent someday, and I applaud that, really I do. But, it's very stressful. Maybe if I had a career.

MICHAEL: Well, actually you do have a—

JENIFER: Baking brownies is not—

MICHAEL: You make the best wheatless, dairyless, sugarless brownies I have ever tasted. And you sell them to specialty stores all over New York City. That's a career.

JENIFER: They're not sugarless.

MICHAEL: Of course they're sugarless.

JENIFER: I put sugar in them.

MICHAEL: You put sugar in them? You lie about putting sugar in them?

JENIFER: Just a little. I just put a little in. Brown sugar. And fructose.

MICHAEL: Well, you have to stop doing that. Take the sugar out. I'm serious. What about the diabetics? It's false advertising.

JENIFER: They're just brownies.

MICHAEL: They're not just brownies. They're wheatless, dairyless and supposedly sugarless brownies.

JENIFER: Jonathan thinks I've become a culinary prostitute.

MICHAEL: Please. This is coming from a man who played a rapist in "Brute Force II." He doesn't like the brownies because he's scared of the brownies. He's afraid the brownies are going to be more successful than he is. Did you know he used to make me sit in his driveway and watch him shoot basketballs for an entire afternoon? Literally. He wouldn't let me go home.

JENIFER: He likes an audience.

MICHAEL: Fine. He has an audience. He was in "Brute Force II." He disappeared into the crowd at Jones Beach at the end. Maybe they'll put him in "Brute Force III." He's desperate. It's his mother's fault. Send him to therapy.

JENIFER: Everything is not his mother's fault.

MICHAEL: His mother's an annihilator.

JENIFER: His mother is not an annihilator. Every mother is not an annihilator.

MICHAEL: I didn't say every mother—

JENIFER: But, that's what you think. That's what all social workers think.

MICHAEL: What?

JENIFER: Just forget it. Drop it. Let's go to the beach.

MICHAEL: I think you're an incredible mother. Don't I always say that you are an incredible mother?

JENIFER: That's not what I was saying. Stop thinking you understand people all the time. I want to relax. Can we please go to the beach?

MICHAEL: Are you crying?

JENIFER: No.

MICHAEL: Jen? Are you alright?

JENIFER: Yes.

MICHAEL: What's wrong?

JENIFER: Emma threw up twice last week.

MICHAEL: I know.

JENIFER: And I'm sitting out here in a fucking bikini. Oh, shit.

MICHAEL: I don't want to sound perceptive, I'm sorry, but it seems to me that you've got some major anxiety going on here.

JENIFER: Okay, let's change the subject. I want to change the subject.

MICHAEL: Kids throw up.

JENIFER: I don't understand why people don't listen to me. I said I want to change the subject.

MICHAEL: I'm listening to you, I just—

JENIFER: I mean, if I want to be an actress you should just hear that.

MICHAEL: You seem like you're in pain, so I'm trying to help.

JENIFER: God, I hate when you play doctor.

MICHAEL: Look, if you want to be an actress, fine, go be an actress.

JENIFER: I don't want to be an actress. I hate acting. I've always hated acting. It fills me with nothing but self-loathing. There, I said it. And you know, you do your affirmations, you know, your prayers that you'll be like, you know, so filled with self-love, that all that won't matter. What am I saying? The whole thing's a joke. You know why I don't want to act? And don't tell Jonathan this. I've never told anybody this. I started to stutter. On stage. Can you believe that? Honestly. I would get to a word in the script, and when I came to it, I wouldn't be able to say it. I would freeze. Every time I would get to it. I couldn't get it out.

MICHAEL: You started to stutter?

JENIFER: I get fixated on a word. Last time, I was playing the blind Mexican flower vendor in "Streetcar Named Desire." Don't ask me why. And all I had to do was say, "Flores para los muertos." There, I said it now. "Flores para los muertos." I had nothing else to say, just that. I sat around waiting all night. "Flores para los muertos." "Flores para los muertos." I couldn't say it. Now I can say it. It's pathetic.

MICHAEL: What couldn't you say?

JENIFER: Muertos. I couldn't say, Muertos. It wouldn't come out. I ended up saying, "Flores para los dead people." Blanche Dubois accused me of sabotaging her performance.

MICHAEL: Well, fuck her. You adapted under difficult circumstances. What did she want you to do? Not say anything?

JENIFER: She wanted me to say the line right. That's what I was not getting paid to do. And Jonathan made me feel so…You know, why don't I just leave him? I really should just leave him. *(Beat.)* Michael?

MICHAEL: What do you want me to say? You should have just married me. That's your problem. I would have taken much better care of you.

JENIFER: You didn't want me.

MICHAEL: I wanted you. I was just young and stupid. And gay.

JENIFER: You're so sweet, you know that? Gary's going to remember that, and come running home.

MICHAEL: Mm, mm.

JENIFER: I guarantee in five weeks they won't even be talking. The guy's a jerk. He's a cipher. What's his name again?

MICHAEL: Gary.

JENIFER: I know Gary, stupid head. I'm talking about the other guy.

MICHAEL: His name's Gary. I told you this.

JENIFER: His name's Gary?

MICHAEL: Yes.

JENIFER: His name's Gary, too? Well, that's ridiculous. It won't last five minutes.

MICHAEL: He's everything Gary ever wanted. From all accounts Gary, his Gary, hereinafter referred to as Gary two, is not very smart, and apparently looks like Italian furniture. And the great thing is he's totally discreet. Nobody has to really be gay. It's perfect.

JENIFER: So be grateful he's gone. You deserve better.

MICHAEL: Oh. Okay.

JENIFER: I love you, Michael.

MICHAEL: I know you do.

JENIFER: I'll always love you. No matter what.

MICHAEL: Well, thank you.

JENIFER: I think we should say that.

MICHAEL: Say what?

JENIFER: That I'll love you no matter what, and you'll love me. No matter what. I think we should say that.

MICHAEL: Out loud?

JENIFER: Yes.

MICHAEL: Why?

JENIFER: Because I want to.

> (*Jonathan enters from the front door. He throws his jacket and briefcase down.*)

MICHAEL: How'd it go?

> (*Jonathan doesn't answer. He starts to take his shoes and socks off.*)

JENIFER: (*After a while.*) Did they put you on tape?

> (*Nothing from Jonathan.*)

JENIFER: Do you wanna go to the beach?

MICHAEL: Yeah, we're going to go to the beach.

> (*Taking his time, and without saying a word, Jonathan heads into the kitchen.*)

JENIFER: Shit.

MICHAEL: Oh God. Just stand up for our rights. Okay? We're just going to stand up for our rights. (*Michael starts to put books into one of the boxes.*)

JONATHAN: (*Offstage.*) There's absolutely nothing in the icebox. Excuse me, there's canola oil.

> (*The leaf blower starts up again. Jonathan comes in from the kitchen and goes to the window.*)

JONATHAN: COULD YOU PLEASE TURN THAT THING OFF BEFORE I FREAK OUT! (*To Michael.*) Didn't they pass some ordinance? (*Back outside.*) IT'S AGAINST THE LAW. AMIGO.

> (*The leaf blower stops.*)

JONATHAN: Michael, there's nothing in the icebox.

MICHAEL: What does it look like I'm doing, Jon?

JONATHAN: Holding your school books like a girl.

MICHAEL: I'm packing my books. I have a week to leave this house because I can't afford to pay the rent any more. Excuse me if there's nothing in the refrigerator. Sir. Corporal. Commandant.

JONATHAN: Fuck you, Michael. God it's so hot. Did you see the taxi I got out of? They bring you there in a limousine, and send you home in a Buick. Did anybody call?

JENIFER: Jon?

JONATHAN: (*He's picked up the phone and is dialing.*) What?

JENIFER: What happened?

JONATHAN: I auditioned. Where's the answering machine?

MICHAEL: I packed it.

JONATHAN: What? That is so rude. *(Into the phone.)* Hi, it's me. Is he there?…It's Jonathan…Dryver. *(The other person obviously doesn't know who he is.)* Jonathan Dryver. *(He's been abruptly put on hold.)* Fucking L.A. office.

MICHAEL: *(Calling out to the gardener.)* Hi. Muy Caliente!

JONATHAN: What the fuck was that noise?

MICHAEL: It was the Nelson's gardener using a leaf blower. You didn't have to scare him.

JONATHAN: This is a city with no seasons. Why does he have to use a nuclear device to rake leaves?

JENIFER: Nobody called you yet. What happened at the meeting?

JONATHAN: You can't breathe in this town. You can't see people through the smog. It's like a fucking ecological disaster area out here. How could you have moved here? Don't you have an air conditioner?

MICHAEL: No, I don't. I'm trying not to contribute to the disaster, actually. They give off fluorocarbons.

JONATHAN: Stop baiting me. *(Into the phone.)* Yeah, well tell him to call me…What's your name?…Cyndy?…Yeah, well this is Jonathan Dryver, and he's got my phone number, Cyndy, okay?…Thank you too. *(Jonathan hangs up.)*

JENIFER: Sweetheart?

JONATHAN: I'm starving, honey. I just want to eat, alright? *(Jonathan goes into the kitchen.)*

MICHAEL: Have some canola oil.

JONATHAN: *(Offstage.)* That stuff's big out here, huh?

JENIFER: Jon.

JONATHAN: *(Offstage.)* What, does it have a low fatty acid profile?

JENIFER: Stop ignoring me! I'm asking you a question!

JONATHAN: *(Re-entering.)* What? I auditioned. I don't know. Stop yelling. *(The phone rings. Jonathan quickly answers it.)*

JONATHAN: Hello…They did?…Well, I thought it went well, yeah…They loved me?…They really loved me?…

JENIFER: This is not normal behavior, right?

JONATHAN: Uh huh…Uh huh…So who runs Fox?…Uh huh…So we wait. Hold on one second… *(He presses the flash button to get the other line.)* Hello…Can he call you right back?…Okay, bye. *(He presses the flash button again.)* Alan?…

MICHAEL: Who was that?

JONATHAN: *(Into the phone.)* Sorry…Fine…No, I can stay…We're at a friend's
house….

MICHAEL: Who was that?

JONATHAN: *(Into the phone.)* Great…Uh huh…Fine…I'll talk to you later.
(He hangs up. Big smile.) I'm going to get this movie, I swear to God.
(Nobody responds.)

JONATHAN: Did anybody just hear me?

MICHAEL: Who was on the other line?

JONATHAN: Jenifer, did you hear that? That was Alan David. The director
wants me. I just have to be approved by Fox. I might have to meet some
vice-president.

JENIFER: How long are you going to have to stay?

MICHAEL: Was that a girl on the other line?

JONATHAN: What? No. A few days maybe. Wednesday. I'll know by
Wednesday. I have to. They start shooting Friday. I got this Jenifer.

JENIFER: We're going to leave Emma till Wednesday?

JONATHAN: It's one more day.

JENIFER: It's two more days.

JONATHAN: Look, honey, if you're so worried, you shouldn't have come out
here in the first place.

JENIFER: That's really helpful.

JONATHAN: Well, then go back. Go back tonight. I don't care.

JENIFER: You can be such an asshole sometimes. *(Jenifer goes down the hall
toward the bedrooms.)*

JONATHAN: What did I do?

JENIFER: *(Offstage.)* Nothing. You didn't do anything.

JONATHAN: I mean, what do you want from me? I just got great news, I don't
need this shit. You decided to come out here. Be supportive. She's being
totally ridiculous now, right? This is not normal behavior.

JENIFER: *(Re-entering. To Michael.)* I'm going to get some lunch. Do you want
anything?

JONATHAN: What did I say?

MICHAEL: No, thank you.

JENIFER: Could I have the keys, please?

JONATHAN: Where are you going?

JENIFER: I'm going to the deli.

JONATHAN: Where? Where is there a deli?

JENIFER: Just give me the keys.
>   *(Jonathan hands her the keys. Jenifer exits, slamming the door on the way.)*

JONATHAN: *(Yelling out to her.)* I thought we were going to the beach. Get me some chicken salad. I'm starving. *(To Michael.)* What did I do? You were here. Tell me. I mean, we're not exactly on Sixth Avenue. It's probably fifty miles to a deli. A deli????

MICHAEL: Please shut up. Just shut up. Okay? Shut up. Shut up. Shut up. Shut up.

JONATHAN: I don't know what it is. I'm obviously a terrible human being or something. I mean, everybody seems to be in agreement on this.

MICHAEL: The tragedy is you're a very decent human being. You just act like, I don't know, a Neanderthal man.

JONATHAN: What did I do?

MICHAEL: You didn't listen. You never listen.

JONATHAN: I listen. I had things on my mind. I just came back from a major audition, excuse me if I wanted a little stroking.

MICHAEL: She asked you how it went ten times.

JONATHAN: You know, let me tell you something. All she does is complain about this disgusting apartment we live in. She can't stand New York anymore, which, what can I say, she's right, sewer rats live better than we do. It's a fiasco with a child in Manhattan, you have no idea. The girl's always sick. We have no money. Do you know how hard that is?

MICHAEL: I work with kids that eat cat food on Sunday, don't look at me.

JONATHAN: Could you spare me the commie-pinko stuff, please. I can almost taste six digits, okay. A trailer, a fucking perdiem, a movie with a modicum of intelligence, and she slams the door in my face.

MICHAEL: She needs to feel good about her life. She's jealous of your life. I told you this already.

JONATHAN: So, what am I supposed to do, Doctor? Fail so she can feel better about herself? I can't force her to go to an audition.

MICHAEL: She doesn't want to go to an audition.

JONATHAN: So what does she want to do? And don't say make muffins.

MICHAEL: Brownies.

JONATHAN: She's an actress, she's not a caterer. You don't choose to bake brownies. You do that when all else fails.

MICHAEL: She makes the best wheatless, dairyless…brownies I have ever tasted. And, if she ever committed to it, she'd probably be completely famous and make more money than you ever dreamed of. And they're good brownies. A lot better than your movies, I can tell you that.

JONATHAN: Fuck you. Now let me tell you something, she hates baking brownies. She doesn't know what she wants. That's the problem. She's been a basket case all summer. About everything. This is not just about me. I don't care if she wants to bake a billion brownies. Bake them. I don't give a shit. I wish everyone would just shut up about the whole thing.

MICHAEL: Fine. Then stop making her feel bad about it. Just because you want to see your face on the cover of some sycophantic magazine, doesn't mean she—

JONATHAN: Don't talk like that. You're not that smart. "Sycophantic." You don't know what you're talking about. Do you think you would handle the whole situation a lot better? Is that what you're saying?

MICHAEL: That's not what I'm saying.

JONATHAN: You know, you really shouldn't go on like this, or I'm going to tell you something you don't want to hear.

MICHAEL: What?

JONATHAN: Forget it. I'll just be yelled at for being insensitive.

MICHAEL: I don't yell.

JONATHAN: No. I just think…I don't think you completely understand how hard it is to be married.

MICHAEL: Yes?

JONATHAN: I just think…Look, I've been married for ten years, Michael. I've had sex with the same woman for twelve years. The three of us live in a space about the size of your Toyota. Okay? I just think you romanticize how easy it is sometimes. *(Beat.)* Just that you shouldn't get on my case. I make an effort. I do the best I can. I'm not always a perfect person. But marriage is not always easy.

(Beat. Michael keeps looking at him.)

JONATHAN: I mean look what happened to you. *(Beat.)* You're alone, that's all. I just don't think you're in a position to talk, that's all. Relationships are hard. At least I'm still in one.

MICHAEL: I can't believe you just said that.

JONATHAN: *(Feeling terrible.)* I'm sorry. Immediately I'm sorry.

MICHAEL: That is incredible.

JONATHAN: You asked me to say it!

MICHAEL: You have to win at everything, don't you?

JONATHAN: I'm sorry. Why do people even talk to me? I'm unrelenting.

MICHAEL: You paid your little sister to lie when she measured my penis that day. Do you remember that? Why are you like this?

JONATHAN: I don't know. It's genetic. I read in the New York Times I might have too much testosterone and not enough oxytocin.

MICHAEL: Then get a shot Jon, get an injection, because you really have to change.

JONATHAN: I was brought up this way. My father only believed in two sayings. "Money is the report card of life." What do you expect?
(Beat.)

MICHAEL: And? What was the other saying?

JONATHAN: "Let them hate, so long as they fear."

MICHAEL: I know, it's terrible, I understand, but you have to fight it, Jon.

JONATHAN: Scratch my back.

MICHAEL: *(Scratching his back.)* Try to remember when your hair was long and your eyes were red.

JONATHAN: Why? We were thirteen. Do you think all that Visine meant anything?

MICHAEL: Don't. Don't make fun of it. You meant it. You were the one who asked me if I wanted to help you plant that tree.

JONATHAN: Big deal.

MICHAEL: It was a big deal. That's why I became your friend.

JONATHAN: It was a nice gesture. Your mother was in a coma.

MICHAEL: It was a nice gesture. There was a time, just for a second, when that was done. The gesture. The nice gesture. We put a plaque on it. Do you remember? "We are all in this together. A symbol of hope. Wilson Junior High."

JONATHAN: It was Earth Day. We were trying to be cool.

MICHAEL: Right. For one lousy second that's what it meant to be cool. You didn't always have to win. It was, for one brief moment, alright to just plant a tree.

JONATHAN: We weren't just planting a tree, Michael. We were also getting high. Extremely high. How else could we come up with a slogan like that and nail it to a three foot sapling?

MICHAEL: No. You were not kidding. You stood in front of the cafeteria and you meant that. You can pretend anything you want, but you stood there in your bleached blue jeans, and a shovel, and you had a chain around your neck, and you were a hero.

JONATHAN: I was your hero.

MICHAEL: I'm going to take Shirley for a walk. *(He goes to get a leash and a tennis ball.)* I don't know why, but I would kill to speak to an animal right now.

JONATHAN: Why are you taking this stupid dog for a walk?

MICHAEL: The Nelsons went to Oaxaca.

JONATHAN: The Nelson's again. These people are very annoying. Why can't they put the dog in a kennel? They can afford a state of the art gardener, and a week in Oaxaca. Why can't they afford a kennel?

MICHAEL: It's better for Shirley.

JONATHAN: I don't care about Shirley. I care about you. I wish you would care about you. How much are you getting paid?

MICHAEL: Nothing. I'm not getting paid anything.

JONATHAN: Nothing? You see? This is exactly why the sixties failed, Michael. There will always be people like you, and there will always be people like the Nelsons.

MICHAEL: Can I go now?

JONATHAN: Gary called.

MICHAEL: *(Beat.)* When?

JONATHAN: Just now, when I was on the phone.

MICHAEL: Why are you telling me this now? Why didn't you tell me this then?

JONATHAN: I was on the phone then.

(Michael goes out the front door.)

JONATHAN: He called this morning, too.

MICHAEL: *(Re-entering.)* This morning? Thank you, Jonathan. Can I process something here?

JONATHAN: Sure.

MICHAEL: One day I'm going to take the piggy things you say and do personally, so could you try and be a little more considerate of my feelings. This has been the worst month of my life.

JONATHAN: I'm sorry.

MICHAEL: Did he leave a message?

JONATHAN: He said to call him. He said he needed to talk to you.

MICHAEL: He did? Well, I'm not calling him. And stop looking at me like that, I'm not going to call him.

JONATHAN: *(Crossing to the phone.)* Come on, you're gonna call him eventually. You have to. He's wants to come back, I could tell from his voice.

MICHAEL: I am not going to call him. I am not going to put myself in that position. Put the phone down.

JONATHAN: *(Dialing.)* Relax, I'm checking my messages. Is that alright?

MICHAEL: Contrary to popular opinion, I'm not a saint. I don't forgive everything.

JONATHAN: Michael, Jesus could take lessons from you.

MICHAEL: Use your calling card number.

JONATHAN: I am.

MICHAEL: I'm not always nice, you know.

JONATHAN: I'm complimenting you.

MICHAEL: Nice is not a compliment to you, it's a swearword.

JONATHAN: This is incredible. I have seventeen messages.

MICHAEL: Where was he? At the radio station?

JONATHAN: *(Looking through drawers.)* Do you have a pen?

MICHAEL: You know, I'm not even allowed to call him at the radio station. God forbid anybody should even know I exist at the radio station.

JONATHAN: Minorities hate themselves. It's a drag.

MICHAEL: Like he's the only gay disc-jockey in the history of the world.

JONATHAN: There are fags everywhere.

MICHAEL: Exactly. Do you remember Carl Ellis?

JONATHAN: No. *(Pointing to the phone.)* This is my mother.

MICHAEL: He was Gary's teacher at school. Remember?

JONATHAN: Yes. He's a fag disc-jockey.

MICHAEL: Was. He died last year.

JONATHAN: Wait. Quiet. She's quoting from the newspaper again. *(Listening.)* When an actor gets a part I really wanted, she does this. She begins to follow his career. Track it for me. *(Listening.)* She's quoting from a review. *(Listening.)* Phenomenal review. She leaves these on my machine. She scours the country for them. She's showing interest. I swear, she thinks she's showing concern. *(Listening.)* This is why I don't get a fax machine. Do you have a speaker phone? *(Holding the phone out.)* You really should listen to this.

MICHAEL: *(Sympathetically.)* I know. Ignore her.

JONATHAN: She's my mother.

MICHAEL: Do you want to hear about Carl or not?

JONATHAN: Yes.

MICHAEL: Then, put the phone down.

JONATHAN: I'm damaged goods, that's why I act like this.

MICHAEL: Put the phone down.

JONATHAN: Fine. *(Puts the phone in his lap.)* How did he die?

MICHAEL: He had a heart attack.

JONATHAN: I'm sorry.

MICHAEL: He and Gary were very close. He was like a father to him. A lot of people went to the service. A lot of important radio and television people.
(Jonathan looks preoccupied.)

MICHAEL: Go on, check.
(Jonathan checks the phone.)

MICHAEL: Is she finished?

JONATHAN: No. *(He puts the phone on his shoulder.)* Go on, I'm listening. I am.

MICHAEL: So, Gary and I go. I mean, I knew him too. I'd been to his house for dinner.

JONATHAN: Yes.

MICHAEL: It was such a big deal for Gary that I even went. He wanted to take separate cars.

JONATHAN: Uh huh.

MICHAEL: Anyway, we had always admired this oil painting he had. It wasn't anything great. You're not listening.

JONATHAN: I am. Hold on. *(He puts the phone back to his ear.)*

MICHAEL: Is she done?

JONATHAN: I think the machine cut her off.

MICHAEL: How many more do you have?

JONATHAN: It's endless, Michael.

MICHAEL: I'll wait till you're done.

JONATHAN: I'm listening. This is a dentist telling me my teeth have to be cleaned. What?

MICHAEL: He left us the oil painting in his will.

JONATHAN: No kidding? So, that's lovely. Hold on one second *(Beat.)* Fuck! I have an appointment tomorrow in New York. How could my own agency not get I am in Los Angeles? *(Yelling into the phone.)* I'm not there Steve!

(Michael groans.)

JONATHAN: Don't you have a pen in this house? Come on, Michael.

MICHAEL: Do you think you'll be kinder and gentler when you're famous?

JONATHAN: Who is Sharon Stark?

MICHAEL: Sharon Stark? Sharon Stark, Sharon Stark? She went to high school with us.

JONATHAN: Why is she calling me?

MICHAEL: I have no idea. She lost her virginity to you.

JONATHAN: You're kidding me.

MICHAEL: No. You don't remember that?

JONATHAN: No.

MICHAEL: You don't remember that? She was so upset, she got psychosomatically pregnant.

JONATHAN: I haven't a clue who this girl is.

MICHAEL: That's insane. You know, you can be so self-absorbed sometimes, it's pathological. Go to a shrink.

JONATHAN: I don't know what's more pathological, Michael, that I don't remember some girl I fucked in high school or that you apparently have a vivid picture of the entire event etched in your mind forever.

MICHAEL: I don't have a vivid picture. I just remember it, that's all. The girl cried on my shoulder for an entire semester. Please, I was never that interested in your sex life. Don't flatter yourself.

JONATHAN: Oh come on, you were in love with me. Admit it. You could sit in my driveway and watch me shoot baskets for an entire afternoon. Literally. You would never go home. You worshipped me Michael, admit it.

MICHAEL: You are so smug, it's unbelievable.

JONATHAN: Finish your story.

MICHAEL: Why should I? What do you care? You have half the free world checking in with you. I'm just one more fan lying prostrate on your driveway.

JONATHAN: Sssh. This is Jenny's sister. *(Listening.)* My daughter threw up again. Why is she taking this tone of voice with me? It's like she never saw a baby throw up before.

MICHAEL: She's not a baby anymore, she's six years old.

JONATHAN: So what? It's not grown-up puke. There's not beer in it or anything.

MICHAEL: What's wrong with her? Is she sick or something?

JONATHAN: She's always sick, she's a kid.

MICHAEL: Don't tell Jenifer, please. She's going to have a heart attack.

JONATHAN: This is why I'm not a better husband. I get blamed for everything.

MICHAEL: You're easy to blame.

JONATHAN: Fuck you, Michael, just finish the story.

MICHAEL: I don't think we get along as well as we used to.

JONATHAN: Fuck you. I try. I call you once a week. You just want to get off the phone.

MICHAEL: You're exhausting. I don't always have the energy.

JONATHAN: You always have the energy to talk to my wife.

MICHAEL: I talk to both of you equally.

JONATHAN: Total lie.

MICHAEL: Well, she's nicer than you. It's easier to talk to her.

JONATHAN: I'm your best friend. You're supposed to talk to me whether I'm nice or not.

MICHAEL: Then hang up the phone, and I'll talk to you.

JONATHAN: Fine, hold on one second. This guy has some Dodger tickets.

MICHAEL: I'm going to walk the dog. *(Michael starts to go.)*

JONATHAN: Michael, hold on.

(*Michael's out the door.*)

JONATHAN: Michael. Michael. Alright. (*Hangs up the phone.*) Michael. Michael. Look. (*Michael stands outside looking through the window.*) There. I probably erased the rest of them. Fuck the Dodgers. How can I make you like me again if you won't give me a chance? I'm listening. What happened to the oil painting? Did Gary take the oil painting? Do you want me to get it back for you?

MICHAEL: (*Re-entering.*) I don't want the oil painting. It's not my oil painting.

JONATHAN: Then what are you saying?

MICHAEL: If you listen, I'll tell you. About six months after the service we got a letter from the lawyer who's handling Carl's estate, and everybody who was a distributee of the will was printed at the top. Gary and I were there on a line together. We were a couple. And we were next to a lot of other names, some of them very important people in radio.

JONATHAN: And he totally freaked out.

MICHAEL: Yes. He totally freaked out. To tell you the truth, he freaked out more over this letter than the fact that one of his best friends had died.

JONATHAN: He's a climber, Michael. He didn't want to end up canceled like Ellen DeGeneres.

MICHAEL: Why are you defending him? You're always defending him.

JONATHAN: I'm not defending him.

MICHAEL: He's overly ambitious. He keeps everything inside. He's a workaholic. He's selfish. He's completely afraid of intimacy. He's stunted and immature.

JONATHAN: Michael, this is a guy. You're describing a normal guy here. I thought you liked men. I'm trying to help. Really. You expect too much from people.

MICHAEL: I thought I was like Jesus.

JONATHAN: I know. That's the problem. Who can live with that? You told me you had a huge fight because he didn't wash the aluminum foil.

MICHAEL: Well he should have saved it and re-used it.

JONATHAN: That's why you broke up?

MICHAEL: The planet's burning up, I thought you noticed.

JONATHAN: He's a guy. If you want selflessness, and decency, and things like that, you should be with a woman.

MICHAEL: This is why I don't talk to you.

JONATHAN: Alright, aside from, you know, recycling, what was the problem?

I'm trying to understand, but relationships are a struggle. I'm not putting you down, but maybe if you compromised.

MICHAEL: I wanted to adopt a child.

(Beat.)

JONATHAN: Excuse me?

MICHAEL: I wanted to adopt a child. And that was basically it for us. I don't know. Maybe he just needed an excuse.

JONATHAN: Michael, Michael, Michael. *(Sitting down for a heart to heart.)* Why didn't you…Listen to me. Gary doesn't want to have a family, he wants to be Howard Stern. Why didn't you tell me this? I just don't understand you. You have been blessed, through a miracle of nature, with a sexual interest in men. This generally limits the possibility of childbirth. Why would you deliberately go out of your way to fuck that up? I am knee deep in Beanie Babies and Play-Doh, alright? I am drowning in responsibilities. There's a school that's fucking me for twelve thousand dollars a year, and this is kindergarten. My daughter can't stop throwing up all over my sister-in-law's furniture. Everybody want's me to listen more. I would love to have a relationship with a stunted and immature man. It sounds marvelous. What I don't understand is how you managed to be queer. Really. It's just not fair. I should have been queer. You're totally ungrateful. Do you remember that waiter you were fucking in New York?

MICHAEL: Do you mean dating?

JONATHAN: Stop sanctifying it, Michael, you were fucking him. Do you have any idea how jealous I was? He was twenty-two years old. How often do you think I have the chance to touch a twenty-two year old?

MICHAEL: What do you want me to do, feel sorry for you?

JONATHAN: I just want you to appreciate your situation. I don't go around plugging twenty-year old's. I've been completely faithful. And nobody pats you on the back for that either.

MICHAEL: Why should they? You're married. It's not some ordeal.

JONATHAN: Why don't you go to a doctor and become straight, if that's your attitude. Really, when was the last time you were with a woman? When was the last time you had a proper fuck? Maybe it was a bad experience. We can fix it.

MICHAEL: You're being such an idiot.

JONATHAN: Who was the last woman you fucked?

(Beat.)

MICHAEL: I don't remember.

JONATHAN: You don't remember?

MICHAEL: No.

JONATHAN: You don't remember? And you call yourself a mental health professional?

(Jenifer re-enters throwing Jonathan a sandwich.)

JENIFER: They put some mayonnaise on the bread. You can scrape it off if you don't want it.

JONATHAN: Did you know he wanted to adopt a girl?

JENIFER: Yes. Mariama.

JONATHAN: Oh. Mariama. Who is Mariama?

JENIFER: Michael, I got you a froze-fruit.

MICHAEL: Yay.

JONATHAN: Come here.

JENIFER: No.

JONATHAN: Come here. I'm sorry I don't listen enough. I apologize. Michael thinks I was ghastly.

JENIFER: You're always sorry.

JONATHAN: Do you want me to tell you about the audition?

JENIFER: I thought your problem was listening.

JONATHAN: Jenny, you gotta forgive people.

JENIFER: Do you want some of my sandwich, Michael?

MICHAEL: No, thank you.

JONATHAN: It's part of being a woman.

JENIFER: Maybe I've just run out of forgiveness. Do you want my pickle?

JONATHAN: You're not going to ask me if I want the pickle?

MICHAEL: I don't want the pickle.

JONATHAN: Well, good. Because I'm her husband, and I should really have first choice on whether I want the pickle.

JENIFER: But I'm not offering you the pickle. I'm offering him the pickle.

JONATHAN: Why don't you two just get married, for Christ sake.

JENIFER: Maybe we should. At least he behaves like a normal human being.

JONATHAN: Like a normal human being? He can't even remember the last woman he fucked.

MICHAEL: Jenifer, give him the pickle.

JONATHAN: I don't want the pickle.

MICHAEL: I don't know about you, but I'd really like to hear about the audition.

JONATHAN: Who cares? She wouldn't even give me a pickle.

MICHAEL: She offered you the pickle.

JENIFER: Here. *(Throws him the pickle.)* Take the pickle.

JONATHAN: Thank you. *(He starts to eat the pickle.)* How could you not remember the last woman—

MICHAEL: Why don't you tell us about the audition? We really want to hear about the audition. Don't we, Jenifer?

JENIFER: Yes. We do.

(Beat.)

JONATHAN: Alright. I'll cut to the chase. It's between me and somebody else. I know him, he used to go to my gym, and I am objectively more talented than he is. Also he's older than me. Plus, he just got panned in a ludicrous remake of "Picnic," and while he was reading the reviews, he got fired from this movie about a blind monkey because he couldn't get along with the chimp. And he tried. Went out of his way. But the monkey hated him. And she's big this monkey. She has casting approval. Plus he's fat. I forgot to tell you. He's definitely put on weight. He's a pig. He doesn't look good. It was pathetic.

MICHAEL: When do you get to the part when he dies?

JONATHAN: He should have been so lucky. We're sitting in the hallway, right? Listen to this, Jenifer, and it's hot, and he's sweating, so I try to be nice. I say, "God it's hot." You know what he says? "Yeah, but there's no humidity." What does he mean by that, Michael? We're in a hallway with no windows, and a broken air conditioner. I mean, it's like the only thing they have to be proud of out here.

JENIFER: He asked you how the audition went. This is character assassination.

JONATHAN: It's not enough to win. I take pleasure in watching the other guy lose.

JENIFER: *(Crossing to the phone.)* He's just provoking you.

JONATHAN: I'm trying to help him. He's too nice.

JENIFER: What time is it in New York?

JONATHAN: What are you doing? Put the phone down. *(Takes the phone from her and hangs it up.)* Stop worrying. You're in California. They arrest people who worry. Come on. Chill. We have to chill. You people get too taciturn. See. Fuck you. Sycophantic. Here, we'll put on… *(He crosses to the stereo and begins to look through the cd's.)* How long have you two been discussing whether he should adopt a child?

JENIFER: Mariama.

JONATHAN: I know it would be nice to have one of those "Baby on Board" signs bouncing in your back window, Michael, but it's a lot more than that.

MICHAEL: Has it ever occurred to you that I might love her? That she might love me. Homosexuals can love children too, you know.

JONATHAN: Believe me, I know homosexuals can love children. *(Starting to laugh.)* Everybody knows homosexuals can love children.

MICHAEL: Why did you marry him?

JONATHAN: Oh, my God, Michael. What is this? James Taylor? Joni Mitchell? This is frightening. "The Lion King?" I know. That's good.

MICHAEL: Put it down.

JONATHAN: Liza Minnelli in "Cabaret?" I'll make a deal with you. You destroy this right now and I won't tell anyone you bought it.

MICHAEL: You gave it to me.

JONATHAN: I gave it to you. That's ridiculous. You're insane. *(He picks up a different cd.)* Here, we'll live with this. *(Turns on the cd player.)* You probably gave it to me, and I gave it back to you a year later. That's what probably happened. *(He's having trouble with the cd player.)* Does this work?

MICHAEL: I'll do it.

JONATHAN: No, no, no. I get it. Jenifer, did I ever tell you the story about when Michael tried to check the oil in the front of his Karmen Ghia?

JENIFER: Yes.

JONATHAN: He was looking for the engine in the front of a Karmen Ghia.

MICHAEL: Why don't you publish this story?

(We begin to hear a slow song from the eighties.)

JONATHAN: Come here.

JENIFER: No.

JONATHAN: Come here.

(He seductively takes her by the hand and leads her into the middle of the room. They start to dance. Jenifer is reluctant.)

MICHAEL: Ferdinand and Miranda.

JENIFER: Michael, stop it.

MICHAEL: It was not that bad, Jenifer. You were very good.

JONATHAN: She was great.

JENIFER: I was fired. How great could I have been? They fired me.

JONATHAN: They fired everybody. They fired the ticket taker.

JENIFER: He died, Jonathan. They didn't fire him. And you quit.

JONATHAN: I had no choice. I was defending your honor.

(They continue dancing. Closer now. It's beautiful to watch. Michael looks a little left out.)

JONATHAN: *(Opening one of his arms.)* Michael, come here.

MICHAEL: What?

JONATHAN: Come here. I'm asking you to dance.

MICHAEL: No, thank you.

JONATHAN: You can be Michael York.

MICHAEL: No.

> (Jonathan approaches Michael playfully. Michael backs away.)

JONATHAN: Why don't you dance? I really don't understand this. You looked so fantastic in tights. I'm serious. What were you afraid of? Everyone was going to call you a fag? They called me a fag for being in drama club. They were imbeciles. They peaked in high school. Dance! Come on, dance! *(Jonathan chases him.)* Go into first position. Pliet! God damn you, pliet! Dance! Dance!

MICHAEL: No.

JONATHAN: *(He's pinned him down on the sofa.)* You're why I act! You were magnificent. You were strong and decisive. Why did you stop? Why?

> (Jenifer turns the music off, and moves to the phone.)

JONATHAN: If you're calling your sister, don't. Emma lost her lunch on the sofa.

MICHAEL: Don't tell her like that.

JONATHAN: I'm sorry. She threw up.

JENIFER: Did you call her?

JONATHAN: Yes, I was about to call her.

JENIFER: Yes, you called her, or you were about to call her?

JONATHAN: She just threw up. Don't get upset. They took her to Doctor Reed's.

JENIFER: Doctor Reed's? Why? *(Into the phone.)* Wendy, it's Jenny. Are you home?…Wendy?… *(Leaves a message.)* I'm here at Michael's. Call me when you get back from Reed's, alright? I want to go over her medication schedule. She takes the blue pills…Oh, just call me. *(She hangs up.)*

MICHAEL: You could have brought her out here, you know.

JENIFER: She has an ear infection. She's not supposed to fly.

MICHAEL: She has an ear infection, too? How long has she had an ear infection?

JONATHAN: She has an ear *ache.*

JENIFER: *(Looking through her purse.)* Where's Doctor Reed's number?

JONATHAN: Jenifer, ear infections are common in children.

JENIFER: Ear infections, and vomiting, and weight loss, that is not common in children, alright. *(Jenifer heads into the bedroom.)*

JONATHAN: Do you understand this now? This is what I'm dealing with. *(Calling out.)* What are you doing?

JENIFER: *(Re-entering with a bag.)* I'm going to the airport.

JONATHAN: Jenifer, stop it. Stop it. Jenifer. What is your problem?

JENIFER: I don't have a problem. I have a daughter who isn't well, and I may not know how to take care of myself, but I will walk across this country if I have to.

JONATHAN: Emma is fine. Stop it. If I didn't think our daughter was completely and positively okay, do you think I would have left her in New York? I love her. When she had tests, what did they say? They said not to worry about anything. She's a kid. She's fine. You have to stop giving her cancer. Just because they can't explain something, doesn't mean she has cancer. Everything's going to be fine. You know what I think? Jenny? I think we should go to the beach. Michael.

(Michael doesn't answer.)

JONATHAN: Michael, wake up, I'm talking to you. Let's go to the beach. You can watch the boys play volley ball. We are all going to not be so anxious, okay? Let me just call Alan and tell him where I am. *(He crosses to the phone.)* Sweetie, smile. *(Into the phone.)* Hello…It's Jonathan Dryver. Is he in?…Thank you. *(To them.)* She remembered me. *(Into the phone.)* Hello…I'm fine, Alan…Well I feel a little like I'm sitting on the space shuttle waiting for it to take off.

MICHAEL: What kind of tests did she have?

JONATHAN: *(Into the phone.)* No, I've never met him. Of course I watched the show.

JENIFER: They tested her for colitis.

JONATHAN: *(Into the phone.)* I would love to but I can't.

MICHAEL: Colitis? Why?

JENIFER: She lost weight over Christmas. I worry too much. I don't know what I'm talking about. Forget it.

JONATHAN: *(Into the phone.)* No, really I can't. My daughter is not feeling perfect, to tell you the truth, and I'm feeling a little guilty for leaving her…Tell him I'm sorry…Fine, I'll call you at the end of the day… Thank you, Alan. *(He hangs up.)* I was just invited to a poker game at Jay Leno's this weekend, Jenny, and I dissed the man. How about that? Where's my bathing suit?

JENIFER: It's in the green bag. It's still in the trunk.

(Jonathan exits.)

MICHAEL: It's not possible.

JENIFER: But—

MICHAEL: Jenifer.

JENIFER: I just wanted to talk about it. Forget it.

MICHAEL: There is no possible way—

JENIFER: Did you ever—?

MICHAEL: You know, this is what I can't stand.

JENIFER: I just thought by now you—

MICHAEL: This is not my problem. Am I the only other person you ever slept with? Are you going to do this to everybody? Why didn't you just talk to your doctor? What do you want me to do? Is this why you came out here?

(Jonathan approaches the front door.)

JENIFER: Michael, quiet.

JONATHAN: *(Re-entering.)* Can I wear your basketball shoes?

MICHAEL: Yes.

(Jonathan keeps going into the bedroom.)

JENIFER: Shit. I'm sorry. I'm so guilty. I'm going crazy.

MICHAEL: *(Shutting the hallway door.)* Do you know what the odds are?

JENIFER: I know.

MICHAEL: There weren't that many people then.

JENIFER: There was that dancer.

MICHAEL: Brendon is fine. He's fine. Look at me, Jen. You're the best mother I've ever known in my life. This is not a problem.

(Jenifer starts to cry. Michael goes to comfort her.)

MICHAEL: Jen, come on. Look, you can go somewhere and take a test. If you really think you need to.

JENIFER: Do you want to take it with me?

MICHAEL: Now? Jenifer, you don't have…There is nothing I did way back then that—

JENIFER: Forget it.

MICHAEL: *(After a while.)* I'll go with you. I'll go with you to the center.

JENIFER: You don't have to. I don't w-w-w-ant you…I just stuttered. I can't believe I just stuttered. In real life.

MICHAEL: You stumbled on a word. Relax.

JENIFER: What are we going to do about Jonathan?

MICHAEL: You can't tell him this. You're not going to tell him this now.

JENIFER: Where am I going to tell him we're going?

MICHAEL: We'll go to the beach. There are a lot of people. We'll lose him in the crowd.

JENIFER: Oh God. It's like the last scene in *Brute Force II.*

MICHAEL: You're not going to tell him this. That was a promise. I mean it. You can't ever tell him.

JENIFER: I don't tell him anything, why would I tell him this? Oh, Michael. We never did much packing, did we?

JONATHAN: *(Re-enters in a bathing suit, basketball shoes, and a Knicks t-shirt.)* You know what I can't stand about my life? I have to just sit here until Wednesday. Waiting. *(Looks at them.)* Don't sit so close to my wife. *(The lights fade.)*

END OF ACT I

ACT II
SCENE I

Wednesday afternoon. Michael is alone, packing, listening to the radio.

RADIO: *(Music fades.)* That was the end of a thirty minute rock block. Smash Mouth, The Wallflowers, Verve Pipe. Edna Swap finished it off. This is Gary Singleton, The Single Man. *(Sound effect: "Oh Yeah.")* And this is KROCK. Welcome to the boom town. I gotta say last night I went down to Costa Mesa to the opening of their club, The Ash Tray… *(Laughter.)* What is so funny, Larry? Larry is doing a manic depressive thing today. *(More laughter from Larry.)* Let me tell them, please. So I go down there and we're playing ping pong. And I end up playing the queen of their table, a Ms. Julie Dawson. *(Larry's voice.)* "End up"? You were begging her all night. *(Gary again.)* That is obvious. That is duh. So duh. She was, well she was beautiful.

MICHAEL: Oh, God.

RADIO: She was simply magnificent. And she trounced me. Simple as that. So in honor of your victory, Ms. Julie Dawson, I would like to ask you a Simple question. Will you marry me?

(Larry howls. Michael can't take it anymore. He goes for the radio.)

RADIO: I'm coming to get you, Julie. I love you. I'm heading for your home. This is Gary Singleton, The Single Man—

(Michael snaps off the radio. He moves over to a box.)

MICHAEL: *(Singing.)* "Gloria. I think they got your number." *(He finds the phone machine in the box and takes it out.)* "I think they got the alias that you've been living under." *(He plugs the machine back in.)* "But you really don't remember." "Was it something that they said? All the voices in your head." *(He presses the message button.)*

PHONE MACHINE: You have no new messages. You have one saved message.

MESSAGE ONE: *(Mariama's voice.)* Michael, it's Mariama. What's up? I'm basically so pissed right now because I think one of the nurses stole my Entertainment Weekly. That is so shady, right. So, like why don't you call me at least? I get out of here in a few days. Did you tape Dawson's Creek? Okay, like I would kill for a cheeseburger—

(He turns off the tape. While he was listening to Mariama, A Young Man has come to the screen door. He's got a knapsack, and is dressed by Urban Outfitters.)

YOUNG MAN: Hello.

MICHAEL: *(Startled.)* Yes.

YOUNG MAN: Hi.

MICHAEL: Yes. Hello. Can I help you?

YOUNG MAN: I'm sorry. I'm bothering you. No, it's just…To tell you the truth, I know your landlord. He told me…Well, I guess you're moving.

MICHAEL: Yes. I am.

YOUNG MAN: Well, he told me maybe I could look at the house. But if you're busy. I didn't mean—

(The phone rings. Michael doesn't move. It rings twice more.)

YOUNG MAN: Do you want to get the phone?

MICHAEL: *(Picking up the phone.)* Hello…Just make him go to the baseball game…We'll get rid of him…I can't hear you…Jenifer, you're breaking up…Shit. *(He hangs up. He seems to have forgotten about the Young Man.)*

YOUNG MAN: Hello.

MICHAEL: Yes, I'm sorry. My landlord said you could look at the house?

YOUNG MAN: Yes, he told me to call first, but I happened to be down the street. Sorry, I'm bothering you. I'll come back later. You seem all wound up. He called you though, right? He said he was going to call you. Did he call you? I feel terrible right now. I feel like a complete idiot right now. I mean, he said he was going to call you and tell you I wanted to look at the house. I'm sorry. I shouldn't be here right now. I should have called. I'm sorry. You seem overwhelmed. Do you want to call the girl on the cell-phone back?

MICHAEL: No, it's okay, thank you. Look, if you want to look around quickly.

YOUNG MAN: Oh, okay. Thanks. Thank you. *(Opens the screen door and slowly comes into the house.)* But, if this isn't cool, I'll come back. You look really exhausted. You should get some rest, chill. Are you eating well and everything?

MICHAEL: I'm sorry?

YOUNG MAN: No, it's just you seem really busy. People don't eat right, bingo, they get really tired.

MICHAEL: I'm not tired.

YOUNG MAN: And then, bang, they get sick.

MICHAEL: Wait. Why do you say that? I'm not tired. I'm not tired at all. Why do you think I look tired?

YOUNG MAN: You don't. Forget it. Don't listen to me. I'm studying to be a nutritionist. I'm trying to practice. I should just shut up. I talk too much. *(He looks around the room.)* This is a really nice house. Great light. I love light. Well, that's cause I have cactus. Why are you leaving?

MICHAEL: I can't afford it anymore. I'm sorry, I didn't catch your name.

YOUNG MAN: Gary.

MICHAEL: Excuse me?

GARY: Gary.

MICHAEL: That's really your name?

GARY: Yes. Last time I checked. Are you okay?

MICHAEL: Yes, I'm fine. I happen not to like your name, that's all. It's nothing. It's no big deal.

GARY: This is definitely an outstanding house. *(He takes his knapsack off.)* To tell you the truth, this is sort of exactly what I'm looking for. I don't like it where I am, that's the thing. I want a change. With everything. I'd like to open up a nutritional corporation. I think that would be really great. Right now I'm a bag boy at Whole Foods. At least I'm in food, right? But I'm going to school. Are you alright? I mean do you want me to leave? I'll leave.

MICHAEL: Yes, I'm alright. Why do you keep asking me that? I mean, do I look like there's something not right about me?

GARY: No.

MICHAEL: Then please stop asking me that.

GARY: I'm sorry. This happens at school a lot. I make people nervous. I get too excited. I have immediate gratification problems. That's what my shrink in high school said. It's like, I just want to follow my bliss, that's all. Can you hear the freeway from here?

MICHAEL: No.

GARY: Good. Did you see that? That show? It was an interview with this guy about doing what makes you feel good? It was about myths. Happiness. Bliss. Screw guilt, basically.

MICHAEL: Yes, I saw the show.

GARY: Did you like it?

MICHAEL: No. I thought it was delusional, actually.

GARY: Wow. Really. Why?

MICHAEL: Because I think guilt is a good emotion. It keeps us from doing terrible things to each other.

GARY: That's true, I guess. I never thought of that. I was like ten when I saw it. Huh. Well, semi-screw it then. Have a good time, but keep the reins in. I'll tell you where I'd like to go. I mean total following my bliss, but pure at the same time. The desert near Santa Fe. You know that one? I mean on the sand. Just a sleeping bag. No house. No offense, house. But

I'd like to just live outdoors. *(Opening a drawer.)* This is a lot of cabinet space. Can I just say one thing about guilt though?

MICHAEL: Sure.

GARY: Everybody has a song, I think, and if they're lucky, they start playing it, and really enjoying it. But eventually, they've got to notice that a whole bunch of people don't even have an instrument, or a voice, and that there are like, starving people in India and stuff. And some people, they feel guilty, and some people, well they quiet down, or they stop playing, completely. You know in like… *(Trying to find the word.)* that guy from Poland…Solidarity, for the other people. But what I'm saying is, I think that's wrong. People should keep playing. The truth is, it's not going to help anyone if they stop. And maybe, all those voiceless people, they might even enjoy listening to the music. I mean, if someone's really playing *their* song, it's beautiful. And you know, we could be dead at any moment.

MICHAEL: You should be a psychiatrist. You should be my psychiatrist.

GARY: No way. I'll just be some deluded spiritual guy and live in the Mojave. I would also like to be a movie star, but that kind of conflicts.

MICHAEL: Well, breathe deeply, 'cause you found the right house.

GARY: Why? What? Did a movie star live here?

MICHAEL: Does the title "Brute Force II" mean anything to you?

GARY: Great movie.

MICHAEL: You saw it? Really? You actually went to that movie?

GARY: I see everything. "Brute Force I," "Brute Force II." I'll even see "Brute Force III." Wait. Was it shot here?

MICHAEL: No. I have a friend in it, that's all.

GARY: Wow. I live in L.A. and I don't know one actor. I know actors, but they're carpenters. But I think actors, I mean real actors, or performance artists, you know people who perform in front of a lot of people and feel no fear. Zip. I think that's amazing. I could never do it. Never. And I grew up here. I'm a native. California native. Where are you from?

MICHAEL: Connecticut. I'm a Connecticut native.

GARY: These are the heating ducts, huh? People don't think it gets cold in L.A. but—

MICHAEL: You know, that's what I used to…Not…I didn't act…But, you know…

GARY: What?

MICHAEL: I was a dancer. I was a ballet dancer.

GARY: You were? God. When?

MICHAEL: Oh…In New York City.

GARY: You must have great legs.

MICHAEL: No, it was a long time ago. When I was a kid. It was nothing. *(Beat.)* I danced at Lincoln Center. I was the Prince in "The Nutcracker."

GARY: Cool.

MICHAEL: I was a student at S.A.B. The School of American Ballet.

GARY: You were. What was that like?

MICHAEL: What was it like? God, it was… *(Beat.)* It was a long time ago, I don't remember.

GARY: Was it just unbelievably hard? You practiced like twenty-four hours a day, right?

MICHAEL: Yeah, but that's easy. You don't have to think. You just have to move. Exactly as your told. Or jump.

GARY: How high did you jump?

MICHAEL: High. *(Beat.)* No, it was great. *(Beat.)* You know when your body starts to…? I was a kid. Your arms, your legs, they start to change. But when you dance, it doesn't feel like nature. It's like you're inventing it. You are forcing your body to be what you want it to be. You create it. When I was twelve years old, I completely understood God. *(Beat.)* Class was always quiet. All you could hear were feet sliding on the floor. It was the most perfect sound you could hear on this earth. I still dream of it.

GARY: Why did you stop?

MICHAEL: Why? *(Beat.)* Solidarity, I guess. My mother died. I didn't feel much like jumping.

GARY: What do you do now?

MICHAEL: I'm a social worker.

GARY: Cool. Do you have a kid? You have a copy of *The Lion King* so…

MICHAEL: No, that's…That's a client's. A girl I know.

GARY: She likes cartoons.

MICHAEL: And movies. It doesn't much matter.

GARY: Did she like *Brute Force II?*

MICHAEL: Too violent. I wouldn't let her see it.

GARY: She would come over here and watch 'em? The movies?

MICHAEL: Yeah. And t.v. She loves that guy Joshua Jackson.

GARY: "Dawson's Creek." But not the guy who plays Dawson. That's fierce.

MICHAEL: Yep.

GARY: That's what you do? Look after kids in fucked up situations?

MICHAEL: Yeah. Some people do adults. I do kids.

GARY: I wish I had someone like you when I was a kid.

MICHAEL: Sure. Well.

GARY: This girl. Is she your favorite?

MICHAEL: Yes. She is.

GARY: Why?

MICHAEL: I don't know. She knows about things I don't know about. She can tell you what kind of haircut looks good on you. She's very into sunglasses. She's fun.

GARY: And you don't know a lot about fun?

MICHAEL: Ha, ha.

GARY: What's her name?

MICHAEL: Mariama. Her name is Mariama.

GARY: How's she doing?

MICHAEL: She's in the hospital, actually.

GARY: Oh. You're kidding. Why?

MICHAEL: She got hit a little. Someone beat her up.

GARY: God. Is she alright?

MICHAEL: She's fine. I'm not allowed to see her, or talk to her even, but…I've been sort of taken off the case.

GARY: Why?

MICHAEL: I…I got too involved. I…Anyway, she's much better. She looks much better I've been told.

GARY: Well, that's great. Yea. No, to tell you the truth, I like kids. How can you get too involved with a kid?

MICHAEL: I don't know.

GARY: Well…She must love you very much.

MICHAEL: Thank you.

GARY: Well…Tell her to eat good. *(Beat.)* Do you have a roommate? I mean, is the house big enough for two? I say that 'cause, no way, I can't afford this on my own. I mean, have you ever lived with anybody?

MICHAEL: Yes, I have.

GARY: Oh. But not as a roommate?

MICHAEL: No.

GARY: Is that over now? I mean, do you live with anyone now?

MICHAEL: I don't even know you, Gary.

GARY: Sorry. I'm sorry. *(Beat.)* Do you have a fireplace?

MICHAEL: Yes.

GARY: Oh, well. Okay. I've never been in a relationship before. It's probably up and down, right?

MICHAEL: Right.

GARY: The bedroom's down there?

MICHAEL: Yeah.

GARY: Can I?

MICHAEL: Sure.

> *(Gary goes down the hall toward the bedrooms. Michael wanders over to a mirror hanging on the wall. He looks at himself, and then, with a little spit, tries to comb his hair.)*

GARY: *(Re-entering.)* So.

MICHAEL: Where do you live, Gary?

GARY: Me? Um. The Valley. A condo. Oakline. Right across the street from Whole Foods. Ah…Well, I wrote down some questions, um… *(Takes a piece of paper out of his pocket.)* Do you have a dryer washer? Washer dryer.

MICHAEL: Yes.

GARY: Ha. And no fireplace. Oh I can't. I can't. I'm sorry. I'm going to have a heart attack. I have a mitral valve prolapse. Oh, God. Listen, I'm Gary. Gary, Gary. Gary's staying with me. Oh, you're a really nice guy. I'm sorry. I just wanted to know you. I'm sorry. I wanted…I saw you at the Beverly Center. You didn't know, but…I just admire you so much. You're so good and devoted to your work. I really was just driving by here when I wrote down these stupid questions. Can I sit down? I'm sorry. *(He sits. Beat.)* I'm sorry Mariama's in the hospital, I didn't know. Gary told me all about her. She seems like such a good kid. She obviously loves you so much. And I think it's really cool that you wanted to maybe adopt her. I disagree with Gary on this. I really like kids, so…See, he asked me if he could move in, and that's a really big decision. I've never been in a relationship before, and sometimes I don't know. *(Beat.)* He called you, right? Gary said he was going to call you. *(Beat.)* I shouldn't have done this. God, I feel really stupid right now.

> *(Jonathan and Jenifer enter.)*

JONATHAN: Michael, do you think I should be represented by a man who goes to not one, but three separate twelve-step programs?

JENIFER: *(Noticing Gary.)* Hi.

JONATHAN: Apparently he's got three separate, altogether autonomous addictions. Or diseases as he puts it. What a fucking lunch. The guy's insane. Did anybody call me? You unpacked the answering machine. *(Finally noticing Gary.)* Hi.

GARY: Hi. I'm just leaving.

JONATHAN: *(Beat. With a smile.)* Did I interrupt anything?

    (Nobody responds.)

JONATHAN: Michael?

    (Nothing.)

JONATHAN: *(Turning to Gary.)* How are you?

GARY: Me? Fine.

JONATHAN: Why are you looking at me like that?

GARY: I'm not.

JONATHAN: I'm an actor, if that's what you're thinking.

GARY: I know. Are you going to do "Brute Force III?"

MICHAEL: Why don't you get his autograph?

GARY: I'm sorry, I have to leave. *(Gary heads for the door.)*

JENIFER: Goodbye.

JONATHAN: Where are you going? Where's he going? *(Going after him.)* Are they casting "Brute Force III?"

    (Gary leaves.)

JONATHAN: Did I fuck this up? Michael?

JENIFER: I'm sorry we're late. I was just saying to Jon that if he wasn't going to the ball game, that this would be a good time for him to go to your health club. Why don't you give him your gym card?

JONATHAN: Just tell me who it was.

MICHAEL: He was a client.

JONATHAN: You have cute clients, Michael. What's he addicted to? The Gap?

JENIFER: I'm sorry we're late.

JONATHAN: We're not late! Stop saying we're late. Where is the fucking schedule that says we're late? Michael, don't even talk to her. She's been a black hole all day.

MICHAEL: Excuse me, I'll let you two fight. *(Michael heads down the hallway.)*

JONATHAN: Hey, I'm sorry we disturbed you. What's wrong with him?

JENIFER: Maybe he's got things on his mind.

JONATHAN: Isn't it funny how he has things on his mind, while I'm always venal and self-centered?

JENIFER: *(Heading down the hall.)* Michael.

JONATHAN: He was here trying to get laid. That's what was on his mind. We interrupted him.

    (Gary comes back to the screen door.)

GARY: I'm sorry. I forgot my knapsack.

JONATHAN: Oh. So, come on in.

    (Gary cautiously comes in, heading for his knapsack.)

JONATHAN: I'm sorry we just, you know, barged in. You don't have to worry
    about me. I'm family. Really, stay if you want.
GARY: I think I should probably go.
JONATHAN: Why? I'm just leaving. Stay. You want a Snapple?
GARY: Me? No.
MICHAEL: *(Re-entering.)* Jon.
GARY: I forgot my knapsack.
JONATHAN: So, how do you two know each other?
MICHAEL: I thought you wanted to go to a baseball game.
JONATHAN: They're at Atlanta. You got it wrong. *(Thinking he's getting the
    hint.)* But, oh yeah. Cool. *(Calling out to her.)* Jenifer, I'll go to the gym.
    If you want to go to the gym. *(Smiling at the two of them.)* So, what have
    you guys been doing all day?
    (No answer.)
JONATHAN: Nice Volkswagen you got out there. You don't see many Bugs in
    New York. I remember once Michael and I were driving down to
    Washington in his Karmen Ghia.
MICHAEL: Don't, Jon. You don't know what's going on here.
JONATHAN: Relax. Let me tell a story. He always afraid I'm going to embar-
    rass him. So, we're driving down to the march on Washington. I'm not
    gay myself. I always wanted to be, but you can't have everything. So we're
    driving and we stop for gas and I say, you know, I'll check the oil. And
    I go straight for the front of the car. Michael goes, "Genius, the engine's
    in the back of a Karmen Ghia."
JENIFER: *(Re-entering.)* Michael, where's your gym card?
    (An uncomfortable pause, as everyone stands there.)
MICHAEL: This is Gary, Jenifer. He lives with Gary. Gary, this is Jonathan and
    Jenifer.
GARY: Can I just say something here?
JENIFER: You're Gary? This is Gary?
GARY: Listen, I made a terrible mistake everybody. I'm a moral person, I
    swear. I didn't want to hurt anyone. It was nice to meet everybody. I'm
    sorry about Mariama. I hope she's okay. I really do. *(Gary starts to leave.)*
JONATHAN: Wait, wait, wait. What the fuck is he talking about?
GARY: Goodbye.
JONATHAN: *(Firmly.)* Wait. Did you invite him over here, Michael?
MICHAEL: Just let him go, alright?
JONATHAN: This is *Gary?* Why is he here? Why did you let him in?
MICHAEL: He just came in. I didn't know who he was.

GARY: I think I—

JONATHAN: Shut up. You see, you don't get to talk right now. I'm here. Are you okay, Michael?

MICHAEL: Jon—

JONATHAN: *(To Gary.)* Why did you come over here?

(*Gary says nothing.*)

JONATHAN: Do you want him to leave? Michael? *(He grabs Gary and pushes him out the door.)* Okay, get the fuck out of here—

MICHAEL: Jon.

JONATHAN: …before I put your face through a leaf blower. Go. You fucking vampire.

(*Gary runs away.*)

MICHAEL: You didn't have to do that. He was leaving.

JONATHAN: Excuse me? The fucking Trojan Horse comes through the gate.

MICHAEL: It was very Clint Eastwood, and I'm grateful, but you didn't have to get violent. He was just a kid.

JONATHAN: WHAT DOES SOMEONE HAVE TO DO TO YOU TO GET A REACTION?

JENIFER: Calm down.

JONATHAN: I CAN'T CALM DOWN! I'M THE ONLY ONE STANDING BETWEEN YOU TWO AND EXTINCTION! *(Beat.)* Will you please tell me who this Mariama girl is?

MICHAEL: She's an eleven-year-old girl. She lived here for three months until my supervisor forced her to go home.

JENIFER: What? You told me—

MICHAEL: Her mother, who unfortunately had a habit of bringing tricks home for crack money and then fucking them in front of her daughter, got arrested. So Mariama stayed there alone, eating Spaghetti O's, until inevitably some crack addict beat the shit out of her. And now she's in the hospital. Of course, I know it was highly inadvisable and unprofessional for her to have stayed here. In the words of my supervisor, I'm a kidnapper.

JONATHAN: Wait a minute. This girl *lived* here? Did you know this?

JENIFER: She's in the hospital?

MICHAEL: She'll be fine. Fine. I didn't tell you, because there is nothing I can do. They won't even let me see her. *(Taking out his wallet.)* My gym card's in here.

JONATHAN: I don't want your gym card.

MICHAEL: Fine. I'm going to walk the dog.

JENIFER: He's just trying to save you money.

JONATHAN: I'm not going to the gym. Shut up. Will you please shut up.

MICHAEL: Don't. Don't say shut up to her. Don't treat her like that.

JONATHAN: I don't want to go to the gym right now.

MICHAEL: Just do as you're told. For once in your life, just do as you are told. People are trying to help you and you don't listen. *(Michael goes out the front door.)*

JONATHAN: *(Calling out to him.)* I'm sorry I took a fucking interest. I won't do it again. *(To Jenifer.)* What did I do? *(Jonathan picks up the phone and dials.)*

JENIFER: Jon, sweetie, you just had lunch with him. Nothing's changed in twenty minutes. Hang up and go to the gym, okay? It's beyond your control now.

JONATHAN: *(Hangs up the phone.)* Thank you. I don't want to go to the gym. I want you to tell me why I can't call our phone machine and you can call home twice, sometimes three times a day. I want to know where you draw the line there. What are you doing?

JENIFER: I'm trying to find Michael's gym card.

JONATHAN: I'm talking to you. Why are you trying to get rid of me?

JENIFER: I'm not trying to get rid of you.

JONATHAN: At the beach I was like fucking poison ivy.

JENIFER: I wanted some frozen yogurt.

JONATHAN: Okay, so you say, "I want some frozen yogurt," and then we walk over and buy some. You two don't have to vanish.

JENIFER: I'm sorry. I told you I was sorry a million times. I don't know what else you want me to do. We looked for you, honestly.

JONATHAN: Crap. You ditched me. You two have entered some…What? Some sorority. It's like I'm not here.

JENIFER: Jonathan.

JONATHAN: Fine. *(Goes and gets a script out of his bag and begins to read it.)* Did you like Alan?

JENIFER: Who?

JONATHAN: Alan. David. Alan David my agent. We just had lunch with him.

JENIFER: Yes, I did.

JONATHAN: What did you like about him?

JENIFER: He's very nice. He's…I don't know, he seemed very nice. He has a good sense of humor.

JONATHAN: He's not at all nice. As a matter of fact, he's an opportunistic lit-tle prick. He's an evil piece of shit without any sense of humor, and anybody who was half conscious would see through his, "I'll have the iced tea. How do you like the Roy Lichtenstein in the lobby," like it was clean glass.

JENIFER: I don't know what you want me to say.

JONATHAN: JUST BE THERE WITH ME. I'm out here eating cilantro with these vultures, trying not to retch, because I'm trying to do something with my life. I do not like *Brute Force II* anymore than anyone else does. But everything is not out of our control. Do you two understand that?

JENIFER: Jonathan, what kind of person do you want me to be? Because obviously I'm failing as I am.

JONATHAN: Oh, I don't think that's fair. I think everybody thinks you're perfect.

JENIFER: Nobody thinks I'm perfect.

JONATHAN: Michael thinks you're perfect, and if I would just listen more, you wouldn't have such a miserable existence.

JENIFER: Jonathan, please.

JONATHAN: But if you checked the record, you'd realize you didn't do anything today to help me. You didn't listen. I finally have lunch with this monster, and you just sit there comatose. I thought you were dead.

JENIFER: Don't do this. You don't know what you're talking about.

JONATHAN: I know what I'm talking about. I know exactly what I'm talking about. Don't tell me I don't know what I'm talking about.

JENIFER: Will you please s-s-s-stop shouting. I-I-I-I…

JONATHAN: These people will kill you, alright. They'll roll you up with seaweed. I need a little support system here. Why is it so hard for you to be friendly in front of one of the most important agents in Hollywood? Do I offend you so much—

JENIFER: It had nothing to do with you. I-I-I-I-I…I'm sorry. I should have been more up.

JONATHAN: Did it ever occur to you he could have helped you? You want a life? Get a life. It was sitting right in front of you. Open mouth and talk. Nobody's going to give you an acting career.

JENIFER: I'm not asking anybody to.

JONATHAN: Then what do you want?

JENIFER: I-I-I-I…

JONATHAN: What?

(She stops trying.)

JONATHAN: What is the matter with you? You can't talk now? What? *(Beat.)* Fine you want to be a caterer be one. Be an optometrist. Just stop blaming me because you're a failure. I'm not responsible. And I'm not going to roll over and starve because you can't get out of bed in the morning. Say something. Alright, fuck you. I'll go to the gym. You want to get rid of me, I'll go. *(He starts to gather his things.)* And I don't need the fucking card, I'll pay the ten fucking dollars.

JENIFER: Your fly's open.

JONATHAN: What?

JENIFER: There, I said something.

JONATHAN: Fuck you. What do you mean my fly's open? *(He checks it, and pulls it up.)* Are you crazy? You've been looking at my fly, open, all day?

JENIFER: I was looking at your underwear.

JONATHAN: You sat at The Ivy and watched my underwear? What is going on with you? Are you sick? Do you have a fever?

JENIFER: I don't want to talk to you anymore.

JONATHAN: You're crazy now.

JENIFER: I'm terrified now. I'm terrified.

JONATHAN: Why? And don't say I'm mean. I'm not mean. I'm just trying to get through the day here. I have a temper, I'm sorry, but this is life. I am in the real world. I am not going to apologize for protecting myself.

JENIFER: What difference does it make? There's nothing left of you to protect. You've killed everything in you worth saving. You're just a series of pre-emptive strikes. It's not self defense. You're the monster now, Jonathan, there's no bigger prick than you. And in case you haven't noticed, I don't like standing in front of a lot of people and shaking. And that's what I do, I shake on stage, and sometimes I can't talk, which I guess you did notice. I stand there waiting for my line to come, knowing I won't be able to say it. And that can be a nightmare, that kind of doom. Really, that's what it is, impending doom, and I don't want to feel that anymore. I slept with Michael. I had sex with him.

JONATHAN: You did what?

JENIFER: You don't know me.

JONATHAN: You did what?

JENIFER: I'm afraid Emma's sick. I've been worried since January.

JONATHAN: *(Barely audible.)* Oh my God. Jesus Christ.

JENIFER: I don't know anything. I took a test. That's all I know.

(Jonathan very slowly sits down.)

JONATHAN: *(Very cautiously.)* When did you take a test?

JENIFER: Monday.

JONATHAN: Jenifer, is Michael…? Do you know that Michael is…?

JENIFER: I don't know. We're supposed to call now.

JONATHAN: But Michael doesn't know he's…?

JENIFER: No. We're supposed to call them.

JONATHAN: So you both took a test?

JENIFER: Yes.

JONATHAN: Because you thought it might be a possibility?

JENIFER: Yes.

JONATHAN: And it's ready today?

JENIFER: Yes.

JONATHAN: And you call them?

JENIFER: Yes, you call.

JONATHAN: And they tell you?

JENIFER: It depends what…Where's my purse? The number's in my purse. And a code. I have a code thing. I need for you to go to the gym.

JONATHAN: Jenifer.

JENIFER: I promised Michael we would call together. He didn't want to do this. I made him take this, and I need for you to go to the gym.

JONATHAN: Calm down.

JENIFER: I am very calm.

JONATHAN: You're getting hysterical.

JENIFER: I don't want you here when he comes back. He doesn't want you to know this.

JONATHAN: Jenifer—

JENIFER: I'm not hysterical.

JONATHAN: Jenifer.

JENIFER: What? *(She finds the code in her purse.)*

JONATHAN: Will you listen to me?

JENIFER: Oh God, I'm going to lose my mind.

JONATHAN: Can you just sit down?

JENIFER: No.

JONATHAN: Fine. Just listen then. I'm not going to the gym. Okay? I'm talking calmly right now, but inside I want you to know I am not calm. I am far from calm. Okay? I am glad you're calm, but I am not calm.

JENIFER: Stop patronizing me, I don't want you to patronize me.

JONATHAN: Can I ask you a question? You slept with Michael?

JENIFER: Yes.

JONATHAN: When?

JENIFER: In 1988.

JONATHAN: In 1988? And this is why you think Emma's sick? I don't think Michael was even sleeping with men in 1988.

JENIFER: He did.

JONATHAN: But the doctors would have told us if they thought it was a possibility.

JENIFER: They didn't know all the information.

JONATHAN: But the chances—

JENIFER: I know what the chances are.

JONATHAN: It's been eleven years.

JENIFER: It incubates—

JONATHAN: I know, but the chances—

JENIFER: I know what the chances are if you don't use…

JONATHAN: If you don't… *(Long beat.)* We were married in 1988.

JENIFER: It was before. The last time was three months before.

JONATHAN: The last time? *(Beat.)* Alright, I don't think any of this is a problem. Okay? I think this has all been built up in your mind and before we all have a heart attack here, I think we should just call. So give me the number.

JENIFER: I'm waiting for Michael. I have to.

JONATHAN: *(Trying not to explode.)* Jesus fucking Christ, Jenny. You know, I'm trying to do the right thing here, but you are making this almost impossible. I'm holding on to us by nothing. Do you understand? By less than nothing.

JENIFER: If you want to stay here—

JONATHAN: This is my family! I'm about to snap. Really I am. *(Trying to remain calm.)* Yes I want to stay here. I want you to call. That's what I want you to do. I just want you and I to make this call together. I'm your husband. Michael is not your husband. You had no right to sleep with him, Jenny. God damn you, it's just completely faithless.

JENIFER: Jonathan, please stop it.

JONATHAN: *(Exploding.)* NO, YOU STOP IT, I'M NOT DOING ANYTHING! OKAY? YOU'RE THE ONE WHO FUCKED HIM! I DIDN'T FUCK HIM! YOU FUCKED HIM! YOU WERE FUCKING MY BEST FRIEND, JENIFER! THREE MONTHS BEFORE OUR WEDDING. FUCK YOU! THAT'S COMPLETELY UNBELIEVABLE. HE'S MY BEST FRIEND. FUCK YOU! I COULD BE DEAD RIGHT NOW! FUCK YOU!

(Jenifer looks at him for a long time and then crosses to the phone. She dials a number.)

JENIFER: *(Into the phone.)* Yes. Hello, I'm calling about…Pardon me?…Yes.

JONATHAN: I didn't mean it. Hang up.

JENIFER: *(Into the phone.)* Yes, I'm calling about a test result.

JONATHAN: Hang up. Please hang up.

JENIFER: *(To Jonathan.)* What are you going to do if something happens right now? *(Into the phone.)* Hello…Yes, I'm holding.

JONATHAN: I lost control. Please, hang up. I love you. I don't want you to find this out right now.

JENIFER: *(Into the phone.)* Yes, hello…Yes I'm calling about a test result…Yes. *(Checking the piece of paper.)* L798. No, I'm sorry. L7998…Yes L7998… I know it matters, that's why I'm saying it slowly, and I don't need your attitude, alright. You're being critical and completely inappropriate. So just listen. L7998…Thank you.

JONATHAN: Jenifer—

JENIFER: *(To Jonathan.)* No. Don't say anything. That's all. *(Long pause. Then into the phone.)* Yes…Oh. Thank you. *(She slowly hangs up.)*

JONATHAN: Jenifer?

JENIFER: I'm fine. I feel like I'm going to cry or something.

JONATHAN: Oh, God.

JENIFER: You see your whole life.

JONATHAN: Come here.

JENIFER: Flash before your eyes. Just like that. And you realize what it is. *(Michael comes in the front door. His hands are covered with blood.)*

JENIFER: Jesus, Michael, you're bleeding.

MICHAEL: No, I'm okay. I'm not bleeding.

JENIFER: Yes you are. You're bleeding.

MICHAEL: Shirley's bleeding. I'm not bleeding. The dog's bleeding. She got bit. One of the neighbors took her to the vet. Excuse me. *(Long pause.)* You told him.

JONATHAN: Can we all just calm down now, okay? We're just all having nervous breakdowns over here now.

JENIFER: I'm okay. They said I was okay.

MICHAEL: You called? Good. Everything's okay.

JENIFER: I should have waited. I'm sorry.

MICHAEL: Why are you sorry? Just be happy. I don't know why we were even worried about it.

JONATHAN: Michael.

MICHAEL: You should see Shirley. She got part of her leg taken off. It was horrible.

JENIFER: Do you want to call now?

JONATHAN: No. Come on, now stop it. What is the matter with you people? You just don't do that at a moment like this.

MICHAEL: What kind of a moment would you like, Jon?

JONATHAN: A calmer one.

JENIFER: I'm sorry.

JONATHAN: One that's a little more planned.

MICHAEL: We were trying to plan a moment, actually.

JONATHAN: I don't want to get into this now, Michael. I really don't think you want to start this right now.

MICHAEL: Thanks a lot, Jenifer. *(Michael heads into the kitchen.)*

JONATHAN: We'll be lucky not to end up on Jerry Springer, the three of us.

JENIFER: You know if you called, it would feel really good to know you're okay.

MICHAEL: *(Re-entering, wiping his hands clean with a towel.)* How do you know I'd be okay?

JENIFER: It will make you feel so much better, I swear.

MICHAEL: No, it will make *you* feel so much better, that's all. You want to know I'm going to be fine, and then you can go on with your life.

JONATHAN: I resent that.

MICHAEL: Well.

JONATHAN: We wouldn't be talking about this if it weren't for you.

JENIFER: Oh, shit.

JONATHAN: The point is you weren't responsible. You should have dealt with this a long time ago.

MICHAEL: Is that the point? You have no idea what it's like to be me right now. No idea.

JONATHAN: *(Quietly.)* You could have at least said you were sorry. You could have said, you're sorry. You're a fucking asshole, you know that?
(The phone rings. Nobody answers it. The machine picks up.)

PHONE MACHINE: Hello, you have reached Michael. If you want to leave a message, please do so at the sound of the beep.

A MAN'S VOICE: Jon-o, it's Alan David. Call me. We have good news. I don't know what to tell you, kid, but congratulations. I need for you to come over tonight. I'm having a party, ironically. No big deal, but you've just become the center of the universe. You got it. You got "Mortal Fusion."
(Michael goes out the front door.)

MAN'S VOICE: Seriously, people over at the studio want to meet you. I'm so deeply proud of you, Jon. Call me.
(The machine clicks off. Jenifer exits down the hall. Jonathan is alone on stage. The lights fade.)

SCENE II

The next morning. Empty stage. Michael comes in front door with a brown paper bag. He empties the contents on the table. Jonathan comes out from the hallway carrying an overnight bag. He sets it down.

MICHAEL: Where are you going?

JONATHAN: Jesus, Michael.

MICHAEL: What?

JONATHAN: You scared me.

MICHAEL: I'm sorry.

JONATHAN: You can't just walk into a room like that and start talking. You scare people when you do that.

MICHAEL: I was already in here.

JONATHAN: Well, you should make your presence known or something.

MICHAEL: I just did.

JONATHAN: Where were you?

MICHAEL: Out.

JONATHAN: *(Calling out to her.)* He's here, Jenifer. *(Goes down the hall.)* Jenifer. *(He returns.)* She's in the shower. Where did you go? I thought you—

MICHAEL: I was out.

JONATHAN: —had an accident or something.

MICHAEL: Where are you going?

JONATHAN: Me? I'm going to the airport. I'm late. I overslept. I couldn't figure out your alarm clock.

MICHAEL: I'm sorry.

JONATHAN: Yeah, well.

(Michael heads down the hall. Gary enters from the front door.)

GARY: Good morning.

JONATHAN: Good morning. *(Beat.)* Talk to me. Please.

GARY: He needed a ride home. His car broke down. He ended up at my house.

JONATHAN: Your house?

GARY: I guess he had a really bad day. You should be nice to him.

JONATHAN: I should be…That's pretty fresh coming from you, kid.

GARY: Last night I was watching "Access Hollywood."

JONATHAN: If this is about my movie, I really don't want to hear it.

GARY: And they were talking about Elizabeth Taylor. Did you know she's had a pretty rough time of it?

JONATHAN: You're kidding me, right?

GARY: She's had her ups and downs. During the seventies she got so fat she was choking on chicken bones on Saturday Night Live. She couldn't get any good movie roles. Richard Burton dumped her. Again. She ended up marrying a Republican. That woman was snakebit. But she fought back. And I gotta say, I really appreciate what she's done. I never liked the perfume. But I really appreciate that she's always given a lot of the money to research. I'm positive. Shut up. I'll be fine. I eat good. They have drugs now. I'm on a cocktail. I don't sleep through the night, because I have to take pills every three hours, or worry whether they're going to stop working, or try and figure out how I could have gotten…I'm just saying, be nice to him. Cause even with everything, he's probably still pretty scared.

JONATHAN: What are you telling me?

GARY: Just be nice.

JONATHAN: Don't lie.

GARY: No. I don't know. I swear.

JONATHAN: Why did he go over to your house?

GARY: I don't think he knew where else to go. I think Gary got a little tense.

JONATHAN: Why didn't Gary bring him home?

GARY: He didn't want to see you. He hates you. You told me not to lie.

MICHAEL: *(Re-entering with a video tape.)* Here. I didn't tape the commercials. It's all "Dawson's Creek." She's in room 1701.

GARY: Sure. And…I'll tell her you said hi. *(To Jonathan.)* Bye. Good luck with "Mortal Fusion."

JONATHAN: Yeah. Good luck with…

(Gary leaves.)

JONATHAN: God, I could never talk to a guy who was fucking my wife. I would have to kill him.

MICHAEL: Yeah, well.

(Beat.)

JONATHAN: Look, I have to leave. I have to go to Vancouver. We start night shooting at a nuclear waste dump tomorrow.

MICHAEL: I didn't read the script. *(Michael starts to open a box of he's taken out of the brown paper bag.)*

JONATHAN: You'll be glad to know the party was awful. It was just guys we wouldn't have eaten lunch with in high school. They run studios now, so

of course I'm on the floor cackling at their jokes. They're incredibly excited about the picture, by the way. "We're giving 'em what they want. Lesbians with guns." That's what they said, "Lesbians with guns."
(Michael is ignoring him.)

JONATHAN: You know, what is your problem?

MICHAEL: Pardon?

JONATHAN: Well, I'm trying to meet you half way here, Michael. I am trying to talk to you. I was not the one who…I was so angry last night I ate an entire bundt cake. What are those?

MICHAEL: Brownies.

JONATHAN: Brownies? Who made them?

MICHAEL: Little Debbie. They're loaded with wheat, dairy, and sugar. Want one?

JONATHAN: Well. Sure, what the fuck. *(Goes over and takes one.)* They're great, right? *(Savoring a bite.)* Who knew brownies could taste like this. Why can't people just eat a brownie? I ate a bundt cake. I lived. Do you know how worried she was?

MICHAEL: My car overheated. I took a bus. I got all the way to Ventura Blvd. before I realized where I was.

JONATHAN: Where were you?

MICHAEL: The Valley. Whole Foods. Right across the street from Gary's. You don't have to be Freud.

JONATHAN: Well, you didn't have to go in.

MICHAEL: You should go on the radio. No, really. You could have a call-in help show. Simplify everything, and then hang up.

JONATHAN: What was I supposed to say? No, tell me. What would have been appropriate? You two drop these bombs on me, and then get mad because you don't like the way I blow up. I mean, come on. I'm trying to listen. How am I supposed to listen, if no one will tell me anything?

MICHAEL: I'm sorry.

JONATHAN: You're sorry. You were sleeping with my wife three months before I was married. Don't say anything. I don't want you to say anything. I forgive you. I don't know why. I must be crazy. It was ten years ago. We were children. I just think there have been too many secrets at the table. Listen, last night I finally decided to go to a shrink.

MICHAEL: *(Beat.)* Am I supposed to say something?

JONATHAN: Tell me all the complaints you'd like me to address. We need to communicate. I'm serious. I didn't know you were queer until we were twenty-six years old. That's pathetic, Michael.

MICHAEL: We were twenty-four or five.

JONATHAN: Actually you were twenty-seven. I remember because we had a big fight over Cher in "Moonstruck." I remember the Oscars.

MICHAEL: There were hints all the way back to "Silkwood." You weren't listening.

JONATHAN: Well, what do you think? People had nothing better to do than sit around and figure out your sexuality? I was your best friend. What did you think? I was going to reject you? Why do gay people think they have cornered the market on shame? Other people feel shame. I jerked off on that chair lift, but I told you that. You should have trusted me. I loved you. I love you. You should have talked to me when you were twelve years old, helped me out.

MICHAEL: I didn't know anything when I was twelve years old.

JONATHAN: What are you talking about? You were cool. You were going into Manhattan. You had friends named Clover and Lute. I was playing little league. I drank Yoo-Hoo. You were ordering lemon peels with your espresso. You knew more when you were twelve than you know now. You should have taught me stuff. Why was I fooling around with Danny Gibson when I should have been fooling around with you?

MICHAEL: *(Beat.)* You fooled around with…What?

JONATHAN: Danny Gibson.

MICHAEL: Danny Gibson? From Berndale Drive?

JONATHAN: What do you think teenagers do? I want us to be closer. I'm going to cure myself. I have to. Nobody likes me anymore. My wife won't talk to me. I think she wants to leave me. *(Beat.)* I used to be your hero. What happened? *(Beat.)* Do you remember when you found out about your mom and I hugged you? I was a better person then.

(Jonathan slowly walks over to Michael and hugs him. Michael barely responds, and eventually lets his hands hang down to his sides. Jonathan continues holding him for a moment, and then lets go.)

JONATHAN: Okay. Fine. I have to try and find these up-grade stickers.

(Jenifer comes in from the hallway.)

JENIFER: Hey. Are you alright?

MICHAEL: Yes.

JENIFER: Are you sure?

MICHAEL: Yes.

JENIFER: I have to call home. Just a second.

JONATHAN: Have you seen those up-grade coupons.

JENIFER: *(She crosses to the phone.)* You scared me, you know that. I thought you were hurt or something.

JONATHAN: Don't tell her I'm not coming home. I'll explain it to her myself. Okay? Jen?

JENIFER: *(Ignoring him. Into the phone.)* Hey, Wendy, it's me…I'm fine. How are you?…Is she okay?…Sometime around eight…I don't know exactly, the ticket's in the bedroom.

JONATHAN: I'll get it. *(Jonathan heads down the hall.)*

JENIFER: *(Into the phone.)* Really?…Oh…No, Wendy, please. I can't talk to her right now. Shit. *(To Michael.)* Where did you go?

MICHAEL: Around.

JENIFER: All night? You should have called me. Doctor Reed thinks Emma might just be lactose intolerant.

MICHAEL: *(Beat.)* Great.

JENIFER: I didn't mean to put you through this. Forget it happened. Really. If you don't want to call, don't call. I don't want to pressure you. That was never my intention. Did you call?

MICHAEL: No.

JENIFER: Okay. *(Into the phone.)* Hi, sweetheart, how are you?…In a few hours…And did you land in all the boxes…

(Jenifer continues on the phone with Emma. Jonathan re-enters with the ticket and some shampoo.)

JONATHAN: Here's the ticket.

JENIFER: *(Into the phone.)* Oh, that's so good.

(She continues on the phone. Jonathan puts the ticket on the table next to her.)

JONATHAN: *(Holds up the shampoo.)* Is this ours?

(Jenifer continues to ignore him.)

JONATHAN: *(To Michael.)* Is this your shampoo or ours?

MICHAEL: It's not mine.

JONATHAN: *(Throwing the bottle in the bag.)* Fine.

JENIFER: Michael, tell him his daughter wants to talk to him.

(Jonathan moves over to the phone.)

JONATHAN: *(Into the phone.)* Hi, Emmy…

JENIFER: Where did you sleep?

MICHAEL: I didn't.

JONATHAN: *(Hangs up.)* She hung up. She's fine, she just hung up. She got bored. *(Long pause.)*

MICHAEL: Look, I'll take you to the airport if you want.

JONATHAN: What? No, forget it. You don't have to do that. You don't even have your car. I…I called a cab. *(To Jenifer.)* You haven't seen the upgrade coupon have you?

(Jenifer ignores him. Jonathan goes into the bedroom.)

JENIFER: I wish you had told me Mariama was in the hospital.

MICHAEL: Don't you have to pack?

JENIFER: Are they going to fire you?

MICHAEL: Just forget it. Drop it.

JENIFER: They would actually fire you if you went to see her? Isn't there some review board you can—

MICHAEL: I DON'T KNOW WHY PEOPLE DON'T LISTEN TO ME! I SAID DROP IT!

JONATHAN: *(Re-entering.)* You know, it's a lot like taking your s.a.t.'s. You don't have a choice.

MICHAEL: Oh, my God.

JONATHAN: Well, that's what we're thinking about. So, can we have a little objectivity here. This is not random. You've got to be in it to win it. You were a prude. You're the most restrained person I've ever met.

MICHAEL: How do you know that?

JONATHAN: Michael, you would leave Dance-ateria at midnight. People called you grandpa.

MICHAEL: Straight people called me grandpa. You don't know where I went after Dance-ateria. For all you know I went to the piers. I walked up and down West Street till four in the morning. For all you know I had sex on the street.

JENIFER: You weren't doing that.

JONATHAN: West Street? Where is West—

MICHAEL: The river. The Anvil. The Ramrod.

JENIFER: Stop it.

MICHAEL: Don't re-test yourself. It was after. You were married.

JONATHAN: Is that what you did?

MICHAEL: Yes. I have done that. Secrets at the table.

(Beat. A horn sounds.)

JONATHAN: Shit. I have to…Look, I'm sure it's nothing to worry about.

(Jonathan stuffs some more things in his bag. Michael walks over to the window and looks out.)

MICHAEL: I thought you ordered a cab.

JONATHAN: Right. The thing is…I didn't order a cab. They sent a car. You know, a, limo. I didn't want to show off. It's no big deal. They always do this. I hate limos. They make me nauseous.

MICHAEL: I don't care.

JONATHAN: It's the way they turn or something.

MICHAEL: I don't care! God, how do you get through the day? The effort it must take to just explain yourself. It'll be so much easier when you have a press agent.

JONATHAN: Fine. Goodbye. I was just trying to help.

MICHAEL: Yeah, well some people can't be helped, Jon. Open your eyes. Some people *do not have hope.* That's the truth. And it doesn't get better. It gets better for you, because you're healthy, and all you have to do all day is obsess over your stupid meaningless life. And you plot, and you conquer, and you get your six digits, your trailer, and a fucking perdiem. You end up with exactly what you want. But some people grow up with crack whores for mothers. Doesn't that mean anything to you? Some people end up in hospitals, alone, with tubes running through her veins!

JONATHAN: And whose fault is that? Once you let a child live in your house, you don't send them packing because a bureaucrat gets mad, or your boy friend wants to leave you. You fight. You fix it. You imagine a solution besides martyrdom. You know, you paint yourself into this corner, and you just stand there feeling morally superior. It's all the same to you. My limousine, the health care system, Mariama. It's all ammunition. Evidence of everybody's infamy. You hate when things get better, because you have no one left to blame. What happened to you? You're lost. Do something! Get a map! You don't have to be a victim to prove the world sucks. *(Beat.)* You know, if I could learn to be a little more like you, and you could be a little more like me. Who ever did that first, that's who would win.

(The sound of a car horn again. He struggles to close his bag.)

JONATHAN: GOD DAMN IT, SON OF A BITCH, MOTHER FUCKER!

(Giving up, Jonathan sinks to the ground and starts to cry.)

JENIFER: *(After a long while.)* Honey. Take your sneakers off and wear your boots. You can't pack your boots.

JONATHAN: Okay. *(Changing his shoes.)* On my desk, on the left side is a note book. They are some notes for this part. When you get home, I need for you to fed-ex them to the hotel. Is that okay?

JENIFER: Okay.

JONATHAN: I was supposed to take Emma to the circus Friday, but you have to take about ten other kids.

JENIFER: I know.

(*He stands up.*)

JENIFER: Your shirt's buttoned wrong.

(*She moves over and buttons his shirt properly. He kisses her on the forehead.*)

JONATHAN: Michael. (*Beat.*) I'll call you. (*Jonathan goes out the door.*)

JENIFER: Do you want me to stay for awhile? Michael. Do you need me to stay?

(*Silence. Michael crosses to the phone. He takes out a piece of paper from his pocket, and dials.*)

MICHAEL: (*Picking up a paper.*) I found your up-grade coupon. (*Into the phone.*) Yes, I'm calling about a test result…Thank you… (*Beat.*) Yes, I'm calling about a test…L7999 (*Beat.*) Yes…Yes, thank you. (*Beat. To Jenifer.*) Do you remember the piano player at the reception?

JENIFER: At my wedding?

MICHAEL: After a particularly horrible rendition of "Evergreen"—

JENIFER: My mother insisted.

MICHAEL: Our eyes met. He looked at me with this yearning sort of terror. I imagined all the weddings he must have sat through. All those toasts. Poems. Declarations of love. And I knew he was all alone in the world. Not getting any younger as they say. I mean he was probably sixty. I went home with him thinking, this is exactly what I deserve. (*Beat.*) Did you strip your sheets?

JENIFER: Did I…Yeah.

MICHAEL: (*Standing up.*) I'm going to the hospital.

JENIFER: Why?

MICHAEL: Can I take the car?

JENIFER: Why?

MICHAEL: (*Into the phone.*) Yes…Okay. Thank you. (*Michael hangs up. He goes over to the table and picks up the car keys.*)

JENIFER: Michael? What…?

MICHAEL: I'm going to get Mariama.

(*The lights fade.*)

END OF PLAY

KILLER JOE
by Tracy Letts

Killer Joe is dedicated to the memory and spirit
of Holly Wantuch, my partner, my conscience, my love.

How often have I lain beneath rain on a strange roof,
thinking of home?

Darl

from *As I Lay Dying* by William Faulkner

Killer Joe was produced by the Next Lab in Evanston, Illinois, on August 3, 1993. It was directed by Wilson Milam; the set and lighting designs were by Robert G. Smith; the costume design was by Laura Cunningham; the sound design was by Chris Peterson; the fight choreographer was Chuck Coyle; and the stage manager was Justin Holmes. The cast was as follows:

Chris Smith . . . . Michael Shannon
Sharla Smith . . . . Holly Wantuch
Ansel Smith . . . . Marc A. Nelson
Dottie Smith . . . . Shawna Franks
Killer Joe Cooper . . . . Paul Dillon

Killer Joe was produced in New York by Darren Lee Cole and Scott Morgee on October 18, 1998. It was directed by wilson Milam; the set design was by George Xenos; the lighting deisng was by Greg MacPherson; the costume design was by Jana Stauffer; the sound design was by Hired Gun/One Dream; the fight choreographer was J. David Brimmer; and the stage manager was Richard Hodge. The cast was as follows:

Chris Smith . . . . Michael Shannon
Sharla Smith . . . . Amanda Plummer
Ansel Smith . . . . Marc A. Nelson
Dottie Smith . . . . Sarah Paulson
Killer Joe Cooper . . . . Scott Glenn

DEBTS

Acting: Fairuza Balk, Scott Glenn, Jan Leslie Harding, Sarah Paulson(!), Lori Petty, Amanda Plummer, Seth Ullian, Michelle Williams

Agenting: Danielle Ausrotas, Jason Fogelson

Artistic Directing: Ian Brown, Dexter Bullard, Dominic Dromgoole, Harriet Spizziri

Believing, with money: Gary and Teddi Cole, Kelly Curtis, Steve Martin

Casting: Kris Nicolau

Criticizing: Richard Christiansen

Designing: Tim Fletcher, Luke Grimm, One Dream, Chris Peterson, Bob Smith, Jana Stauffer, George Xenos

Potato Peeler Designing: Tim Reinhart

Familiarizing: M & P, S & S, D & D, G & G, G & G

Fighting: David Brimmer, Chuck Coyle
Producing: Michael Codron, Darren Lee Cole, Laura Cunningham, Scott Morfee
Publicizing: Shirley Herz
Stage Managing: Siofra Campbell, Richard Hodge, Justin Holmes, Adrian Pagan
Understudying: Christine Ashe, Allen Burroughs, Mim Drew, Mary Hammett

BIGGER DEBTS

Paul Dillon, Shawna Franks, Marc Nelson, Mike Shannon, Holly Wantuch, Eric Winzenried, and especially Wilson Milam: the six actors and director who helped create this play
Without their work, talent, faith, and love, *Killer Joe* would not exist.

THE AUTHOR

Tracy Letts was born and raised in Oklahoma. *Killer Joe,* his first play, premiered in 1993 at the Next Lab Theatre in Chicago. That production, under the auspices of Hired Gun Theatre, traveled to the Traverse Theatre in Edinburgh, Scotland, and subsequently transferred to the Bush Theatre in London and the Vaudeville Theatre in the West End. *Killer Joe* has since been performed in ten countries in over a dozen languages. His second play, *Bug,* premiered at the Gate Theatre in London in 1996. Mr. Letts is an actor who currently resides in Los Angeles.

PRODUCTION NOTES

No pre-show music. Only static from the T.V.

No "incidental" or "atmosphere" music within the scenes.

All music and sound should be sourced, with the exception of intermission, curtain call, and the scene changes (see below).

Blackouts between the scenes should be covered by the sound of the following scene. For example, Act II, Scene I ends; blackout, sound of evangelist on house speakers; once scene change is completed, lights rise on Scene II, and evangelist cross-fades from house speakers to on-stage radio.

Scene changes should be as quick and quiet as possible.

Lighting should appear to be sourced.

The final dinner is wholly improvised, and may take as long as two or three minutes.

As written, the final fight is a map of the dynamics of the scene.

Directors and fight choreographers worth their salt will change it as necessary to meet their staging needs.

A NOTE TO THE PLAYERS

The published edition of *Killer Joe* contains many stage directions designed to help a reader visualize this material. Although you will inevitably incorporate many of these stage directions into your production, you are encouraged to start from scratch, inhabit the characters, and make the play your own.

Ellipses (…) indicate an incomplete thought, or a trailing off.

Dashes (—) indicate an interruption and overlapping.

CHARACTERS

CHRIS SMITH: twenty-two years old

SHARLA SMITH: Chris's stepmother, early thirties

ANSEL SMITH: Chris's father, thirty-eight years old

DOTTIE SMITH: Chris's sister, twenty years old

KILLER JOE COOPER: mid-thirties

PLACE

A trailer home on the outskirts of Dallas, Texas.

Two entrances: a door leading outside, and a hallway leading to the bathroom and two bedrooms.

The living room occupies two-thirds of the set; the kitchen occupies one-third. There is no separation between the rooms, unless it is a small counter extending from the wall. The playing area should be quite small and cramped. A low ceiling is helpful.

The furnishings and decorations in the trailer are seedy and cheap: walls covered with ugly wood paneling; tattered, smoke-stained plastic shades covering the windows; kitchen filled with dirty, mismatched cups and utensils, many of them fast-food giveaways; a hide-a-bed, stained, torn, burned with cigarettes; a coffee table covered with fast-food debris, empty beer cans, and filled ashtrays; grimy refrigerator, filled almost solely with beer; a monstrous television, topped by a snarled and intricate antenna made of coat hangers and tin foil; Taco Bell refrigerator magnets, Dallas Cowboy cheerleader calendar, ZZ Top poster, and other detritus of the poor.

ACT I
SCENE I

Lights slowly rise: faint glow of the streetlights bleeds through the window shades…flickering ghost light spills from the t.v., tuned to snow. Lightning. Thunder. T-Bone, a neighbor's pit bull with a bad attitude and a chain a few links too long, snorts and barks ferociously outside. Footsteps. Doorknob. Tap on the door.

CHRIS: Dottie? *(Beat.)* Dottie?

(The tap grows louder. T-Bone keeps barking.)

CHRIS: Dottie, wake up. It's me.

(The tap grows even louder. Chris raises his voice slightly, but he tries to be quiet.)

CHRIS: Come on, Dottie, it's me, goddamn it. Let me in. I'm cold. I gotta piss. Let me in.

(Pause. The voice impatient, almost yelling. The knock gets louder.)

CHRIS: Shut up, T-Bone! Dottie, goddamn it, wake up! Don't make me wake up the whole goddamn neighborhood! I'm about to piss in my pants!

(Pause. The voice bellows and the pounding on the door threatens to tear down the entire wall.)

CHRIS: GODDAMN IT, OPEN THIS GODDAMN DOOR BEFORE I BURN THIS WHOLE GODDAMN TRAILER PARK TO THE GROUND! GET OUTTA THAT FUCKIN' BED, RIGHT! FUCKIN'! NOW!

(During the above, Sharla appears from the hallway and scampers to the door. She wears only a man's sweat-stained tee-shirt that falls above her ass.)

SHARLA: Hold on, hold on—

(She unlocks the door and Chris bursts in.)

CHRIS: Goddamn it—! *(Sees Sharla, heads down the hallway.)* Put some clothes on, for Christ's sake.

SHARLA: Well, hell, I didn't know who you were.

(But he's gone. We hear Chris's urine splash in the toilet bowl.)

SHARLA: Close the goddamn door!

(He doesn't. She gets a soda from the fridge, stocked only with a few Cokes, a dribble of milk, and a lot of beer. She finds a cigarette, lights it. Chris returns.)

CHRIS: Why don't you put somethin' on? My God—

SHARLA: I didn't know who you were—
CHRIS: You answer the door like that if you don't know—
SHARLA: Just relax, it's nothin' you haven't seen before, I'm sure—
CHRIS: Nothin' half of Dallas County hasn't seen before, Sharla—
SHARLA: —shut up—
CHRIS: —but that ain't the point. It's freezin' in here—
SHARLA: What do you want?
CHRIS: Is Dad here?
SHARLA: He's asleep.
CHRIS: Dottie's here, isn't she?
SHARLA: Everybody's asleep, it's almost three o'clock in the—
CHRIS: I can tell time, all right?
SHARLA: Adele throw you out?
CHRIS: Yes, goddamn it. I need to talk to Dad—
SHARLA: Why'd she throw you out? Did you—?
CHRIS: —that bitch—
SHARLA: —hit her again?
CHRIS: No, I didn't—look, will you please put some clothes on?
SHARLA: My God, I never heard so much—
CHRIS: I'm sorry, it's just a bit distractin' tryin' to talk to your stepmother with
    her bush starin' you right in the face—
    (Ansel, wearing just his underwear, turns on the lights as he enters from the
    hallway.)
SHARLA: All right! Jesus—
CHRIS: Thank you.
    (Sharla whacks Ansel as she exits. Chris has grabbed a beer from the fridge
    and pulled the pot stash from under the couch. He rolls a joint.)
ANSEL: Help yourself.
CHRIS: What'd you do, chop up some clover? Where'd you get this shit?
ANSEL: I bought it from you.
CHRIS: This is that?
ANSEL: What are you doin' here?
SHARLA: (Offstage.) Adele threw him out!
ANSEL: So?! The boy can talk!
CHRIS: So I needed a place to stay, all right?
ANSEL: How come she threw you out?
CHRIS: It's a long story.
ANSEL: Sharla, get me a beer!

(During the following, Ansel crosses to the t.v., flips channels, finds a monster truck rally.)

ANSEL: You didn't hit her again, did you—?

CHRIS: No, goddamn it, I didn't hit her—

(Sharla returns, wearing a pair of Ansel's underwear.)

SHARLA: It's not like you never hit her before—

CHRIS: I didn't hit her, okay?

SHARLA: So why'd she throw you out?

CHRIS: None of your goddamn business, Sharla—

SHARLA: ANSEL:

  Hey, I live here—!   Calm down—

CHRIS: Well, Jesus Christ, Dad, I get thrown out in the middle of the night, and I come over here and have to listen to your naked wife givin' me the third degree—

SHARLA: I'm not naked—

CHRIS: Why do you let her walk around here like that?

SHARLA: ANSEL:

  Like what?   It's the middle of the—

CHRIS: She answered the door with her beaver puckered out like it was tryin' to shake my hand—

SHARLA: Hush your mouth—

ANSEL: She didn't know who you were—

CHRIS: That's not the point, goddamn it! I don't want Dottie havin' to look at her own stepmother's pussy!

SHARLA: That's it! I'm goin' to bed! I've heard all—!

CHRIS: Good night.

SHARLA: *(Going for Chris.)* You listen to me—!

CHRIS: Good night. Sweet dreams.

SHARLA: ANSEL:

  Ansel—!   Hey, now—

CHRIS: Don't let the bedbugs bite.

ANSEL: *(Between Chris and Sharla.)* Stop it, Chris—!

SHARLA: He can stay here tonight—!

ANSEL: CHRIS:

  Sharla, honey, now don't   Hey, I'll stay as long as
  get like that—!   I by God feel like!

SHARLA: —but if he stays any longer, I'm liable to hurt the little bastard!

ANSEL: Sharla, don't go to bed all mad—

SHARLA: Good night! *(She exits.)*

CHRIS: *(Calling to her.)* Don't die in your sleep!

SHARLA: *(Offstage.)* GODDAMN HICK!

> *(Chris lights the joint, takes a long drag, passes it to Ansel. They smoke the joint throughout the scene.)*

ANSEL: Now look what you did. I'm in the doghouse.

CHRIS: Fuck her.

ANSEL: Yeah, well, you don't live here—

CHRIS: I need to talk to you about somethin'.

ANSEL: I don't have any money for you—

CHRIS: I don't need a lot, but I'm in some trouble—

ANSEL: You're not listenin' to me, Chris—

CHRIS: —and if I can just get a little something to get me back on my feet—

ANSEL: No, goddamn it, you're not suckin' any more money outta me—

CHRIS: It's important, Dad—

ANSEL: It always is.

CHRIS: It's a matter of life and death, really.

ANSEL: It always is.

CHRIS: I need six thousand dollars, or some guys are gonna kill me.

ANSEL: Boy, you better get outta town, and quick.

CHRIS: If you could just give me a thousand—

ANSEL: —I don't have it—

CHRIS: I could hold these guys off with a thousand—

ANSEL: Chris. I don't have it.

CHRIS: I wouldn't be in this mess if it weren't for Mom, y'know—

ANSEL: Oh, I doubt that.

CHRIS: I'm in a jam cause of her, then she kicks me out.

ANSEL: Well, what'd you do to her? She wouldn'ta kicked you out for no reason—

CHRIS: She's a fuckin' bitch, Dad—

ANSEL: You hit her, didn't you?

CHRIS: Goddamn it, NO! I didn't hit her, I told you—

ANSEL: Then why'd she throw you out?

CHRIS: I threw her up against the fridge.

ANSEL: That's pretty much the same as hittin' her, wouldn't you say?

CHRIS: No, it's not. I barely threw her. There's not a mark on her.

ANSEL: But she threw you out anyway—?

CHRIS: You wanna know why I threw her?

ANSEL: No.

CHRIS: She stole two and a half ounces of coke from me.

ANSEL: Now that's bullshit. Your mother doesn't snort cocaine.

CHRIS: I know that, goddamn it, she sold it. Or gave it away to that goddamn Rex. Cause the shit was gone, and she's the only other one who knew where it was. Then tonight, after I find it missin', she comes back to the house with her Pinto runnin' like a watch.

ANSEL: You're shittin' me. That piece of shit hasn't run in years—

CHRIS: Y'see? What'd I tell you? So the blow I was plannin' on sellin' to pay these guys back is gone, and now they're gonna kill me. My own mother, for Chrissake. *(Beat.)* So?

ANSEL: Hm? What?

CHRIS: The money. Are you gonna loan me the money?

ANSEL: No.

CHRIS: That's great. That's just great. You're a regular what's-his-name. I'm fucked—

ANSEL: I never had a thousand dollars in my life—

CHRIS: How would you like to?

ANSEL: What?

CHRIS: Would you like to have fifteen thousand dollars?

ANSEL: Aw, Jesus, another one of your stupid—

CHRIS: Now just hear me out, I got another plan here—

ANSEL: Every goddamn time. How about that farm—?

CHRIS: Hey, now just leave the farm out of it, all right? I'm talkin' about somethin' a lot easier than that.

ANSEL: This oughtta be good—

CHRIS: You ever hear of Killer Joe Cooper?

ANSEL: Huh-uh.

CHRIS: He's a cop.

ANSEL: Yeah?

CHRIS: Well, a detective, actually.

ANSEL: Yeah?

CHRIS: And he's got a little business on the side.

ANSEL: What's he do?

CHRIS: He's a killer. He kills people.

ANSEL: Yeah? So?

CHRIS: Mom's got a fifty-thousand dollar life insurance policy.
    (Beat.)

ANSEL: What are you sayin'?

CHRIS: You know what I'm sayin'. Don't look at me like that.

ANSEL: Who's the…?

CHRIS: Beneficiary. Dottie.

ANSEL: The whole thing?

CHRIS: The whole thing.

ANSEL: All fifty-thousand.

CHRIS: Yep.

ANSEL: She didn't leave nothin' to me?

CHRIS: Of course not, you dipshit. Why would she do that?

ANSEL: I'm her ex-husband.

CHRIS: She hates you, Dad. You know that.

ANSEL: Yeah, but still—

CHRIS: What do you think?

ANSEL: About what?

CHRIS: My idea.

ANSEL: How much does a thing like that cost?

CHRIS: I hear he charges twenty-thousand.

ANSEL: Jesus Christ—

CHRIS: This really isn't somethin' we can afford to cut corners on. I'd say it's worth it if we know we're not gonna get caught. Killer Joe's a professional, and he'll do this right.

ANSEL: How do you know? Who told you about this?

CHRIS: Never mind that.

ANSEL: Where are we supposed to get that kind of money?

CHRIS: I wanna hire him on spec. Ask him to do it for free, then give him a cut of the insurance money.

ANSEL: Look, after you pay this guy, you're only talkin' about clearin'…

<table>
<tr><td>ANSEL:</td><td>CHRIS:</td></tr>
<tr><td>…thirty thousand.</td><td>…thirty thousand.</td></tr>
<tr><td>Split that four ways—</td><td></td></tr>
</table>

CHRIS: Three ways.

ANSEL: How do you figure?

CHRIS: You, me, and Dottie.

ANSEL: What about Sharla?

CHRIS: What about her?

ANSEL: She gets a cut.

CHRIS: The hell she does. She's not family.

ANSEL: She's been my wife longer than Adele has.

CHRIS: It's less money.

ANSEL: It's less money for you.

CHRIS: And it's more money for you.

ANSEL: Yeah? I am the father here, y'know. We're talkin' about my ex-wife. I'm the one who found her. Not you, and not Dottie.

CHRIS: Okay, all right, fine, we can split it four ways—

ANSEL: Hold on just a second here. I haven't agreed to nothin' yet. This is murder we're talkin' about, and I'm not just gonna sit here, noddin' my head—

CHRIS: Look at it this way. Is she doin' anybody any good?

ANSEL: Whattaya mean?

CHRIS: Is anybody gonna really care if Mom's not around anymore?

ANSEL: Rex.

CHRIS: You think that dumb son-of-a-bitch would care? He screws anything that can draw breath—

ANSEL: That don't mean he don't care—

CHRIS: Tell you the truth, I think he'd be tickled pink. You should see how she treats that poor bastard.

ANSEL: 'Bout like she treated me, I bet.

CHRIS: Anyway, who gives a fuck about Rex?

ANSEL: Right—

CHRIS: Who else?

ANSEL: Dottie, maybe.

CHRIS: Right, Dottie. Now think of it this way: which do you think would be better for Dottie, havin' ten thousand dollars so maybe she could go to that Amazon school, or havin' a beat-up, old, ugly, naggy alcoholic mother for another twenty years or so?

ANSEL: I see what you're sayin'—

CHRIS: Exactly. So as long as Dottie never knows what we're talkin' about… we're really doin' her a favor.

ANSEL: Yeah…

CHRIS: Let me just call him. Let's just set up a meetin' with the guy, and talk to him. We don't have to decide anything right now.

ANSEL: Okay.

CHRIS: Okay. Okay. Okay, good. Okay, now this's just between you and me, now.

ANSEL: I know.

CHRIS: Cause if Sharla or Dottie find out—

ANSEL: —right—

CHRIS: —they'll be considered accomplices—

(Dottie enters, wearing a nightgown and robe.)

DOTTIE: Hey, Chris. What're you doin' here?

CHRIS: I got in a fight with Mom.

DOTTIE: Did you build this city all by yourself?

CHRIS: What? Uh, yeah. Sure did. Brick by brick.

DOTTIE: I heard that at the wedding.

ANSEL: *(To Chris.)* She's asleep.

DOTTIE: I'm not asleep, I'm just workin'. *(She exits.)*

CHRIS: You think she heard us?

    (Ansel shrugs.)

CHRIS: Scared the shit outta me. That sleep talkin' gives me the creeps.

ANSEL: She's gotten worse and worse about it. 'Bout every night now.

CHRIS: I don't suppose she's seein' anybody yet.

ANSEL: No, and I wouldn't hold your breath, neither.

CHRIS: I don't understand it.

ANSEL: You wanna know the truth, I think she's still…you know…

CHRIS: What. A virgin?

    (She reenters, gets a comic book.)

DOTTIE: I heard y'all talkin' about killin' Momma. *(Beat.)* I think it's a good idea. *(She exits.)*

    (Beat.)

CHRIS: There you go.

ANSEL: Yeah…

CHRIS: …so…

    (Long silence.)

ANSEL: She got that piece of shit Pinto runnin' again, huh?

    (Blackout. Sound of the karate movie from the next scene plays over the blackout.)

SCENE II

Lights rise. Two days later: the shades are up and daylight streams through the windows. Rain falls outside…an occasional distant rumble of thunder. Dottie is alone, "exercising" in the living room, matching moves with an action sequence from a poorly dubbed karate movie on t.v. The volume is earsplitting. The door to the trailer opens and Killer Joe Cooper enters, wearing a raincoat and cowboy hat. Dottie does not hear him. He shuts the door, stands motionless, watches her.

JOE: Looks hard.

> (*She sucks in her breath, runs into the kitchen. They shout to be heard over the television.*)

DOTTIE: Jesus—!

JOE: I didn't mean—!

DOTTIE: Who are you?!

JOE: Joe Cooper, I'm a friend of—! Joe Cooper—! Excuse me! *(Turns off t.v.)* Joe Cooper, I'm a friend of—

DOTTIE: How'd you get in here?

JOE: The door. I knocked, but you had the t.v. turned up too loud to hear me. I decided not to stand in the rain.

DOTTIE: Well, you scared me to death—

JOE: And I apologize.

DOTTIE: That's okay. It's okay.

JOE: Looks hard. From the t.v. like that. You should get a teacher.

DOTTIE: Yeah…

JOE: *(Extends his hand.)* I'm Joe Cooper.

DOTTIE: *(Shakes his hand.)* Hi.

JOE: I was supposed to meet Chris here at ten-thirty.

DOTTIE: He's not here.

JOE: I'm a little early.

DOTTIE: He's usually late.

JOE: *(Beat.)* Could I trouble you for a cup of coffee, or—?

DOTTIE: Oh, yeah, sure. I'm sorry. Why'n'tcha sit down? Can I take your—?

> (*Joe removes his raincoat and hands it to Dottie, who drapes it over the back of a chair. She prepares a pot of coffee.*)

JOE: Can I ask your name?

DOTTIE: I'm Dottie.

JOE: Hello, Dottie.

DOTTIE: Hi.

> (*He stands, stares at her. She feels his eyes on her, wheels, faces him.*)

DOTTIE: What.

JOE: Hm?

DOTTIE: Why are you—what?

JOE: Nothin'. I'm just…standin'.

DOTTIE: Okay. *(Beat.)* What are you? I mean, what do you do?

JOE: I'm a detective.

DOTTIE: Really? Like Mannix?

JOE: Uh…no. He's a private detective. I'm in the Dallas Police Department.

DOTTIE: He's not real, either.

JOE: No. I'm real.

DOTTIE: I read it's nothin' like the shows, with car chases and all.

JOE: Lot of paperwork.

DOTTIE: I read some policemen go their whole lives without shooting their guns.

JOE: Probably true.

DOTTIE: Have you ever drawn your gun?

JOE: Oh, sure.

DOTTIE: What happened?

JOE: I've drawn my gun lots of times.

DOTTIE: You ever shot anybody?

JOE: Yes.

DOTTIE: Who?

JOE: Nobody you'd know.

DOTTIE: Did they die?

JOE: They have, yes.

DOTTIE: Wow. I bet you don't like to talk about it.

JOE: No, no. Not that I like to talk about it, but it doesn't keep me up nights. You know.

DOTTIE: Yeah. *(Beat.)* What's the most exciting thing that ever happened?

JOE: Hm. The most exciting. I don't know. I don't know.

DOTTIE: *(Beat.)* I bet it's more exciting than anything I ever—

JOE: Oh, wait, I can tell you the funniest thing—

DOTTIE: —okay—

JOE: —well, maybe not the funniest, but the…oddest.

DOTTIE: Okay—

JOE: When I was a patrolman—do you want to hear this?

DOTTIE: Yeah, sure—

JOE: When I was a patrolman, my partner and I got a call there was a domestic disturbance in progress. Which is kind of misleading, if you ask me, because "domestic" sounds awful homey, and "disturbance" sounds like just an argument. But cops know that domestic disturbances are the calls where you're most likely to get hurt.

DOTTIE: Uh-huh.

JOE: So we took the call, and I was a little nervous. (I hadn't been on the force long, and I still got nervous about domestic disturbances.) When we got to the house, we heard this awful screaming from inside, this shrieking.

DOTTIE: Wow.

JOE: We went into the place, and it was completely dark, and we just followed
    the sound of this scream back to the back bedroom. I didn't know what
    the hell to expect—

DOTTIE: —yeah—

JOE: —and we open the door, and suddenly, this huge guy is on top of me,
    knocks me to the floor, just screaming and clawing at me—

DOTTIE: Oh my God—

JOE: And then it turns out…there's no one else even there. And he wasn't try-
    ing to hurt me…he wanted me to help him.

DOTTIE: Why?

JOE: He was in terrible pain. It turns out…he had gotten into a fight with his
    girlfriend. She had been having an affair…so, in order to "teach her a les-
    son," (That's what he said, "teach her a lesson.") he had doused his gen-
    itals with lighter fluid, and set them on fire.
    (Dottie stares at Joe. He laughs. She joins in the laughter.)

DOTTIE: Oh, I get it. I thought you were serious.

JOE: I am.
    (She stops laughing. He continues.)

JOE: That poor, miserable bastard set his genitals on fire to teach his girlfriend
    a lesson. Do you believe that? Guess he showed her. I wonder if she ever
    got over it.

DOTTIE: Was he all right?

JOE: No. No, he wasn't all right. He set his genitals on fire. *(Beat.)* Oh, boy.

DOTTIE: I had an aunt who set herself on fire—

JOE: Yeah, okay—

DOTTIE: —but not on purpose. She was wearin' a long lace dress and she got
    it caught in the furnace and she died before they put out the fire.

JOE: Really.
    (She pours his coffee.)

DOTTIE: They say she's the one in the family I look most like.

JOE: Hm.

DOTTIE: Her name was Viva. Isn't that a great name? She never got married,
    I don't think. *(She hands him his coffee.)* Are you gonna kill my momma?

JOE: I'm not sure. Why?

DOTTIE: Just curious. *(Beat.)* My momma tried to kill me when I was real lit-
    tle. She put a pillow over my face and tried to stop me from breathing,
    cause she cared more about herself than her little baby, and she didn't
    love me like a mother loves a little baby. And she thought she'd done it,
    and she was happy, cause then she didn't have to worry about me eating

her food, and sleeping in her bed, and growing up to be the part of her that was cut out and grown into a better thing than she had been, had ever been. Cause that would mean the best part of her was me. But she hadn't done it, she didn't give me back to Him, she only made me sick, made me not be for a while, but then I was and she was sad that I was, and that I always would be.

> *(T-Bone barks as Chris and Ansel approach from outside.)*

<table>
<tr><td>JOE:</td><td>CHRIS: (Offstage.)</td></tr>
<tr><td>(Studies her for a moment, then.)</td><td>(Laughing.) You charged him how much?</td></tr>
<tr><td>How do you know that?</td><td></td></tr>
<tr><td>DOTTIE:</td><td>ANSEL: (Offstage.)</td></tr>
<tr><td>Know what?</td><td>Fifty bucks.</td></tr>
<tr><td>JOE:</td><td>CHRIS: (Offstage.)</td></tr>
<tr><td>That your mother tried to kill you.</td><td>For a lousy spark plug!</td></tr>
<tr><td>DOTTIE:</td><td>ANSEL: (Offstage.)</td></tr>
<tr><td>Cause I remember.</td><td>Hell, he didn't know the difference, dumbass Yankee.</td></tr>
</table>

(Chris enters, soaking wet. Ansel, dressed in grease-stained auto mechanic's overalls, is behind Chris on the stairs, so he does not see Joe standing in the kitchen.)

ANSEL: About sucked my dick for havin' the right-sized wrench. *(Ansel now sees Joe and freezes behind Chris.)*

JOE: Hello.

CHRIS: Oh, Jesus, you must be Joe.

> *(Chris goes to him and they shake hands.)*

CHRIS: Chris Smith. This is my father, Ansel.

JOE: *(Shaking hands with Ansel.)* Ansel.

ANSEL: Hey there.

CHRIS: I guess you met Dottie.

JOE: Oh, yes.

CHRIS: Dottie, would you excuse us?

DOTTIE: Yeah, sure.

CHRIS: I mean, could you leave the house? We've got some business to discuss with Mr.—

DOTTIE: I know. *(To Joe.)* Good-bye.

JOE: Good-bye, Dottie.

(She grabs her coat and Joe opens the door for her. She exits, giving Joe a final look.)

CHRIS: *(In the fridge, getting beers.)* She's a sweetheart, isn't she?

JOE: Yes, she is.

CHRIS: Like a beer?

JOE: No…no, listen, I don't have a lot of time—

CHRIS: All right, sir, let's get down to it.

JOE: If that's all right—

CHRIS: First off, let me say that me and my father here have never done anything like this before, and…well, to be honest, we don't want to do it, but it's gotta be done.

JOE: That has nothing to do with me.

CHRIS: Okay. Uhh…well, sir, instead of me starting this off, maybe you could sort of tell us the questions we need to ask, or—

JOE: It's really pretty simple. You're going to pay me some money for a service I'm going to perform.

CHRIS: Uh-huh.

JOE: You'll give me particulars about her whereabouts, her schedule, her habits, and I'll act on them accordingly. I won't give you many details about my activities, because the less you know about them, the better for everyone concerned.

CHRIS: All right—

JOE: I only have a couple of rules that I insist on sticking to. Insist.

CHRIS: Okay, yeah—

JOE: If you are caught, if you are implicated in this crime, you are not, under any circumstance, to reveal my identity or my participation.

CHRIS: Oh, of course—

JOE: If you break this rule, you'll be killed. Do you understand?

CHRIS: I—

JOE: I don't mean to sound melodramatic, and I don't want our business relationship to get off on the wrong foot. But I want to be absolutely clear on this point.

CHRIS: I understand.

JOE: *(To Ansel.)* Do you understand?

ANSEL: Yeah.

JOE: My payment is twenty-five thousand dollars, in cash, in advance. No exceptions.

ANSEL: Twenty-five?

JOE: Yes, sir.

ANSEL: *(To Chris.)* You told me twenty.

CHRIS: *(To Ansel.)* I was told twenty.

JOE: Twenty-five. Is that a problem?

CHRIS: We don't have a problem with twenty-five—

ANSEL: Now hold on a second here—

CHRIS: We don't have a problem with twenty-five. That's not our problem.

JOE: What is your problem?

CHRIS: We have a problem with the advance.

JOE: No exceptions.

CHRIS: Sir, I'd just like…let me explain. One of the reasons we're interested in having this done is that my mother holds a very large insurance policy—

JOE: *(Standing to leave.)* They usually do.

CHRIS: —and we thought we could interest you in the job if we guaranteed payment after the policy had been covered.

JOE: This really isn't open to discussion. Our conversation is finished.

   (Joe gets his coat, moves for the door. Chris reaches for him.)

CHRIS: Please, this is important—

   (Joe turns and fires.)

JOE: What did you think this was? "Let's Make a Deal"? This is serious business you're fuckin' with here, boy—

CHRIS: I'm aware of that—

JOE: I don't think you are. I don't take you seriously.

CHRIS: This is gonna get done, one way or another—

JOE: Our conversation…is finished. I never met you. You never met me.

   (Chris gives up, goes to the kitchen.)

JOE: *(To Ansel.)* Thank Dottie for the coffee. *(Joe turns to the door, his back to the room. Long pause. He slowly turns around to face Chris and Ansel.)*

JOE: Of course, we never discussed the possibility of a retainer.

CHRIS: Whattaya mean?

JOE: You know how to reach me. Call me if she's interested. *(Again, he starts for the door.)*

CHRIS: Hey, man, are you talkin' about my sister?

JOE: Is that who she is? *(Joe exits.)*

   (During the following, Ansel checks Joe from the window, lights a joint, turns on the t.v., finds some auto racing.)

CHRIS: Jesus—

ANSEL: What's he mean, "retainer?"

CHRIS: Whattaya think he means, Dad? He means Dottie.

ANSEL: Yeah, but retain what, exactly?

CHRIS: Just how stupid are you? Are you really that stupid?

(Ansel grabs a plastic troll, hurls it at Chris's head. Chris dodges, and the troll smashes into the wall.)

ANSEL: You watch your goddamn mouth!

CHRIS: What are we gonna do, Dad? We gotta think of somethin'.

ANSEL: We could do it ourselves.

CHRIS: You gonna kill somebody? You can't even tell time.

ANSEL: What do you think we should do, smart ass?

CHRIS: We can forget about the whole thing, or we can…give him Dottie.

ANSEL: GODDAMN IT! *(Ansel jumps off the couch, fusses with the t.v. antenna until his reception improves. Then.)* Y'know, it might just do her some good.

(Blackout. Sound of the lottery drawing from the next scene plays over the scene change.)

SCENE III

Lights rise. Sharla talks on the telephone, smiling, examining a sheaf of photographs. She wears the red-and-white checkered uniform of a Pizza Hut waitress. The Texas Lottery drawing plays on t.v.

SHARLA: Don't be silly. Nobody's gonna see 'em. *(Beat.)* What're you so worried about, anyway? It's not like you can see your face in any of 'em. *(Laughs.)* I doubt it. *(Beat.)* That little photo shack out in front of the mall. *(Beat.)* Oh, hell, you worry too much. Just some little pimply-faced girl, never saw one before in her life. *(Beat.)* None that big, anyway. *(Nasty laugh.)* What time are you gonna pick me up? *(Beat.)* eleven-thirty? What do you expect me to—?

(Dottie comes out of her bedroom, wearing a pair of blue jeans and a sweatshirt, crosses to the t.v., changes channels, finds Wheel of Fortune. Sharla casually puts the photographs in a rainbow-colored packet.)

SHARLA: Hold on, Jennie.

(Sharla covers the phone and speaks to Dottie, who is now setting the table for supper.)

SHARLA: Why don't you put on your new dress, hon?

DOTTIE: What for?

SHARLA: We're havin' a guest for supper.

DOTTIE: Who?

SHARLA: I don't know. Some friend of Ansel's. *(Back to phone.)* Huh? No, it's Dottie—

DOTTIE: We have to dress up?

SHARLA: I just think you look real pretty in your dress.

DOTTIE: I'd rather save it for somethin' special. I'd feel silly just wearin' it for supper.

(Sharla pauses, then returns to the phone.)

SHARLA: Jennie? I'll call you from work, all right? No, I can't—no, I have to— uh-huh, you me, too. *(Sharla hangs up, sticks her finger into a hole in Dottie's sweatshirt.)*

SHARLA: Look at that:

DOTTIE: What? It's a sweatshirt.

SHARLA: Why don't you put on your dress?

DOTTIE: I don't feel like it. Is everybody else dressin' up?

SHARLA: I don't know what everybody else's doin'. I'm goin' to work.

DOTTIE: Then what difference does it make?

SHARLA: It doesn't, really. Your daddy just wanted you to look nice.

DOTTIE: Where are they?

SHARLA: They'll be here. They better be. I gotta get to work. *(Sharla prepares for work, putting on make-up, fixing her hair.)* What're you fixin'?

DOTTIE: Just some casserole.

SHARLA: What kind? Smells like tuna.

DOTTIE: It is.

SHARLA: You gonna make a salad?

DOTTIE: I could, if people're hungry enough.

SHARLA: Some rolls or somethin'?

DOTTIE: No.

SHARLA: I think we got some biscuits in there.

DOTTIE: We got plenty.

SHARLA: Okay. I was just sayin'…

DOTTIE: Was that your boyfriend on the phone?

SHARLA: What do you mean?

DOTTIE: Wasn't that your boyfriend?

SHARLA: I'm married, silly.

DOTTIE: I won't tell Daddy.

SHARLA: I don't know what you're talkin' about. That was Jennie, my friend
    from high school.

DOTTIE: Is he cute?

SHARLA: Stop talkin' like that.

DOTTIE: I hope he's cute. You should have a cute boyfriend.

SHARLA: Listen—

DOTTIE: I had a boyfriend in the third grade, but I never told nobody. His
    name was Marshall and he was fat. But he loved me.

SHARLA: You should go out more often—

DOTTIE: It was our little secret, me and Marshall. All the other kids would
    always make a big show of goin' together, writin' their initials on their
    notebooks and holdin' hands at recess, but me and Marshall kept it a
    secret. Nobody at that school ever knew we were goin' together and
    nobody at home knew either, even though nobody ever asked. We never
    saw each other at recess and we didn't have any lunch together and we
    didn't write notes and he didn't walk me home from school.

SHARLA: When would you see him?

DOTTIE: In class. At school.

SHARLA: I mean alone.

DOTTIE: We didn't see each other alone.

SHARLA: Ever?

DOTTIE: That would've spoiled the secret.

SHARLA: How did you all decide you were goin' together if you never spent
    any time alone?

DOTTIE: We just knew.

SHARLA: Wait—

DOTTIE: We never had to talk about it. If we'd talked about it, it wouldn't've
    been what it was, which was true.

SHARLA: What was true?

DOTTIE: Love. We loved each other.

SHARLA: How do you know he loved you if y'all never talked about it?

DOTTIE: He loved me with a pure love.

SHARLA: Well, there's not many like that around, I guess.

DOTTIE: It's Joe, isn't it? Joe's comin' over.

SHARLA: Joe who?

DOTTIE: I don't remember. His eyes hurt.

SHARLA: Huh?

DOTTIE: What?

SHARLA: I don't remember his name, but it was important to Ansel you put on your dress. I guess he wanted to make a good impression. *(Beat.)* You met him?

DOTTIE: Uh-huh.

SHARLA: What's he like?

DOTTIE: He told me I should get a teacher for my kung fu.

SHARLA: Yeah…

DOTTIE: He had me make him some coffee.

SHARLA: What's he like?

DOTTIE: I don't know…

SHARLA: *(Beat.)* Well. Anyway. Why don't you put on your dress?

DOTTIE: Okay.

    (T-Bone barks outside.)

SHARLA: And you just forget about Jennie, all right? She's just an old friend and I don't wanna have any trouble with your daddy over an old friend.

DOTTIE: You should have a cute boyfriend.

    (Ansel enters.)

SHARLA: I bet your ears were burnin'.

ANSEL: You all talkin' about me?

DOTTIE: No, sir—

SHARLA: I was just tellin' Dottie how you wanted her to put on her dress for dinner tonight.

ANSEL: *(As he changes channels on t.v., finds an episode of* Cannon.*)* Would you, honey?

DOTTIE: Is everybody dressin' up?

ANSEL: Yeah. Yeah, we're all gonna dress up.

DOTTIE: Okay. *(She exits.)*

SHARLA: Ansel Ray, get in this kitchen.

ANSEL: What?

SHARLA: When are you gonna tell that girl?

ANSEL: Tell her what?

SHARLA: That it's just gonna be her and Joe.

ANSEL: She's not stupid. She'll figure it out.

SHARLA: You gotta tell her. She doesn't know what to expect.

ANSEL: There's nothin' to expect—

SHARLA: That girl's not like other people, goddamn it. She doesn't put two and two together, like you and me and Chris—

ANSEL: There's nothin' to get worried over—

SHARLA: She's never even been on a real date before—

ANSEL: It's not a date—

SHARLA: Well, it's the closest thing she ever had to one, except for some fat
     kid who didn't even know it—

ANSEL: What fat kid?

SHARLA: Give me the keys. I gotta get to work.

ANSEL: There's no reason to get all bent outta—

SHARLA: You talk to that girl, Ansel, cause you're liable to blow this thing real
     good—

ANSEL: *(Fishing keys out of pocket.)* What'm I gonna say?

SHARLA: Tell her the story, for God's sake. Don't make everything so compli-
     cated—

ANSEL: What story?

SHARLA: The situation. Tell her why he's comin' over tonight.
     (He is having difficulty extricating the keys from his pocket.)

ANSEL: How the hell am I supposed—?

SHARLA: I don't know, but if she—look at it this way, if she doesn't know why
     he's—what've you got in your pockets?!

ANSEL: It's like gum or somethin'—

SHARLA: If she doesn't know what's expected of her, then she might disap-
     point him. Now did you think of that?

ANSEL: I can't tell the girl how to behave—

SHARLA: Oh, you can't tell anybody anything! Give me those goddamn keys!
     *(He finally jerks the keys from his pocket, along with a shower of loose change
     that falls to the kitchen floor. She snaps the keys from his hand, flings the
     door open.)*

ANSEL: Wait, Sharla—
     (Sharla leaves. Ansel steps out, calls after her.)

ANSEL: —what fat kid?! *(Then, to a neighboring trailer.)* Would you tie up that
     fuckin' dog?!
     *(Unseen to us, the dog attacks. Ansel retreats quickly into the trailer, slams
     the door just in time. T-Bone snaps and growls outside, but eventually gives
     up. Ansel angrily picks up a chair, considers throwing it, reconsiders, becomes
     hypnotized by the cop show on t.v.)*

ANSEL: Cannon, you fat bastard… *(He stoops, collects his change, pockets it, gets
     a beer from the fridge, kills a bug, cackles as he washes its remains down the
     sink.)*
     (Dottie enters, wearing a sexy black evening dress.)

DOTTIE: Daddy?

ANSEL: Oh, honey…

DOTTIE: What do you think?

ANSEL: You look like a goddamn movie star. Come on over here.

    (He grabs a chair, helps her stand on it.)

ANSEL: Turn around.

    (She does.)

ANSEL: Like a goddamn movie star.

DOTTIE: I feel funny.

ANSEL: Why?

DOTTIE: I don't know. I feel like I went to school naked, like that dream you told me about.

ANSEL: Don't feel funny. You're beautiful.

DOTTIE: My butt's too big.

ANSEL: Let me let you in on a little secret: guys like big butts.

DOTTIE: They do not.

ANSEL: *(Feeling her butt.)* I'm speakin' from experience.

DOTTIE: *(Getting down from chair.)* Sharla doesn't have a big butt.

ANSEL: Give her some time.

DOTTIE: Why aren't you dressed yet?

ANSEL: I'm not gonna stay for dinner.

DOTTIE: What do you mean?

ANSEL: Me and Chris have some business to attend to—

DOTTIE: Where's Chris?

ANSEL: He's on his way—

DOTTIE: Then where—

ANSEL: So it's just gonna be you and Joe for dinner.

DOTTIE: *(Beat.)* I should change.

ANSEL: No—

DOTTIE: Yeah, I should—

ANSEL: No, I think it'd be nice for Joe if he—

DOTTIE: Yeah, I'm gonna go change—

    (She heads back to the bedroom. Ansel grabs her arm.)

ANSEL: Whoa, whoa, hold up, honey—

DOTTIE: Let me go, I need to change—

ANSEL: Just listen for a second—

DOTTIE: I have to change—

    (She tries to pull away, but Ansel grabs her around the waist. T-Bone barks again.)

DOTTIE: I have to change, I have to change, I have to change—

ANSEL: Now, calm down, Dottie, just—

DOTTIE: I have to change, I have to change—

ANSEL: *(More violent.)* Hold still, you little bitch—!

DOTTIE: *(Hysterical.)* I HAVE TO CHANGE!

    (Chris bursts in, immediately separates Ansel and Dottie. She collapses to the floor.)

CHRIS: What the hell's goin' on—?!

ANSEL: She wants to get out of her dress!

CHRIS: So?!

ANSEL: Well, I told her I thought it'd be nice for Joe if—!

CHRIS: Let her change if she wants!

ANSEL: Don't you think she looks nice?!

CHRIS: *(To Dottie.)* You put on whatever you like—

ANSEL: Now wait a goddamn second—!

CHRIS: Let her change, Dad—

ANSEL: Who the hell do you think—?!

    (Chris is suddenly in Ansel's face.)

CHRIS: LET HER CHANGE! *(To Dottie.)* Go change.

    (She exits down the hall.)

ANSEL: She looked great.

CHRIS: It's bad enough we gotta give the son-of-a bitch a present. We don't have to gift-wrap it.

ANSEL: You listen to me—

CHRIS: This whole thing makes me sick.

ANSEL: This is my home—

CHRIS: You don't have a home—

ANSEL: —and I call the shots around here—

CHRIS: Shut up.

ANSEL: Just so you know.

CHRIS: She knows it's just gonna be the two of 'em?

ANSEL: She does now.

CHRIS: Great. Goddamn it. Too bad he didn't meet Sharla first, huh? He coulda dated her instead, and I wouldn'ta minded—

ANSEL: That's my wife you're talkin' about.

CHRIS: Yeah, right.

ANSEL: Look, are you ready? Joe told us to be gone half an hour ago.

CHRIS: Fuck Joe.

ANSEL: He's runnin' this show, ain't he?

CHRIS: I'll leave when I by God feel like it.

ANSEL: Chris…? If we're gonna do this, we should do it right.

CHRIS: Yeah, okay.

(A knock at the door.)

CHRIS: Poop.

ANSEL: Dottie?

DOTTIE: *(Offstage.)* I'm not ready!

CHRIS: Answer the door, for God's sake.

(Ansel opens the door and Killer Joe enters, wearing a double-breasted suit, a new cowboy hat, and a pair of lizard-skin boots. He carries a bouquet of spring flowers.)

JOE: What are you doing here?

CHRIS: We're on our way out.

JOE: We discussed this—

CHRIS: Don't push it, we're leavin'—

JOE: Hey. That's right, Junior. Don't push it. When we make arrangements, I expect the details to have some attention paid to them.

CHRIS: Let's go, Dad.

JOE: You understand me?

CHRIS: Yeah…

JOE: Good boy. Where is she?

CHRIS: She's changing.

(Chris and Ansel leave. T-Bone barks. Joe takes off his hat, holds it, calls into Dottie's bedroom.)

JOE: Dottie? It's me. Joe Cooper. We're alone now. *(Beat.)* It's okay if you don't want to come out. You stay in there as long as you like. *(He hangs his hat, turns off the t.v., puts down the flowers, lights a cigarette. Goes to the kitchen, checks the food in the oven.)* Your casserole smells nice. I think you got a good scald on it. *(Beat.)* I wish I had a funny story about blind dates or casseroles, but I don't. *(Beat.)* Maybe one will come to me later. *(Beat; to himself.)* Maybe not. *(He finds a radio on the kitchen counter, turns it on, flips the dial, finds a Hank Williams song.)* Hank Williams. From Oklahoma. I don't have a funny story about Hank Williams, either. Or Oklahoma. Well, Oklahoma's kinda funny anyway, right? I grew up lookin' at Oklahoma. From the south bank of the Red River. That's where I grew up. See, when I was a boy, the border between Texas and Oklahoma was actually the middle of the river. If you were fishing on the north bank, you were catching Okie fish. But I caught Texas fish. They probably tasted the same. Some time since then, we gave our half of the river away. Now the whole damn thing belongs to Oklahoma. South bank: that's the border. I'm not sure why we did that, but it makes me mad. Kind of like giving away your…your front porch.

(Dottie emerges from her bedroom, wearing her jeans and sweatshirt.)

JOE: Good evening.

(She moves past him, into the kitchen, checks the food in the oven.)

DOTTIE: You said it was scalded.

JOE: No, I said, "You got a good scald on it." Just an expression.

DOTTIE: Oh.

JOE: How are you?

DOTTIE: Fine.

JOE: Do you want to know how I am?

DOTTIE: How are you?

JOE: I'm fine, thank you. *(Joe gets the flowers, gives them to Dottie.)* You look very nice.

DOTTIE: Thank you.

JOE: You're welcome.

DOTTIE: I changed.

JOE: Oh?

DOTTIE: I didn't know just you and me were gonna have dinner.

JOE: Somebody should've told you.

DOTTIE: They did. Just now.

JOE: What did you change from?

DOTTIE: A dress.

JOE: I'd love to see it.

DOTTIE: Are you hungry?

JOE: Famished. *(Beat.)* Yes, hungry.

DOTTIE: Are you ready to eat?

JOE: Whenever you are.

DOTTIE: Your eyes hurt.

JOE: I beg your pardon.

DOTTIE: Huh?

JOE: May I have a beer?

DOTTIE: Oh, sure.

JOE: I'll get it. *(He gets a beer from the refrigerator.)*

DOTTIE: Well…I'll serve dinner.

JOE: That would be lovely.

DOTTIE: What did you say?

JOE: I said, "That would be lovely."

(She begins to set the table for two.)

JOE: Can I help you?

DOTTIE: No, that's okay.

JOE: How old are you?

DOTTIE: Twenty.

JOE: And Chris…?

DOTTIE: Twenty-two. *(Beat.)* You're wonderin' about Daddy.

JOE: Hm?

DOTTIE: Daddy was sixteen when Chris was born. Momma was fifteen.

JOE: So young.

DOTTIE: It was an accident.

JOE: Really.

DOTTIE: They didn't want to get married.

JOE: Why did they?

DOTTIE: I don't know. That's just what they always said. "We didn't want to get married."

JOE: Do you trust me?

DOTTIE: Not quite.

JOE: Good.

DOTTIE: Have you ever been married?

JOE: Maybe.

DOTTIE: What does that mean?

JOE: It means no.

DOTTIE: How come?

JOE: Because women are deceitful, and lying, and manipulative, and vicious, and vituperative, and black-hearted, and evil, and old.

DOTTIE: *(Beat.)* Yeah…

JOE: What are you drinking?

DOTTIE: Nothing.

JOE: Can I get you something?

DOTTIE: No, thank you.

JOE: A tall glass of cold beer, perhaps?

DOTTIE: No, thank you. *(She finishes setting the table. She takes the casserole out of the oven, places it in the center of the table.)*

JOE: Lovely.

DOTTIE: I'm a virgin.

JOE: I know.

DOTTIE: Okay.

> *(He helps her into her seat, lights a candle, places it on the table, turns off the lights, takes his seat.)*

JOE: A. Tuna. Casserole.

DOTTIE: Yes.

JOE: May I serve?

DOTTIE: Please.

> *(He slices some casserole and puts it on her plate, then does the same for himself.)*

JOE: It looks delicious.

DOTTIE: Thank you.

JOE: Thank you.

> *(He waits for her to take the first bite. She gestures, "After you." He takes a polite bite, eyes her, takes a larger bite, growls hungrily, and digs in. She begins eating.)*

JOE: I'd really like to see that dress.

DOTTIE: It wasn't right.

JOE: May I see it anyway?

DOTTIE: How are you gonna kill Momma?

JOE: Ohhh…that's not…appropriate dinner conversation.

DOTTIE: Not unless you poison her.

> *(He freezes, food in his mouth. She laughs.)*

JOE: I'm not sure I'm going to kill your mother.

DOTTIE: How come?

JOE: Because I rarely do that sort of thing. I have operatives.

DOTTIE: What's an operative?

JOE: An agent. An assistant.

DOTTIE: Oh.

JOE: Yes. Someone else will take care of it. *(Beat.)* Unless, of course, I do it myself.

DOTTIE: So you might…?

JOE: Yes. I don't know.

DOTTIE: How will you do it? Or the operatives?

JOE: Well…well, it'll be taken care of.

DOTTIE: When?

JOE: I don't know.

DOTTIE: Will you be the detective who investigates?

JOE: Probably not, but sometimes.

DOTTIE: Is that a problem?

JOE: That's a convenience.

DOTTIE: That's a convenience.

JOE: Yes.

DOTTIE: So are homes.

JOE: Yes.

DOTTIE: I love my brother. I remember when Momma and Daddy were havin' a divorce, and they, Momma had just told us (she was drunk), "I don't love your Daddy no more. I never loved him," and I screamed somethin' that didn't make any sense, and I ran out of the house, and into the yard, under the streetlight, and I was crying, Chris came out (he hadn't said anything), and he just…laid on top of me. He stretched his body out, like this, and laid on me, until I stopped cryin'—

JOE: Dottie—

DOTTIE: —and we haven't talked about it, ever.

JOE: Bring the dress.

DOTTIE: Now.

JOE: Yes.

(They rise. She exits. A moment later, she enters, carrying the dress on a hanger.)

JOE: Why wouldn't you wear that for me?

DOTTIE: It's not me.

JOE: Not when you're not in it.

DOTTIE: I once had a boyfriend—

JOE: Put it on.

DOTTIE: *(Beat.)* All right. *(She heads for the bedroom.)*

JOE: Where are you going?

DOTTIE: I'm going to put the dress on—

JOE: I said put it on.

DOTTIE: I was—

JOE: Here.

DOTTIE: I—

JOE: Put it on, please.

(She hesitates.)

JOE: Put it on, Dottie.

(She lays down the dress, takes off her sweatshirt, hesitates again.)

JOE: I want to see you put it on.

(She takes off her tennis shoes. He stares at her. She peels off her jeans.)

JOE: Stop.

(She stops.)

JOE: Take off your socks.

(She does. He turns his back to her.)

JOE: Take off your brassiere.

(She hesitates.)

JOE: Take off your brassiere.

(She does…lets the brassiere fall to the floor…covers her breasts…then drops her arms to her sides.)

JOE: Take off your underwear.

(She does.)

DOTTIE: *(Very softly.)* Babies.

(His back is still turned to her.)

JOE: Put on the dress.

(She pulls the dress over her head.)

JOE: Come here. Right behind me.

(She does. He unfastens his belt and opens his pants.)

JOE: Reach around and put your hand in my pants.

(She does.)

DOTTIE: I don't remember…

JOE: Do you feel that?

DOTTIE: Yes…

JOE: What does that feel like?

DOTTIE: I don't remember…

JOE: How old are you?

DOTTIE: Twelve.

JOE: So am I. *(Stillness, then.)* Switch places with me.

(She moves in front of him. Their eyes do not meet.)

JOE: Your boyfriend?

DOTTIE: Marshall.

JOE: Marshall.

DOTTIE: He was fat…

JOE: Uh-huh…

DOTTIE: He loved me. With a pure love.

(Joe slowly begins to lift her skirt.)

DOTTIE: Our secret.

JOE: Nobody.

DOTTIE: Home.

(Blackout.)

END OF ACT I

ACT II
SCENE I

Lights slowly rise: late at night. Thunder. Lightning. Footsteps. T-Bone. Chris unlocks the door, but a metal chain keeps him from opening it. He moans, mutters. He kicks the door open, snapping the chain off the wall. He staggers inside. His shirt and pants are soaked with blood. One eye is blackened, and blood streams from his nose and mouth. Suddenly, Killer Joe, naked and holding a gun, grabs Chris's hair from behind and forces him to the floor.

JOE: CHRIS:

ALL RIGHT, GET DOWN THERE   I'm sorry! I'm sorry!
NOW! GET DOWN!

    (Joe relaxes, his foot planted in Chris's back.)

JOE: Chris…

CHRIS: Oh, fuck…

    (Sharla, wearing a t-shirt and a pair of men's underwear, runs in from the hallway. Ansel is behind her.)

SHARLA: What the hell—?!

    (She turns on the light and Chris's condition is visible to all of them.)

SHARLA: Good God, what happened—?

ANSEL: You look rough, boy—

JOE: Excuse me.

    (Joe exits to Dottie's bedroom. Sharla and Ansel keep their distance from Chris, examining him from across the room.)

CHRIS: Dad—?

ANSEL: Them old boys caught up to you.

CHRIS: —my hand—

SHARLA: What happened?

CHRIS: I think they broke my hand—

ANSEL: What'd they do to your face—?

CHRIS: I got—

SHARLA: —Jesus—

CHRIS: —I got—

ANSEL: You wanna go to the hospital—?

SHARLA: I think he better—

CHRIS: I got beat up—

ANSEL: I can see that—

CHRIS: Oh, God—

> (Dottie enters, wearing a robe. She rushes to Chris. Joe emerges again, now wearing a pair of slacks.)

DOTTIE: What happened to you?

CHRIS: Some guys—

DOTTIE: *(To Sharla.)* Will you get a wet rag?

CHRIS: —I got beat up—

> (Sharla gets a dishrag, soaks it, and wrings it out.)

ANSEL: They do all they were goin' to, or—?

CHRIS: Huh—?

ANSEL: Did they—?

JOE: If they'd wanted to kill him, he'd be dead.

> (Sharla gives the dishrag to Dottie, who gently wipes blood from Chris's face.)

CHRIS: Oh, God—

DOTTIE: Your nose is broken—

JOE: Is that all?

CHRIS: What the fuck, man—?

ANSEL: What'd they say to you?

CHRIS: What the fuck you think they said?

ANSEL: They want their money.

CHRIS: No shit.

SHARLA: You want a beer?

JOE: Where'd they find you?

CHRIS: Wild Bill's. They jumped me in the parking lot.

ANSEL: *(Stepping over Chris to turn on t.v.)* D'ja see Bill there?

CHRIS: I don't…I don't know, why?

ANSEL: He owes me ten bucks.

CHRIS: Christ—

SHARLA: I'm goin' back to bed—

DOTTIE: *(To Chris.)* You sure you don't wanna go to the hospital?

CHRIS: Yeah, I—

SHARLA: C'mon, Ansel—

DOTTIE: That cut on your head looks pretty deep—

JOE: He's fine. He just got a whipping.

CHRIS: *(To Joe.)* Listen, buddy, I'm—

JOE: No, I'm saying, it could happen to anybody—

ANSEL: We'll turn in then, I guess—

SHARLA: Ansel, come on—

CHRIS: Just go—

ANSEL: —all right—

SHARLA: —good night—

CHRIS: Dottie—

> *(Sharla exits.)*

DOTTIE: You feel any better—?

CHRIS: I didn't mean—

JOE: Come on, Dottie, you should get back in bed.

CHRIS: Wait just a minute here—

SHARLA: *(Offstage.)* ANSEL!

ANSEL: Okay, goddamn it, I'm comin'. *(Ansel exits.)*

JOE: *(To Dottie.)* Come on, Dottie.

CHRIS: Dottie, I want to tell you: I never meant—

JOE: Dottie.

> *(She stands and exits without turning back.)*

JOE: *(To Chris.)* Good night.

> *(Joe turns off the light and goes to bed. Chris is left in the middle of the floor, bleeding by the light of the television.)*

CHRIS: *(Calling off.)* Joe? *(Beat.)* We need to talk.

JOE: *(Offstage.)* Tomorrow.

CHRIS: Now.

JOE: *(Offstage.)* It can wait.

CHRIS: Right now.

> *(Joe reemerges from the bedroom, turns on the light, turns off the t.v.)*

JOE: Shoot.

CHRIS: I wanna know what kinda progress you're makin' on your job.

JOE: It's being taken care of.

CHRIS: Yeah, it sure as hell is. You been here a week now, fuckin' my sister, and my mother's a helluva lot healthier than me at the moment.

JOE: Cut to the chase, Junior.

CHRIS: I'm havin' second thoughts.

JOE: You want me off the job?

CHRIS: I don't know—

JOE: Say the word.

CHRIS: Huh?

JOE: Say the word. Your call.

CHRIS: When are you plannin' on doin' it?

JOE: Tomorrow.

CHRIS: Really.

JOE: Yes.

CHRIS: How?

JOE: I won't tell you.

CHRIS: Where?

JOE: I won't tell you.

CHRIS: Am I the customer here?

JOE: Tomorrow. That's all you need to know.

CHRIS: So you'll be leaving tomorrow.

JOE: No, of course not.

CHRIS: Why not?

JOE: The retainer isn't for the job. It's for the money. I'm not leaving until I get my money.

CHRIS: I don't like that.

JOE: I don't care.

CHRIS: I don't want you near my sister.

JOE: I don't care.

CHRIS: And if I tell you the deal's off—

JOE: I'll leave right now and you'll never see me again. Your call.

CHRIS: "Say the word."

JOE: Who are you into for this money?

CHRIS: I won't tell you.

JOE: Digger Soames?

CHRIS: How'd you know that?

JOE: Digger Soames. What did he say he'd do to you if you don't pay him?

CHRIS: You know that too?

JOE: He'll do it. I used to work with an old boy on the force…can't remember his name. He and Digger came to cross purposes. Digger warned him; he didn't believe Digger would really do it. He went to sleep one night…woke up six feet under. We found him a couple of months later… like this: (*Joe mimics the position of a man found buried alive: hands hooked into claws, eyes and mouth wide open.*)

CHRIS: Why didn't you arrest him?

JOE: I like Digger.

CHRIS: Aren't you supposed to arrest people who commit murder?

JOE: Where would you suggest I start, Junior?

CHRIS: Do it.

JOE: What are your plans for tomorrow?

CHRIS: Why?

JOE: Don't be around here tomorrow.

CHRIS: I'll be wherever the hell I feel like—

JOE: For the safety of the job…make yourself scarce. Do you understand?

CHRIS: You'll never get my mother to set foot in this trailer—

JOE: Do you understand?

CHRIS: Yeah, but you'll never get my mother to set foot in this trailer.

JOE: You let me worry about that.

CHRIS: Okay.

JOE: Okay. Get some sleep. (*Joe starts for the bedroom.*)

CHRIS: Joe?

 (*Joe stops, turns.*)

CHRIS: You better not hurt my sister.

 (*Joe laughs.*)

CHRIS: What's so funny?

JOE: Oh, I don't know. That just…struck me.

 (*Dottie enters.*)

DOTTIE: How many?

JOE: How many what, sweetie?

CHRIS: (*Sweetie?*)

DOTTIE: I'm sorry, it's been a long time…

CHRIS: She's asleep.

DOTTIE: You'd fuck a snake if you could hold its head.

 (*Joe turns to Chris and smiles.*)

JOE: That's fun. (*Joe puts his arm around Dottie and pulls her down the hallway.*)

CHRIS: Dottie…

 (*Blackout. Sound of the evangelist from the next scene plays over the blackout.*)

SCENE II

 Lights rise: daylight streams through the windows. Killer Joe sits at the kitchen table, listening to an evangelist on the radio. His gun lays on the table. T-Bone barks crazily. Pounding on the door. Joe lifts his gun, cocks it.

CHRIS: (*Offstage.*) Joe?! Joe?!

 (*Chris rushes in, sweating, out of breath, panicked. His head and hand are bruised, bandaged. Joe holsters his gun.*)

CHRIS: Ah, thank God! I was afraid…I wouldn't get here, and…it'd be too late…ah, thank God…

Listen. We gotta stop this thing. We can't… *(Chris turns off the radio.)* I been in a lotta trouble, all my life, but I never tried nothin' like this before.

I'm sorry. I didn't mean to waste your time.

I hate that bitch. I've always hated her. I just…I can't be the one, y'know?

But more than that, the main thing, really, is, is, is Dottie. I mean, my sister…she never did nothin' to nobody, y'know? And for me to…I can't be…responsible.

And you can't have her. I can't let you have her. You gotta give her up, cause I can't look her in the eyes otherwise.

Do you understand, Joe? I don't want my sister to see you again. I don't think you're a good influence.

I mean, come on, Joe, you kill people, for Chrissake. Y'know?

No offense. I mean, it's not like me and Dad or Mom have been especially good influences. But Dottie managed to turn out all right anyway. And it just seems like the best thing I can do for her now is to keep her away from people who won't do her any good.

So I think it'd be best if you and me just shook hands and forgot any of us ever met. Is that okay? Can't we just walk away from it before it goes too far? None of us are any better off, but we're really no worse off, either.

I'm no better off. I owe Digger Soames six thousand dollars. I'll never have that kinda money, not ever.

And, you know, even if I had it, wouldn't that suck, handin' it over to these guys? I'd wanna keep that money, try to make somethin' with it.

I tried startin' a farm once. That seemed like the kind of life I want. Workin' for myself, outside a lot, make my own hours, live in the country, smoke dope, watch t.v. That's all I really want.

So I started a rabbit farm. I built the whole thing, by myself. I was livin' with a coupla guys out near Mesquite, but they didn't help me; I built it, with my own two hands. Lumber, chicken wire, water bottles, pellets. Rabbits. I loved those little bastards. They smell like shit, and they fuck all the time, but they're awful easy goin' animals.

I left for a coupla weeks, cause of this girl down in Corpus, and when I got back, a rat, or a skunk, or somethin' had got in the pen, and it was rabid. Awful hot out, too.

They just tore each other apart. Their eyes were rollin', and foamin' at the mouth, and…and screamin'. Did you know rabbits can scream? They sound just like little girls.

It was disturbing.

I started sellin' dope for a living. I knew more about it.

(Joe checks a beeper affixed to his belt, then goes to the door, looks outside.)

CHRIS: So I can't pay this guy, and I don't even really want to.

That means you gotta get out, Joe. You gotta get outta here, and leave my sister alone, forever. Otherwise, you and me're gonna have some trouble.

Do you understand?

Do you understand?

(A long silence. Chris slowly turns and looks at a large, overstuffed garbage bag sitting by the other garbage in the kitchen. Chris walks to the bag, starts to open it.)

JOE: Don't open it. *(Beat.)* Do you want to help me get her in the car?

(Blackout. Sound of the Road Runner cartoon from the next scene plays over the blackout.)

SCENE III

The lights slowly rise. Daylight streams through the windows. Chris staggers back and forth from the bedroom to the living room, doing a poor job of selecting mourning clothes. Dottie watches a Road Runner cartoon, and the volume seems incredibly loud. Chris reaches his limit and snaps off the television.

CHRIS: Goddamn coyote!

DOTTIE: I was watchin' that, Chris…

CHRIS: Listen, honey—

DOTTIE: I was watchin' the show.

CHRIS: I know—

DOTTIE: I wanted to see how it turned out.

CHRIS: HE DOESN'T CATCH THE BIRD, OKAY?! IT JUST GOES ON AND ON AND ON!

DOTTIE: Yeah?

CHRIS: Dottie. I know you know what's goin' on. I don't have to tell you anything; you know.

DOTTIE: Uh-huh.

CHRIS: I want you to understand somethin', though: I didn't mean to hurt you. I never meant to do that.

DOTTIE: Yeah…

CHRIS: Arrangements just kinda broke funny, and…if I had known how all of this was gonna fall out, I might've done things a little different.

DOTTIE: No…

CHRIS: Well, maybe not, but I might have. Anyway, this's just about over and he'll be gone soon.

DOTTIE: He will?

CHRIS: Soon as this money comes through, and we pay the son-of-a-bitch—

DOTTIE: That's where they are now?

CHRIS: Dad and Sharla. Yeah, they're talkin' to Kilpatrick.

DOTTIE: He won't pay them today, will he?

CHRIS: Nah, they're just goin' over the policy—

DOTTIE: Joe's not leavin' just yet, right?

CHRIS: No, but soon, and then you won't ever have to see him again.

DOTTIE: See him…

CHRIS: We're gonna be better off after this, honey. I'm gonna get outta this trouble I'm in, set things right. Get a job. Get married. I'm gonna do things right, from now on. I've gotta pay for things I've done wrong. You don't pay for that kinda stuff, and it comes back to you. Always.

DOTTIE: Uh-huh…

CHRIS: Dad'll be able to…oh, I don't know, you know Dad.

DOTTIE: Yeah.

CHRIS: And Dottie, you're finally gonna get to go to that modelin' school. You remember how you always wanted to do that? Like those girls in the thing?

DOTTIE: Christie Brinkley…

CHRIS: Y'know how long it'd take you to do that, answerin' phones for that chiropractor?

DOTTIE: Yeah, oh, I don't do that no more.

CHRIS: Why not?

DOTTIE: I got fired a few months back.

CHRIS: What for?

DOTTIE: Stopped goin'.

CHRIS: I didn't know that. Nobody told me that. Why didn't I know that?
(She picks up a comic book. He strides to her, rips the comic from her hands.

CHRIS: Why didn't I know that?

(She tries to pull away, but he grabs her, forces her to listen.)

CHRIS: Maybe you don't like me so much anymore. Maybe you don't think I did right by you, but by God, I did the best I could. Nobody can accuse me of not havin' people's best interests at mind. People do the best they can. Anybody says he doesn't's lyin'. *(Beat.)* I did the best I could. I didn't want to hurt anybody. Ever.

(He grabs her, buries his head in her lap. She holds him.)

CHRIS: Oh, God…fire…

DOTTIE: Will there be a trial?

CHRIS: Huh?

DOTTIE: Will there be—?

CHRIS: I don't know. I don't know. I doubt it. Joe knows what he's doin'—

(T-Bone barks.)

DOTTIE: I never been to a trial.

CHRIS: D'ja see the shot in the paper? Her car?

DOTTIE: Uh-huh.

CHRIS: Yeah, he knows what he's doin'. They couldn't even do a real autopsy cause there wasn't much left to speak of—

(Ansel and Sharla enter, wearing mourning clothes. Chris pulls away from Dottie.)

CHRIS: How'd it go?

ANSEL: You little bastard…

CHRIS: What?

ANSEL: You little son-of-a-bitch…

CHRIS: What's the matter?

ANSEL: I'm not talkin' in front of Dottie—

SHARLA: Oh, hell, Ansel, she knows what's goin' on—

ANSEL: I'm not talkin' in front of her!

CHRIS: What are you talkin' about? What happened with Kilpatrick?

ANSEL: Sharla, take Dottie for a drive—

SHARLA: You take her—

CHRIS: Will you please tell me—?

ANSEL: I'm not talkin' in front of—

DOTTIE: They're not gonna pay you the money, are they?

(Silence.)

CHRIS: Dad?

SHARLA: Tell him, Ansel.

CHRIS: Tell me.

SHARLA: Tell that idiot—

CHRIS: Just tell me—

ANSEL: Who told you about Adele's policy?

CHRIS: Rex. Rex told me. He just mentioned it. In conversation.

ANSEL: Rex…

CHRIS: Will you for the love of God tell me—?

ANSEL: When did he tell you?

CHRIS: In conversation—

ANSEL: Not how! WHEN!

CHRIS: A coupla weeks ago. Me and Mom just had a big fight—

ANSEL: Oh, Christ—

SHARLA: I told you, Ansel.

CHRIS: What happened?

SHARLA: I told you from the start—

CHRIS: Shut up, Sharla—

SHARLA: Don't tell me to shut up, I'm not the one who blew this thing—!

CHRIS: What happened, Dad?

SHARLA: You come in here—!

CHRIS: Dad?

SHARLA: —tell people what to do, how we're all gonna see a hundred grand—!

CHRIS: *(Advancing on Ansel.)* Goddamn it, you tell me, right now—

ANSEL: Dottie is not the beneficiary. Rex is the beneficiary.

CHRIS: I don't understand.

ANSEL: It's not real tough—

CHRIS: Explain it to me.

ANSEL: Dottie does not get the money. Rex gets the money.

CHRIS: Wait, I—

ANSEL: Dottie does not get the fifty thousand dollars. Rex gets the fifty thousand dollars.

CHRIS: That's not right.

ANSEL: That's the way it is.

CHRIS: That can't be.

ANSEL: Go talk to Kilpatrick yourself.

CHRIS: That can't be. I don't—what do you, what do you—what do you mean? Because I was told! Because—because I was told! Because Rex told me! He told me! Rex told me!

DOTTIE: Rex was Momma's boyfriend—

CHRIS: JUST—SHUT UP, DOTTIE! He told me—

SHARLA: He was lyin'.

CHRIS: Why would he do that?

SHARLA: Why do you think?

CHRIS: No, no, he couldn't've known! He couldn't've known I'd do this!

SHARLA: He's the one who put the idea in your head—

CHRIS: I don't fucking believe this—

ANSEL: Who told you about Killer Joe?

CHRIS: *(It hits him.)* Oh…oh, God…

SHARLA: *(To Ansel.)* I told you. Did I tell you?

ANSEL: Yeah…

CHRIS: Oh my God…I'm fucked…piece of fucking fuck suck cake…

ANSEL: He really played you like an accordion fish, didn't he, boy?

CHRIS: No, God—

SHARLA: *(To Chris.)* You make me sick.

CHRIS: I don't believe you, God—

> *(Ansel grabs Chris, shoves him, holds him.)*

ANSEL: Well, you better believe it. Sooner you start believin' it, sooner you can figure a way to pay Killer Joe his money—

SHARLA: We gotta get goin'—

ANSEL: —not to mention Digger Soames—

SHARLA: We gotta get goin', y'all.

ANSEL: What for?!

SHARLA: Funeral's in half an hour.

CHRIS: You all go ahead. I gotta think of somethin'.

ANSEL: Oh, I wish you would. We always seem so much better off when you do.

DOTTIE: Where's Joe? Isn't he going to the funeral?

SHARLA: No, huh-uh.

DOTTIE: He's comin' back, isn't he?

CHRIS:	ANSEL:
Yeah…yeah, he's comin' back, all right.	Oh, he's comin' back.

ANSEL: Let's hit it. We gotta get your mother in the ground.

CHRIS: I'll take Dottie.

ANSEL: Dottie?

DOTTIE: We'll be along.

ANSEL: All right. Mrs. Smith?

> *(Sharla is spraying her thighs with some cheap perfume.)*

ANSEL: When you're done fumigatin' the Gates of Hell.

> *(She exits. Ansel follows, stops at the door.)*

ANSEL: *(To Chris.)* Hey. Why don't you do us all a big favor and kill yourself?

> *(They're gone. T-Bone barks.)*

DOTTIE: You feel bad.

CHRIS: Yeah, I do…I think maybe I'm not supposed to be on Earth or somethin'…

DOTTIE: You remember those shows you used to put on? With your knees?

CHRIS: Hm?

DOTTIE: We'd be layin' in bed, late at night, and you'd get a flashlight, and put your knees up, and you'd put a pair of sunglasses on one knee, and some kind of hat on the other?

CHRIS: Yeah…

DOTTIE: And you'd put on a little show. "The Greatest Show on Earth." That's what you called it.

CHRIS: Yeah…

DOTTIE: "Into Time and Forever From Now On. No Ventures, or Time-Outs, or King's-X's, Everlasting, One More Than You Can Say, Into Infinity, and Outer Space. Amen."

CHRIS: Nothin's worse than regrets. Not cancer, not bein' eaten by a shark, nothin'.

DOTTIE: Joe is comin' back, isn't he? Cause I think maybe I'm—

CHRIS: I'm leaving.

DOTTIE: I think maybe I'm—

CHRIS: Will you come with me?

DOTTIE: *(His eyes hurt.)*

CHRIS: I'm leaving. And I want you to come with me.

DOTTIE: Where?

CHRIS: Mexico. No. Further. Peru. In South America.

DOTTIE: How do we get there?

CHRIS: We'll drive. We can drive it. Dottie, we can do this. It may not be livin' it up, exactly, not for a while—do you like Texas? I never liked this goddamn state. You hear these people talk about it like it's such a great place and all, but it's really just a bunch of goddamn hicks and rednecks with too much space to walk around in.

DOTTIE: It's warm.

CHRIS: Let's go. Let's just…go. Now.

DOTTIE: To the funeral.

CHRIS: No, Dottie, listen, if we're gonna pull this off, we gotta gas up—

DOTTIE: I have to see Joe.

CHRIS: No, no, Dottie, if we see Joe—

DOTTIE: I have to see him.

CHRIS: We have to go to Peru *now.*

DOTTIE: Then you go by yourself. I have to see Joe.

CHRIS: All right, I'll make you a deal. We'll go to the funeral, and you can see Joe.

DOTTIE: Good.

CHRIS: But you can't tell him we're plannin' on leavin'. You can't tell him good-bye. Not outright.

DOTTIE: Okie-doke.

CHRIS: And you can't tell Dad or Sharla either, cause they're mad at me right now and they might try to screw up our trip.

DOTTIE: Right.

CHRIS: We'll go to the funeral. You'll see Joe after.

DOTTIE: I understand.

CHRIS: Are you excited? Do you want to go?

DOTTIE: I'm always excited.

CHRIS: We can do this thing, Dottie. We can pull it off.

DOTTIE: Not if somebody makes me mad.

CHRIS: What?

(*Blackout. Sound of thunder during the blackout.*)

SCENE IV

The lights slowly rise. The daylight is dark blue and fading. (By the end of the scene, it should be dark outside.) The lights inside the trailer are off. No one is on stage. Thunder. Lightning. T-Bone. Footsteps. A moment later, the door opens and Sharla and Ansel enter, still wearing their funeral clothes. Sharla carries a bucket of fried chicken.

ANSEL: It's dark.

SHARLA: Dottie?! It's us!

ANSEL: I can't find the light.

(*Sharla turns on the lights, sets the chicken down in the kitchen. Ansel empties his pockets of keys, wrappers, lint, a pint bottle, and a mountain of change onto the kitchen table. He struggles out of his coat and shirt, then turns on the t.v.*)

ANSEL: Christ...

SHARLA: Dottie?! We stopped by the K-Fry-C! You hungry?! (*Beat.*) Dottie?! (*Beat.*) Chris?!

ANSEL: Fetch me a beer.

(Joe emerges from Dottie's bedroom.)

JOE: He's not here.

ANSEL: Hi, Joe—

SHARLA: Is Dottie here?

JOE: She's asleep.

SHARLA: Where's Chris?

JOE: I don't know.

SHARLA: You want some chicken? Stopped by the K-Fry-C.

JOE: Yes, please.

SHARLA: Help yourself. It's on the stove.

ANSEL: Get it for him, would you, hon?

SHARLA: Sure. White or dark?

JOE: Leg.

SHARLA: You need a plate?

JOE: No, thank you.

(She wraps a chicken leg in a paper towel and hands it to him.)

ANSEL: Want a beer?

JOE: Yes, please.

ANSEL: Honey, would you—?

(She gets beers for Ansel and Joe, then gets a piece of chicken for herself. Ansel grabs his pint from the kitchen table, offers Joe a swig.)

SHARLA: Funerals make people hungry for some reason.

JOE: Hm.

SHARLA: I'm starvin'.

JOE: *(Beat.)* Hm.

SHARLA: *(Beat.)* Dottie told you about the insurance.

ANSEL: Sharla—

JOE: Yes. She did.

ANSEL: *(To Joe.)* I don't know what to say.

SHARLA: You don't have to say anything. Not your fault.

ANSEL: Yeah, but—

SHARLA: *(To Joe.)* Chris. That Chris is so stupid. I coulda told you he'd fuck this up.

JOE: Why didn't you?

SHARLA: Why didn't I?

ANSEL: *(To Joe.)* Just an expression, really.

JOE: What is?

ANSEL: Well…what she said. That she coulda told you he'd fuck it up.

JOE: I've never heard that expression.

ANSEL: Manner of speakin', is what I mean—

SHARLA: I've never liked that little bastard.

JOE: You haven't.

> *(During the following, Joe collects Ansel's discarded clothing, carries it off, down the hall.)*

SHARLA: You can't trust him. He's just no good.

ANSEL: They never really hit it off—

SHARLA: All he cares about is himself.

ANSEL: That's not fair, really—

SHARLA: Bullshit fair. It's true.

ANSEL: Well, that's all anybody really cares about, isn't it?

SHARLA: No wonder.

ANSEL: No wonder what?

SHARLA: No wonder Chris wound up like he did.

ANSEL: What did I do?

SHARLA: Just shut up—

ANSEL: Hey, now—

SHARLA: *(To Joe, as he reenters.)* I mean, how stupid do you have to be to let an idiot like Rex take advantage—

JOE: Rex.

SHARLA: Yeah, Rex…

JOE: What about Rex?

SHARLA: I said…I said, "How stupid do you have to be to let an idiot like Rex—"

JOE: Yes, I heard what you said. Tell me about Rex.

ANSEL: *(To Joe.)* Rex is Adele's boyfriend.

JOE: Was.

ANSEL: Was Adele's boyfriend—

JOE: *(To Sharla.)* Tell me about Rex.

ANSEL: What do you want to know—?

JOE: *(To Ansel.)* Not you. *(To Sharla.)* You.

SHARLA: What.

JOE: You. Tell me about Rex.

SHARLA: What do you mean?

JOE: You know the man, right? I mean, you've met him.

SHARLA: Yeah, of course—

JOE: Tell me about him.

SHARLA: I don't know what you—

JOE: Is he tall? Is he fat? Is he Chinese? Where does he work? How old is he? Do his ears hang low? Is he unlike other men? Tell me about Rex.

SHARLA: Uh…Rex is…I don't get this, really—

JOE: Who told you about our arrangement?

SHARLA: What arrangement?

JOE: The contract made between myself and this family. Who told you about it?

SHARLA: Ansel.

JOE: Why?

ANSEL: Joe, she's my wife, you know—

JOE: I wasn't addressing you, sir.

ANSEL: Okay.

JOE: Why did he tell you?

SHARLA: Cause I'm his wife, like he said, he tells me—

JOE: Were you supposed to get a cut of this money?

SHARLA: Sure—

JOE: Why?

SHARLA: Why?

JOE: Why?

SHARLA: Cause—cause I'm his wife, like he said—

JOE: Did you advise Ansel against the idea?

SHARLA: No—

JOE: Why? You could've told him Chris would fuck it up.

SHARLA: It's none of my business—

JOE: But it is, isn't it? It is your business.

SHARLA: Look, what is this all—?

JOE: If you were going to share in the money, it is your business. Isn't it?

SHARLA: Yeah, I don't know—

JOE: Yet you didn't advise against it.

SHARLA: No. No, I didn't.

JOE: Why not?

SHARLA: I'm trying to tell you—

JOE: Why didn't you advise against it?

SHARLA: Cause I wanted some of that money, all right? I mean, if, if Chris could pull something like that off—

JOE: Were you going to split Ansel's third? Or were the four of you going to split it up evenly?

SHARLA: We didn't discuss that—

JOE: Oh, now, I'm sure you did. You're a practical woman.

SHARLA: I don't know, I assumed I would take…a fourth—
JOE: Not one-half of one-third—
SHARLA: No, one fourth, four ways—
JOE: —instead of one sixth—
ANSEL: —one-sixth—
SHARLA: No, four ways, to even—
JOE: So then the four of you would—
SHARLA: Right—
JOE: —would split the remainder of the money, after I had been paid—
SHARLA: Right—
JOE: —paid my fee of twenty-five thousand dollars—
SHARLA: Uh-huh, after you were covered—
JOE: What?
SHARLA: I say, after you were covered—
JOE: Which means, equal shares, you wanted that money, what would those four equal shares come out to, that's—
SHARLA: I haven't done the math—
JOE: Well, than, do it with me, now.
(*During the following, Joe takes a seat at the kitchen table and uses Ansel's pile of change to visualize his calculation. Sharla reluctantly joins him.*)
JOE: The insurance policy gets covered, the agent, Kilpatrick, cuts you a check, or cuts Ansel a check—
SHARLA: —Dottie, that would be—
JOE: —right, best of all possible worlds, Dottie—
SHARLA: I don't even know why we're goin' over all this, since we're not—
JOE: Please, just watch my feet here, all right—?
SHARLA: All right—
JOE: So Ansel gets the—
SHARLA: Dottie—
JOE: —Dottie—
SHARLA: If the check is for a hundred, we pay you twenty-five—
JOE: How much?
SHARLA: —twenty-five—
JOE: But how much, the policy was for—?
SHARLA: However much. (*To Ansel.*) How much?
ANSEL: Fifty-thousand.
SHARLA: That much, so fifty minus your twenty-five—
JOE: Right, minus my twenty-five, but you said a hundred, didn't you?
SHARLA: A hundred what.

JOE: You said a hundred, the check is for a hundred—

SHARLA: However much, minus your twenty-five, leaves twenty-five four ways—

JOE: But you said a hundred.

SHARLA: Yeah. However much.

ANSEL: She was mistaken. It's fifty.

JOE: Is it.

ANSEL: Yeah.

(A long silence. Joe rises from the table, turns off the television.)

ANSEL: Idn't it?

JOE: No.

ANSEL: Wait a minute…

JOE: In case of accidental death…the figures double.

SHARLA: Oh, right, Kilpatrick told us that this morning. Didn't he, Ansel?

ANSEL: Huh-uh.

SHARLA: Yeah, I think he did.

JOE: Ansel? Did he?

ANSEL: No.

SHARLA: I think he did—

ANSEL: So…it's not…fifty.

JOE: No. (To Sharla.) It's a hundred.

SHARLA: Like I say. However much.

JOE: However much.

SHARLA: Look, what are you gettin' at?

JOE: What do you mean?

SHARLA: I made a mistake, all right—?

JOE: Yes, you did—

SHARLA: —so it's fifty, or a hundred, or however much—

ANSEL: Hey, you all don't do this now—

JOE: You said you never cared for Chris—

SHARLA: —and I haven't. I don't—

JOE: —and you said Rex is an idiot—

SHARLA: uh-huh, right—

JOE: —and you said, "the check is for a hundred"—

SHARLA: —"or however much"—

JOE: —and I was just wondering—

SHARLA: —what are you gettin' at—?

(Joe reaches in his pocket and takes out the rainbow-colored packet that Sharla had at the beginning of Act I, Scene III.)

SHARLA: —oh, fuck—

(He takes the sheaf of photographs from the packet and shows one to Sharla.)

JOE: Whose dick is that?

SHARLA: Where'd you get those?

JOE: That's not Ansel's dick, I bet. (He hands one of the photographs to Ansel.) Is that your dick?

ANSEL: No.

SHARLA: Oh, hell, yes it is, darlin', you were drunk—

JOE: (Showing Ansel another photo.) How about that one?

ANSEL: No.

JOE: That one? Make sure, now. Might've been drunk.

(Ansel shakes his head.)

JOE: (Examining a photo.) So whose dick is that? Is that your little step-son's cock in your mouth?

SHARLA: Just stop it—

JOE: Or does that particular dick belong to your boyfriend?

SHARLA: Please—

JOE: To your boyfriend: Rex: "That idiot."

SHARLA: Please, now, just—

JOE: The man who's getting all that money.

SHARLA: I didn't—

JOE: All "hundred grand."

SHARLA: I said stop it—

JOE: That's a nice photo, really. You should frame that. (To Ansel.) What do you think? Look nice on the bedroom dresser?

SHARLA: I didn't know, I swear—

JOE: (To Ansel.) Were you aware of this?

ANSEL: I'm never aware—

JOE: Of course not. (To Sharla.) Whose is it?

SHARLA: You son-of-a-bitch—

(Joe grabs her by the throat with one hand.)

JOE: There's no need for name-calling. I haven't called you any names. You be polite to me. I'm a guest. Now tell me whose little dickie that is, and don't lie to me or by God it'll be the last lie you ever tell.

SHARLA: Rex. It's Rex.

JOE: Correct.

SHARLA: Ansel, please—

JOE: Oh, I don't think Ansel is too inclined to give you any assistance at this point in time. Are you, Ansel?

ANSEL: No, I'm not.

JOE: In fact, you're content to just sit there, aren't you?

ANSEL: Yes, sir.

JOE: That's what I thought.

SHARLA: Let me go, you motherfucker—

(Joe tightens his grip on her throat.)

JOE: What did I say about insulting me?

SHARLA: (Choking.) Let me go—I can't breathe—

JOE: What was that? I'm sorry, I can't quite hear you.

SHARLA: Let…me…

(Dottie emerges from the bedroom.)

DOTTIE: Joe?

JOE: Go back to bed, honey.

DOTTIE: Did you take out the trash?

JOE: No, but I will.

DOTTIE: Well, your eyes are just black as night.

JOE: All right, just go back to sleep.

DOTTIE: I can't sleep with Momma in there. (She goes back into the bedroom.)

(Joe relaxes his grip on Sharla.)

SHARLA: We'll give you the money. I swear, I'll talk to Rex and we'll give you as much of the money as you want.

JOE: I'm afraid that's impossible.

SHARLA: No, it's not—

(Ansel moves to the television.)

JOE: Rex picked up the settlement this afternoon.

SHARLA: What?

JOE: (As Ansel reaches t.v.) Don't touch that television. (Joe takes a cashier's check from his pocket.) He gave it to me before he left. (Hands check to Ansel.) "A hundred grand."

ANSEL: God amighty…

SHARLA: Where did he go?

JOE: It's worthless, of course. Made out to Rex.

ANSEL: Oh my God…

SHARLA: Where did he say he was goin'?

JOE: He was unavailable for comment. (Joe peels off his watch and pockets it as he approaches Sharla.)

SHARLA: I don't understand, why didn't you get him to—? I can…I can get him to sign it over—

(He punches her squarely in the face. She falls to her knees.)

JOE: Looks like you need a new boyfriend.

> *(She crawls away from him, toward Ansel, toward the living room. He follows, puts the toe of his boot in her ass, pushes her down.)*

JOE: I'll be your boyfriend. Just for a little while. *(Joe walks back to the kitchen, grabs another chicken leg.)*

ANSEL: *(Terrified whispers to Sharla.)* Stay down…just stay down there…

> *(Joe strides back to Sharla. Ansel shreds the check: a plead with Joe. Joe stands above Sharla, holds the chicken leg in front of his crotch.)*

JOE: Suck this.

SHARLA: Go fuck yourself—

> *(Joe reaches down, one-handed, grabs her hair, slams her head onto the floor, screams in her face.)*

JOE: You insult me again, and I'll cut your face off and wear it over my own! Do you understand?!

SHARLA: *(Crying.)* Ansel—!

> *(Ansel rockets off the couch, about to attack. Joe drops Sharla, spins to face Ansel, who quickly retreats to the kitchen sink.)*

ANSEL: Hey, you made your bed—

JOE: That's right. Now lie in it.

SHARLA: Ansel, please—

JOE: *(Grabbing her hair again.)* Are you going to insult me again?! Do you want me to wear your face?! *(Holding her head with one hand, the chicken leg in front of his crotch with the other.)* Now suck it.

> *(Shaking, crying, she hesitantly takes the end of the chicken leg in her mouth.)*

JOE: Ohhhh, yes… *(To Ansel.)* Hey. What do you think?

ANSEL: I don't.

> *(Joe bobs her head back and forth on the chicken leg.)*

JOE: Now, you listen to me, and I want you to listen very carefully, both of you. I performed a service for this family, and I deserve my payment in full. As a result of the misunderstanding regarding the insurance, I'm not going to receive any cash for my services. And that's unfair.

> I don't care to hear excuses, or the placement of blame. I hold you all equally responsible.

> Reach around and grab my ass.

> *(She does.)*

JOE: I was fortunate, however, in thinking ahead. I secured a retainer for my services. Since I fulfilled my obligation, and since my cash is not forthcoming, that retainer is now mine. It belongs to me. And I'm taking it with me when I leave.

(He bucks his hips, jams the bone further into her mouth. She is sobbing.)

JOE: You're very good at this. Please moan.

(She begins an awkward humming.)

JOE: Chris doesn't agree with the concept of the retainer. He's coming back here tonight and he's going to attempt to take it with him. I can't allow him to do that. This family can't allow him to do that.

(He's now ramming the bone into her mouth up to its hilt. He finally groans and pushes the chicken leg all the way in. She gags. He gasps, lets her go. She falls to the floor, coughs out the leg.)

JOE: Do you understand?! If this family allows Chris to leave this trailer, I'll slaughter all of you! Like pigs! Do you believe I'd do that?!

(He drops to the floor, straddling her. She screams.)

JOE: I'm asking for your help. Will you give it to me?

(She nods.)

JOE: Ansel?

ANSEL: Yes, sir.

JOE: Good. *(He traces a finger around Sharla's breasts.)* You know, you're a very beautiful woman. *(To Ansel.)* Don't you think so?

ANSEL: I haven't given it much thought—

(Joe places the point of his finger over her windpipe.)

JOE: No. Wrong answer.

ANSEL: *(Weeping.)* Yes. She is a very beautiful woman.

JOE: *(To Sharla.)* That's sweet. Don't you think so?

(She nods. He grabs her under the arms and hoists her to her feet.)

JOE: Now, get your ass in that kitchen and set the table for a proper meal. Then we'll all sit down and eat. Just the four of us. Just the family.

(She moves away slowly. He playfully whacks her on the ass; she runs to the kitchen sink and vomits. Ansel sits at the kitchen table. Joe lights a cigarette.)

JOE: How are you, guy?

ANSEL: Where'd you get them photographs?

JOE: Oh, that's hardly important.

ANSEL: I guess…

JOE: All she did was suck his cock and try to steal your money. It could've been worse.

ANSEL: How?

JOE: *(Beat.)* Well, no. I suppose that's about as bad as it gets. *(Then, privately.)* Spend time with your wife. *(Joe exits down the hallway.)*

ANSEL: Sharla…

SHARLA: Yes?

ANSEL: Are you okay?

SHARLA: Yes, Ansel, I'm fine.

ANSEL: Are you sure?

SHARLA: Yes, I'm sure.

ANSEL: Okay.

>*(He weeps. T-Bone barks.)*

ANSEL: He's home.

>*(Chris enters the trailer.)*

CHRIS: Hey there.

ANSEL: Hello, son.

CHRIS: Dottie here?

ANSEL: She's in the bedroom.

CHRIS: *(Eyeing the chicken bucket.)* Thank God, I'm starvin'. You hear from Joe?

ANSEL: He's in his bedroom.

>*(Chris picks up the chicken leg from the floor, carries it into the kitchen.)*

CHRIS: *(To Sharla.)* You eat already?

>*(Dottie comes out of the bedroom.)*

DOTTIE: Hi, Chris.

>*(Joe emerges from the bedroom.)*

JOE: JUNIOR! YOU'RE HOME!

CHRIS: Hi, Joe.

JOE: Hey, I heard about the money, and I gotta tell you, I'm all broke up things didn't work out—

CHRIS: —yeah, me too—

JOE: —but that's the way the world turns, right?

CHRIS: Huh—?

JOE: That's the way the cookie crumbles?

CHRIS: Yeah, okay—

JOE: Caveat emptor, you know what I mean?

>*(Sharla rakes change, keys, everything from the kitchen table onto the floor.)*

JOE: A place for everything. *(Extends his arm to Dottie.)* Shall we dine?

>*(She takes his arm and he ushers her to the table. Sharla sets the table with paper plates and the bucket of chicken.)*

JOE: It smells heavenly. Ansel? Chris? "K-Fry-C?"

ANSEL: I'm not hungry, really…

JOE: You should join us, though. All of us.

>*(The family gathers at the table and takes their seats. Sharla continues setting the table with paper towels and plastic silverware.)*

JOE: Come on, Sharla, take your seat.

(She does.)

JOE: Let me see if I can't scare us up some music. *(He turns on the radio, finds music. Stands back, observes the family at the table.)* This is lovely. *(Takes his seat.)* Who would like to say grace?

(No response.)

JOE: Dottie? Will you do the honors?

(The family clasps their hands, lowers their heads. They do not close their eyes.)

DOTTIE: Dear Jesus: Thank you for the food. Thank you that we're all here, together, and safe. We're sorry Momma's dead. We hope you'll give her a place to stay in Heaven. Please forgive us for anything we did wrong. We would all like a place to stay in Heaven, too. In the Lord's name which is Jesus Christ, we say, "Amen."

JOE: Amen. *(To Dottie, privately.)* That was beautiful.

DOTTIE: Thank you.

JOE: *(To all.)* Let's eat. Sharla, we need some drinks, please.

(They eat. Sharla gets plastic cups, a plastic pitcher of iced tea, a case of beer from the fridge, a carton of non-dairy creamer. The others pass chicken, mashed potatoes, coleslaw. Joe directs the action, asking for iced tea, passing the food around, commenting on the meal, directing Sharla to finally sit and eat. The others respond as they are addressed—although Sharla is silent. Finally, Joe taps his iced tea cup with a plastic "spork," stands, and extends his cup.)

JOE: I have an announcement to make: You've all probably noticed by now that Dottie and I have been spending an awful lot of time together. The fact is: we've fallen in love. So it's my privilege to tell you that I've asked her to be my bride. And she has accepted. Isn't that true, dear?

DOTTIE: Yes.

(Silence.)

ANSEL: Well, I, for one, am very happy for—

CHRIS: Shut up.

JOE: A toast: to my future wife.

(Joe drinks. All but Chris follow suit.)

CHRIS: When's all this supposed to take place?

JOE: *(Taking his seat.)* We're leaving after this delicious meal.

CHRIS: *(To Dottie.)* Is that right?

DOTTIE: Yes.

CHRIS: You can't have my sister, Joe.

JOE: What do you mean?

CHRIS: I mean I can't let that happen. You're not going to marry my sister. You
    can't have her.
ANSEL: Now, Chris, I don't think it's up to you—
CHRIS: Shut up.
ANSEL: Don't tell me to shut up—
CHRIS: Say another word, old man, and I'll rip your head off your shoulders.
JOE: Chris, I can certainly appreciate your love for your sister, but you have
    to cut the old apron strings sometimes—
CHRIS: I'm not gonna discuss it. She's my sister. I'm takin' her with me. We're
    leavin' here.
JOE: Maybe we should let Dottie decide—
CHRIS: Dottie doesn't have a say in the matter.
JOE: I believe she does—
CHRIS: You believe wrong. Dottie, go get your stuff.
JOE: *(To Dottie.)* Stay seated.
CHRIS: Dottie?
JOE: Dottie.
    (She stands.)
JOE: Take your seat, Dottie.
CHRIS: Go get your stuff.
JOE: Take your seat.
CHRIS: Dottie?
    (She walks toward the bedroom.)
JOE: Dottie.
CHRIS: Go on, Dottie—
JOE: Stop—
CHRIS: Dottie, go get your stuff, now—
JOE: Dottie.
CHRIS: That a girl—
    (She reaches the hallway.)
JOE: *DOTTIE!!!*
    (She stops in the doorway.)
JOE: She's my retainer.
CHRIS: The deal's off.
JOE: No, it's not.
CHRIS: It didn't work out. You're gonna have to eat this one.
JOE: You know…you know I'll kill you.
CHRIS: Go fuck yourself.
    (Silence. Joe drops his napkin on his plate, slowly stands up from the table.

Chris raises his hand from beneath the table. He is holding a .45. Ansel and Sharla jump from the table, back into the kitchen. He cocks the gun, steadies it with his left hand, keeps it aimed at Joe's head.)

CHRIS: Take your seat, Joe.

(Joe slowly sits down as Chris rises and backs around the table.)

CHRIS: Get your stuff, Dot—

(Sharla grabs a knife from the kitchen counter, screams, buries it in Chris's upper chest, near his shoulder. The knife handle snaps off in her hand. Chris reels, shocked. The gun fires, striking the floor. Joe flips the table over, charges Chris, buries his shoulder in Chris's stomach, and drives him into the wall. The gun flips out of Chris's hand into the living room. Dottie picks it up.)

DOTTIE: Stop it!

JOE: *YOU'RE DEAD, MOTHERFUCKER! YOU'RE DEAD!*

(Joe grabs the lamp cord, wraps it around Chris's neck, and heaves. Choked, dazed, Chris flies into a kind of seizure, doing anything he can to get free.)

DOTTIE: Stop it, Joe! Stop it!

JOE: *DEAD! DEAD! DEAD!*

DOTTIE: STOP IT!

JOE: ANSEL, GRAB HIS LEGS!

(Ansel falls on Chris's kicking legs, holds them tight under his arm. Chris looks in horror at his father as the three men writhe toward the living room.)

ANSEL:	DOTTIE:
I GOT HIM, JOE—!	STOP IT, DADDY—!

(Sharla grabs a potato peeler from the sink and charges at Chris, who tries to twist his body out of the path of the blade. She sticks the potato peeler blade in his side, one, two, three times. Chris flails, kicks off Ansel. Joe flings him around the room by the cord, smashing him into cabinets, counter, table, television, refrigerator.)

JOE: *DIE, MOTHERFUCKER, DIE!*

DOTTIE: *(Shrieking, hysterical.)* STOP IT, STOP IT, GOD!

ANSEL: HOLD HIM STILL, GODDAMN IT!

(Chris backs up suddenly, smashing Joe against the wall. Joe loosens his grip momentarily and Chris elbows him sharply in the ribs. Joe gasps, lets go of the cord, falls to the floor. Chris approaches Dottie, his hand out.)

CHRIS: Dottie, the gun—

(Ansel grabs Chris from behind, picks him up, squeezes him, throws him into the kitchen. Sharla smashes a beer bottle over Chris's head. Ansel shoves him into the refrigerator, holding him down.)

DOTTIE: GOD, STOP IT, PLEASE, STOP IT!

(Chris flails inside the refrigerator. Shelves, beers tumble out of the fridge.)

ANSEL: JOE, KILL HIM! I GOT HIM!

(Chris tries to struggle out of the refrigerator, but Joe is suddenly there, beating hell out of Chris.)

ANSEL: SHARLA, GRAB HIM—!

JOE: *GODDAMN YOU, DIE!*

(Sharla jumps on Chris's feet, pins them to the floor. Ansel holds Chris down while Joe continues beating on him.)

ANSEL: DO IT, JOE, KILL HIM!

SHARLA: KILL HIM! KILL HIM!

DOTTIE: I'M GETTING ANGRY!

JOE: *DIE, DIE, DIE!*

(Dottie fires the gun, striking the radio. Joe, Ansel, and Sharla immediately roll out of the way and look at Dottie. Chris pulls himself out of the refrigerator and looks at her also. She points the gun at him.)

CHRIS: Dottie?

(She fires, strikes him squarely in the chest, rockets him back into the refrigerator. Sharla screams.)

ANSEL: Jesus—

(Dottie pivots, shoots Ansel in the stomach. He falls to his knees, clutching the hole in his stomach. Blood spills from his mouth. Sharla screams again.)

ANSEL: Oh, my Christ, honey…

SHARLA: *(Hysterical.)* DON'T KILL ME, DOTTIE! *(Sharla scrambles behind Ansel, wraps her arms around him.)*

SHARLA: PLEASE DON'T LET HER KILL ME!

(Joe starts toward Dottie. She pivots, points the gun at his head.)

JOE: Now, Dottie…just take it easy.

(He advances. She aims carefully.)

JOE: Hold on, now. Be safe.

(He advances. She cocks the gun.)

JOE: Oh, God…

(She tenses, squeezing the trigger slightly.)

DOTTIE: I'm gonna have a baby.

(Joe looks at her, uncertain.)

JOE: A baby? *(Beat.)* A baby? *(He smiles broadly, proudly.)* A baby!

(Ansel holding his stomach, Sharla crying behind him, Joe smiling, Dottie with her finger tensed on the trigger, Chris dead in the refrigerator.)

(Blackout.)

END OF PLAY

THE ONE-EYED MAN IS KING
by Carter W. Lewis

THE AUTHOR

Carter W. Lewis is currently working as Literary Manager and Playwright-in-Residence at Geva Theatre. Prior to moving to New York he was co-founder and Literary Manager for the new play development theatre, Upstart Stage, in Berkeley, CA. He is the winner of several national playwriting awards including: The Live Oak Theatre Best New American Play Award (1993), A Delaware Center Theatre's Connections Award (1994), A Beverly Hills Theater Guild/Julie Harris Playwriting Award (1994), The Lois and Richard Rosenthal New Play Prize (1995), The New Dramatist L. Arnold Weissberger Award (1996), and most recently The Mildred and Albert Panowski New Play Award and The Charlotte Repertory Theatre New Play Prize (1998). He was awarded a playwriting residency at the Playwrights' Center in Minneapolis where his play, *An Asian Jockey In Our Midst,* was selected for the 1995 Playlabs Conference. *Asian Jockey* had its world premiere at the Cincinnati Playhouse In The Park in January of '96 and went on to subsequent productions at The Live Oak Theater (TX), The Round House Theatre (MD) and Oakland Ensemble Theatre (CA). His award winning play, *Golf With Alan Shepard,* has been produced at The New Conservatory Theatre (CA), The Sacramento Theatre Company, The Berkshire Theatre Festival (MA), The Pope Theatre (FL), Syracuse Stage, Geva Theatre (NY), Studio Arena Theatre, Dorset Theatre Festival, The Barter Theatre, and The Phoenix Theatre and has upcoming productions at The Barksdale Theater, Western Stage, Playhouse on the Square, The Watertown Theatre and The Virginia Stage. Carter's play *Soft Click Of A Switch* was workshopped at ASK Theatre Projects (LA), New Dramatist (NYC), and The Royal Court Theatre (London) before premiering at The Northwest Actors Theatre in Seattle and The Source Theatre in Washington DC. *Soft Click Of A Switch* was recently published by Samuel French. His new play *The One-Eyed Man Is King* received it's world premiere at Geva Theatre (1998), with subsequent productions at The Forest Roberts Theatre and The Fulton Opera House. He is currently working on two commissions: one for ASK Theatre Projects in Los Angeles entitled *Longevity Abbreviated For Those Who Don't Have Time;* and one for Otterbein Theatre in Ohio (untitled).

The developmental journey of *The One-Eyed Man Is King* began with the discovery of a wonderful and passionate short story by H.G. Wells. I had been compiling notes for a play centered around the character of a blind thief, when I stumbled across an out of print collection of Mr. Wells' short stories. As I leafed through the collection, I was intrigued by a story entitled, "The Country of the Blind." I read it from beginning to end, standing amongst stacks of antique volumes in a used-book store in Berkeley, California. It was the idea of "inversion of normalcy" that drew me to write about a blind thief, and it was that same sense of inversion that I found so captivating about the Well's short story. In the play, "The Country of the Blind" is loosely adapted and re-told by the character of Ludviccio; consequently, the play will forever be indebted to the great H.G. Wells.

H.G. Wells was only the first of many collaborations that brought the play into being. Great leaping *thank you's* are in order for Artistic Director Mark Cuddy, New Plays Coordinator Jean Gordon Ryon, and the entire staff at Geva Theatre for their continued support of this play during my years as Playwright-In-Residence. And thank you to friends and artists, whose love and wisdom kept me in motion on the play: Andrew Traister, Karen Radcliffe, Shelley Russell, and all the folks at the Tantleff Office. And a thank you to those blind collaborators who taught me so much about the play, and who shared a reality of their world that holds true in all worlds: "When we stop moving or speaking, we cease to exist."

The One-Eyed Man Is King was originally developed and produced at Geva Theatre in Rochester, New York. Artistic Director, Mark Cuddy, New Plays Coordinator, Jean Ryon.

Geva Theatre Workshop, February, 1997:

Lise . . . . .Karen Radcliffe*
Bendalli . . . . .Jonathan Putnam*
Elliot . . . . .Christine Murphy
Ludviccio . . . . .Sam Gray*

Geva Theatre World Premiere, September, 1998:

Lise . . . . Julie Eccles*
Bendalli. . . . . Steven Memran*
Elliot. . . . . Careena Melia*
Ludviccio. . . . . Jim Mohr*

Director . . . . Andrew Traister
Set Design . . . . Rosario Provenza
Costume Design. . . . . Clare Henkel
Lighting Designer . . . . F. Mitchell Dana
Sound Design . . . . Dan Roach
Stage Manager. . . . . Frank Cavallo

*Actors Equity Association

The One-Eyed Man Is King was the winner of the 1998 Charlotte Festival—New Play in America Series and was workshopped by the Charlotte Repertory Theatre.

The One-Eyed Man Is King was the winner of the Mildred and Albert Panowski Playwriting Award, James A. Panowski, Director.

CHARACTERS

LISE: a woman, late thirties
BENDALLI: a thief, blind, thirties
ELLIOT: Lise's stepdaughter, teens
LUDVICCIO: old Italian immigrant, boisterous, peasant class

SETTING

The living area of a house in upstate New York. Tall cathedral ceilings; rich oak bookshelves with hardcover volumes dignify the room from floor to ceiling. Light-colored glistening hardwood floors with antiques floating on Persian rugs. Stretching exotic plants, abstract sculptures and contemporary artwork inform us that young wealth has invaded old tradition.

It is important that *The Country of the Blind* is somehow represented during the storytelling portions of the play. In the premiere this was handled with a light box that brought up a mountainscape above and around the set, the story itself being underscored with distant flute. It is also a good idea that Ludviccio is amplified as he speaks so that the story "told" envelops the story on-stage. During the present day portions of the play, the light box appeared to be a curved atrium skylight above the walls of the room.

The two worlds are storytelling worlds, and should appear so. The worlds of two fables colliding.

NOTE

The description of the room, given by Bendalli in the first scene, may be altered to accommodate the scenic designer, but should not be compromised in its statement of wealth and elegance.

The story told by Ludviccio is loosely based on the H.G. Wells story, *The Country of the Blind.*

ACT I

Of light and darkness: music. A lone spot comes up on Ludviccio. Although he speaks toward the audience, he is speaking to Bendalli, silhouetted in half light on another part of the stage.

LUDVICCIO: Please, listen to me. There are no clear stars shining out of the darkness for you. There are no mountains, no azure sky. There is no lost valley of wonder. You are not a child anymore, it is time to stop this.

BENDALLI: Tell it.

LUDVICCIO: No. Never again.

BENDALLI: Why?

LUDVICCIO: Because the story has become a sad story for you. You are not a boy anymore, you've grown, you've changed. The story does not change. And this saddens you.

BENDALLI: TELL IT!

LUDVICCIO: It is not your story.

BENDALLI: YOU TOLD ME IT WAS.

LUDVICCIO: You were a child then. Now you must make a new story. You're own story.

BENDALLI: No.

LUDVICCIO: Bendalli.

BENDALLI: NO!

LUDVICCIO: This is not good for us. You get worse and worse. It has all become too dangerous.

BENDALLI: The Country of the Blind, tell me about the Country of the Blind.

LUDVICCIO: I cannot.

BENDALLI: Tell me!

LUDVICCIO: NO!

(Bendalli disappears into the darkness.)

LUDVICCIO: Bendalli? Where are you going? Bendalli, you stay home tonight, it is too dangerous. You will get caught again. You will get hurt! Bendalli! *(Loud sound of glass breaking. Music change. A wealthy household in upstate New York. The room is dark. Only light from the hall and night through a window illuminate Lise, standing in the archway—a quiescent silhouette in a translucent nightgown. At the end of her arm is the end of a drink. She stares into the room. High above her, clinging to the bookshelves, is Bendalli. She does not see him, we do not see him. Dark on dark, lost in the shadows.*

Lise drains her drink. The glass hangs loose, she lets it drop. She enters and slowly begins to re-arrange furniture. An urgency takes over. She puts the furniture in absurd positions. Throwing pillows, objects. Grunting. Breathing. Crying.)

LISE: Move. There. There. Move. MOVE. AH! CHANGE!
(She slumps to the floor, exhausted, sobbing. Pause. Then…from the darkness.)

BENDALLI: Put it back.

LISE: Wha? Hello?

BENDALLI: Change it back.

LISE: Who's there? Who's in here?! *(She turns on the light, a chandelier? The room is illuminated, but Bendalli is still shadowed.)* Where are you? My husband's right upstairs.

BENDALLI: Please!

LISE: *(She sees Bendalli. He is up high, above her. The lights should gently bring him into our focus, as if our eyes were adjusting.)* Who? What the hell are you doing up there? *(Grabs for something ridiculous, a sculpture of a pig, or…?)* I know how to use this!

BENDALLI: I didn't mean to scare you.

LISE: *(A lie.)* I'm not scared.

BENDALLI: I won't hurt you.

LISE: There's an alarm system, the police are probably on their way right now. My husband has…many guns.

BENDALLI: There are no guns.

LISE: Dogs, I meant dogs.

BENDALLI: I didn't notice dogs either.

LISE: They're…in the hall. Stay, Seabiscuit, stay!

BENDALLI: That's a horse's name.

LISE: He's a very large dog. What are you doing up there?

BENDALLI: Stealing, I steal things.

LISE: Those are books. You steal books?

BENDALLI: I'm not a reader. I heard you coming, I climbed up.

LISE: If I wake my husband, he'll kill you. He'll…

BENDALLI: Please, no, let's be reasonable.

LISE: I live here, I don't have to be reasonable!

BENDALLI: Philosophical then.

LISE: How lovely, I'm being robbed by Socrates.

BENDALLI: We can dignify our situation with a little perspective.

LISE: Ok, I'll dignify our situation. I am here and you're not, or shouldn't be,

here…or…or there or anywhere near here. Or up there. Therefore I
am…a little drunk.

BENDALLI: Scotch. Lagavulin. I can smell it.

LISE: Stinking drunk then. Thank you for dignifying my situation.

BENDALLI: You spilled it. Two ice cubes. You should be more careful, the glass
is crystal.

LISE: You can't have the crystal.

BENDALLI: I wasn't…

LISE: *(She grabs the glass.)* They're my wedding glasses. My husband and I
drank White Star in a thunderstorm on the beach of the Hotel Del
Coronado. I was still in white, and there were stars you see. Have you
ever been to the Hotel Del Coronado? Perhaps, stolen something from
the Hotel Del Coronado? We stole these. As a professional, you should
respect that.

BENDALLI: I don't want the crystal.

LISE: What do you want?

BENDALLI: Could you change it all back?

LISE: What?

BENDALLI: Could you put the room back in order?

LISE: You don't like it? I call it Still Life With Drunk Rich Lady.

BENDALLI: I'm sure it's very nice.

LISE: You're a bit particular for a thief.

BENDALLI: I'm blind.

LISE: *(Beat.)* You're what?

BENDALLI: Blind. I don't know what's below me.

LISE: Blind? But how did you…? *(Beat. Lise bursts out laughing.)* Oh, God,
that's splendid. A blind thief. *(Continues laughing, picks up her glass,
crosses to the cabinet.)*

BENDALLI: It's all right to laugh. It is funny. A blind man clinging desperately
to your bookshelves. I could take my chances and just drop, but I could
get hurt—and you have some very valuable things here. Irreplaceable by
what I could tell from a cursory fondling.

(A renewed burst of laughter.)

BENDALLI: What?

LISE: *(Uncontrollable. Pointing at him.)* "I'm not a reader!" You said… *(She
goes off. Stumbles to the chair, with a new drink, sits.)* Interesting career
choice. The blind thief. *(To herself.)* "But what I really wanted to be was
an art critic."

BENDALLI: I can't stay up here forever.

LISE: Why not? Chaucer has. Alfred Lord Tennyson has. Stay put, every few
    years we'll stiffen your binder.
BENDALLI: Just tell me what's below me.
LISE: *(Peers up.)* Vonnegut. *(Beat.)* God I hate Vonnegut. But you've got to
    keep him, don't you, it's like saving your prom corsage.
    (Bendalli drops a book.)
LISE: *(Jumps.)* What was that?
BENDALLI: It didn't hit anything. Is it clear below?
LISE: No.
BENDALLI: What's down there!?
LISE: My husband's javelin collection.
BENDALLI: You're lying.
LISE: Go on, call up and ask him, his name's Vlad.
    (Spider-like, Bendalli quickly climbs higher and across.)
LISE: What are you doing?
BENDALLI: Moving toward the arch. My guess is you didn't put anything in
    the entry way.
LISE: You're making me dizzy.
BENDALLI: You wouldn't block the arch, you're not stupid.
LISE: Stay where you are!
    (He stops.)
LISE: What do you know about what I'd do? And it's rude to underestimate
    the stupidity of your host.
BENDALLI: *(He drops another book.)* There's nothing there.
LISE: Hardly an unusual conclusion from a blind man. *(Beat.)* How did you
    know there was an arch?
BENDALLI: You came in.
LISE: It could have been a door.
BENDALLI: Hinges and knobs, I hear them.
LISE: You've been here before. To…case the joint. Is that the proper bur-
    glarese? Or for the blind it's more… *(She demonstrates with her hands.)*
    …get the feel of the joint.
    (He drops another book.)
LISE: Still looking for a drop spot?
BENDALLI: That was more to annoy you.
LISE: Ah, now we're getting along.
BENDALLI: You seem to be enjoying this.
LISE: Other than doctors and lawyers, there's been no one here in years. I
    should feel violated, but deep down, I think you've actually perked the

old place up. It's all so mysterious and sexy. So tell me, have you been running your fingers over my life, touching my fabric, fondling my bric-a-brac?

BENDALLI: I know the room.

LISE: Knew. You knew the room. It's different now. And it was a trick question. I'm rich. I don't have bric-a-brac, I have art.

BENDALLI: Matisse stencil prints, and Wicker Warhol in the atrium. Stippled and gilded Tuscan columns with Doric entablature by the arch. Desk lamp, Donghia. Desk chair, Jack Lenor Larsen. Desk, Florian Papp. The far wall has a display of 1930's tractor seats interspersed with African masks, which to the blind touch is like discovering a tiara on a hotel maid. A pair of carved marble sphinxes on plinths, a seventeenth century gold leafed mirror, an art deco side table with a nineteenth century bronze monkey and in the corner, what I assume is a Segal of a woman sitting in a chair. Approximately eight-hundred books, a great many of them read. One family picture, no albums. Taffeta draperies, brass holdings, Pollack splatter above the mantel and you have mice, actually just one, it lives behind the sideboard.

LISE: What's his name?

BENDALLI: It's a she.

LISE: Being blind, I shudder to think how you determined that.

BENDALLI: Why were you crying?

LISE: Perhaps seeing's not all it's cracked up to be, Mr…?

BENDALLI: Nunez. Call me Nunez.

LISE: But it's not your real name.

BENDALLI: Your husband won't be coming to your rescue, is that it?

LISE: If you know the sex of my mice, surely you know that he won't. Is that why you chose me?

BENDALLI: You don't have dogs.

LISE: You're frightened of dogs?

BENDALLI: They move around. I choose environments based on their reliability. And you drink.

LISE: That comes under reliability. How often have you come?

BENDALLI: Every night this week, three nights last week.

LISE: *(Surprised.)* Well, I should put out cookies like we do with Santa. *(Beat.)* Have you seen me before?

BENDALLI: I'm blind, remember?

LISE: You know what I mean. Have we, crossed paths before?

BENDALLI: Once you came out of the bathroom, I was in the hall.

LISE: The bathroom…Oh, dear…was I…?

BENDALLI: A blind Peeping Tom is beyond even my comprehension.

LISE: Yes, I suppose if I was stark naked you wouldn't know.

BENDALLI: I didn't say that.

LISE: *(She closes her nightgown.)* Well, I haven't noticed anything missing.

BENDALLI: I haven't taken anything.

LISE: But you will?

BENDALLI: Perhaps you've failed to notice a subtle change in our situation.

LISE: Yes, it's no longer about breaking in, it's about breaking out. It's about leaving. *(Pause. She strolls, thinking.)* Do you hurt people…Mr. Nunez?

BENDALLI: No, not in the way I think you mean.

LISE: Is there something you want other than my…things? Some sociopathic satisfaction or agenda fulfilled perhaps?

BENDALLI: We all have reasons for what we do.

LISE: Is what you do, something you do FOR yourself…or TO others. Should I be afraid of you?

BENDALLI: No.

LISE: I think you should proceed as planned then.

BENDALLI: Excuse me?

LISE: You're obviously an intelligent man. You're not the type who robs convenience stores or stuffs burritos down his trousers at the local grocery. And I have to assume it's not the money, but the necessity. The personal necessity; there are easier things for a blind man to do.

BENDALLI: Am I to understand…

LISE: What you see before you is still life. A world whose parameters are grand but fixed. A waiting room with no entrances, exits or expectations. You can enter my house, but you can't see me, see who I am. But I can see you, there, hanging above me, trying desperately to define yourself, your situation. I can affect your world, but you can have no effect on mine. So who's intruding on whom?

BENDALLI: You didn't break into my world, I broke into yours.

LISE: An odd claim from a man trapped on my periphery. You're not successfully "in" until I put the furniture back, now are you?

BENDALLI: I refuse to function in an environment that accommodates me!

LISE: If I just move the one chair…

BENDALLI: *(Overlap.)* I don't need any help!

LISE: Fine. All right then, if I see you take anything, I'll have you arrested, how's that? And I'll call the police after you've gone. *(Beat.)* You'll come back then?

(No response. Finishes her drink.)

LISE: Mr. Nunez. I'm going to bed. Take what you want, when you want. There are no javelins. The crystal is mine, please. If you drop straight down, you'll be quite safe. *(Stops.)* One more thing. In the darkness, does anything change? Or is it always the same, no shading, no difference, day to day, year to year?

BENDALLI: Sometimes the darkness moves, sometimes it breathes and whispers as if someone else is there, but no one is. Someday there will be, and that will be change.

(She turns out the lights, exits. Daylight. The room is still in disarray. Lise has a cup of coffee and is staring out the window. A moment. Door slam. Elliot runs in the arch. She stops.)

ELLIOT: Wow. What happened?

LISE: We had a break-in.

ELLIOT: Cool.

LISE: Yes, very exciting.

ELLIOT: Did they get anything of mine?

LISE: Yes, dear, he went straight past the Pollack and the Chagall right to your collection of ceramic doorknobs.

ELLIOT: What have I told you about sarcasm?

LISE: That it's only myself I'm deceiving?

ELLIOT: No, that was lying.

LISE: It takes one to know one?

ELLIOT: That was name-calling.

LISE: Please, it's too early, don't be a little snot.

ELLIOT: Ok, that was name-calling. If you had said, "Don't be such a little angel," that would be sarcasm. If you'd said "Good morning, Elliot, how nice to see you," that would be a lie.

LISE: It is good to see you.

ELLIOT: Is that why you send me away?

LISE: I don't send you away.

ELLIOT: That's right, you hired a shrink to do it for you.

LISE: You're right next door. And how are the Wentworths?

ELLIOT: Happier stick figures were never drawn.

LISE: You should be grateful for a healthy environment.

ELLIOT: Unhunh. This morning Mrs. Wentworth told me she was going to stop taking her Prozac because the buzz from the refrigerator was keeping her perfectly calm.

LISE: They don't have children of their own.

ELLIOT: Of course they don't, that would require sex.

LISE: Dr. Reasoner wants you to fraternize with the living.

ELLIOT: Then maybe we should try going out, go to a restaurant or a movie.

LISE: I think that would be good for you.

ELLIOT: I meant together.

LISE: I'm too tired to go out.

ELLIOT: We could invite friends over then.

LISE: And who might these friends be?

ELLIOT: Then just me, I could spend the night and—

LISE: *(Overlap.)* Dr. Reasoner thinks.

ELLIOT: *(Overlap.)* —Ok, fine, never mind. Did you call the police?

LISE: They just left.

ELLIOT: And?

LISE: They said they'd double up on patrols for a week.

ELLIOT: *(She picks up a couple books.)* Why would he throw books?

LISE: He's not a reader.

ELLIOT: I don't see anything missing. There's so much expensive stuff here, what is he, blind?

LISE: Wouldn't that be amusing.

ELLIOT: Did he wake you up?

LISE: No.

ELLIOT: Did he wake Dad up?

LISE: He was a burglar, not a magician.

ELLIOT: Dad wakes up. Last week he looked straight at me and said, "Janie, take the candle out of your mouth." Janie's his younger sister.

LISE: Yes, I'm family, remember?

ELLIOT: Janie used to suck on candles and skin the wax off with her teeth. Dad says that's what scared away all her boyfriends.

LISE: Did he say anything else?

ELLIOT: Just some druggy-headed stuff. "Bobo, get the bonzo, Bobo, come, Bobo go." Bobo was…

LISE: *(Snapping, rattles off.)* His dog. Yes, I know. Bobo slept at the foot of Adrian's bed until he was nineteen when a UPS truck accidentally backed over him. Bobo, not your father. I loved your father—

ELLIOT: *(Overlap.)* Did you?

LISE: *(Overlap.)* —he was a part of my life.

ELLIOT: Was?

LISE: Is, am, whatever. Please.

ELLIOT: Have you been up yet?

LISE: Not yet.

ELLIOT: I'm gonna go say hi. You wanna come?

LISE: I'll go up later.

ELLIOT: He said something else.

LISE: What was that?

ELLIOT: Something goofy, like…"Seal bark…that seals it."

LISE: What? He said that?

ELLIOT: Yeah. Does it mean something? Lise?

LISE: *(Distracted, a lie.)* I…I don't know. You probably misheard him.

ELLIOT: No. Cause he kept saying it over and over. "A seal barked…that seals it." Is that like a joke or something?

LISE: Sometimes I don't think he's there at all, then all of a sudden, I know exactly where he is.

ELLIOT: Does it mean something?

LISE: It was a long time ago.

ELLIOT: *(Annoyed, starts out.)* Great. Then I'll just have to ask him.

LISE: No. When you're sick, you just say things. He probably doesn't remember, he…

ELLIOT: Then I'll help him remember.

LISE: I DON'T WANT YOU BADGERING HIM WITH SILLY QUESTIONS!

ELLIOT: *(Angry.)* Fine.

LISE: Elliot. I'm sorry, I'm…I'm not myself today.

ELLIOT: Oh, that's cool. "I'm not myself today." The carte blanche every self pitying bitch needs. Did I say that? Sorry, I'm not myself today.

LISE: I was apologizing.

ELLIOT: Okay then, me too.

 (Stalemate.)

LISE: Maybe you could help me put the furniture back in order.

ELLIOT: All right.

LISE: But I want it the way it was. Okay? I want everything exactly the way it was.

 (The lights dim, half light, as they move the furniture back to it's original position. A light isolates Ludviccio. He holds a large book.)

LUDVICCIO: You no write in the journal. Every night you are supposed to write in the journal! You no sleep in your bed! Where are you? Are you in the shadows? Hiding like when you were a boy? "I'm invisible, Poppa. Who is the blind one now, Poppa?" Are you there? All right, Bendalli, you listen. I will tell it! The Country of the Blind, yes. Are you there?

(He crosses down, begins. Music.)

LUDVICCIO: Three hundred miles and more from the great Seas of Perception, miles below the snow blind crests of the Visionary Mountains, nestled along the wildest tributary of the river Perspective, there lies a mysterious valley, cut off from all the world, called, The Country of the Blind. *(Music softens, In the half light. A chair.)*

LISE: It wasn't there.

ELLIOT: It was.

LISE: No. I'm sure it was further right.

ELLIOT: I can't see any difference.

LISE: There's a difference. It needs to be exactly the same. Exactly.

ELLIOT: Aunt Janie says people who rearrange furniture too often are sexually inactive.

(Music restores.)

LUDVICCIO: The Country of the Blind was a land whose beauty could only be imagined by its inhabitants, because you see, one thing marred the country's perfection. A strange disease had come upon all who lived there and had made the people of the valley, and all the children born to them, blind.

(Lise looks out window, exits.)

LUDVICCIO: As generation followed generation, the very concept of sight was lost forever and the darkness was embraced by all. AND THEN…Are you listening, Bendalli, it is your favorite part. AND THEN something wonderous and strange happened. It chanced that a man, an explorer from beyond the mountains, stumbled into this valley.

(Bendalli appears in the arch.)

LUDVICCIO: His name was Nunez. This is the story of that man.

(The light goes out on Ludviccio. Moonlight. Bendalli enters. His movement is smooth, but measured. His feet check where the carpet ends, where the wood floor begins. He checks the bulbs of lamps for heat. He uses his body to measure. He touches an object and uses it to pivot towards another, pivot to pivot, piece to piece. As he moves into the room, his hip nudges the chair that Lise and Elliot struggled with. He adjusts it.)

BENDALLI: You did your best. *(He approaches an area of the room that he's unfamiliar with. He starts to feel the area from the ground up. A table. An object. A picture frame. Touches it, concludes, puts it down. Another object. A flat glass sculpture of a face. Confused.)* Cutting board, cheese plate. No. Ashtray. No. (Laughs.) Art. *(He moves to a standing abstract sculpture of a* man. *To himself.*) Sorry, being a bit personal here. Not a Hargrave, not a Toscan. No signature, no symbol, no technique. Must be local.

LISE: *(Steps out from behind the curtain by the window. Abrupt, loud.)* IT'S A SCARBONI.

(Bendalli jumps, falls over a piece of furniture, hits his head.)

LISE: Are you all right?

(Nothing.)

LISE: Mr. Nunez? Mr. Nunez? *(She tentatively crosses to him.)*

BENDALLI: I'm all right.

LISE: Are you sure?

BENDALLI: I'm… *(Rising, stops, softly.)* …oh, God.

LISE: What?

BENDALLI: Wait. *(Beat.)* Incredible.

LISE: What is it?

BENDALLI: Good God in heaven. I think.

LISE: Mr. Nunez?

BENDALLI: I'm getting images…I can see images.

LISE: You mean…?

BENDALLI: Yes. *(Focusing.)* Are there reds and greens in the rug?

LISE: Yes.

BENDALLI: And plants…flowering ivy there…along the sideboard.

LISE: Yes! The Nasturtium.

BENDALLI: You're standing by the window.

LISE: Yes. Can you see me moving?

BENDALLI: I CAN see movement, wind fluttering curtains. A dark outline, you watching me.

LISE: This is so exciting, yes, I'm by the window!

BENDALLI: There by the window, watching me. Fascinated by me. I can even see the twinkle of ownership in your eyes. Wait! Something else. I can see the future too! I see great crowds gathering, come one, come all, and I see you in the middle. In the middle of it all, telling the neighbors the circus has come to town, this little blind clown who wants to be a thief! *(Flat.)* Yes-oh-God-oh-God-I-can-see.

(Beat.)

LISE: Ah. Then you're still.

BENDALLI: As—a—bat. A blow to the head only cures the blind in cartoons.

LISE: That was mean.

BENDALLI: I once described the contents of a dentist's office so accurately, the dentist was convinced he'd cured me during a periodontal exam.

LISE: You should learn to use your gift with less cruelty.

BENDALLI: It's a cruel gift. God gave me a photographic memory, but no camera.

LISE: Do you mind if I turn on some light?

(Bendalli "looks" at her. Lise remains a bit afraid.)

LISE: Of course. Sorry. I'm not used to.

BENDALLI: The optically challenged?

LISE: Company. *(She turns on the chandelier.)* Would you like a drink?

BENDALLI: I'm not a drinker.

LISE: Are you hungry?

BENDALLI: I'm not much of an eater either.

LISE: Not a drinker, not an eater, and definitely not the circus I was hoping for. What am I to think of you, Mr. Nunez?

BENDALLI: Think of me as the potential loss of everything you own.

LISE: I've caught you twice, Mr. Nunez and I'm hardly Hercule Poirot.

BENDALLI: I don't consider this being caught.

LISE: I could shoot you now and no one would bat an eye.

BENDALLI: You don't own a gun.

LISE: What makes you think that?

BENDALLI: I suspect you are someone who fears her own potential for rash decisions.

LISE: Is this legendary blind insight or just testimony that you've ransacked my sock drawer. *(She begins to hand him a glass, but she is still afraid. She sets it on the coffee table.)* Here. I made you a gin and tonic. You don't have to drink it, just clink the cubes a bit, so it feels like a party.

(Bendalli doesn't touch it. She backs off, maintains a distance.)

BENDALLI: What is it you want?

LISE: A blind thief. Have you always been blind?

BENDALLI: No, I was born deaf, I found it tedious, so I switched.

LISE: I suppose I deserved that.

BENDALLI: Why did you want me to come back?

LISE: As you accused, the novelty of it all.

BENDALLI: The risk suggests it's more than that.

LISE: I will admit, I was a bit more comfortable with you trapped on the bookshelf and myself *(Refers to drink.)* …the blinder of the two, but here we are. So, do you get caught a lot?

BENDALLI: Once.

LISE: A homeowner?

BENDALLI: A Bassett Hound.

LISE: He barked?

BENDALLI: He lay down in an area I had already translated. I tripped over him. My head hit the edge of a Sicilian armoire. When I woke up, two officers and a family of six were watching the dog eat my belt.

LISE: Did you go to prison?

BENDALLI: Fourteen months sentence. Out in seven.

LISE: Good behavior?

BENDALLI: Pity is a blind man's perk. I liked prison. A large block of time to concentrate on a very small area.

LISE: To translate it?

BENDALLI: You've been paying attention.

LISE: What does that mean? Translate?

BENDALLI: Seeing is a language. A visual language. I have to translate my surroundings into a language that I understand. I can't see, but I can hear, touch, taste…sense.

LISE: Sense?

BENDALLI: Intuition is a derivative language. A form of slang, found somewhere in the cracks between seeing and hearing, between hearing and touching. But as with any derivative it asserts itself where others fail. It's a more difficult translation, but by far the most honest. Why are you moving around?

LISE: I'm nervous, sorry, I don't mean to make you uncomfortable.

BENDALLI: It doesn't, I know where you are, I can hear you.

LISE: Why did you come back?

BENDALLI: For the "loot."

LISE: "The risk suggests it's more than that."
    (A moment.)

BENDALLI: I was invited, that's a rarity in my profession.

LISE: So, here we are, both of us willingly separated from what we know to be safe.

BENDALLI: Does this feel dangerous to you?

LISE: I don't know what I feel, but I do know that I feel anxious about feeling it.

BENDALLI: Please be careful, Mrs. Radcliffe…

LISE: (Shaken.) You know my name.

BENDALLI: I'm very good at what I do.

LISE: Then call me by my first.

BENDALLI: Please be careful, Lise. Understand that in spite of your anxious feelings and gracious hospitality, neither will deter me from my objective.

LISE: Which is, I assume…to rob me blind.

BENDALLI: Yes.

LISE: What's it like?

BENDALLI: What?

LISE: Real darkness. No light. No exit. What does it feel like?

BENDALLI: It's constant. Always dangerous, at times comforting.

LISE: But do you ever lose your sense of direction? Slip somehow into the eye of the darkness? And although you know life is whirling around you, you don't quite know how to step back in?

BENDALLI: It's not an uncommon feeling for the blind.

LISE: Being blind, does that make it less terrifying?

BENDALLI: Less terrifying than what?

LISE: I find myself in a similar place, where I'm aware of life but I have no real desire or capacity to re-engage.

BENDALLI: Am I supposed to feel sorry for you?

LISE: No, but my instinct is to grab onto you. To grab onto a blind man and let him lead me. Out, up, down, away. Do you know what I dream of, Nunez? Emptiness. A desert where I can't even grab a handful of sand, because the desert is empty of itself. There's nothing to indicate where I came from. Nothing indicates direction. And when I finally do start to move, everything…begins.
(Realizes her glass is empty, she crosses to the bar. He follows. She reacts, still not trusting.)

BENDALLI: What's wrong with your husband?

LISE: He has a degenerative nerve disease.

BENDALLI: Is he going to die?

LISE: Unfortunately, no. Not for quite a while. But he is, by all accounts, not living. When he's awake he can speak, but he's in a great deal of pain. We keep him on a morphine drip. Now he pops in and out like biographical sound bytes on a cheap radio. He's only forty seven.

BENDALLI: How long has…

LISE: Three years.

BENDALLI: How long have you…

LISE: Three years and two months. We hadn't even sent out the fucking thank you notes.

BENDALLI: Do you love him?

LISE: Well. Isn't that the nine point five million dollar question. Did your blind eyes brighten? And as I suspect you already know, a great deal of that wealth is in this room.

BENDALLI: You didn't answer the question.

LISE: I believe I loved him. But the lights were very bright, our time was very short.

BENDALLI: Do you resent him?

LISE: No, I'm not bitter, Mr. Bendalli, just cynical. I take care of him. I sit with him everyday. I wonder where he is. I wonder if he's ok. I wonder if I'm ok. Of course the booze helps.

BENDALLI: And you have a daughter.

LISE: His.

BENDALLI: And she blames you.

LISE: I suppose she does.

(Beat.)

BENDALLI: Well, I should go.

LISE: I thought we were getting along.

BENDALLI: I've got work to do.

LISE: I thought you would stay longer, translate things.

BENDALLI: In crime, being caught usually indicates the end of the criminal activity. *(Exiting.)*

LISE: Why are you leaving?

BENDALLI: Let's come to an understanding. You are not my host. This is not a visit. We are not going to be friends!

LISE: If you found me likable it would be difficult to steal from me, is that it?

BENDALLI: There is very little chance that I'll find you likable.

LISE: Why?

BENDALLI: You're not afraid.

LISE: You want me to be afraid of you?

BENDALLI: Not of me. Of loss. What is there that I could take from you that you would fear losing?

LISE: Well, I can't think of anything off hand.

BENDALLI: Exactly, it's all too rudely accommodating. I have standards.

LISE: Well compromise them. If you steal something, I promise to experience some sort of excruciatingly painful post loss epiphany.

(He starts out, she grabs a sculpture.)

LISE: Wait. Wait, I like this!

BENDALLI: You do?

LISE: I would rather die than part with it. It's an original.

BENDALLI: An original what?

LISE: It's…African. Ah, Northern I think. It belonged to a very Great Warrior. They call it the Sacred Sculpture of the…the …very Great Warrior.

BENDALLI: Goodnight, Lise.

LISE: There are things that I value!

BENDALLI: I won't be back.

LISE: THERE ARE THINGS THAT I VALUE! *(Beat.)* Please. Don't go.

BENDALLI: Crystal. There was crystal.

LISE: No.

BENDALLI: A wedding set, I think you said.

LISE: You can't take the crystal.

BENDALLI: I can't make you any promises. Do you still want me to stay?

LISE: Yes.

BENDALLI: My name isn't Nunez.

LISE: No.

BENDALLI: My name is Bendalli.

> *(They meet.)*

LISE: Hello, Bendalli.

BENDALLI: I left my drink.

LISE: I'll…

> *(She gets the drink. Bendalli "translates" the sculpture.)*

BENDALLI: This isn't African. It's Mayan, twelfth century. The Mayan Indians placed them around the pens where they kept goats, they thought it would sweeten the milk. You were right to value it so.

LISE: Yes, I knew there was something about it I liked. *(Brings him the drink.)* Do you need the things you steal?

BENDALLI: No.

LISE: The money?

BENDALLI: Not at all.

LISE: Is being a thief then, your act of vengeance?

BENDALLI: I'm not looking for vengeance.

LISE: What then?

BENDALLI: I don't think you'd understand.

LISE: I've tried to be frank with you.

BENDALLI: In school, I couldn't do the things that other kids could do. Ride a bike, catch a ball, cheat off another student's test paper. Consequently I wasn't considered…normal. So one night I locked myself in an abandoned meat locker behind our house so that I could die. As the air got thinner and I began to get dizzy, I quietly slipped away. I drifted through clouds, over mountains, floated across seas. I'm sure I would have slipped away completely, but I suddenly became aware of a voice in the darkness. It was my father's voice. He was talking to me, he was telling me a story. It was a story about a man who could see and how this sighted man named Nunez accidentally stumbled into a lost valley where all the inhabitants were blind. In this valley, because Nunez was the only one who could see, it was Nunez who wasn't normal. In this valley, Nunez was trapped like me. Nunez was running out of air like me. And soon, Nunez wanted to be normal, to be blind—blind like me. I don't know when I came out of the meat locker. I just remember my father was holding me as he finished the story.

LISE: And that's why?

BENDALLI: Sometimes you have to travel a great distance in order to return. At that moment, I decided I wanted to be blind. And I begin to search for others who I was sure existed in my world, for that one other person who understood the darkness as I did.

(The lights black out. The stage is completely black.)

LISE: Oh, God. What happened? Did you do that?

BENDALLI: Do what?

LISE: It's completely dark in here!

BENDALLI: Is it?

LISE: I can't see anything. You did this to me, didn't you?

BENDALLI: Are you implying that I'm contagious?

LISE: You must have used a timer.

BENDALLI: I'm not that high tech.

LISE: Where are you? Stop moving.

BENDALLI: I'm right here.

LISE: Turn the lights back on.

BENDALLI: It wasn't me, Lise.

LISE: TURN THEM BACK ON!

(Crash.)

BENDALLI: Careful.

LISE: I'm trying to get to the desk, there's a flashlight.

(Crash.)

BENDALLI: Lise, stop.

LISE: Then turn the lights on.

BENDALLI: I'm sure it's just a power outage.

LISE: I don't believe you.

(Crash.)

BENDALLI: Please! Stop moving before you destroy something else.

LISE: It's just an old tea set. I hated it.

BENDALLI: Yes, well, I was rather fond of it.

LISE: What am I supposed to do?

BENDALLI: Keep still until I tell you to move.

LISE: Great, what now?

BENDALLI: Stay calm.

LISE: I'm in a pitch dark room with a criminal. At least Audrey Hepburn had the refrigerator light.

BENDALLI: Your husband's life support—is he ok?

LISE: He can be off the system for several hours. Where are you? You're moving again!

BENDALLI: I'm right here.

LISE: What's that sound?

BENDALLI: I'm closing the drapes.

LISE: Why are you closing the drapes? Is this about sex?

BENDALLI: I don't want you to have the advantage.

LISE: Oh, God, it is about sex.

BENDALLI: No, it's about cars with headlights.

LISE: You'll never get them closed, they aren't meant to close.

BENDALLI: Each object has a chronology. You start with a single part of that object. A gathering of cloth, an interruption, a brass holding sequences into a bracket on a wall. If there is a logic to the object you learn its logic sequentially. How it feels, what it is, and by default, how it functions. They're closed.

LISE: Very impressive.

BENDALLI: Can you see anything?

LISE: I couldn't see anything before.

BENDALLI: Good. Are your eyes open, Lise?

LISE: What difference would it make!?

BENDALLI: What do you see?

LISE: Nothing.

BENDALLI: Welcome to the desert, Lise.

(Music. A light comes up on Ludviccio. It is important that the light does not spill into the pitch black room.)

LUDVICCIO: So Nunez greeted the people of the village. "Over the mountains I come," said Nunez, "out of the country where men can see." And the villagers held Nunez and felt his face, and then a finger touched his eye. "Carefully," he cried. "I can see," Nunez said again. But these people knew nothing about seeing. Murmurs rose from the crowd; "What does he say? What is this seeing? Look, he stumbles around like an oaf." And they all laughed, and above the laughter one man proclaimed: "Tell us fool, what is this thing called seeing?!"

(Lights dim, Ludviccio stays in half light. The stage is still dark but as our eyes adjust, the lights should also adjust so we can see faint images moving in and out of shadow. This is best accomplished through a pitch dark stage, with areas of "gobo" light, as opposed to a "grey" wash.)

BENDALLI: Do you know where you are?

LISE: I'm afraid to move. It's frightening in here.

BENDALLI: You say "in here" like you're in a new place.

LISE: It feels like I am.

BENDALLI: But if I turn on the light, you'll find yourself at home.

LISE: But I'm not there now. I'm somewhere else, between worlds.

BENDALLI: I think you're beginning to understand the desert, Lise.

LISE: Show it to me.

BENDALLI: Your eyes are open?

LISE: Yes.

BENDALLI: Feel the floor, are you on the rug?

LISE: No. Wood.

BENDALLI: Then take a step. Not a small step. A normal step. Learn the distance you travel in one step.

LISE: What if...

BENDALLI: I won't let you get hurt.

LISE: *(Crash.)* Ahhhh! I went too far.

BENDALLI: It's all right.

LISE: No, I broke something, I...

BENDALLI: Lise.

LISE: I should have moved slower, I...

BENDALLI: Lise...listen, what do you hear?

LISE: Nothing.

BENDALLI: Without movement or sound everything ceases to exist. What just happened, is no longer happening. In the dark, we live in bursts of sound and touch.

LISE: Isn't it natural to be afraid of the dark?

BENDALLI: Ask yourself what you need to move through it.

LISE: Electricity.

BENDALLI: Tell me where you are now?

LISE: I've reached the rug. I can feel it.

BENDALLI: Can you sense what's around you.

LISE: I remember where everything is.

BENDALLI: Don't remember, Lise. Sense the space around you. Feel it holding you.

LISE: I'm trying.

BENDALLI: Now reach out, straight out from your shoulder. And the picture of your husband, the one on the table, will be there.

LISE: All right. Oh, God. Okay. Uhhh.

BENDALLI: Stop.

LISE: What?

BENDALLI: Pull you arm back. We'll try it another day.

LISE: What's the matter?

BENDALLI: You're afraid.

LISE: You said you wanted me afraid.

BENDALLI: You're afraid of moving. You're afraid of the motion. You want to stand there safely, tucked into the darkness, but the dark is only safe when you can move through it, Lise!

LISE: Why are you angry?

BENDALLI: Because it's my world, you can't hide in it!

LISE: Please. I'm trying not to be afraid. Please, teach me.

BENDALLI: Look toward me, Lise. I'm right here. But what you see is blackness. When you look, there's no difference between me or a chair or the empty space next to me. We are part of the darkness. You and I are the same now. Like your desert we are empty of ourselves. And unless we move or touch, we cease to exist.

LISE: I want to understand.

BENDALLI: Then move your arm, move reach touch. You'll graze the photograph with your fingertips. Do it swiftly. Eyes open. You know it's there.

LISE: Yes.

BENDALLI: It's there.

LISE: Yes.

BENDALLI: Now. Do it now.

LISE: Yes. Ah! I touched it! Just like you said. Just with the tips of my fingers. *(She laughs.)* It was really there.

BENDALLI: Movement without sight is faith.

LISE: I like this. Oh, God, I really like it. Thank you for bringing me here. Bendalli?

BENDALLI: Everything's where you think it is.

LISE: Except you. You keep moving.

BENDALLI: *(He is some distance away.)* I'm right here.

LISE: Stay close to me. I feel better when… *(Gasps.)* Ahhhh! You touched me. You just touched me.

BENDALLI: It wasn't me, Lise, I'm still over here.

LISE: No, it must have been you.

BENDALLI: It's just the darkness, Lise.

LISE: Someone touched my cheek.

BENDALLI: It swirls up sometimes, like sand in the desert. Sometimes you feel alone, sometimes you swear someone is there, someone is very close. But it's just the desert.

LISE: Who's there? WHO'S THERE?!

(Music. Lights come back up on Ludviccio. The stage is dark.)

LUDVICCIO: "Who is he? Why is he here?" cried the villagers. "The man is a lunatic!" But Nunez was convinced that he would be loved by these people, because he could see! With one good eye, he could help them, lead them. After all, they were all blind! So Nunez proclaimed loudly, so they would know they were not alone in the darkness anymore, he proclaimed for all to hear:—"In the country of the blind the one-eyed man is king." And with two, he thought to himself, I am like…a God.

(Music out. Ludviccio exits. Lights up on the room. Elliot is in the arch holding a paper sack. Lise is asleep on the sofa. The room is still in disarray from the previous night.)

ELLIOT: He wants to die! Wake up, Lise.

(She crosses to the drapes and opens them. Sunlight.)

LISE: *(Jars awake. Groggy, hungover.)* Oh! Wha? Morning. Is it morning?

ELLIOT: He wants to die. He told me so. He told me he wants to die.

LISE: Who wants to die?

ELLIOT: Dad.

LISE: Wait. Wait. What? Wait. Nobody dies before coffee.

ELLIOT: And he wasn't groggy. He made complete sense. He knew who I was. Are you listening to me? He said he wants to die.

LISE: Elliot.

ELLIOT: And I want to come home.

LISE: Dr. Reasoner thinks…

ELLIOT: Dr. Reasoner's dead. Oh, didn't you hear? He was talking to himself and he died of boredom.

LISE: *(Dazed.)* Was I asleep a really long time?

ELLIOT: When you go to bed drunk, it's not unusual for mornings to feel abrupt and unfamiliar. Dr. Reasoner calls it the Ripped Van Winkle syndrome.

LISE: I thought Dr. Reasoner was dead.

ELLIOT: *(Picks up the ice bucket by sofa.)* He'll prescribe from the grave when it pertains to you.

LISE: You don't have to do that.

ELLIOT: Are you through with it?

LISE: Leave it, you don't have to do that.

ELLIOT: I want to talk and I don't want to do it over a bucket of vomit. *(Lise, aware. Rises, looks around. Crosses to the window, looks for Bendalli. Elliot returns.)*

ELLIOT: You have a bad night?

LISE: No, I had a lovely night.

ELLIOT: You sure broke a lot of stuff for a lovely night. Jesus, are you smiling?

LISE: Am I?

ELLIOT: Yeah, cut it out. So what are we going to do?

LISE: About what?

ELLIOT: Dad wants to die. He's knows he's not going to get better.

LISE: *(Opening the bag. Coffee.)* He doesn't know that.

ELLIOT: And we know he's right.

LISE: You want him to die?

ELLIOT: No. I want him the way he was before.

LISE: Before what? Before I came?

ELLIOT: I think we should pay attention to what he wants.

LISE: He's delusional, he doesn't know what he wants. Chocolate?

ELLIOT: It's for me. *(Takes doughnut.)* He's barely been out of that room in three years. He's barely been conscious for the last two. Would you want to be alive under those conditions?

LISE: I am alive under those conditions. *(Beat.)* Look, can we just have a quiet little breakfast and…it's not just my decision, it's a family decision.

ELLIOT: No it isn't.

LISE: Who's then?

ELLIOT: It's yours. He needs to know you'll be all right.

LISE: And what about you?

ELLIOT: He promised me he would visit me. He said when I closed my eyes and thought of him, or when I was asleep at night he would come to me. And he promised he wouldn't be at all like he is now, but like he used to be. And we'd talk all night. And he wouldn't stop coming. Ever. And it would be like he'd never left. So I said it was all right.

LISE: That was brave.

ELLIOT: But I want to come home so he knows where I am. Lise, can I come home?

LISE: Let's give it some time. Maybe things will change.

ELLIOT: *(Flaring.)* What's going to change? He's not going to suddenly join us for breakfast.

LISE: I can't do this now.

ELLIOT: You hate me. That's it, isn't it? If Daddy dies then I'll come home and you don't want that. You couldn't live with that.

LISE: No…

ELLIOT: You want this house to yourself…

LISE: God no.

ELLIOT: That's what you always wanted. Daddy and you and this house. It's just like Aunt Janie says, you probably knew he was sick. You probably married him 'cause he was sick!

(Lise slaps her, crosses to the bar, pours a drink.)

ELLIOT: It's a little early isn't it? *(Beat.)* I'm not sorry I said it.

LISE: I'm not sorry I hit you.

ELLIOT: What happens if he dies? What would happen if he died today?

LISE: Just eat your doughnut.

ELLIOT: Would you leave? You would, wouldn't you? I'd have to go live with Aunt Janie the candle sucker. I'd have to walk that stupid dog of hers. I'd have to go to those cybercafes and watch her get all sweaty on the chat network. *(Beat.)* I'm right aren't I?

LISE: Yes.

ELLIOT: I wish I was a grown up.

(Beat. A lone spot up on Ludviccio.)

LUDVICCIO: Bendalli? I am telling the story. Are you there?

LISE: I don't hate you. You said I hated you and it's not true. But I don't love you either. It would be a lie to say I did, and if I said it, you would know I was lying. But I don't want you to be hurt. That is the truth.

LUDVICCIO: Bendalli?

LISE: We've never known each other. You can't see me. You can't see me as I was. And I don't know what you look like when you're happy. I want to walk towards you, but I can't seem to find the way.

LUDVICCIO: Where are you?

LISE: And I'm not sure I ever will.

LUDVICCIO: Where are you?

ELLIOT: I'm right here.

(Lights fade.)

END OF ACT I

ACT II

The room is the same as the first scene. Elliot is standing in the middle of the room, holding a candlestick. After a moment, a shadow appears at the window. Elliot speaks to herself.

ELLIOT: Aha. Gotcha.
  (The shadow suddenly falls out of vision. A crash.)
ELLIOT: He's blind all right.
  (The window opens and a figure tumbles in—gasps, struggles, caught in the curtains. Beat.)
ELLIOT: FREEZE, HOLD IT RIGHT THERE. *(Elliot runs to another part of the room. A different voice.)* DON'T MOVE OR I'LL SHOOT! *(Another area. Another voice.)* WHAT DO YOU THINK, JOE, SHOULD I RELEASE ALL THESE DOGS? *(Runs. First area, first voice.)* YOU HAVE THE RIGHT TO REMAIN SILENT, YOU HAVE THE RIGHT TO…TO CALL SOMEBODY, YOU HAVE THE RIGHT TO LIFE, LIBERTY, AND THE PURSUIT OF HAPPINESS.
  (Ludviccio peeks out from under the curtain.)
ELLIOT: *(Runs, second area, second voice.)* STATE YOUR NAME OR WE'LL SHOOT!
LUDVICCIO: My name is Ludviccio.
ELLIOT: YOU'RE NAME'S BENDALLI, YOU'RE A THIEF! TELL THE TRUTH!
LUDVICCIO: You want the truth, I tell you the truth. My name is Ludviccio, I'm not a thief and you are not three policemen.
ELLIOT: What?
LUDVICCIO: You are just a boobalini. Just a baby. And I'm just an old man who fell through your window.
ELLIOT: You're not Bendalli the thief? You're not blind?
LUDVICCIO: *(Holds up three fingers.)* How many fingers I got?
ELLIOT: Three.
LUDVICCIO: You are right, see, I am not blind.
ELLIOT: *(Runs, turns on the lights.)* If you're not the thief, who are you?
LUDVICCIO: What I look like, his sister? I'm his poppa.
ELLIOT: You're his father?
LUDVICCIO: Whatever, I'm the one who had the fun with his momma. So, you seen him or no? *(Crosses into the room.)*

ELLIOT: I thought you were him.

LUDVICCIO: *(Impatient.)* I am not him, I tell you this already.

ELLIOT: I've never seen him.

LUDVICCIO: He has seen you! Hah, maybe you are the blind one. *(Up into the arch.)*

ELLIOT: How do you know he's seen me?

LUDVICCIO: Because he writes about you in the journal, everything goes in the journal. I poke the holes you know. He is the blind one, but I, Ludviccio, I am the one who must poke the holes.

ELLIOT: You mean Braille.

LUDVICCIO: He does not like the word. When he was little, he called it stabby stabby, now it is called poke the holes. For fifteen years we write in the journal everything. And now he stops!

ELLIOT: Why did he stop?

LUDVICCIO: If I know this, would I be here!? This is the last thing he writes, about the beautiful woman who is not your momma and…the ANNOY-ING little girl.

ELLIOT: If he's blind how does he know she's beautiful?

LUDVICCIO: Is not important question.

ELLIOT: Yes it is.

LUDVICCIO: Why is important?

ELLIOT: Because you don't want to answer it.

LUDVICCIO: You no trust me, is that it? Ok, because I come before, I do the appraisals. She gave me a tour of the house.

ELLIOT: So you do the appraisals and he comes later.

LUDVICCIO: I just say this, didn't I just say this?!

ELLIOT: We invite you here and then you steal from us?

LUDVICCIO: Is not a personal thing. For your poppa's will they gotta know what is worth—all these things. So I do the appraisals. My son comes and he steals these things, you get the insurance—Ah!, and just like that everybody is happy.

ELLIOT: Like Robin Hood.

LUDVICCIO: Robin Hood is a putz. We do it for the honor. So she has seen him?

ELLIOT: I caught her standing by the window the other night. "Bendalli, where are you?" Over and over. "Where are you?"

LUDVICCIO: And does he come?

ELLIOT: I think he's come every night for two weeks now.

LUDVICCIO: Aha.

ELLIOT: She sends me away, so…

LUDVICCIO: Yes, I know, the Wentworths, we almost rob them. The furniture, like it was new, still has the plastic on—but is not new, is trick! *(Proudly.)* So I choose you.

ELLIOT: I'm sure we're the envy of the neighborhood.

LUDVICCIO: I choose you because I know who you are. I wouldn't let my boy come if I no like you. We don't steal from bad people, bad people steal from themselves. You understand?

ELLIOT: Yeah, you've got more loose screws than a hardware store.

LUDVICCIO: I thought you understood! YOU TELL ME YOU UNDERSTOOD!

ELLIOT: *(Frightened.)* Don't come near me! Stay away!

LUDVICCIO: My son who could walk a maze of light in his sleep, loses his way. Here! Why, Boobalini, why in this house, should I lose my son?

ELLIOT: I don't know, I wasn't here!

LUDVICCIO: *(Command.)* A drink. I need a drink.

ELLIOT: I don't get people drinks.

LUDVICCIO: I am guest, you are host.

ELLIOT: You're a thief, you threatened me.

LUDVICCIO: Is small detail. In Italy, first thing, you give glass of wine to your guest.

ELLIOT: Welcome to New York.

LUDVICCIO: I steal it then. I steal it and you shoot me in the back. *(He goes to the bar. Looks.)*

ELLIOT: How can a blind man be a thief?

LUDVICCIO: If my son was afraid of water, he would live on a boat. If he was afraid of heights, he would sleep on a cloud. Is his way. He lives in the country of the blind and is his desire to be king. Fernet. You do not have Fernet! Is terrible country. *(Drinks from a wine bottle.)*

ELLIOT: Does his mother know he's a thief?

LUDVICCIO: *(Not sentimental.)* His mother was from Long Island. This is in your country. Is not so long, this Long Island. I come to this Long Island from a small village above Florence. I come as a car person. I drive the car I wash the car I fix the car. I come because my blessed Aliondra died of the weak heart with my child in her belly. My child suffocates in the corpse of the woman I love, so I come. This woman on the not-so-Long Island, is named Amanda, she is widow. She had the fun with Ludviccio and then she is big with his child. I beg her. On my knees I beg, "My child, please, give me my child." She carried him and she bore him. She is dead now. On his neck, he has a locket. Aliondra and Amanda. He is the son of two mothers. His blind eyes are his gift from each.

ELLIOT: You can't have two mothers.

LUDVICCIO: He has two mothers. What is wrong with you!?

ELLIOT: Your mother is the one who gives you life.

LUDVICCIO: And what is life to you, Boobalini? Life is just eat the spaghetti, burp the spaghetti and *(Raspberry.)* the spaghetti in the toilet!

ELLIOT: Amanda is your son's mother. The other woman wasn't even there.

LUDVICCIO: *(Angry.)* Why do you speak of Aliondra? She is here, Boobalini! My heart was torn from my chest when she died! So I try each day to bring the love back. And is because of THIS that Bendalli comes to me. Because of my love. What is life, Boobalini? Life is who we love on the day of our death. Just LIVING is not life. LIFE is LOVE with DEATH. LIFE IS LIFE!

ELLIOT: So is this where you start snapping your fingers and dancing like Anthony Quinn?

LUDVICCIO: I like you better when you were three policemen.

ELLIOT: I'm not a child, I have my own therapist.

LUDVICCIO: Ah, this is where I make my mistake.

ELLIOT: I graduated at the head of my class at Martin Middle School, I saved eight hundred and fifty dollars.

LUDVICCIO: I make this much playing pinochle on weekends.

ELLIOT: But the fact that I've saved it, at my age, should inform you that I will be a force on the open market.

LUDVICCIO: In Italy, open market is a place to sell vegetables, to be a force there you must have many children…and a truck.

ELLIOT: I'm going to be a great financial wizard.

LUDVICCIO: You want to be like your poppa, big fancy rich fellow.

ELLIOT: My Father's sick, don't make fun of him.

LUDVICCIO: I would like to be a big fancy rich fellow!!

ELLIOT: *(Snaps.)* I said don't make fun of him!

LUDVICCIO: *(Pause, realizes she is hurt. He speaks more formally, directly.)* Yes. I am sorry. You are right, Boobalini. And I am very sorry too about his sickness. He will get better?

ELLIOT: No.

LUDVICCIO: Is hard for you, eh?

ELLIOT: He told me he wants to die.

LUDVICCIO: Ah, Boobalini, I have heard these words before, these are the hardest of all words to hear. You talk to him?

ELLIOT: I try. When he's strong he pinches the drug tube so his head will clear and we talk just like we used too. But there's not much time before the pain starts and he has to go away again. But I want to tell him so many things, like about the squirrel in our basement, and that Outside Charlie at the Texaco station says hi, but I can't remember everything fast enough!

LUDVICCIO: For him, he has died many times. He has lost you each time. This is his pain, is no drugs to stop this pain.

ELLIOT: Is that why he wants to die?

LUDVICCIO: What is a life, Boobalini?

ELLIOT: She won't let him go.

LUDVICCIO: She loves him very much.

ELLIOT: She barely knows him!

LUDVICCIO: If there was a single moment when she felt his love, it is that moment that she keeps alive.

ELLIOT: Do you think it's all right for me to want him to die?

LUDVICCIO: Is not what you want. Is for him you want this?

ELLIOT: Yes.

LUDVICCIO: Then is all right. For your notamomma, maybe she's afraid it is what she wants, and so—she cannot allow it to happen.

ELLIOT: *(Beat.)* Could you come for dinner sometime? Maybe if you came for dinner, I could stay too.

(Music. Ludviccio continues his story.)

LUDVICCIO: In time and much to his surprise, Nunez discovered that in the country of the blind, he was not a God at all. He was just a man. Nunez longed for his old world, for books to read, for films to watch, but none of the people of the village understood this. Except perhaps, one. She had an instinct that reached beyond the darkness. And Nunez found her beautiful…the most beautiful thing of all creation. He was convinced it was she that brought him to the village, it was she that he had been searching for all his life. So he began to trust her. And very tentatively and timidly he spoke to her of sight.

(Music out. Lights come up on Lise and Bendalli. Lise is pointing a gun at Bendalli. Ludviccio exits.)

LISE: There are people living here, a family! But that doesn't mean anything to you, does it. We're just another job, some—

BENDALLI: Lise…

LISE: *(Overlap.)* —some open house for burglars!

BENDALLI: Lise, please…

LISE: Stay where you are! I have a gun!

BENDALLI: I don't believe you.

LISE: The loud sound and the sharp pain in your chest should convince you.

BENDALLI: He was my father, he was looking for me.

LISE: She's been hurt enough already!

BENDALLI: Not by us!

LISE: I could kill you right now and no one would blink.

BENDALLI: You don't really have a gun.

LISE: Is it so hard to believe you were wrong? A woman who fears her potential for rash decisions, I think you said. Well maybe rash decisions are all I have left! Should I prove it?

BENDALLI: Yes.

LISE: *(Cocking the gun.)* Tempt me. Go on, tempt me.

BENDALLI: Put the barrel in my mouth.

LISE: What?

BENDALLI: If I can't see, or touch, short of shooting me, what's left? *(He puts his hands behind his back and opens his mouth.)*

LISE: My pleasure. *(She puts barrel in his mouth.)* Keep still, toothless and blind is no way to go through life.

BENDALLI: *(Mouth full.)* How do I know it's a gun?

LISE: You're right, Bendalli, it's a dog. What part of the dog do you think it is? *(Beat.)* Was he really your father?
(Bendalli deftly disarms her and turns the gun on her.)

LISE: Ahhhh! Damn you. *(Recovers.)* You're a little high and to the right. If you're going to shoot me, I may have to talk you through it.

BENDALLI: *(Using the rug or furniture, he calculates stance as he speaks.)* There was a famous Armenian General, Basil, Slayer of the Bulgars. He earned the dubious surname from a battle in which he defeated the Bulgarian army and took fifteen thousand prisoners. After the battle, Basil ordered that all the captured Bulgars should have their eyes put out. Except for every hundredth man. Every hundredth man had only one eye put out, so that they could lead his comrades home. As the story goes, the men with one eye, failed to recover their sense of being, their sense of wholeness. But most of the others, who'd lost all attributes of sight, became better soldiers. Duck.

LISE: What?

BENDALLI: I'm going to fire, I suggest you get out of the way. One. Two. Three.
(Lise stares. Pause. She casually steps out of the line of fire. Bendalli fires.)

LISE: You missed.

BENDALLI: How far?

LISE: Six inches. Left.

> (*Bendalli adjusts using a piece of furniture or the rug to calculate his stance, fires again. He hits the first in a line of small sculptures on the mantle. He continues firing. The sculptures explode down the line. Returns the gun to Lise.*)

BENDALLI: Yes, I should have trusted you. It's a gun all right.

LISE: Why didn't you do it?

BENDALLI: What?

LISE: Shoot me. A perfect crime. Comatose husband, estranged daughter, who'd have suspected anyone would want me dead more than me.

BENDALLI: This is about your husband, isn't it?

LISE: This is about thieves, people who come into this house and then leave.

BENDALLI: You don't talk about your husband.

LISE: You are leaving aren't you? That's the plan, isn't it?

BENDALLI: I know you spent your honeymoon by the ocean. He has a "penchant" for the ocean?

LISE: I like the ocean. I have a penchant for oblivion.

BENDALLI: And Adrian…?

LISE: Adrian likes the mountains. He talked endlessly of mountains! Is this necessary?

BENDALLI: Yes. It's when you're the most vulnerable. It's when translating is least effective. It's when I wonder what you look like.

LISE: *(Beat.)* It was you.

BENDALLI: What was me?

LISE: In the dark. It was you who touched my face.

BENDALLI: No.

LISE: You wanted to know what I looked like. You still do. All right then, I'm excruciatingly beautiful. I have china white skin, jet black hair and a bosom so full that my feet have never felt the sun.

BENDALLI: Now you've frightened me.

LISE: I would like to see you frightened.

BENDALLI: It happens.

LISE: Sleeping dogs.

BENDALLI: No.

LISE: Not heights, not mice, not the undeserving rich.

BENDALLI: Italy.

LISE: What?

BENDALLI: Italy. My Father tells me Italy's my home.

LISE: And that frightens you?

BENDALLI: He left because his family died. Now he has a new family, me— and he says it's time to go back. Different sounds, rhythms. I would be translating a language I didn't know, into a language I was still learning. I'd lose too much time.

LISE: You come you steal you leave? Isn't that the M.O.?

BENDALLI: Translating isn't just touching, it's cumulative, it's learning an instinct for an environment that allows me closer. Without time, I'll forever hear the beating, but never find the heart.

LISE: But when you reach the heart, the exit begins. *(Beat.)* What will you do with my things after you've stolen them?

BENDALLI: My father sells them.

LISE: And after the physical objects are sold, do the translations remain in your head? Is your darkness cluttered with my things?

BENDALLI: I have no visual sense of your things so…

LISE: But you have a cumulative sense.

BENDALLI: The knowledge stays with me, the objects, no.

LISE: So, you steal homes and make them disappear.

BENDALLI: Vengeance is mine. Is that what you're getting at?

LISE: You think you have special rights, some sort of exclusivity.

BENDALLI: Being excluded is hardly a benefit.

LISE: Unless it's a choice. *(Beat, reload.)* If you could be cured would you want to be?

BENDALLI: I can't be cured. There's nothing partial about my blindness.

LISE: That's not what I asked.

BENDALLI: Yes.

LISE: I'm not sure I believe you.

BENDALLI: Are you feeling excluded, Lise?

LISE: I think you've convinced yourself that you are a part of some transcendent land where language is intuition.

BENDALLI: It's a blind world, I exist within it.

LISE: Exist yes, "live," I'm not so sure. I know the grey areas. I am the queen of the cul de sac, remember?

BENDALLI: I'm more than a blind man with a cane. I haven't allowed my blindness to dictate anything.

LISE: And a blind man with a cane has?

BENDALLI: I do have a cane, Lise, I don't translate myself to the supermarket and back, I tap my way down the street just like all the others.

LISE: And you hate it.

BENDALLI: Yes, I hate it. I imagine the looks, people dodging me, a wake of lurching pedestrians, like I was some runaway speed walker with his throttle stuck. Do you feel better now?

LISE: Why should I feel better?

BENDALLI: Because that's what you want. My misery acknowledged. So you can feel safe, whole. Better yet, magnanimous, you can compensate your pity by proclaiming my other senses magical. Like the blind wine maker who can detect a cloudy day from the taste of a grape. The blind safe-cracker who can hear the tumblers touch. YES, I hate being blind, not because I can't see! I hate it because I've been told that a part of me is missing.

LISE: So you choose to succeed where sighted people fail.

BENDALLI: I chose it because there were very few choices.

LISE: You chose it because it's dangerous!

BENDALLI: I chose it because I'M ALONE IN HERE! Why are you doing this?

LISE: Because if I can't hide in your world you can't hide in mine. Because after you take my things and most of my life with you, I'll be alone too.

BENDALLI: *(Beat.)* Part of the job is to disappear.

LISE: Even now you're planning your exit.

BENDALLI: My exit begins the moment I enter.

LISE: It doesn't have to.

BENDALLI: Eventually there's nothing left to steal.

LISE: I'm rich. I can replace everything.

BENDALLI: And then?

LISE: And then we do it all again. And then again. And when you're tired, I'll just buy things and have them fucking delivered to you. But don't leave! *(Bendalli turns away.)*

LISE: And don't turn away.

BENDALLI: Sometimes I forget you can see.

LISE: Sometimes I forget you can't. Isn't that the way it should be?

BENDALLI: I need to know the obstacles.

LISE: Have you ever made a move without knowing?

BENDALLI: Never.

LISE: I can't even begin to clear a path for you. How can I point you toward the heart when I don't know myself where it is?

BENDALLI: *(He walks away quickly to the periphery. Touching something secure. Beat. Then he slowly makes a circuitous route through the room, using the furnishings.)* I know that if I walk here, skirting the edge of the room, I learn the periphery. I know there is no risk to the room or myself. I start a sequential interpretation of the space, this table leads to that chair, this chair to the Segal, the Segal to the Banana Tree and so on. *(He starts toward her.)* But if I move inward. The risk is greater now because the sequence has deepened. Now my retreat is no longer direct, it's a translation in itself. A translation without obstacles. But I've... *(Brushes against lamp, it falls.)* Sorry, I wasn't concentrating.

LISE: Break anything. Break everything.

BENDALLI: I'm all right.

LISE: Do you need…

BENDALLI: *(He jumps, disoriented, lost.)* NOOO! You asked me what I was afraid of. This. This is terrifying for me. I've spent days, weeks, understanding the various paths toward the center and out again. It's why I come. To discover the sequence that would bring me closer. I know I can't translate you. The obstacles are larger than I've ever encountered. There is no sequence. There is no logic. If I get close, there may be no way out. That's why I'm afraid. *(He removes his gloves.)* But I want to see you!

(Pause. She steps to him. He traces her face. When he gets to her eyes….)

BENDALLI: Your eyes are closed. Lise, open your eyes.

LISE: No, please. This is the world that I try to find each night. I try to drink my way to some soft place between my life and dying. I always thought, eventually, I'd find my way back. *(She takes Bendalli's hand and puts it to her cheek.)* But then you came and now I don't want to move. I want to stay with you, here. *(She kisses him.)*

BENDALLI: No. Please. Lise, open your eyes.

LISE: I never want to open my eyes again.

BENDALLI: Open your eyes.

LISE: Stay with me. Stay. *(Kiss.)* Stay.

(Music. Ludviccio enters, continues the story. Lights eventually fade on Lise and Bendalli.)

LUDVICCIO: Even from the beginning, their love was in great conflict with itself. How could the darkness love the light? And what good is the light if there is no darkness to illuminate? So Nunez stood before her hearing her plea over and over, stay, stay! And he knew then he was not a God nor even a man, but a poor tortured soul who had finally found the love he had been searching for. And she spoke to him gently, "Those queer things that you call eyes, are your confusion, my sweet. All we need is a simple operation—remove the irritant bodies! Put an end to this curse called "seeing"! The next morning the sun rose with quiet intent, first peeking cautiously over the mountains, then gently it began to caress the rich green valley. Suddenly the sun splintered violently through the forests and over the jagged cliffs of the village, shafts of gold careened off the black diamond waters of the river Perception, a performance of light for Nunez, celebrating his last day of sight.

ELLIOT: Wait, wait, wait!

(The lights come up. Informal dinner Italian style. Clattering plates, over-lapped conversation. Ludviccio enters the scene. Bendalli somewhere in the room, "translating.")

LISE: Elliot, don't interrupt.

ELLIOT: It's stupid.

LISE: *(Overlap.)* Elliot.

LUDVICCIO: Is okay.

ELLIOT: He wants to be blind? He wants them to take out his eyes?

LUDVICCIO: Yes, "remove the irritant bodies," is part of the story.

ELLIOT: Why would Nunez do that?

LUDVICCIO: Because he loves the beautiful girl. Because love is more power-ful than sight.

ELLIOT: It's dumber than Disney.

LISE: Let him finish the story.

ELLIOT: You told this story to your son? No wonder he's a criminal.

LISE: It's a wonderful story.

ELLIOT: *(Flat.)* Yeah, a real eye popper.

LUDVICCIO: Here, you eat more, maybe with a full mouth I don't hear you! Each night Bendalli would not sleep unless I tell him. Sometimes two, three times. "The Country of the Blind, Poppa, tell me about…"

BENDALLI: It's an old story, a child's story.

LUDVICCIO: *(Surprised.)* Yes, it is. But still you want to hear it.

BENDALLI: No more, Poppa, I'm sick of it.

LISE: But how does it end?

BENDALLI: *(A bit too violently.)* It will end the same way it always has!

LUDVICCIO: *(Staring at Bendalli, shocked.)* Yes, it will. And so, that is that, eh Bendalli? This will be the last telling?

BENDALLI: Yes. *(Beat. He continues translating.)*

ELLIOT: Blind people are weird.

LISE: Elliot, that's enough.

LUDVICCIO: She is right, they are. *(To Elliot.)* But is exactly the point of the story. Nunez wants to be less as you say, "weird." He wants to be normal, so he can love the beautiful girl.

ELLIOT: But blind isn't normal.

LUDVICCIO: This, Boobalini, is the question you have to ask yourself. Who in the story has the illness? Who in the story sees?

ELLIOT: Yeah, yeah, it has two sides like a paradox.

LUDVICCIO: Exactly. Two ways of looking, a pair of stories, like your pair of doxes.

LISE: *(To Bendalli.)* Why don't you join the party? It's embarrassing, my first party in years and my guest of honor is perched on my mantle strategizing how to rob me.

LUDVICCIO: He no get out much.

LISE: At least come down and eat something.

LUDVICCIO: Come eat, you never eat! You don't eat, someday you'll be so skinny you'll slip through your asshole and hang yourself.

BENDALLI: *(Jumps down.)* Poppa.

LUDVICCIO: She knows! Asshole is not bad word! You got one, right? Is only bad word when you are one. *(Laughs.)* Is true, no!?

BENDALLI: I'm sorry, I didn't mean to be rude.

LISE: Come, it's a party. It's the first time I've felt good in this room in years.

ELLIOT: Hey, Bendalli… *(Putting her plate down.)*

LISE: And I think there's someone here who is as taken by you as I am.

ELLIOT: *(Crossing to him.)* Do you want to see?

LISE: Elliot, that's rude.

BENDALLI: It's all right. *(To Elliot.)* I do see.

ELLIOT: Do not.

BENDALLI: Do to.

ELLIOT: Ok, how many fingers? *(Elliot holds up three fingers.)*

BENDALLI: Five.

ELLIOT: Three.

BENDALLI: Five. Three straight and two curled.

ELLIOT: Ok, you mean "seeeeing," *(Spooky.)* like, is the glass half empty sort of thing.

LUDVICCIO: Is stupid expression. What does it mean? If glass is half empty, it only means someone is not doing they're job. *(He tips an empty wine bottle.)*

LISE: Sorry sorry. Elliot, could you light the candles?
  (She exits for wine. Elliot lights the candles. Ludviccio approaches Bendalli, sotte voce.)

LUDVICCIO: What is wrong with you, why are you still translating?

BENDALLI: I have work left to do.

LUDVICCIO: We eat cannelloni, we drink wine, we no rob them now. This would not be polite.

BENDALLI: We begin the story, we finish the story.

LUDVICCIO: What has one got to do with the other? You disappear for weeks and then I find you like this. These are good people, what is wrong with you!?

BENDALLI: You don't understand.

LUDVICCIO: This woman loves you, I can see this, this I understand.

BENDALLI: No.

LUDVICCIO: You will not hurt these people. I will not let you!

BENDALLI: Then I'll finish the story alone!

ELLIOT: Hey, what's the matter?

LUDVICCIO: Is nothing.

LISE: *(Returns with a bottle of wine, fills Ludviccio's glass.)* Here we are.

LUDVICCIO: Ah, you see, Boobalini, she brings wine to her guest, she is good host, probably Italian.

LISE: Bendalli, if you don't have a glass of wine, I'm going to have the entire room redesigned and then where will you be?

LUDVICCIO: You have a glass of wine and you relax.

LISE: I'll fix you a plate, you don't have to eat it.

ELLIOT: *(Crosses, sits with Ludviccio.)* Hey, finish the story.

LUDVICCIO: Oh, yes, it is not important that I eat, only that you eat.

ELLIOT: How do they take out his eyes? I saw a movie once where they did it with a can opener!

LUDVICCIO: You do not want me to eat at all, is that it?

ELLIOT: In cartoons they just smack the characters head and they pop out on springs. Bawarrrrrrng.

LUDVICCIO: Is not a cartoon, is important story of life!

LISE: *(Handing Bendalli a plate, a private exchange.)* They share the darkness together. They have each other and that's all they really need. I'm right, aren't I?

BENDALLI: Yes. But before he can give up his sight, he must know that in the darkness, it is truly him that she sees.
(Beat.)

ELLIOT: Daddy used to tell me a story about a very beautiful Princess who lived in the mountains.

LUDVICCIO: Many times I have tried to tell my son about a very handsome

prince who lived there also. ME! But it is always the same story he wants
to hear.

BENDALLI: Someday we will go back to Italy, Poppa.

LUDVICCIO: Someday. Someday is when my brain is a pineapple.

LISE: Your son claims he has trouble finding the heart.

LUDVICCIO: You want to find the heart, is right here! *(Heart.)* I tell him over
and over again! I do not want to die in this country. If a man doesn't die
in the right place at the right time, the angels do not sing.

BENDALLI: The angels will sing.

LUDVICCIO: No. In America, it will be a lounge act from the Holiday Inn.

ELLIOT: Will the angels sing for Daddy?

LISE: Of course they will.

ELLIOT: But he's only alive because of a machine. How strict are they?

LUDVICCIO: Very strict! Take away the wings, and angels are just like the nuns
at school.

ELLIOT: Daddy didn't die at the right time. The machines kept him alive.

LISE: But that doesn't mean…

ELLIOT: Maybe it means they won't sing!

LISE: No, Elliot, it's just an expression. He's just…please… explain it her.

LUDVICCIO: But is not expression…the angels are very serious thing.

LISE: But it's not about our lives, it's just a story.

BENDALLI: Sometimes a story is the more honest of the two.

ELLIOT: I knew it, they won't sing!

> (*Lise stares at Bendalli. Bendalli turns to Elliot.*)

BENDALLI: Elliot, your father likes the mountains, doesn't he?

ELLIOT: So?

BENDALLI: When your father dies, that's where he'll go. He'll float up to the
mountains.

ELLIOT: What's that got to do with the angels?

BENDALLI: I happen to know that's where the angels live…and that's where
they sing.

ELLIOT: How do you know?

BENDALLI: I was there once. But I was too young, so they sent me back. But
your father, when he's ready, will hear the angels, and he will stay with
them.

ELLIOT: He's ready now, he told me!

LISE: Elliot please!

LUDVICCIO: *(Trying to lighten things up.)* The angels will take ALL of this into
consideration. For instance, we are having a party, right! So the angels

know your poppa is not ready. Angels no spoil a party. But a nun, a nun
could spoil a party from two miles away.

ELLIOT: But Daddy's not at the party.

LISE: Elliot, we can talk about this later.

ELLIOT: You always say that. It's like he's not even here.

BENDALLI: Then maybe we should invite him down. I'm sure he would enjoy
the change in scenery.

ELLIOT: You mean bring him down here?

BENDALLI: Yes, invite him to the party. You said he could be off the machine
for several hours.

ELLIOT: We could tell him the story!

BENDALLI: Yes.

LISE: Please Bendalli, you're not helping.

ELLIOT: It would be so cool, Lise. He hasn't been down here in so long.

BENDALLI: I could carry him. You could help me.

LISE: It's…it's too dangerous.

BENDALLI: What is it you're afraid of, Lise? He'll be perfectly safe. He'll hear
our conversations, he'll smell the cannelloni, maybe even feel the touch
of his wife's cheek on his hand.

ELLIOT: It would be so cool.

LISE: *(Upset. Blows out the candles.)* I'm sorry, but I think the party's over.

ELLIOT: I want to tell him the story.

LISE: You don't know the story. I think it's time for everyone to go home.
(Starts cleaning up.)

ELLIOT: Down here it would be different.

LISE: What would be different?

ELLIOT: You could see how tired he is.

LISE: He's not tired, he's sick.

ELLIOT: He told me he was tired. Don't you talk to him? What do you do up
there?

LISE: I sit with him. Elliot, stop it, this isn't the time…

ELLIOT: I want to bring him down…

LISE: You're not bringing him down here, I said no!
(Elliot slams her plate down, sits in a chair. Long silence.)

LUDVICCIO: In Italy, when no one talks, it means they are all dead. America
is different. *(Rises.)* Andiamo, Bendalli. Thank you for inviting us.
(Crosses to the arch.) Bendalli?

BENDALLI: *(Pause. He faces Lise. Then he feels his way to the sofa. He feels the
surface. He props a pillow up, and then describes with his hands, a body, a*

head resting on the pillow.) It's a strong face. He's very handsome. He's smiling, I think he knows it's a party. *(He extends hand toward Elliot.)* Come on. Don't you see him.

(She tentatively takes his hand. He leads her to the sofa.)

BENDALLI: It's just a different way of seeing.

ELLIOT: *(She looks at Bendalli then down at the sofa. Hesitant.)* Daddy? *(Sits by him on sofa. Beat.)* Everyone's here, Daddy. Me, Lise. Bendalli. He's a thief, but you'd like him anyway. Say hi, Daddy.

BENDALLI: Hello, Adrian.

ELLIOT: And that's Ludviccio.

LUDVICCIO: Is very nice house. Don't worry, we no steal anything.

ELLIOT: Ludviccio used to live in the mountains. He wants to go back there, just like you. *(Looks up at Lise.)* Lise is standing right over there, I think she dressed up because she knew you'd be here. I wish you could see her, I wish you could see how pretty she is.

LISE: Elliot stop.

ELLIOT: *(With difficulty. Confessing.)* Daddy? Ludviccio says that you've died over and over cause we keep saying good-bye to each other. I didn't mean to hurt you. It's just…I didn't want you to go. I'm not going to hurt you anymore. So, I'm saying good-bye. But, you have to come visit me, like you promised. Please don't forget, okay? *(She gets up and stares at Lise. Then quietly.)* Lise, if you don't let him go, he won't be able to come see me. I'll be at the Wentworths. *(She runs out.)*

LISE: Elliot.

LUDVICCIO: I will go with her.

LISE: It's the second house on…

LUDVICCIO: Yes…eh, I have been there. *(Ludviccio exits.)*

    (Pause.)

BENDALLI: Should I help clean up?

LISE: Why did you do it?

BENDALLI: I thought it was important for you to see him.

LISE: I see him everyday. I sit up there with him everyday.

BENDALLI: But he's not up there. He's down here. Across from you at dinner, next to you at night, he pours your drinks for you, Lise.

LISE: Why are you doing this?

BENDALLI: I'm a thief, remember. I need to know the room. What's here, who's here!

LISE: What about us? What about last night?

BENDALLI: He was here.

LISE: *(Goes to him, touches him.)* I want to be with you, only with you.

BENDALLI: No one can blind themselves.

LISE: What?

BENDALLI: Last night, in the dark, are you sure it was me, Lise?

LISE: Of course it was you.

BENDALLI: But you refused to look.

LISE: I'm looking now. I see you now.

BENDALLI: But in the dark. Who was it, Lise?

> *(The stage goes dark. A low, almost indiscernible drum beat, heart beat.)*

LISE: Ah! Did you do that? Are you testing me, Bendalli?

BENDALLI: Did the lights go out again?

LISE: You know they did.

BENDALLI: Who's here in the dark, Lise? Is it Adrian?

LISE: It's you.

BENDALLI: Or is it Elliot sneaking back from the Wentworths?

LISE: What are you talking about?

BENDALLI: She used to sneak back just to talk to her father, but now she goes straight for the basement.

LISE: What?

BENDALLI: That first night Elliot hadn't planned on you staying awake, but you were waiting for me.

LISE: It's you doing this.

BENDALLI: I've caught her myself! I heard her whispering "good-bye" over and over. She was standing there staring at the fuse box. Trying to gain the courage.

LISE: I don't believe you!

BENDALLI: She's asking you to help her!

LISE: I can't.

BENDALLI: Have I found something you value, Lise?

LISE: Where's the flashlight?

BENDALLI: I've got it. I've got the lighter too.

> *(Crash.)*

BENDALLI: Careful, Lise.

LISE: Turn on the lights.

BENDALLI: You can't move without my help, Lise.

LISE: I'll find the arch, I'll find my way…

> *(Crash.)*

BENDALLI: YOU'RE IN MY WORLD NOW! I can keep you here. I can

make the room swirl up around you and hold you. I can change where
you came from, and where you're going. I can hold you, Lise!

LISE: Why are you doing this!

BENDALLI: BECAUSE I NEED TO SEE YOU!

LISE: *(Soft.)* Why couldn't it just be us?

BENDALLI: Can you feel him? The darkness is where he lives.

LISE: He's not here!

BENDALLI: Each night for three years. It's where you find him.

LISE: No.

BENDALLI: Let me see you, Lise.

LISE: I can't, I'm not here, none of us are here.

BENDALLI: Then let me see who you were.

 (Beat.)

LISE: Who I was. Ask Adrian's family. They knew. They came to their own
early conclusions. Younger woman, rich widower, that was my story.

BENDALLI: And Elliot, is that what she believed.

LISE: No. But like you said, sometimes a story can become the truth.

BENDALLI: Did something happen? What happened?

LISE: It was after Adrian fell ill.

 (We see her silhouetted in the light and shadow.)

LISE: We were in his bedroom. We were taking turns reading to him. It was
Elliot's turn to read and…suddenly she stopped. She…just stopped, and
she asked me.

BENDALLI: Do you love him?

LISE: Such a simple question. But I wanted to give her an answer that was real.
I wanted to tell her that love owns moments of not loving, moments
when you look down at the man you loved, lying there, never to be quite
who you loved again. I wanted to give her an answer that would live
through his death and into our lives, an answer that neither sister Janie,
or any of them could ever take away from her.

BENDALLI: What?

LISE: I closed my eyes. I closed my eyes to find him, find the words. *(Breaking.)*
But they weren't there. The words weren't there. What did that mean? I
closed my eyes and I…I didn't say anything. And when I opened
them…she was gone.

BENDALLI: Did you go after her?

LISE: I couldn't.

BENDALLI: Why not?

LISE: Because he was there. Adrian. Lying there, alone in the night. He was
    there, waiting to hear my voice, waiting to hear my answer.
BENDALLI: Why didn't you…
LISE: It was too late. It was all suspended there in the silence.
BENDALLI: *(Moves center, behind her.)* If we don't move or speak in the dark-
    ness, we cease to exist.
LISE: Yes.
BENDALLI: Now you keep him alive.
LISE: Yes.

    (Bendalli is right behind her. We see his silhouette.)
BENDALLI: Sit with him each night.
LISE: Adrian.
BENDALLI: *(He brings his arms up behind her, without touching her.)* And he
    waits, holding you in the darkness.
LISE: *(Reacts, as if being held.)* Ohhh. Yes, please hold me. Don't let go of me.
BENDALLI: He never let go, he never would.
LISE: He would touch me, like you're touching me.
BENDALLI: Like he's touching you now. Moving past the edge of your skin.
    He's waiting, Lise. *(He backs out of the light.)* How does the story end?
LISE: Where are you? You were holding me…?
BENDALLI: *(He lights the candle.)* Open your eyes, Lise.
LISE: Bendalli?
BENDALLI: Who's in the darkness with you?
LISE: Bendalli?
BENDALLI: No, Lise, it's not me, it's never been me. *(He disappears.)*
LISE: Where are you? *(She runs to the window.)* Bendalli! NOOOO! Don't
    leave. Oh, God, don't leave me! Don't leave me alone! *(Tears the pillows
    from the sofa, destroying the outlined Adrian.)* He's not here! He's not!
    BENDAAAALLIIII! *(She slumps next to the sofa.)* You're not here,
    Adrian. You're not in the darkness. *(Beat.)* I know where you are. You're
    there where the light found us. Do you remember The Hotel Del
    Coronado? We stood on the beach sipping champagne. That's where I
    remember us. Standing in sea air and moonlight. Do you remember?
    Out of the darkness, the night, a seal barked at us. *(Smiles.)* "That seals
    it," you said. You told me you'd never been so happy. Because of me. You
    can hear me, can't you. Keep listening. Tonight I'll whisper and you'll
    hear. Tonight you'll go to the mountains.
    (Music. Ludviccio continues the story.)
LUDVICCIO: "Good-bye," he whispered. "Good-bye." Morning was approaching.

But for Nunez, the morning would become night, and it would stay night forever. As he walked toward the lonely place where he should sacrifice his gift of sight, the birds sang to him in the voice of angels, and his eyes drifted up to heaven. He was seeing the morning for the last time, the morning like an arc of immeasurable light. He saw the mountains and the sky above, a blue transparence, a thin veil between himself and God. Sight became joy and joy became thought. He thought of the young girl. He thought of the morning. He thought of darkness and he thought of light. He thought of home. He soon realized what he had known in his heart all along. Even for love, he could not blind himself. The voices sang to him as he continued walking, until he reached the foot of the very peak down which he had come so long ago. He set his eyes on the highest peak, the spire closest to the angels and, seeing clearly where he had to go, he began to climb.

(Light fades, Ludviccio exits. Music fades. When the lights come up on the room, Lise and Elliot are standing in the arch. They are dressed in dark colors, funeral colors. The room is empty. The artwork, furniture, rugs, curtains, books, everything is gone. The hardwood floors glisten against the backdrop of empty walls. Lise steps into the room.)

LISE: He did it.

(Pause.)

ELLIOT: Everything's gone. He took everything.

(Pause.)

LISE: I never really thought he could do it.

ELLIOT: I think he even cleaned.

LISE: *(Enters.)* So much light.

ELLIOT: It looks like no one ever lived here. It's creepy.

LISE: It's all right.

ELLIOT: All Dad's things. The sculptures, his chair, even his tractor seat collection. Lise, they took the crystal.

LISE: Nothing left.

ELLIOT: I wanted to sit in his chair. When we were standing at the grave, that's all I could think of. I wanted to come home and sit in his chair.

LISE: It's ok.

ELLIOT: No it isn't. I hate Bendalli. I wish he never came. I just wanted to sit in his chair.

LISE: Then sit. Just sit there.

ELLIOT: No.

LISE: Try.

ELLIOT: *(Plops down, belligerent.)* It's not the same. Why did they have to take
    everything?

LISE: They're thieves.

ELLIOT: The floor's cold.

LISE: *(Hands her coat to Elliot.)* Sit on this.

ELLIOT: Would you sit with me?

    (They sit together.)

ELLIOT: What are we going to do?

LISE: About what?

ELLIOT: About everything. Are you going leave?

LISE: I don't know.

ELLIOT: I don't want you to leave.

LISE: Close your eyes, Elliot.

ELLIOT: What for?

LISE: Just close them.

    (Their eyes remain closed. Slow fade to a spot on Lise and Elliot.)

ELLIOT: Are you closing yours?

LISE: Unhunh.

ELLIOT: What do we do now?

LISE: Pretend you're warm.

ELLIOT: But I'm not, I'm cold.

LISE: Think of the desert, Elliot. Feel it on your skin, the sand all around you.

ELLIOT: It's making me thirsty.

LISE: Hmmm.

ELLIOT: I wonder where they went?

LISE: I think they're very far away.

ELLIOT: We should find them. We should go rob them. Steal everything.
    Wouldn't that be cool?

LISE: That would be cool.

ELLIOT: Let's do it. Okay?

LISE: We'll see.

ELLIOT: I'm starting to feel better now.

LISE: When you're in the desert there's only sand. Nothing to tell you where
    you are or where you've been. Nothing to tell you what to do next.

ELLIOT: What are we going to do?

LISE: Sit a while. Feel warm. And when it's time, we'll choose a direction…
    we'll open our eyes…and we'll begin.
    *(Music. Lights up on Ludviccio and on Bendalli silhouetted. Of light and
    darkness:)*

LUDVICCIO: When sunset came, Nunez stopped climbing. He had left the valley of the blind, where he thought he might be king. And the glow of the sunset passed, and the night came. And he looked up at the…
LUDVICCIO AND BENDALLI: …cold, clear stars shining out from the darkness.
BENDALLI: There was a smile on his face. And he whispered a secret that he had held deep in his heart since he was a child. He whispered it to no one, only to the night. He whispered, "Sometimes we must travel a great distance, in order to return."
(*Music. The lights fade.*)

END OF PLAY

BOBBY SUPREME

by J.B. Miller

THE AUTHOR

J.B. Miller grew up in Massachusetts and London before moving to New York. He is the author of the novel *My Life in Action Painting* (Grove Press), cowrote the film *Gringuito,* and has written for *The New York Times* and *Salon Magazine.* Staged readings: *Rainbow Park* (Dramatists Guild), *Risk* (Naked Angels, Grace Rep), *Bravado* (Workhouse, Stageplays Theatre Company, Loading Zone). Productions: *White Lies* (Naked Angels, One Dream, Stageplays Theatre Company), *Bobby Supreme* (Open Door Theater, 29th Street Rep), *Shirkers* (Orenda Theater). Miller is a member of the Dramatists Guild and a recipient of a MacDowell Fellowship.

AUTHOR'S NOTE

I remember, when I was twelve years old, seeing a revival of John Osborne's *Look Back in Anger* at the Young Vic in London. The play was a jolt to me, as was the description in the program of its original production. People had apparently walked out in protest to the rawness depicted on stage, and I remember feeling exhilaration over the idea that someone could be moved enough to, well, actually move out of the theater.

Actually, I'd forgotten about that revelation until I watched people walk out of my play *Bobby Supreme.* I hadn't intended for that effect, and the walk-outs happened early—during the opening monologue, to be exact. But everyone who got past that opening, stayed.

The play came about from my fascination with certain kinds of person-alities. Shock jocks, gutter comics—these people take on a character only to have it sometimes take over *them.* As Vonnegut says, "You are what you pretend to be."

ORIGINAL PRODUCTION

Bobby Supreme was first presented at the ArcLight Theatre in New York on November 5, 1997. It was directed by David Millman. Produced by Allen Dennis and Filippo Anselmi for the Open Door Theater, with the following cast:

Bobby . . . . David Burke
Angelina . . . . Joanne DiMauro
Douglas . . . . Julius Bremer
Riggs . . . . Barry J. Hirsch
Janet . . . . Lisa Collins
Brandy . . . . Lisa Anne Sclar

A subsequent, slightly revised version of the play opened at the 29th Street Rep in New York on April 23, 1998. It was directed by Tim Corcoran. Produced by the 29th Street Rep with the following cast:

Bobby . . . . David Mogentale
Angelina . . . . Paula Ewin
Douglas . . . . Charles Willey
Riggs . . . . Leo Farley
Janet . . . . Elizabeth Elkins
Brandy . . . . Moira MacDonald

CHARACTERS

BOBBY: comic
ANGELINA: muse
RIGGS: manager
DOUGLAS: journalist
JANET: advocate
BRANDY: groupie

SETTING

Action takes place in a hotel room and bar in New York, plus various comedy clubs and an arena stage. Staging should be as minimal as possible.

TIME

The present

SCENE I

Spotlight on Bobby, late thirties. He's wearing all black: jeans, leather jacket, Doc Martens, and a leather codpiece. He addresses the audience directly.

BOBBY: So now the bitch is unconscious, right? So I figure, what the hell? She won't make so much noise. So I'm giving her a quick fuck, and I'm thinking, hey, something's not right here. I mean—she's cold inside. She doesn't feel right. So I take her pulse, okay? And...the bitch is gone. She's dead. But, you know—what the hell? I'm in mid-screw here. It's not like I'm going to ruin her day. So I'm going at it, and I feel something tighten around my prick. It's like her muscles are contracting in the rigor mortis state. Ooooh! What a feeling. Awwwhhhh! I'm really getting my rocks off. My balls are as hard as walnuts. I'm jazzing in Cinemascope. This is a Technicolor, Quadraphonic, Surround-sound fuck, here. And I come like a fire hose. I come for about twenty minutes—I could fill up a gas tank. It's high test, unleaded. It's Saudi crude. So I keep coming—squirt, squirt, squirt, squirt—until I'm spent. I'm overdrawn. Just blew my credit rating. And I'm about to, you know, dismount, when I find that it won't go. I'm stuck. My dick is locked in the glove compartment, know what I mean? I'm in cement city, here. It's what you might call a sticky situation. I mean, how to explain this to the rookies? My dick's been caught in the cookie jar. My prick is jammed in the exhaust pipe. I've misplaced my wazoo. "Oh, uh, hello, officer. Just doing a bit of sit-ups here, with my girlfriend. She's asleep. That's how she likes to exercise. Sleeperobics. Yeah. Say, uh...Do you have a crowbar or a tire iron or something? Yeah, to scrape off the missus—she forgot to take out the cork..." What you might call embarrassing, right? But I can't go on like this. I mean, what'll the guys say when I show up at the pool hall with a dead chick strapped to my lap? And she'll be less than pine-needle smelling by then, I can tell you—I'd be screwed into rotting meat. So what can I do? I reach over to the phone and dial 911...And that's where I'm stuck.

(Lights up on a hotel room. Angelina, his collaborator, is sitting in an armchair behind Bobby. Sitting on another chair is Douglas, a journalist.)

ANGELINA: You're stuck?

(Bobby puts away his walking stick and begins taking off his codpiece, leather jacket, and Doc Martens.)

BOBBY: Yeah, I don't know what should go next. *(He picks up an apple that's sitting on a small table next to Angel and bites into it.)*
DOUGLAS: I hate to be the one to tell you this…
BOBBY: What?
DOUGLAS: Rigor mortis doesn't set in for eight to ten hours.
BOBBY: So what? This is poetic license.
ANGELINA: Oh, is *that* what it is?
BOBBY: *(Re: the apple.)* I can't taste this at all.
　(He offers it to Angel, who waves it off.)
ANGELINA: It's fine.
BOBBY: It's tasteless. *(He take another bite.)* So anyway, what happens? The police show up.
ANGELINA: No, an ambulance.
BOBBY: Yeah?
ANGELINA: Yes, and…a nurse. She…sees the situation…
BOBBY: And she's jealous.
ANGELINA: No, she's angry. You're insulting her gender.
DOUGLAS: *(To Bobby.)* Is this how you work out your routines?
BOBBY: Sure. Jump in.
DOUGLAS: Me? Oh no, I'm just an observer.
ANGELINA: *(To Bobby.)* So you're insulting her gender.
BOBBY: No, the bitch wakes up. With the police around, the dead bitch wakes up. And she says, uh…
ANGELINA: "What, you have me arrested just because I fell *asleep?"* *(She laughs uproariously.)*
　(Pause. Bobby puts the apple down.)
BOBBY: I don't get it. *(To Douglas.)* Do you get it?
DOUGLAS: Well…
ANGELINA: She fell asleep. Because he was such a lousy fuck.
　(Pause.)
BOBBY: So the joke's on him.
ANGELINA: Sure. Why not?
BOBBY: Self-deprecating humor, Angel, isn't exactly Bobby Supreme. That's for old pricks like Dangerfield. I'm a registered asshole. I got a nasty rating— the Surgeon General issued a health warning.
ANGELINA: But if it's funny—the joke works…
BOBBY: No, if the joke *fits.* *(To Douglas.)* Right?
ANGELINA: If it works, it's funny.
BOBBY: But it works against me. Bobby Supreme is a lousy fuck? Where's the

humor in that? I think we've been nice enough to let the bitch stay alive.
She doesn't have to be a surly cunt on top of that.

ANGELINA: Oh, lighten up, Bobby…

BOBBY: Lighten up? This isn't for me, Angel. People *pay* for this. They pay to
laugh *with* me, *at* other people. Not *with* other people, *at* me. (*Beat.*) Do
you think I should ax the codpiece? It's like fag flypaper—I've become a
pansy pin-up. They sit in the front row and try to cop a feel.

DOUGLAS: I've never seen that.

BOBBY: No more fags in the front row. I don't even know why they show up—
I'm nasty enough to them.

ANGELINA: You're nasty to everyone.

BOBBY: Yeah, that's true. Where's my other codpiece? This one's too tight. (*He
goes out of the room.*)
(*Pause.*)

DOUGLAS: You're his assistant?

ANGELINA: Artistic Director. We developed Bobby Supreme together.

DOUGLAS: You don't find any of his material offensive?

ANGELINA: It's just material. Very lucrative material.

DOUGLAS: He must be making a lot of money.

ANGELINA: We got 160,000 on a T-shirt deal alone.

DOUGLAS: A hundred and sixty grand? Jesus.

ANGELINA: That's just one deal. We've got bowling jackets, track suits, caps,
sweat-bands…
(*Bobby comes back into the room adjusting a bright, new codpiece.*)

BOBBY: I like this one. See? It lights up in the dark. (*He laughs, then goes over
to the desk and begins looking over some papers.*)

BOBBY: God, look at these contracts. I wish I'd done better in math in high
school…

ANGELINA: You did just fine in high school, Bobby.

BOBBY: (*To Douglas.*) The future is in pay-per-view. The Tyson-Holyfield
fight, they made fifty-two million on PPV. Bobby Supreme is too hot for
TV, too hot for cable—special-event concerts, 29.95. Say, four shows a
year—extravaganzas—600,000 viewers—eighteen million times four is,
what? A seventy-two million take, of which we get thirty percent. What's
that? Almost twenty-two million dollars. Plus my road work and movie
deals, product tie-ins and commercial endorsements. I might make
thirty million dollars next year. And to think Lenny Bruce died for a
parking ticket.

DOUGLAS: Do you really think people will pay to see you four times a year?

BOBBY: You put a charge on the cable bill and people don't even notice it—
it's a minor blip on their wallet radar, it's hardly even a hiccup. Half their
phone bills are sex lines or fuck numbers or astrology or baseball scores
or the fucking weather. People are too lazy to flip through a magazine or
a newspaper or even look out of the goddam window—they'd rather
poke their telephone. "Gee, is it raining out? I'd better call 1-900-
WEATHER." Twenty bucks for a cable special, for *Bobby Supreme,* isn't
so steep. It's painless. A pinprick. It's a thirty-million-dollar anesthetic.
(He laughs.)
DOUGLAS: That's a big paycheck.
BOBBY: Tell me about it. So, how much time do you need here?
DOUGLAS: Whatever you can give me.
BOBBY: *(To Angel.)* Angel, see if you can find Riggs. He was supposed to bring
me the midwest papers.
ANGELINA: Sure, Boss.
*(She goes out of the room. Bobby picks up the apple again, bites it and
squints as if trying to register some taste. He offers it to Douglas.)*
BOBBY: Can you taste this?
DOUGLAS: Uh, no thanks. *(Beat.)* So. Are you two equal partners in this?
BOBBY: Sure. She's been with me from the start. She's my moral conscience.
DOUGLAS: *(Sarcastic.)* She's doing a great job.
(Bobby laughs. Douglas takes a couple of CDs and books out of his briefcase.)
DOUGLAS: I want to ask you a couple of questions about your work.
BOBBY: You must be my number-one fan. You've got the whole kit. No T-
shirts? I make more money from T-shirts than from ticket sales.
DOUGLAS: I was very interested in your CDs.
BOBBY: Digital Supreme. I give great headphone.
DOUGLAS: How is it selling?
BOBBY: Double platinum. That's for "Public Nuisance." "The Supremacist"
did almost as well.
DOUGLAS: It's pretty strong stuff.
BOBBY: Apple sauce.
DOUGLAS: Actually, I couldn't hear some of it for all the laughter. Did you do
a lot of remixing?
BOBBY: What, you mean use a laugh track? No way. That's the real thing.
Beatlemania. The kids wet their seats. Then they chop them up. We
couldn't go back to Kansas City. They went nuts. Set the arena on fire.
(He laughs.) It was hilarious.
(Douglas sets up a small tape machine.)

DOUGLAS: Mind if I use the machine?

BOBBY: No. I mean, yes, I mind. No machine. I hate machines.

DOUGLAS: Don't you want me to quote you correctly?

BOBBY: No. If I say something awful, I'd just as soon deny it afterwards. As long as there's no tape of the conversation, I can pretty much do that.

DOUGLAS: You've denied a lot of your statements.

BOBBY: It's true, I've denied everything. I'm a complete liar. There, that's your headline: "BOBBY SUPREME IS A LIAR. ADMITS IT. LIES." I don't know what you want. Tell me what it is and I'll say it. Hand me a script. If you give me a script I'll let you turn on the tape recorder. We'll do a radio play. But if I'm on my own, I'd just as well be misquoted.

DOUGLAS: You aren't misquoted on your records, on which you seems to have a propensity to use such words as "kike" and "wop" and "cunt"...

BOBBY: And "nigger."

DOUGLAS: Yes.

BOBBY: Ouch.

DOUGLAS: I was wondering if you use these words in your everyday speech.

BOBBY: What do you mean? My routine is every day.

DOUGLAS: But when you're not on stage.

BOBBY: I'm always on stage.

DOUGLAS: So their use is reflection of how you feel?

BOBBY: What do you mean "how I feel"? Right now I have a headache. That's how I feel. So do I say "nigger" when I have a headache? No. I say "nigger" whenever I want to. Just like whenever I want to, I say "washing machine," "Velcro," and "toothpaste."

DOUGLAS: But listening to your records, the way you say "nigger" makes me think that you're not a real racist.

BOBBY: Why, how do you want me to say it?

DOUGLAS: I don't want you to say it at all, but if you do say it, you should say it right. A racist doesn't say the word "nigger" as a dirty word—it's vocabulary. There's no thought to it. There's malice, maybe, but the malice is injected into a vocabulary word. It's like when your car breaks down and you say, *"Fucking* car!" You don't shrink at the word "fucking"—it's an adjective. It might not be in a high school dictionary, but it's part of the vocabulary.

BOBBY: So?

DOUGLAS: So, when you say "nigger," you trip over it. It gets stuck on your tongue. You're aware of it. You say it self-consciously. It's the wrong inflection. You're acting the word.

BOBBY: Sorry.

DOUGLAS: You're performing it.

BOBBY: So, as I said, I'm always on stage. But it doesn't mean anything to me, these words…they're just words…I don't care if I offend some people. I'm making other people laugh. Laughter is the important thing.

DOUGLAS: You don't care if you offend people?

BOBBY: Offended people will always be offended by something. And the same people are always getting offended. Have you noticed that? If it's not one thing, it's another. So I figure as long as the offenses are sort of bunched up, you know, amongst everyone, I'm not really adding to it much.

DOUGLAS: Everyone being…black people, Hispanics, Jews, gays, the handicapped…

BOBBY: Yeah, the usual suspects. Special-interest groups. *"Them."* Too many people were handling them with kid gloves. It's gotten so quiet lately. So I filled the gap. That's why I'm so successful. I'm the only comic bigot out there.

DOUGLAS: You just said that all the abuse was "bunched up" on the same people—as if you're just one of the gang. Now you're saying you're the only one out there.

BOBBY: The only *comic.*

DOUGLAS: I thought you weren't a comic. I thought you were a performance artist.

BOBBY: I am. That's true. A performance comic. Look, you can't take any of this too seriously. Comedy is not my calling. It's my occupation. Most comics, you ask them, they'll tell you they were the class cut-up, the class clown. They had insecurities, they were skinny, they stuttered. They were short or fat or ugly. I was none of the above. I was smart, but none of the above. In America, if you don't have problems, it's a handicap. Problems are the national fuel. The nation runs by overcompensation. That's what success is: overcompensation. But if you come from a well-adjusted, middle-class background, you might as well be dead. The game is over. The mystery has been solved. There's nothing to go on. If you're born with money and security and support, it's just a big fat bladder, and you'll spend the rest of your life pissing it away. I'm in this for the racket. This isn't therapy—I'm not working through my problems. I don't have any problems. I'm not getting stuff out of my system. I'm not even trying to get stuff out of *your* system. Your system is too fucked to get anything out of it. I'm just studying it. I'm a student. I'm an anthropologist.

(Beat.) Look, where's it say in the Constitution you have to like every-one?

DOUGLAS: Where's it say you have to hate everyone?

BOBBY: This isn't about hate. It's about waking up.

DOUGLAS: I'm just trying to figure out what you're doing making "nigger" jokes to twenty thousand teenagers in Madison Square Garden. Has your mother ever seen your act?

BOBBY: I don't think so.

DOUGLAS: What about your father?

BOBBY: My father died when I was fourteen. We were close. Used to go camping together. He was a scout leader. He was more into the scouts than I was. We'd go to Red Sox games together at Fenway, fishing on the Charles. One day he started coughing. I even joked him about it. "Hey, whaddaya got, Pop—tuberculosis?" And he waved me away, laughing— but he kept coughing, and he couldn't stop. It was cancer. Lung cancer. All his fucking Marlboros. It's why I refuse to smoke. I hate it. *(Beat.)* He died on my fourteenth birthday. Happy birthday, Bobby.
(Pause.)

DOUGLAS: Well, he sends his regards. I talked to him last week. He's living in Phoenix.

BOBBY: I thought you meant my stepfather.

DOUGLAS: You don't have a stepfather.

BOBBY: But if I had one. *(He laughs.)* He'd probably die of lung cancer on my fourteenth birthday. That's what they do. *(Beat.)* Hey, look. If it wasn't me, it'd be someone else. Comprendo? It's a business. All I can say, I deserve it. All the acclaim. Everything. And it couldn't have happened to a nicer guy. And I know. I was there.

DOUGLAS: Where?

BOBBY: Where I was when I was a child.

DOUGLAS: Where was that?

BOBBY: I don't know. Long Island somewhere. Pick a town. Fort Lee.

DOUGLAS: That's in New Jersey.

BOBBY: Whatever. Anytown, U.S.A. A high school with a walk-through metal detector. Teachers who flunked out of college. I think even the gym teacher failed his physical. How's that for the fertilizer of the New Age? I'm surprised anyone even learned how to use a zipper. Everything was Velcro when I was growing up—let it rip. I love America. I really do. But it's a pretty paltry excuse for a country, don't you think? Just because we've got the loudest radios in the world, we think we own the place. Know what I mean?

DOUGLAS: I guess so.

BOBBY: It's one big—and I say this as a true patriotic American—steaming pile of horseshit. And if anyone wants to pay thirty bucks to see me insult them, then the very least I can do is spit in their face.

DOUGLAS: Some people think you're asking for trouble.

BOBBY: Maybe I am. So maybe I'm on a suicide mission. I'm a kamikaze pilot. Take no prisoners—just drive right into the sidewalk and mow down a crowd. Isn't it worth a few innocent bystanders if it wakes everyone else up?

DOUGLAS: What if one of those bystanders gets you first?

(Beat.)

BOBBY: Do you pack?

DOUGLAS: Pack what?

BOBBY: Carry a gun.

DOUGLAS: Me? *(He laughs.)* No. I'm a journalist.

BOBBY: Journalists can't carry guns?

DOUGLAS: No, it's just that—

BOBBY: When *this* could happen to you, any second.

(Bobby has whipped out a gun and is holding it to Douglas' head. Douglas is a little nervous, very quiet, very still. Bobby laughs.)

BOBBY: You're pistol-whipped.

DOUGLAS: Yeah, I see. Uh…is it loaded?

BOBBY: You're pussy-whipped. By a Glock with a kick in it. *(He hands the gun to Douglas.)* Nine millimeter. Standard army issue.

DOUGLAS: It's heavy.

BOBBY: Because it isn't made of soap.

DOUGLAS: You carry this around?

BOBBY: I've been threatened.

(Douglas opens the magazine.)

DOUGLAS: Jesus, this is *loaded.*

BOBBY: *(Takes the gun back.)* Let's hope so.

DOUGLAS: You pointed a loaded gun at my head.

BOBBY: What's the point if it isn't loaded? Why point an *unloaded* gun at someone's head? What's the point?

DOUGLAS: Do you have a permit for that thing?

BOBBY: Sure. I'm a public person. My life has been threatened. Every day. Phone rings. "Hello?" "I hope you die, Supreme. Eat my cock." Nasty stuff. Letters: Pins in my eyes, my balls crushed, a burning stake up my ass. It's amazing, the public preoccupation with my private parts. And who did I piss on? You know? People pay money to see me. It isn't exactly required reading.

DOUGLAS: No one's ever pointed a loaded gun at me before.

BOBBY: There's a first time for everything.

DOUGLAS: That's trouble. A gun is trouble. I wouldn't want one anywhere near me. Not in my house, not anywhere near me.

BOBBY: You'll get used to it. It's a fashion statement. The barrel matches your hair.

DOUGLAS: What's that, a joke?

BOBBY: No, it isn't a joke. I don't like jokes. Anyway, there's no such thing as a joke.

DOUGLAS: What do you mean?

BOBBY: Just what I said. There's no such thing as a joke. It doesn't exist. Every so-called "joke" is a polemic hidden in a laugh. It's a point. A knife. A crowbar wrapped in silk. "What did you say?" "Nothing. It was a joke." If it was a joke, then it wasn't nothing.

(Angel comes in with Riggs, Bobby's manager, who's carrying a small pile of newspapers.)

ANGELINA: Two o'clock in the afternoon, he was already in the Oak Room.

BOBBY: Drinking? Riggs, you're becoming an embarrassment.

RIGGS: I got the papers, Bobby.

BOBBY: Why didn't you come right up?

RIGGS: You said you didn't want to be disturbed. *(He sees Douglas for the first time, and looks at him a little leerily.)* Oh. Hello, sir.

(Bobby laughs at Rigg's nervousness and formality.)

BOBBY: This is Riggs, my manager. Meet Douglas McArthur. Like the general.

DOUGLAS: McCarthy.

BOBBY: Like the senator.

DOUGLAS: No relation.

BOBBY: He's doing a hatchet job on me for the New Yorker.

RIGGS: Oh. *(Pause. Riggs tries to whisper something in Bobby's ear.)*

BOBBY: You can speak freely in front of General McArthur.

DOUGLAS: McCarthy.

BOBBY: We have nothing to hide.

RIGGS: It's just that it's about the…

BOBBY: The what? The drugs? The girls? *(For Douglas' benefit.)* How old was she? Did I knock her up?

RIGGS: No, it's…

(Riggs gestures to one of the newspapers, which Bobby picks up and starts reading.)

ANGELINA: *(To Douglas.)* You think he's joking.

BOBBY: *(To Riggs, not looking up from his paper.)* Give me a kiss, Riggs.

RIGGS: Bobby…

BOBBY: Give me your ten percent kiss.

RIGGS: I really don't—

BOBBY: I said KISS ME!

(After a beat, Riggs nervously steps forward and pecks Bobby on the cheek.)

BOBBY: Faggot. *(He laughs, then refers to the newspaper.)* Hey, look, it's in the news—there's another one.

ANGELINA: Another what?

BOBBY: Another Bobby Supreme crime spree.

ANGELINA: Shit. I hate that.

BOBBY: Yeah, this one's in Baltimore.

ANGELINA: Bobby…

DOUGLAS: What are you talking about?

BOBBY: It's very sweet. It's an homage.

ANGELINA: It's ridiculous.

BOBBY: It's nice. *(To Angel.)* Remember? It happened in Nashville last week.

DOUGLAS: What did?

BOBBY: This guy beat up this old woman. When he was arrested, he said he was Bobby Supreme.

DOUGLAS: I didn't know that.

BOBBY: Well. It's small news on a big planet. But it's been happening.

DOUGLAS: You can't be serious.

RIGGS: He's serious, all right. They arrested him in Salt Lake City.

BOBBY: Yeah. Luckily the real guy came forward.

RIGGS: One of these days you're gonna get nabbed.

BOBBY: Nah.

RIGGS: *(To Douglas.)* That's what I thought you were. I came in here, saw you taking notes, I figured finally they'd got him. I thought you were the FBI. *(Douglas laughs.)*

DOUGLAS: *(To Bobby.)* People on crime sprees really blame them on you?

BOBBY: No, they *attribute* them to me. It's a tribute. A salutation.

ANGELINA: I told him—it's sick.

BOBBY: It's just the fans' way of letting me know I'm getting through.

ANGELINA: We have to stop it, Bobby. We talked about this.

BOBBY: How? I can't control them. They're not my fault. Anyway, it's a tribute. It's like the act is popping up all over the country.

ANGELINA: A crime-wave tribute to Bobby Supreme. That's brilliant.

DOUGLAS: People really do that?

BOBBY: People do anything.

ANGELINA: Bobby, we have to go over your schedule.

BOBBY: *(To Douglas.)* This might be a good time to take a break.

DOUGLAS: Oh, sure. I'll, um, I'll go down and get something to eat. Anyone want anything?

BOBBY: No, thanks. I live by room service.

DOUGLAS: Okay, well. I'll be downstairs then. *(He packs up his briefcase and goes out.)*

ANGELINA: Are you going out tonight after the show?

BOBBY: Yeah. Someone's giving me a party at Venus.

ANGELINA: Well, be careful, won't you? Those death threats are serious.

BOBBY: They're not serious. I send half of them myself.

ANGELINA: *Half* of them. Just don't drink too much. You don't know who gets into those parties.

RIGGS: Bobby, there was a call from the Cincinnati D.A.'s office…

BOBBY: Did you get my note?

RIGGS: What?

BOBBY: I hope you could read it. I used very simple words.

RIGGS: What, *that?* You can't be serious about that, Bobby. It can't be done.

BOBBY: Those aren't words, Riggs. That isn't vocabulary.

RIGGS: It's one thing to be banned from Toronto or…Salt Lake City. But New York? We'd have half the city at our necks.

BOBBY: Who needs 'em? We've got the United States. The States—United. In my fist.

RIGGS: Angel, will you talk some reason into him?

ANGELINA: I don't know what you're talking about.

RIGGS: It just doesn't sound right.

BOBBY: Vocabulary, Riggs…

RIGGS: But what's the point, Bobby?

BOBBY: "What's the point?" "What's the point?" What do you mean "What's the point?" What kind of question is that?

RIGGS: Bobby…

BOBBY: "What's the point?" *(Scoffs.)* What's the point of getting up in the morning? Why not just stay in bed? Why not just slit your throat?

ANGELINA: What are you talking about?

RIGGS: You want to do it just once?

BOBBY: No, it's going to be part of my show. From now on.

RIGGS: So what exactly does this involve, Bobby? You pick out someone from the audience...

BOBBY: Not someone. A chick.

RIGGS: Okay, a chick, from the audience. You invite her up on stage and you...

BOBBY: I beat her.

(Pause.)

ANGELINA: What?

RIGGS: This is ridiculous, Bobby. In all my years in the business...

BOBBY: *(Testy.)* In all your years in the business you've never had a comic like me. Never. I made you a very rich man. In all your fucking years...Don't give me that shit.

ANGELINA: *(Tentatively.)* Bobby...

RIGGS: They'll close down your show.

BOBBY: *(Getting angry.)* No...No, *I'll* close down my show, Riggs. *I'll* close it down. Unless I do this.

(Pause. Riggs thinks about it.)

RIGGS: Beating a girl on stage. What's the...Where's the...the...

BOBBY: With her consent. That's the point. She can even sign a release, if you like. Right on stage. It'll be part of the act. Absolve you of your fucking legal responsibility.

(Pause.)

RIGGS: Would you hit her hard?

(Angel sits down.)

BOBBY: No, not hard. Maybe a few marks. Enough to soften her up a bit. Enough to get her wet.

RIGGS: This is too dangerous.

BOBBY: Riggs? I thought you were my manager. I thought you were on my team. I thought you were a team player.

RIGGS: I am, Bobby...I'm just looking out for your intentions.

BOBBY: I don't need you to look out for my intentions. I can look out for my own fucking intentions. All I need is for you to say yes. You're my yes-man. That's what I pay you for. If I wanted your opinion, I'd give it to you. OK?

RIGGS: Yes, Bobby...

BOBBY: All I need to know is if you're working *for* me or *against* me.

RIGGS: I'm working for you, Bobby. You know that.

BOBBY: That's good. OK. Now. I want you to do an errand for me.

RIGGS: Sure, Bobby.

BOBBY: I want you to go downstairs, and I want to see if you can find me a riding crop.

(This seems to alarm Angelina, but she doesn't move or say anything.)

RIGGS: A riding crop?

BOBBY: Yes. I want you to get me a riding crop. I'm going to need it for tonight's show.

RIGGS: Oh. Okay, Bobby. Sure. *(He goes out.)*

(Pause.)

ANGELINA: What was that about?

BOBBY: That was a test.

ANGELINA: A test.

BOBBY: Yeah, a test. Of the Emergency Broadcast System. I want to see how much of the act he believes.

ANGELINA: He'll do anything you ask him to.

BOBBY: I have no interest in beating someone on stage. But if he brings me the crop, I'll have no choice.

ANGELINA: But it's just an errand.

BOBBY: No, it's more than that. I want to see how far he thinks I'm willing to go.

(Pause.)

ANGELINA: Bobby, I think we're missing the point of the show.

BOBBY: What point?

ANGELINA: The irony. The political subtext.

BOBBY: People don't come to my show for political subtext. They come to my show to laugh. That's what they come to Bobby Supreme for.

ANGELINA: Yes, but I think this is getting out of hand. Remember the deal we made?

BOBBY: What deal?

ANGELINA: When we fill the biggest venue, we retire.

BOBBY: Madison Square Garden isn't the biggest venue. I haven't done stadiums yet.

ANGELINA: You can't do this in a stadium. It's already gotten out of hand. You told me you're beginning to be afraid of your fans.

BOBBY: No no, just some of the louder ones. I don't like the firecrackers. But it's a rock n'roll crowd, I have to get used to that. It isn't like the clubs anymore.

ANGELINA: It's going wrong. Beating someone on stage. People getting hurt in your name.

BOBBY: It's just fistfights. That would have happened anyway.

ANGELINA: Have you seen some of your fans? They're like Nazi Youth.

BOBBY: Well, Hitler. That was some act. Nuremburg was a huge venue.

ANGELINA: Hitler wasn't an act, Bobby.

BOBBY: For fuck's sake, lighten up, Angel, that was a joke.

ANGELINA: There's no such thing as a joke. Remember? You taught me that.

> *(She goes out.)*
>
> *(Blackout.)*

SCENE II

At the hotel bar, Riggs is sitting on a stool next to Janet, an attractive, corporately dressed woman in her thirties. She's ignoring him completely while talking on a cell phone. On the bar, in front of Riggs, is a riding crop.

RIGGS: *(Slightly drunk.)* You ever heard of Bobby Supreme? He's the biggest comic in the world. He's one of mine. My one and only, in fact—I manage him. And boy is he tough to manage. *(A little laugh.)* If you want tickets I could get you one. He's playing the Garden tonight—it's completely sold out. But we always have a few tickets set aside, you know, VIP stuff, for special friends. *(Pause.)* Do you come here often? I'm not trying to pick you up. I'm just saying that because it seems to be the thing to say in a bar.

JANET: What? I'm sorry, were you talking to me?

RIGGS: Um, yeah. What's that you're working on?

JANET: Just business.

RIGGS: Are you from around here?

JANET: Do you come here often?

RIGGS: What?

JANET: I'm feeding you lines.

RIGGS: Oh. *(Confused.)* Do you come here often?

JANET: Yes, that's good.

> *(At another part of the same bar, Angelina is sitting at a table, drinking. Douglas approaches her.)*

DOUGLAS: Can I buy you a drink?

ANGELINA: What? *(Looking up.)* Oh, it's the New Yorker. *(She holds up her drink.)* Thanks, I'm already plugged in.

DOUGLAS: Mind if I join you?

(Angel gestures it's okay. Douglas sits at her table. Pause.)

DOUGLAS: *(Pause.)* How's it going?

ANGELINA: It's after working hours, I don't answer any questions.

DOUGLAS: Did I ask any questions?

ANGELINA: There's another one.

(Riggs and Janet at the bar.)

RIGGS: Are you from New York?

JANET: Should I be?

RIGGS: I don't know where else people come from, L.A. or New York.

JANET: I'll get you a new map.

RIGGS: My guy's on the cover of Rolling Stone this week.

JANET: I don't read Rolling Stone.

RIGGS: When I met him he said he was a performance artist. I told him to get real—he was a comic. Make some money. What's performance art? In the sixties they called them "Happenings." I went to a Happening once. It was John Lennon and Yoko Ono in a paper bag. For two hours we all watched this huge paper bag. Nothing happened. Finally, some guy jumps up on the stage, rips open the bag, and there's nothing inside but this little note. "Glad you could make it. Love John and Yoko." That cost me ten bucks—which was a lot of money in those days. It got a great review in the Times. What did you say your name was?

JANET: I didn't say.

RIGGS: *(Offering his hand.)* Cy Rigger. Everyone calls me Riggs. I'm a talent manager. And there used to be a lot of guys I managed. And they were a lot like horses. Some of them came in last. Now I have only one guy. And he's huge. He comes in first. Every time. He's the biggest horse. He just won the Indianapolis 500…

JANET: I don't think horses run in the Indianapolis 500…

RIGGS: You ever heard of Benny Carton?

JANET: No, I can't say I have.

RIGGS: He was a comedian. But he was the old-fashioned kind. *(Beat.)* He was funny.

(Angelina and Douglas.)

DOUGLAS: Congratulations—the Madison Square Garden's completely sold out.

ANGELINA: *(Automatic pilot.)* He's been selling out every venue in his thirty-six-city tour. Fastest-selling comic in the business. Not since Lenny Bruce has a… *(She realizes she's just slipped into PR mode.)* Whatever. You got the press release.

DOUGLAS: I've got the whole kit.

ANGELINA: So what's your angle?

DOUGLAS: What angle?

ANGELINA: On the Bobby Supreme story. "Symptom of the New America"? Or "The Bigot Facade"? Or is it "The Supreme Idiot"?

DOUGLAS: What's *your* angle?

ANGELINA: I don't have an angle. I'm just an employee.

DOUGLAS: Of a performance piece.

(She looks at him.)

ANGELINA: Right.

DOUGLAS: Seems like an odd business for someone like you to be in.

ANGELINA: Someone like me? What's that? A small-breasted post-preppie with an MBA? Or am I a chick from the boroughs with former big hair and half a real estate license?

DOUGLAS: You're a smart woman. His language is all "fucking cunt."

ANGELINA: It's just language. What do you think this is about?

DOUGLAS: I'm not sure what this is about.

ANGELINA: They're just jokes.

(Riggs and Janet.)

RIGGS: In one day, Bobby Supreme makes more money than Benny Carton made in his entire, miserable lifetime.

DOUGLAS: What was he like when he started out?

RIGGS: He played tiny clubs—hole-in-the-walls. The first time I saw him was in Baltimore.

ANNOUNCER'S VOICE: *(Over P.A. system.)* Let's give a warm, friendly, Philadelphia, give-him-a-break welcome to Bobby Sikowski—his first time on mike at the Comedy Shop.

(Respectable, light applause. Lights up to show Bobby speaking at a mike in a small comedy club.)

BOBBY: Hi. It's always nice to be back in Philadelphia. The City of Brotherly Love. *(Beat.)* The *sisters* get kicked around a bit… *(He freezes in position.)*

RIGGS: Maybe it was in Philadelphia. Anyway, he wasn't very good. But he was so *good* at being not very good that I thought there might be something there. I felt he was just *pretending* to be not very good. Like he knew how good he really was. But that people weren't really ready to hear his best material. So he did the stuff they wanted to hear. And it wasn't very good.

BOBBY: *(Unfreezes.)* Thanks. Actually, I wasn't going to come up tonight because I have this...this thyroid condition... *(Beat.)* I understand that isn't very comical. A thyroid condition. It isn't great real-life material to be working with, but that's what I have. *(Beat.)* I asked for a hernia, but they were all out...

(Light to Riggs.)

RIGGS: *(To Janet.)* Did you know he graduated from Princeton?

(Light on Bobby again. He's at another club, doing his routine.)

BOBBY: It's like that saying: "Don't be depressed. Today is the worst day of the rest of your life." Can't get any worse than that. Am I speaking in platitudes? Well, sorry, it's in my contract...

ANGELINA: We spent all summer driving up and down the East Coast, stopping in comedy clubs. He just improvised, he had no idea what to say. I mean, really, he had no idea what a stand-up comic *was*.

BOBBY: It's always good to be in Baltimore. Why is it good to be in Baltimore? Because it's the thing you say at comedy clubs. "It's always good to be in Baltimore."

ANGELINA: His material began getting a bit philosophical. That's when I started to like it. But nobody else did.

BOBBY: What I mean is, "Good thing I'm not a lampshade. Nice to be in Baltimore." Or, "Glad I didn't get run over by a truck. Oh, I'm in Baltimore? Okay. Why not?" Because bad as things are...they aren't worse.

ANGELINA: What did he tell you? That he never graduated from college? He used to tell me different stories. Riggs thinks he went to Yale or something.

RIGGS: He went to Princeton. Graduated Summer come louder. Or whatever it's called. That thing in Latin that means you did real good. He got that.

ANGELINA: Whatever you've read of the record—the official bio, the PR sheet—I'd scrape it off with a knife. Pure bullshit. Absolute BS. But that's Bobby Supreme, isn't it?

(Under this, we hear Bobby, in a dim light, doing his routine at another club.)

BOBBY: ...That's what I used to do as a kid—I'd invite disaster on myself, because it was exciting. It was something I could use. Anyway, that happened in Boston. Actually, I'm originally *from* Boston...

RIGGS: To tell you the truth, I hardly knew a thing about him—except that he had this odd, covered-up talent. I'd been in the business twenty-five years and I'd never seen anything like him. Once he actually threw up on stage. Right into the front row.

ANGELINA: He had seafood poisoning.

RIGGS: But he was a natural. A *mensch.* Actually we have a word for it in Yiddish, for that kind of play-acting. I can't think of it offhand, but there's a word for it. *Schmeckel.* No, that's not it. Anyway, he had it.

ANGELINA: Then he started going through what he called his "socially conscious" phase.

BOBBY: Let me tell you how to get rid of racism…

ANGELINA: Yeah, "How to get rid of racism." Like he was running for Congress or something. *(She laughs.)*

BOBBY: This is so obvious, it's hurting me. Listen up, I'm only going to say this once cause I can hardly pronounce it: miscegenation. Everyone's got to melt. The white people have got to fuck the black people to make brown people. The brown people have got to fuck the yellow people to make, uh, puce people. The brown people have got to fuck the white people to make darker white people. This will take a couple hundred years, but eventually it will all even out and everyone will look more or less the same. The Irish have got to fuck the Italians…

ANGELINA: There was something about his social commentary that I sort of liked…

BOBBY: *(Continuing.)* The Italians have got to fuck the Jews…

RIGGS: I thought it was disgusting.

BOBBY: *(Continuing.)* We've got to melt everybody—we're not melting.

ANGELINA: It was interesting.

BOBBY: *(Continuing.)* Okay, problem solved. Interracial fucking. It's the only thing that'll work. Everybody's got to fuck everyone else. Except no one's fucking the fags, cause they're too busy fucking themselves. So, next problem: Homophobia. What are you worried about? They're just *fags.* The point is, there are probably more of them than you think. Okay? Everybody who's a fag, put your hand up and say hello. Any out there? *(Points.)* Right, there's one. Okay, fine. That's what we have to do: we have to notice them. They're part of your fucking family, so get used to it. They're your brother, your sister, your boss, your *mother-in-law.* Some of them. You'd be surprised. Okay, message to the homos: Stop flashing your pierced nipples and pink shorts at us—we get the picture, okay? Now sit down and shut up.

ANGELINA: But then it changed. At some point he realized that the nastier and dirtier his material got, the more people liked it. And the more money he made.

(Bobby is smoking an unlit cigar.)

BOBBY: I'm glad to be back in New York. The Big Apple.

RIGGS: Yeah, he liked the money. They both did.

ANGELINA: Hey, we paid off our student loans in six months. No one else did that.

BOBBY: Welcome to my fucking cigar. It's an oral prop—a crutch. George Burns taught me how to do this. You tell a joke, toke on the cigar. The crowd laughs while you do the toke.

(He takes a toke. Silence.)

BOBBY: I said, the crowd laughs while you do the toke.

(Laughter.)

BOBBY: That's better. Like I gotta do all the work myself here? Like I gotta laugh at my own jokes. Like I don't work for a living. Gimme a break. Oh, you'll notice the cigar isn't lit. That's because it's a prop. You think I'm gonna fuckin' kill myself for your pleasure? Fuck you. Fuck you. *(Beat.)* And you and you and you…

ANGELINA: Two months later we bought a loft on Broome Street in SoHo. We were artists. David Byrne. Julian Schnabel. Bobby Supreme.

(A buzz goes off in Janet's pocket.)

JANET: Excuse me. *(She takes a small cellular phone out of her pocket and speaks into it.)* Yes, Dorothy…No, not yet. I'm speaking to his manager now… Right. Okay. Yes, I will. Okay…Right…Bye. *(She closes up phone and puts it back in her pocket.)*

RIGGS: I should, uh…Bobby doesn't let me have one of those.

JANET: They're a nuisance. You'll be having dinner at the Occidental, and your pocket goes off.

RIGGS: The Occidental. That's in…

JANET: Washington.

(Riggs nervously sits up a little straighter.)

RIGGS: What, uh…department are you in?

JANET: Never mind that. When can I see Mr. Supreme?

RIGGS: Uh. Well, I'll, uh, set something up immediately. Of course he's pretty busy, but I know he'll want to see you. He's probably working at the moment. You know, his routine. He's meticulous about his work. *(He gets up off his stool and starts walking away.)*

JANET: Mr. Riggs…

(Riggs stops.)

JANET: You forgot your riding crop.

> (*She takes the riding crop off the bar and holds it out to him. Riggs stares at it. Blackout.*)

SCENE III

Bobby's hotel room, the next morning. Bobby and Brandy in bed. Bobby is asleep. Brandy is sixteen and has a black eye.

BRANDY: Bobby?

> (*No answer. She shakes him.*)

BRANDY: *Bobby?*

BOBBY: *(Wakes up, groggily.)* Wha…What is it?

BRANDY: Bobby Supreme…

BOBBY: What?

BRANDY: Mr. Bobby Su-pre-eme…You're the *supremacist.* Good morning.
> (*She smiles brightly.*)

BOBBY: Where am I?

BRANDY: *(Sing-song.)* In your hotel room. In bed. With Brandy Centerfold. Good morning. Boy did we have fun last night. This morning, actually.

BOBBY: *(Sits up and looks at her.)* God, what happened to your face?

BRANDY: What, did I break out? Shit! *(She touches her eye.)* Oh, the eye? *(She giggles.)* We were sort of fooling around.

BOBBY: I couldn't have done that. Jesus. Let's get some ice…

BRANDY: No no no. Don't bother. I kind of like it. Boy, do you have one insatiable cock. Let me tell you. You're a real hottie. I love you.
> (*Pause. Bobby stares at her.*)

BOBBY: Who are you?

BRANDY: Don't you remember? I guess I'll have to jolt your memory a bit.
> (*She begins fondling him under the covers.*)

BOBBY: Hey!

BRANDY: Gaining altitude…

BOBBY: Will you cut that out! *(He slaps her hand.)* Stop that!

BRANDY: Hmmmm….

BOBBY: Stop it!
> (*She does so.*)

BOBBY: God, my back hurts. It's like I…

BRANDY: I scratched you.

BOBBY: You did?

BRANDY: All down your back. In the heat of passion. You scratched me too. *(Giggles.)* It was a real scratch-out fuckfest!

BOBBY: *(Looks at her strangely.)* Jesus, where did we *meet?*

BRANDY: Venus.

BOBBY: What?

BRANDY: We met at *Venus.* You know, the nightclub. Don't you remember? I'm Brandy. You chased me under the table.

BOBBY: I met you at a *nightclub?* How did you get in? How *old* are you?

BRANDY: Sixteen. But they let me in all the nightclubs. *(Proudly.)* I'm ornamental!

BOBBY: Why aren't you in school, Candy?

BRANDY: Brandy. I got a day off. You were really disgusting last night. *(Giggles.)*

BOBBY: When?

BRANDY: At your show. You were wild! You brought that girl up on the stage and you pretended to fuck her! *(Laughs.)* I almost peed myself laughing! *(She mimes whipping someone.)*

BOBBY: You found that funny?

BRANDY: I fell off my seat!

BOBBY: Why did you find it funny?

BRANDY: Why? *(She thinks for a moment.)* Because it was! *(Beat.)* Why do you have a limp?

BOBBY: Because some asshole shot me when I was a kid.

BRANDY: How'd it happen?

BOBBY: Don't you read the articles? I've told the story about a thousand times.

BRANDY: But it's always different.

BOBBY: I pissed a kid off. He shot me. I limp. The end. *(Squints in pain.)* And now my back's gonna have a limp. Listen, Minky, I think you better go. Now. *(Quietly.)* Where's your underwear?

BRANDY: Destroyed. You ripped it off.

BOBBY: *You* must have ripped it off. I'm not a ripper.

BRANDY: Okay, *I* ripped it off. But you approved…

BOBBY: "Right." *(He reaches over to the phone by the bed, starts poking in a number.)*

BRANDY: What are you doing?

BOBBY: I'm ordering some Band-Aids and new underwear. *(Brandy puts her hand on the receiver, blocking the call.)*

BRANDY: Don't. I'd rather just stay here for a while…with you.

BOBBY: No underwear? Okay, it's your call, Minky, but you're outta here. Subito. *(He gets up from the bed naked, slips on a pair of boxers, goes over to his notebook computer on the desk and starts typing. He has scratches on his back.)*

BRANDY: All my friends at school think you're really great.

BOBBY: Great.

BRANDY: You know, I want to be a comic when I grow up too.

BOBBY: You'll love it.

BRANDY: I wrote a routine. Want to hear it?

BOBBY: Not right now, Mink.

BRANDY: It's about sex in high school.

BOBBY: Not now, Mink. Some other time.

(Brandy takes Bobby's codpiece off the bed, sniffs it and starts stroking it, then licking it.)

BRANDY: I wasn't sure if I should mention this, but…

BOBBY: Your mom wants to me make it with me too.

BRANDY: *(Laughs.)* No! *(Dead serious.)* I've written a screenplay.

BOBBY: Oh, God! Not another one! Everyone wants to give me their screenplay! "Aren't you Bobby Supreme? Would you mind taking a look at my screenplay?" Everyone. Traffic cops. Waitresses. Call girls. My fucking *dentist.* He's not really a dentist—he's really a screenwriter! I suppose I should go to a film studio to have my teeth cleaned, huh!?
(Pause.)

BRANDY: It's about this girl who grows a third breast.

BOBBY: Oh. Sounds great. Is it based on a real experience?

BRANDY: No, I just thought it was interesting.
(Pause.)

BOBBY: Where's it come up?

BRANDY: What?

BOBBY: The third breast.

BRANDY: Oh. Sort of in the middle. *(Beat.)* So you want to read it?

BOBBY: No!

BRANDY: Want me to give you a blow job?

BOBBY: What? No. *(Beat.)* Thanks for the thought.

BRANDY: I could do it under the table. Some guys say it makes them work better.

BOBBY: Some guys? *(Laughs.)* Jesus Christ. *(Mutters.)* "Some guys." "Scratch-out fuckfest…"

BRANDY: Oh, they don't mean anything to me. They're just assholes. Not like you. *(Pause.)* No one will believe I slept with you.

BOBBY: Good. Just as well.

BRANDY: I'll tell them, but they won't believe me. They'll make fun of me.

BOBBY: So what do you want me to do about it? Write you a note?

BRANDY: Will you?

BOBBY: Sure. I'll give you a certificate. You can give it to your teacher. "Please excuse Minky for missing school yesterday. She was busy fucking Bobby Supreme.

(Pause. Brandy laughs.)

BRANDY: You're funny.

BOBBY: Right.

BRANDY: But my name's Brandy, not Minky.

BOBBY: No one's called "Brandy." Not even centerfolds. Not really. It's a made-up name. What do your parents call you?

BRANDY: My parents are dead.

BOBBY: No they're not. They're just confused.

(Brandy laughs.)

BRANDY: What are you writing?

BOBBY: An article.

BRANDY: What's it about?

BOBBY: It's about the importance of getting a secondary education, maintaining a high Grade Point Average, and getting good SAT scores. And don't forget extracurricular activities.

BRANDY: Really?

BOBBY: Yeah, sure.

(Beat.)

BRANDY: *(Coyly.)* I'm pretty good at extracurricular activities, aren't I?

BOBBY: Ace. They should give you a medal.

BRANDY: You think so?

BOBBY: Yeah. A Nobel Prize. Look, Minky…I really gotta work here.

BRANDY: That's okay. *(Beat.)* Are we going to go to the zoo?

BOBBY: *What?*

BRANDY: You said last night you'd take me to the Central Park Zoo. You wanted to see the sea lions.

(Bobby sits on the bed.)

BOBBY: Look, Mink. I don't even know what *country* I was in last night. *(Pause. Bobby stares off for a moment. He looks at Brandy, a sudden recognition.)* Wait a minute. I remember…

BRANDY: You were incredible…

BOBBY: I was a little under the weather last night…

BRANDY: That was the best sex I ever had. I came for twenty minutes.

BOBBY: Look, Mink, last night I was… *(He gets up off the bed.)*

BRANDY: You want me to leave?

BOBBY: Nothing personal.

BRANDY: Say something nice about me.

BOBBY: What?

BRANDY: Before I go, I want you to say one thing really nice about me.

BOBBY: Then you'll go?

BRANDY: I promise.

> *(Pause.)*

BOBBY: You have nice teeth.

BRANDY: I do?

BOBBY: Yeah.

BRANDY: That's because I floss regularly.

BOBBY: Well it shows, Minky. Keep up those teeth. And have a good life. Go to college. Marry somebody. *(Bobby gets up and goes into the bathroom.)*

BRANDY: Can I have a pair of your boxers?

BOBBY: *(From the bathroom.)* No! *(He slams the door.)*

> *(Brandy takes Bobby's underwear and slips it on under the bedcovers, then gets out of the bed.)*

BRANDY: *(Speaking to him through the door.)* My name's not really Brandy. But I read that it was your favorite drink, so that's what I call myself. This is really a dream come true for me—I've wanted to go to bed with you all my life. Ever since I read about you in Sassy. They hated you, but I thought you were cute. I'm sick of Brad Pitt. My girlfriends and I talk about you all the time.

> *(Angelina comes in, unbeknownst to Brandy.)*

BRANDY: Zora bet me ten bucks that you had a cock ring. I won.

ANGELINA: I bet you did.

BRANDY: *(Turning around.)* Oh! Who are you.

ANGELINA: Angelina. And you're Breakfast. And Breakfast is over. *(She starts cleaning up the papers on the desk.)*

BRANDY: Are you his wife?

ANGELINA: No, I'm his mother.

BRANDY: You don't look like his mother.

ANGELINA: Yeah, well he's younger than he looks. He's a baby. And so are you. Why aren't you in school?

BRANDY: I graduated.

ANGELINA: Sure you did. *(Looks at Brandy's face.)* God, what happened to your face? Did Bobby do that?

BRANDY: Yeah. He kind of beat me up.

ANGELINA: Christ. Do you have enough money to get home?

BRANDY: I'm not going home. Bobby's going to take me to the Central Park Zoo.

ANGELINA: Oh, for God's sake. Look, why don't you hop on a bus and scuttle back to New Jersey. Here's twenty bucks.

(She offers a twenty dollar bill to Brandy, who takes it with no reaction.)

BRANDY: I'm not from New Jersey.

ANGELINA: Then Disneyworld, or whatever planet you come from. *Out.* This is business.

(Pause. Brandy doesn't move.)

BRANDY: You don't like me, do you?

ANGELINA: Honey, *like* has nothing to do with it. This is Wall Street. Business. Money. Career. Job. Do you speak English?

BRANDY: You want me to go? Where's Bobby?

ANGELINA: Out. Exit. Scram. Beat it. Dismount. Proceed outside. Tell me which word you don't understand, I'll look it up in Mallspeak.

BRANDY: Bobby doesn't want me to leave.

ANGELINA: Bobby wanted you to leave so much, he left himself. But he doesn't do the traffic work, I do. I'm the traffic cop. The shovel brigade—he makes the mess, I clean it up. It's my job. It's what I get paid to do. You wouldn't want me to get fired, would you?

BRANDY: Bobby wouldn't fire you. You're his mother.

ANGELINA: Einstein fired his mother. Picasso fired his mother. I don't think Brando's mother lasted too long either.

(Bobby comes out of the bathroom, dressed and adjusting another codpiece.)

BOBBY: Angel, I need a copy of this month's Science Digest magazine, there's an article about the breeding habits of Norway rats. And get me some pineapple juice. What's the girl doing here? Did you give her bus fare?

BRANDY: She won't go.

BOBBY: *(To Brandy.)* Next time, Minky. Bobby's got to go to work. *(To Angelina.)* Give her a signed photo.

ANGELINA: She doesn't want a photo.

BOBBY: Sure she does.

(Angelina takes a publicity shot, signs it herself, and hands it to Brandy, who takes it glumly.)

ANGELINA: Here. Hang it on your wall with your other victims.

BRANDY: *(To Bobby.)* Are we going out?

BOBBY: No, Daddy has to work today. *(To Angel.)* She's real 2-D, this one. *(To Brandy.)* Put your clothes on and buy yourself a magazine. *(He takes his wallet out of his pocket and hands her a bill.)* Here's twenty bucks.

ANGELINA: I already paid her.

BOBBY: So we're putting her through college. *(To Brandy.)* I'll count to ten. If you're not gone, Sweetheart, you're in police custody.

BRANDY: What for?

BOBBY: Breaking and entering. Soliciting. Statutory rape.

ANGELINA: He'll do it.

(Brandy looks worried.)

BOBBY: One…two…three…four…five…

(Brandy starts to get up, grabs her clothes, puts them on quickly and—unnoticed by Angelina or Bobby—grabs the codpiece on the bed and slips it into her bag.)

BOBBY: Six…seven…eight…nine…

BRANDY: I LOVE YOU, BOBBY!

BOBBY: Ten.

BRANDY: Bye, Bobby. *(She hands him a scrap of paper.)* That's my number. Don't call me after eleven PM, my mother goes to bed. *(She exits, then quickly sticks her head back in the door.)* You're a great fuck! *(She exits.)*

BOBBY: *(To Angelina, without missing a beat.)* And get me some papers. I didn't get the papers.

ANGELINA: Did you have to beat her?

BOBBY: I didn't beat her. She beat herself.

ANGELINA: On stage. The girl on stage. Why did you do that?

BOBBY: She *volunteered.*

(Angelina stares at him. Pause.)

ANGELINA: Doug McCarthy is waiting outside.

BOBBY: Who?

ANGELINA: The guy from the New Yorker.

BOBBY: Oh, right. I haven't read the papers yet today. I need the *Times, Post, News, Voice.*…And get me an escort, okay?

ANGELINA: Ah, Bobby…

BOBBY: I'm sick of this groupie shit. All they want is literary criticism. I'm not a fucking comedy workshop here, I'm just a comic with hard-on. If I want students I'll get a professorship at Cornell. Get me an escort. Blonde. Black fishnet stockings. No comic. No actress. No model. No

groupie. Just a fucking pro, is that too much to ask for? And don't forget: fishnet. Last escort they sent me had pantyhose. It was like trying to
fuck a muppet.

ANGELINA: You don't want an escort, Bobby.

BOBBY: No, you're right. What could I be thinking of?

ANGELINA: You don't. You never used to be like this. What's gotten into you?
This is *off stage.* You should be off character now.

BOBBY: I'm never off character.

ANGELINA: Bobby, you're talking to *me.* Don't tell me you're never off character. I know you. Shit, I *created* you. I practically built your hard drive.
(Beat.)

BOBBY: Bobby doesn't have a hard drive.

ANGELINA: Seriously, Bobby. We've got the intellectual cachet now. Isn't that
what we wanted? *The New Criterion? The Nation? The New York Review
of Books?* Christ, we've done the Garden and we've got the *New Yorker.*
(Bobby is staring at himself in the mirror, adjusting his codpiece.)

ANGELINA: You never used to need these cartoon hood ornaments.

BOBBY: Well, not everyone's built like a Studebaker. Everything looks smaller
on stage.

ANGELINA: You don't need a stage. *(Beat.)* Remember that first trip we took
down Route One along the coast? Stopping in those little neon, mall
towns? What was that place in Norwalk called?

BOBBY: The Laugh Shop.

ANGELINA: *(Laughs.)* Right. The Laugh Shop. A converted hardware store.
They still had the ladders against the walls. You didn't even have a name
yet.

BOBBY: Bob Sikowski. We didn't get paid.

ANGELINA: They paid us in beer!

BOBBY: Should have paid us in ladders. We could have moved up faster.

ANGELINA: We moved up pretty fast.
(They kiss.)

ANGELINA: Why don't we get out of this? Take our winnings and go home.
(Bobby notices his reflection in the mirror.)

BOBBY: I am home, Baby.

ANGELINA: You aren't, Bobby…

BOBBY: Cover of Rolling Stone.

ANGELINA: *(Notices his distant stare.)* What are you doing?

BOBBY: Angel?

ANGELINA: What?

BOBBY: I want you to do Bobby a favor.

ANGELINA: What?

BOBBY: *(Quietly.)* I want you…to get Bobby an escort…with fishnet stockings.

(Angelina breaks out of the embrace and slaps his arm.)

ANGELINA: Dammit, Bobby! You're a fucking asshole!

(She goes out. Bobby goes to the mirror. He takes the gun out of a drawer and points it at himself in the mirror.)

BOBBY: You're a fucking asshole. You *fuck*. You motherfucker. You fucking *kike*, cunting *asshole, chink-wop-fuck…*

(He puts the barrel of the gun in his mouth. A soft tapping on the door, and then Douglas sticks his head in.)

DOUGLAS: Morning. Am I interrupting something?

(Bobby takes the gun out of his mouth.)

BOBBY: No. No, come in. *(Bobby puts the gun back in the drawer.)*

DOUGLAS: This room's been pretty busy this morning.

BOBBY: It's always like this. It's crazy. What do you want? I thought you were finished with me.

DOUGLAS: Just a few more questions. I checked your bio, and it doesn't click…

BOBBY: It's not meant to click. You have to use a hammer.

DOUGLAS: You said you never did any clubs, but I checked and you have a pretty solid performance record.

BOBBY: I never did the clubs.

DOUGLAS: You claim you started right on television, on Letterman and Leno, and then got your HBO special. It was supposed to be an explosion…

BOBBY: It *was* an explosion…

DOUGLAS: But you started a long time ago and you did the club circuit.

BOBBY: You're mistaking me with someone else.

DOUGLAS: You used the name "Bobby Sikowski."

BOBBY: I've never heard of Bobby Sikowski. *(Beat.)* I'm a *performance* artist, Douglas.

DOUGLAS: Yes, you've claimed that several times. In fact, you've claimed many things, but I did my homework, Bobby, and I've found some inconsistencies. For instance, you're not from Long Island. You're from Connecticut.

BOBBY: Same direction.

DOUGLAS: And you didn't drop out of the Brooklyn Technical Institute. You went to Princeton.

BOBBY: That was Princeton? All I remember is a bunch of buildings covered in weeds. And horsey girls who only talked about horses. And girls.

DOUGLAS: You graduated summa cum laude, majoring in African-American studies. Then you went to medical school at NYU.

BOBBY: Disgusting, isn't it?

DOUGLAS: But you dropped out after a year and started doing the clubs and then performance spaces like Dixon Place and PS 122 in New York.

BOBBY: Oh, right.

DOUGLAS: And a talent scout saw your act—at the Public Theater—and gave you a contract for an HBO special.

BOBBY: I feel like I'm on "This is Your Life." Is the talent scout going to come out from behind a curtain?

DOUGLAS: I don't know why nobody dug this up before.

BOBBY: Because none of it is true.

DOUGLAS: It's an intriguing biography, you have to admit. Why did you fake your resume?

BOBBY: I didn't fake my resume.

DOUGLAS: You gave yourself a Brooklyn-based, blue-collar Italian background. When you're an upper-middle class half-Jewish, half-Italian kid from Hartford, Connecticut, who majored in African-American studies.

BOBBY: What can I say? You got me. I'm a closet nice guy. *(He grins.)* Except that none of this is true.

DOUGLAS: Your parents marched in Selma.

BOBBY: You're full of shit.

DOUGLAS: You marched with them.

BOBBY: I don't even know who Selma is.

DOUGLAS: You were four years old. I even found a picture of you in Life magazine. *(He hands a small cut-out photo to Bobby, who studies it intently.)*

BOBBY: That isn't me. I don't even think it's a boy.

DOUGLAS: It is. It's you.

(Bobby puts the photo in the drawer of the desk.)

BOBBY: So what are you saying?

DOUGLAS: You're a fake. This isn't you. Why are you doing this? What are you covering up?

(Pause. There's a knock on the door.)

BOBBY: *(Calling.)* Door's open.

(Janet comes in.)

JANET: Hello. Mr. Supreme?

BOBBY: That's me. (*He turns around, sees Janet. Smiles.*) Oh, it's you. (*To Douglas.*) Sorry, New Yorker. Nature calls.

DOUGLAS: I still have some questions…

BOBBY: After the show.

DOUGLAS: I've already seen the show.

BOBBY: Then the interview is over. I have nothing else to say.

(*Douglas stares at Bobby a moment, then goes out. Janet is still standing by the door.*)

BOBBY: Come in, come in.

JANET: Mr. Supreme…

BOBBY: "Bobby," please.

JANET: Bobby. I'm Janet Goodman.

BOBBY: Great. You look good. Come in.

(*Janet comes into the room.*)

JANET: Thanks. You let anyone just come in like that?

BOBBY: Sure. My bodyguards have the year off. (*Looking at her legs.*) No fishnet stockings. I told Angel fishnet.

(*Janet looks down at her legs.*)

JANET: Angel fishnet?

BOBBY: That's okay.

JANET: I'm glad you approve.

BOBBY: Yeah, it's fine. Take a seat.

JANET: Thanks. (*Janet sits down.*)

BOBBY: So. Janet. I know there's a two-hour minimum, which is fine, but I don't have the time, so I'll only use an hour…

JANET: I only need a few minutes.

BOBBY: That may be, but what *I* want to do will take more than a few minutes. (*He laughs.*)

JANET: Oh, well. That's very kind. Thank you.

BOBBY: Don't mention it. (*He laughs again.*) I love the briefcase. Nice touch.

(*Janet reaches into her briefcase and looks for some documents. Bobby turns around and begins taking off his clothes.*)

JANET: I have some figures I'd like you to look at, showing that over thirty percent of the nation's children are still living under the poverty level…

(*She looks up and sees Bobby taking his pants off.*) What are you doing?

BOBBY: Oh, I…Jesus. I thought you were my escort. (*He buckles up self-consciously.*)

JANET: Your escort? You mean a prostitute?

BOBBY: Yeah, I ordered one up. When you came in, I…I thought you were my room service.

JANET: You thought I was a prostitute? *(She bursts out laughing.)* That's hilarious. I should be insulted but…No one ever mistook me for a prostitute before.

BOBBY: Yeah, well…First time for everything.

JANET: I'm…I'm Janet Goodman. I… *(She's still laughing.)* I spoke to your manager yesterday… *(Trying to regain composure.)* …about the benefit.

BOBBY: What benefit?

JANET: For the NCH. The National Coalition for the Homeless.

BOBBY: A benefit? A minute ago I thought I was about to get my rocks off, now I'm doing a benefit?

JANET: On the phone I was given to understand you were interested.

BOBBY: You were? Well, it was misinformation. Riggs is a complete imbecile. You have to understand this.

JANET: He told me to visit you in your hotel when you got to New York. God. I can't believe you really took me for a…

BOBBY: I just did a benefit.

JANET: Well, last summer you participated in the Gutter Comics to Save the Rain Forests.

BOBBY: Yeah, I did the Gutterthon. We raised over half a million bucks for the whatever-it-is. The trees.

JANET: Yes, but your track record isn't exactly stellar on charitable causes.

BOBBY: I'm not Bob Geldof. Or Sting.

JANET: Mr. Supreme: You do a lot of comedy at the expense of the homeless. But do you really understand the *life* of the homeless in America? In New York City alone there are an estimated seventy-five thousand men, women and children living on the streets. At the NCH we're raising money to rehabilitate housing on the Lower East Side and give some of these people a decent place to live. By helping them we help ourselves; we get these families off the streets and leading worthwhile lives, working, paying taxes, and contributing to society as a whole. It's a crucial campaign and we have to…to…What are you staring at?

BOBBY: You.

JANET: Me?

BOBBY: Yeah. You know, you wouldn't make such a bad escort…

JANET: What, a whore?

BOBBY: Well, an escort. Businessmen fly into the city for a meeting, they want to relax after work, like to spend time in the company of beautiful, well-turned-out women.

JANET: For sex.

BOBBY: For…No, not always. Well, yes, usually. They need companionship. In a hotel. For a couple of hours. It's a good field. I've steered a lot of women into it.

JANET: You've driven women into prostitution?

BOBBY: No, the *escort* business. God, do you have a chip on your shoulder or what? All I'm saying is, you've got the moves. You move like a cat. Did you know that?

JANET: A cat.

BOBBY: Your gestures are almost…balletic.

JANET: Then why don't I become a dancer?

BOBBY: Escorts *are* dancers. *(Pause. Bobby stares at her.)* Tell me, Janet, have you ever seen my act?

JANET: I saw your TV special last month.

BOBBY: That wasn't my act. That was what I call Mr. Relatively Nice Guy— my broadcast alter-ego. That was Bobby Okay, not Bobby Supreme.

JANET: The Okaymatist.

BOBBY: Right. I'm not sure if you'd like Bobby Supreme to do a benefit for the homeless.

JANET: Why not?

BOBBY: Because Bobby doesn't like the homeless. Bobby is sick of the homeless—infesting the subways, clogging the sidewalks, begging on the streets. Bobby thinks the homeless ought to become Republicans and open wine bars and golf courses and goddam get to work.

JANET: Well, if Bobby Supreme raised some money, he would help to get the homeless off the streets. As for the wine bars…

BOBBY: They could be coffee bars. I'm not partial to alcohol necessarily.

JANET: …That takes experience and bank loans…

BOBBY: They can do it. Just set their minds to it.

JANET: Have you ever been homeless?

BOBBY: I'm homeless right now. I've been living in hotels for two years.

JANET: That's not exactly homeless.

(Pause.)

BOBBY: Are those stockings or pantyhose?

JANET: What?

BOBBY: Are you wearing stockings or pantyhose?

JANET: I don't think that's any of your business.

BOBBY: I know. I'm just interested. I'm doing a survey.

JANET: Well I guess you'll just have to use your imagination.

BOBBY: I am.

JANET: Good.

BOBBY: What are *you* willing to do for the homeless?

JANET: I've devoted most of my working life to the homeless, both in New York and in Washington, where we regularly lobby HUD for better local appropriations and encourage corporations to contribute services and funding.

BOBBY: And how could I help?

JANET: A benefit concert could raise as much as a hundred thousand dollars, depending on the venue we could get and the expenses.

BOBBY: A hundred grand is a lot of money.

JANET: It would make a real difference in a lot of people's lives.

BOBBY: And I'm supposed to sleep better at night, is that it?

JANET: I have no idea how you sleep.

BOBBY: I'd have to interrupt my tour.

JANET: I'm sure you could fit something in.

BOBBY: I suppose I could "fit something in." With a bit of convincing.

JANET: What kind of convincing?

BOBBY: You didn't answer my question before.

JANET: What question?

BOBBY: What kind of stockings do you have on.

JANET: *(Trying not to get flustered.)* They're just normal…

BOBBY: Are you wearing a garterbelt?

JANET: This doesn't sound like Bobby Relatively Nice Guy.

BOBBY: It isn't. It's Bobby Supreme.

JANET: Uh-huh.

BOBBY: So. Are you wearing a garterbelt?

    (Beat.)

JANET: I really don't see what this has to do with the homeless.

BOBBY: Well…It's cause and effect. If you're wearing a garterbelt, a few of the homeless might eat better. The question is: Did you dress for success this morning?

JANET: I don't think we have to continue this conversation.

BOBBY: No, you'd rather fly down to Washington, have a three-star dinner at a famous restaurant, travel around in chauffeur-driven limousines…

JANET: I use taxies.

BOBBY: Why don't you use the subway? The difference adds up.

JANET: What does it matter to you? You've never thought about the homeless.

BOBBY: I'm thinking about them right now.

JANET: Are you?

BOBBY: Why don't you take your clothes off?

JANET: Excuse me, I have to go.

(She heads for the door, but he blocks her way.)

JANET: Get out of the way.

BOBBY: What did you have for dinner? Steak tar-tar? Swordfish? How about sorbet for dessert? Or was it tapioca pudding?

JANET: This is none of your business.

BOBBY: All of this is my business, or you wouldn't have come here. I know your kind.

JANET: You don't know anything about me.

BOBBY: I know you. You like Jimmy Stewart movies. You cry at the end of *It's a Wonderful Life.* You send your Dad a Father's Day card every year. You always mean to buy the organic vegetables in the supermarket, but you never do. You have two Siamese cats, Espresso and Cappuccino. You get the New Yorker, but you never read them and can't seem to throw them out. They're piled up in a corner in your living room. You never did pay for that subscription to Vanity Fair, so they stopped sending you the issues. You're a lousy cook, but you know how to make pesto from scratch. You like Fiona Apple and Cheryl Crow. You're nuts about Woody Allen, or at least you used to be, until he got serious. You like the idea of sexy lingerie, but you're always too embarrassed to go into a shop and actually buy any. You publicly read Milan Kundera and Gabriel Garcia Marquez and, secretly, Stephen King and Anne Rice. You always pay your rent two weeks late and your telephone is usually on the verge of getting disconnected. When you were a kid, you were funny looking and had a goldfish named Ringo. You're an enthusiastic but lousy tennis player. You like to shoot pool and play miniature golf, but you can't Rollerblade. When you were nine years old, if someone had asked you what you wanted to be when you grew up, you probably said "A fireman." You eat too much chocolate and wish you could travel more. You fell in love with Paris. You dropped your hotel keys in a canal in Venice. You were almost raped in Florence. You hate big dogs and guys with ponytails. You spend your usual Saturday night with the Sunday Times, watching Lucy and Mary reruns and eating pints of pistachio-walnut ice cream, sitting in a bathrobe with nothing on underneath… *(Pause.)* Sound familiar?

JANET: Sounds like you.

BOBBY: You're like an open book. When you have sex, you don't make any sounds.

JANET: How would you know that?

BOBBY: I've had sex with people like you.

JANET: What…What am I supposed to say to something like that?

BOBBY: Say whatever you like.

JANET: You're a shit.

BOBBY: That's good.

JANET: A presumptuous, ignorant shit.

BOBBY: It's gotten me where I am today.

JANET: And where's that?

BOBBY: Just where I'm standing. Staring through you.

JANET: Oh yes. Well, how's this for a view? *(She unzips her skirt, lets it fall to the floor. She's wearing pantyhose.)*

BOBBY: What are you doing?

JANET: What does it look like? *(She begins unbuttoning her blouse.)*

BOBBY: What is this, a stunt?

JANET: You tell me. *(She's standing in her underwear. She goes over to the chair, sits down and spreads her legs open.)* Okay, Mister Bobby Supreme. Why don't you come over here and give me a good fucking? For the homeless of New York City. Let's see if there's any cod in that codpiece of yours. *(Bobby freezes. He isn't sure what to do. He tries to grin his way out of it.)*

BOBBY: That's a very provocative pose.

JANET: Oh yeah? So where's the rock n'roll? Why don't you come over here and rip off my pantyhose? Sorry they aren't stockings, but I'm sure you could get through them with your teeth.

BOBBY: I supposed I could.

(But Bobby is frozen in place. Janet glares at him. A stand-off. Finally, he turns away. Janet laughs and starts buttoning up. She picks up her briefcase and heads for the door.)

JANET: That was great.

(She exits. Bobby stares at the door, then goes to the desk and takes the photo out of the drawer. He holds it in his hands, staring at it. He takes out a lighter and ignites the photo, dropping it in the ashtray. It burns as the lights fade.)

SCENE IV

ANNOUNCER'S VOICE: *(In darkness.)* Ladies and gentlemen…the international sensation…banned from radio and MTV…the Supremacist himself… BOB-BY SU-PREME!!

(Huge, rowdy applause. A Heavy Metal, rock n'roll introduction. Lights up to show Bobby hanging on a big wooden cross. He just hangs there for a while, then smiles at the audience and jumps off the cross, heading downstage, where he picks up his walking stick and grabs the microphone off the stand. He saunters around the stage as he speaks.)

BOBBY: Good evening, ladies and gentlemen, boys and girls. Assholes and members of the *industry*…All proceeds from tonight's show go to the National Coalition to Dick Around the Homeless. The check is in the mail. *(Beat.)* So. News flash: Sex is *okay.* The *era*…of *caution*…is *over.* Hear that? The Age of Fear has passed. You have permission to fuck like rabbits. *My* permission. I'll write you a note. But a word of advice: Take the fucking glove off, guys. It'll feel better. Safe sex is for wimps. You won't get it from *them.* They're chicks. And *you* don't have it, unless you're a fag. So, take the fucking glove off. Give her a fresh jab, blow out the pipes. Stick her on the pill. If she gets pregnant, mail her a get-well card and a coat hanger. To you broads in the audience: lighten up, okay? What we had was special, but it was a one-night stand. Okay? A Saturday night special, if you know what I mean. Go back to your boss. Fuck the producer. Blow your super…

(Light change—it's later in the show.)

BOBBY: To the fags in the audience: *One,* I didn't mean what I said in San Francisco. It was a joke, okay? And *two,* what the fuck are you *doing* here tonight anyway? I'm a homophobe. Yeah, right: I'm scared to death of you guys. "Ooooh." Maybe I'm a closet queer. Yeah, right—I'm a secret woof. I've got a gerbil waiting for me in my hotel room. It has on a little pair of stockings and a G-string. And—who knows? Maybe I'll go that way one of these days. Because women are cunts. Hey, I need a woman up here. A chick. Any volunteers? It's part of the act…Yes, m'am, you…

(He mimes an experimental whipping. Lights change to later in the show.)

BOBBY: Let's have a round of applause for the broad with the nice red ass. Nice work, Babe. Let's do it again soon. Actually, you can run into problems, because they can't usually take a punch. Like recently? I was slapping my bitch around, and she banged her head on the wall, and she fell unconscious. So I figured, what the hell? She won't make so much noise, so I'm giving her a quick fuck, but I'm feeling something not quite right. I mean, she's cold inside. She doesn't feel right. So I take her pulse, okay? And the bitch is—

(A shot rings out. Bobby sinks to his knees.)

BOBBY: The bitch is…is…Fuck.

(He collapses. Blackout. Sirens and indecipherable police radio dispatches, blurring to white noise, which then fades.)

SCENE V

Spotlight on Riggs, who reads from a New Yorker magazine.

RIGGS: *(Reading.)* "Like a talk show host or a politician, Bobby Supreme is in love with the sound of his own voice—a love so strong that it's caught the fancy of millions of fans across the country. In the end he is not so much a bigoted, Neanderthal polemicist, as a be-bop, hip-hop musician, his words not information but the peculiar music of our era, wildly discordant and, even to the details of his attempted assassination, supremely American."

(He looks up, smiling. Lights up on the hotel room full of flowers, cards, and balloons. Bobby is sitting up in bed, reading magazines. Angelina is in a chair by Bobby's bedside.)

BOBBY: What crap! Typical New Yorker crap! I spent hours with the guy, and that's what he comes up with?

RIGGS: I liked it. It's really good. "Supremely American."

BOBBY: Yeah, right.

ANGELINA: I like how he got the shooting in there at the end.

RIGGS: They're saying you staged the whole thing.

BOBBY: Who is?

RIGGS: Daily News and The Post. Front page.

BOBBY: I staged the bullet? That's quite a performance piece.

RIGGS: You did it for the publicity. Like when you shot yourself in the foot.

BOBBY: I'm always shooting myself in the foot.

RIGGS: When you were a kid.

BOBBY: I was never a kid.

ANGELINA: Come on, Bobby. You shot your left foot when you were twelve to get out of a gym class.

BOBBY: Who told you that?

ANGELINA: *You* did.

BOBBY: I lied.

ANGELINA: Don't start with that, Bobby, I'm tired of it.

BOBBY: Let me see the papers.

(Riggs tosses a couple of tabloids to Bobby.)

BOBBY: *(Reading a headline.)* "Supreme Staged Shot. Number One with a Bullet." Nice.

RIGGS: When are we going back on tour, Bobby? This is the biggest press we've ever got. You could have sold out the Garden ten times over today with that show—and the riding crop. My riding crop!

(Riggs laughs. The phone rings. Angelina picks it up. Bobby holds his chest in pain.)

BOBBY: Wo…

RIGGS: What is it?

BOBBY: Just a pile of broken glass inside me. I feel like I've lost my transmission.

RIGGS: They took the bullet out of your shoulder.

BOBBY: Jesus, I can feel it…

RIGGS: Look, they saved the bullet for you.

(He shakes a jar containing the bullet taken out of Bobby's shoulder. Angelina is talking silently on the phone.)

BOBBY: Don't lose that. I might want to donate it to the Friar's Club.

RIGGS: You got a nice card from the mayor.

BOBBY: I thought he hates me.

RIGGS: Oh no. When you do a benefit concert for the homeless and then get shot, mayors are very nice to you. Especially in an election year.

BOBBY: Who did it? Did they catch the guy?

RIGGS: Who the fuck cares?

BOBBY: I wish you wouldn't talk like that.

RIGGS: Listen to the boy scout. *(He laughs.)* He doesn't like the language.

BOBBY: I don't like it anymore.

RIGGS: Sure, sure. *(He laughs.)* He wants to drive a Jetta now. Give his limo to the homeless. *(He laughs again.)*

BOBBY: I'M NOT DOING THIS ANYMORE!

(Pause. Angelina hangs up the phone.)

ANGELINA: *(To Riggs.)* Don't you have something to do? Somewhere to go?

RIGGS: I'm just keeping him company.

BOBBY: I don't want your company!

ANGELINA: *(To Riggs.)* Could you wait outside for a moment?

>   *(Beat.)*

RIGGS: Yeah, sure. *(He gets up and goes out.)*

ANGELINA: Bobby…

BOBBY: Jesus, I'm so wide awake, I feel like I've got *coffee* in my veins. *(He laughs nervously, then becomes more serious.)* And I've got some accounting to do, okay? I've opened up the ledger. That's what happens when you get shot. Who did it? Who shot me?

ANGELINA: That's not imp—

BOBBY: Who did it? Did they catch the guy?

ANGELINA: Yes, but they don't know—

BOBBY: Who was he?

>   *(Pause.)*

ANGELINA: He gave his name as Bobby Supreme.

>   *(Pause. Bobby bursts out laughing.)*

BOBBY: Of course! Bobby Supreme! I did it! It was Bobby Supreme! Perfect.

ANGELINA: So. Is this thing over?

BOBBY: What? Yes. I'm out of it. The homeless benefit started out as a joke, but they've called me on it and they've won. They get the money—all of it. Being shot was the best thing that could have happened to me. It sounds funny, doesn't it, but it's true. I refuse to press charges—it was an act of love. The guy was looking out for me. My fans came through after all. And what an act to go out on! Huh? What a performance piece! This one's for the records…

ANGELINA: Bobby…

BOBBY: This was for the Museum of Modern Art. I'll be in the Performance Art Hall of Fame. Forget Karen Finlay and Bogosian and all the others. We did it. We reached the top. Now I'll go work in a gas station or something.

ANGELINA: Are you serious about this?

BOBBY: Sure. *(Beat.)* Until the next step of the piece. I'll repent on TV talk shows. Do the Bible Belt—fill a few football stadiums on the way. Maybe learn a bit of Country music. The Born Again Christian Comic. Football stadiums, Angel. Maybe even do a brief Catholic stint, meet the Pope. Do a gig in St. Peter's Square. Play the Vatican! Think of *those* headlines, Angel… *(He picks up the Gideon's Bible from next to the bed and begins looking through it.)*

ANGELINA: Bobby, we just got a call from the Cincinnati Police Department…

BOBBY: What is it, another bar tab Riggs forgot to pay?

ANGELINA: No, this is serious, Bobby. They've got a warrant for your arrest.

BOBBY: What are you talking about?

ANGELINA: A teenage girl claims you beat and raped her.

> *(Pause.)*

BOBBY: What?

ANGELINA: Is that true? I have to know. I understand you sometimes wanting to keep us in the dark about what you're doing, but did this really happen?

BOBBY: It's nonsense, Angel. It's a Tawana Brawley. I've been through this before. The same thing happened in Phoenix, remember? A girl claimed I knocked her up…

ANGELINA: You *did* knock her up.

BOBBY: It happens to the Heavy Metal bands all the time. Anyway, I've got paternity insurance.

ANGELINA: This is rape and assault, Bobby.

BOBBY: Didn't happen.

ANGELINA: Is this one of your games?

BOBBY: What games?

ANGELINA: Like what you did in Chicago. That staged attack in Grant Park.

BOBBY: That was for publicity. "Supreme Attack Proved a Hoax." Front page, Chicago Daily News. Sold out the Fox Theater.

ANGELINA: I know sometimes you can go a bit far with your "pieces," but please tell me what happened in Cincinnati. This is going to get onto the news any hour now, so I have to know.

BOBBY: It's all part of the act, Angel.

ANGELINA: Did this happen?

BOBBY: Didn't happen.

ANGELINA: The report said she was beaten up real bad. Had a black eye. *(Beat.)* Like that girl you were with the other night.

BOBBY: It didn't happen, Angel.

ANGELINA: I don't believe you.

> *(Pause.)*

BOBBY: What?

ANGELINA: I've gone along with you all the way, but this just doesn't sound right.

BOBBY: It's fine.

ANGELINA: I wish I could believe that.

BOBBY: Then *believe* it. That's all you have to do. What's it *matter* what happened? What matters is the perception. As far as I'm concerned, I only assaulted that girl if people believe I did. If we can prove she's a liar, then I'm innocent. It didn't happen.

ANGELINA: But if they can prove it happened…

BOBBY: With what? Witnesses? DNA? If I whacked off into an envelope and sent it to the Cincinnati Police Department, they still wouldn't have a case. There's no case. It's that simple.

ANGELINA: So what happened?

BOBBY: Nothing happened. A groupie. I don't even remember. Maybe I put her up to it.

ANGELINA: Put her up to what?

BOBBY: Maybe she's part of the act.

ANGELINA: I'm sick of the whole thing. You've begun to *believe* this shit. That last show was frightening. What you did to that woman on stage…

BOBBY: *(He holds up the Bible.)* I've changed.

ANGELINA: We have to respond to the Cincinnati Police.

BOBBY: Ignore it.

ANGELINA: We can't ignore it. It's going to get on the news. There's no way we can ignore this.

BOBBY: It didn't happen.

ANGELINA: But if the perception is that it *did* happen…God, now I'm beginning to talk like you.

BOBBY: Then the perception will have to be changed. *(Beat.)* Look, I'm Bobby Supreme, and Bobby Supreme doesn't hurt people. He *mends* people. He brings them together. The Supreme Being. Saint Bob. The Holy Goof. The One and Only—Bobby Superior. *(He begins crossing himself.)*

ANGELINA: Stop it, Bobby…

(He starts praying, quietly mumbling personal benedictions.)

ANGELINA: Stop it!

(There's a knocking at the door.)

ANGELINA: *(To the knocking.)* Not now!

(Riggs sticks his head in the door.)

RIGGS: There're a couple of people to see—

ANGELINA: Not now! Get out!

(After a beat, Riggs goes out and closes the door.)

ANGELINA: Tell me what happened.

BOBBY: Nothing happened. How could anything happen, Angel? I'm a saint. *(He laughs at the sound of this.)* I'm a fucking saint…

(He's laughing harder now. Angelina starts packing up.)

ANGELINA: What am I, crazy? Cleaning up after your groupies, ordering you whores. It was almost funny when you were playing a part, but I don't know what this is anymore.

BOBBY: What are you doing?

ANGELINA: I don't know when you're joking anymore. I don't get it.

BOBBY: *(Trying to laugh it off.)* You can't go. You're part of this.

ANGELINA: Yeah, well, not anymore. I was in love with you once. With Bobby Sikowski. Now I don't know who you are.

BOBBY: But you're part of this. Angel? You're the only one who really *understands* it…

ANGELINA: I don't understand it anymore. Not when people are getting hurt.

BOBBY: But it was *for* you. It's *yours.* You always said that. This is a marriage, Angel, till death us do part. Till death us do part. If I got killed, you said it'd all be part of it. That's how far we were willing to go.

ANGELINA: I'm not willing to go that far.

BOBBY: *I* did. Angel? I was almost killed…

ANGELINA: And other people are almost getting killed. It's not funny anymore. It's not even interesting.

BOBBY: It *is* interesting…

ANGELINA: Get over it. We've completed the act. It's time to get out. But don't confuse what this is, because it's what it's always been: an act.

BOBBY: THIS IS NOT AN ACT! *(Pause. Whispering to himself.)* This is not an act.

ANGELINA: Bobby…

BOBBY: It's not an act.

(Beat.)

ANGELINA: Then it's over, Bobby. Show's over.

(She leaves. The door is still open. Bobby stands, intensely reading the Bible. Pause. Riggs comes in.)

RIGGS: Bobby, there's a couple of guys out here to see you.

BOBBY: *(Stunned.)* What?

RIGGS: There's a couple of guys here. From the FBI.

BOBBY: *(Dazed.)* What?

RIGGS: Two guys from the…the FBI.

(Bobby doesn't answer.)

RIGGS: I saw their badges. *(A small laugh.)* Part of the show, huh?

(Bobby stares blankly at him. Pause.)

RIGGS: Bobby? ….Bobby?

(The lights begin to fade.)
RIGGS: Bobby?
(The lights continue to fade as Bobby stares out at the audience.)

END OF PLAY

THE UNEASY CHAIR
A Cautionary Tale in Three Volumes

by Evan Smith

THE AUTHOR

Evan Smith was born and raised in Savannah, GA, where he still lives. He attended Benedictine Military School, Vassar College, and the Yale School of Drama. His play *The Ecstasy of Lucy* was performed by the Home for Contemporary Theater at HERE; *Servicemen* was produced by New York Stage & Film; and *The Uneasy Chair* was produced at Playwrights Horizons with Roger Rees and Dana Ivey.

ORIGINAL PRODUCTION

The Uneasy Chair was produced by Playwrights Horizons (Tim Sanford, Artistic Director; Leslie Marcus, Managing Director; Lynn Landis, General Manager) in New York City, in October, 1998. It was directed by Richard Cottrell; the set design was by Derek McLane; the costume design was by Jess Goldstein; the lighting design was by Peter Kaczorowski; the sound design was by JR Conklin; and the production stage manager was Lauri Goldfeder. The cast was as follows:

Captain Josiah Wickett	Roger Rees
Miss Amelia Pickles	Dana Ivey
Miss Alexandrina Crosbie	Haviland Morris
Mr. John Darlington	Paul Fitzgerald
Edward Cagebee and Others	Michael Arkin

CAPT. JOSIAH WICKETT

MISS AMELIA PICKLES

MR. JOHN DARLINGTON

MISS ALEXANDRINA CROSBIE

NELLIE THIMBLE*

PHILIP ARBUTHNOT*

EDWARD CAGEBEE*

REVEREND SOLOMON PINKNEY*

THE JUDGE*

HATTIE*

THE BURGLAR*

*played by the same actor

PLACE
London

TIME
The Nineteenth Century

ACT I
THE UNEASY CHAIR

Before a gold-trimmed red velvet curtain hangs a large map of Telfair Circle in the City of London, c. 18—. Captain Josiah Wickett and Miss Amelia Pickles enter.

WICKETT: As so many of the events chronicled here take place in the neighborhood of Telfair Circle, it is fitting I should describe in some introductory way a bit of the local geography. The word "circle" would indicate to many some circular thoroughfare, as around a park or monument, but more experienced travelers know that "circle" more likely indicates a middle-class dead end. *(He indicates Telfair Circle on the map.)*

PICKLES: A *cul de sac.*

WICKETT: Indeed, even a circular motion is rendered impossible by the proximity of the north facades of Telfair Circle to the south facades, a distance at one point of no more than sixteen feet. Carriages which venture east into the circle from Cross Street, finding their expected egress into Morton Place blocked by Number Fifteen, can hope ever to venture west again only by inducing their horses to walk backwards, for any attempt to turn them around inevitably introduces them into the front parlours of Numbers Eleven and Fourteen.

PICKLES: I wouldn't live in Number Eleven or Fourteen, not for a hundred thousand pounds. Number Fifteen is the only house on the circle in which I would ever consider living.

WICKETT: According to the fashion among the inmates of the circle, residences become more desirable the further they are into the dead end—

PICKLES: *Cul de sac!*

WICKETT: —rendering Number Fifteen the apogee of refined good taste, as numbers higher than fifteen there are none. It is a lucky coincidence that every resident of the circle is living at precisely that number lower than which they will not venture. It must be said, however, that from time to time a certain resentment toward Number Fifteen arises among the lower orders—

PICKLES: I take no notice.

WICKETT: It is often murmured that if Number Fifteen were pulled down, permitting the flow of traffic between Telfair Circle and Morton Street, the circle would be easily assimilated into Belgravia, that elysium of fash-

ionable society. More than a few of her neighbors wonder how the proprietress of the boarding house at Number Fifteen, Miss Amelia Pickles—
(She bows.)

WICKETT: —can be so abominably selfish as to allow her house to remain
standing when it alone blocks their annexation into the fashionable
world. But she only says:

PICKLES: The good Lord protect me from the fashionable world. I had
enough of that in my early youth.

WICKETT: Nowadays, in what we may presume to be her late youth, she cannot be made to discuss the nature of her interaction with the fashionable
world.

PICKLES: I will only say I have had enough of it. That is all I can possibly say.

WICKETT: Here she sighs wistfully, and occasionally will close her eyes and
sway, as if to a distantly remembered waltz.
(She sighs wistfully, and sways.)

WICKETT: Her dear friend Miss Nellie Thimble, on her friend's involvement
with the fashionable world:
(Miss Nellie Thimble enters.)

NELLIE THIMBLE: She's never had a thing to do with the fashionable world, so
if it's possible to have had enough of something you've never had, I suppose she has. *(She exits.)*

PICKLES: Telfair Circle is my retreat from the fashionable world. I would no
more live in Belgravia than in the African Congo.

WICKETT: A statement with which I am in perfect agreement. I consider that
day to be one of the most fortunate of my life when I first crossed the
threshold of the boarding house at Number Fifteen, to inquire about a
room-to-let.
*(The map flies out and the red velvet curtains part to reveal the parlour of
Number Fifteen Telfair Circle. It is genteel, worn, neat and clean. Pickles
and Wickett assume the attitude of having just introduced themselves.)*

WICKETT: Although, upon reflection, our first encounter was moderately
inauspicious.

PICKLES: Yes, I will say that the room is available, Captain—

WICKETT: Wickett.

PICKLES: Captain Wickett. But I hope you understand and will not take
offense, that the fact of its being available in the abstract does not necessarily render it available in the particular.

WICKETT: I understand perfectly, and I am sure you will not be offended

when I say that my inquiry as to availability in no way indicates a deter-
mination to assume a lease.

PICKLES: Of course.

WICKETT: If she desired my tenancy, she could offer me the room, free and
clear, for my due consideration.

PICKLES: If he wanted the room, he had only to tell me, and I would consider
him with the other applicants.

WICKETT: You've had many inquiries?

PICKLES: Heavens, yes. Such a flood.

WICKETT: None to your liking?

PICKLES: I wouldn't say that. And you, you must have seen dozens of rooms.

WICKETT: Oh, there are several I have my eye on.

PICKLES: I suppose you can afford to stay in an hotel until you find something
you like.

WICKETT: I've recently come into a small independence. The weight of mon-
etary concerns has been lessened.

PICKLES: My experience of the rich told me that the smaller they claimed their
fortune to be, the larger it was.

WICKETT: A *very* small independence.

PICKLES: Mmmm.

WICKETT: I suppose you are free to allow your boarding house to go
untenanted when you please?

PICKLES: Oh, I wish I were. I will tell you in confidence, Captain, it is hard
for a woman of my position to be so poor. That's the word I use. Poor.

WICKETT: I'm sorry to hear that.

PICKLES: And still he did not offer.

WICKETT: She did not offer still. There was something in this woman's per-
sonality that both attracted and repelled. I had a brief presentiment of
doom. I was on the verge of leaving and not taking the room, but the
roaring fire, comfortable furniture, and delicious smell from the kitchen
all conspired to keep me in Miss Pickles' parlour.

PICKLES: I tried to think of how to get rid of him. I wanted an excuse of such
transparent falsehood as to be cutting. But in truth, I had had no satis-
factory applicant for the room, and had already spent the next quarter's
rent.

(Pause. Wickett's face suddenly brightens.)

WICKETT: It occurs to me, Miss Pickles, I might be able to do you a favour.

PICKLES: Oh?

WICKETT: You have a room untenanted, and rather than see you undergo the hardship of a tenantless quarter, I am prepared to—

PICKLES: I saw instantly where he was going. It was perfect, but I would get there first. / And perhaps I might be able to do you a favour, also! If your prospective lodgings seem not all you might expect, perhaps I might offer you the room on the second floor on a temporary basis, purely as a favour.

WICKETT: She was trying to outflank me! / My suggestion exactly! Perhaps I might occupy the room on the second floor on a temporary basis, purely as a favour to you.

(Pause.)

PICKLES: I needed words that left it open as to who was doing the favour for whom. / And this situation is agreeable to you?

WICKETT: Indeed. / I only ask, is it possible for a woman of her confessed poverty to do favours for a man in possession of an income of almost two hundred pounds a year?

PICKLES: Let it never be said that Amelia Pickles is proud. A woman in my position cannot afford pride, trying to live in these times on little more than two hundred pounds a year.

WICKETT: Several months later, the following exchange occurred: / Oh, Miss Pickles, I shall be in Bath for a fortnight starting on the twenty-fourth.

PICKLES: Feeling gouty, Captain?

WICKETT: Me? Heavens, no, just visiting a friend. I'm fit as a fiddle. *(He moves about a bit to demonstrate the soundness of his joints.)* But I will be absent on the first, on which date I believe the quarterly rent falls due. Shall I give it to you on the seventh, when I return?

PICKLES: Just as you wish, Captain. / I said. Then immediately asked myself, Why should I wait seven days for what was mine? Why could he not pay me the rent on the twenty-fourth, before he left? The next day I said: / So you'll be taking a holiday in Bath, Captain?

WICKETT: That's right.

PICKLES: And you said, what was it? That you'd pay me on the twenty-fourth, before you left?

WICKETT: She knew exactly what I had said. / Yes, Miss Pickles, either that or on my return, on the seventh.

PICKLES: Oh dear, but it is due on the first.

WICKETT: Yes, but I'm afraid I'll be in Bath on the first.

PICKLES: Yes, of course. What are we to do?

WICKETT: I had thought to give it to you on my return.

PICKLES: And I hoped you might give it to me before you left.

WICKETT: Why should I pay a week early?

PICKLES: Why should I be paid a week late?

WICKETT: How petty; quibbling over a week.

PICKLES: Arguing over seven days. How petty.

> *(They think.)*

WICKETT: There must be some arrangement which would redound to our mutual satisfaction.

PICKLES: Perhaps you could leave behind a bank note? I sha'n't touch it until the first.

WICKETT: That would be the same as giving it to you before I leave, for I shall not be able to use it.

PICKLES: Quite so.

WICKETT: There was a principle involved.

> *(They think.)*

WICKETT: Perhaps I could leave a bank draft, unsigned, which I could sign upon my return?

PICKLES: That would be no use to me on the first.

WICKETT: Yes, I mean, no, it wouldn't. / I couldn't bear the thought that my exemplary domestic situation might be spoiled by so trifling a problem.

PICKLES: You could send it in a letter!

WICKETT: Cash money through the post?

PICKLES: No, that won't do. / I was on the verge of using profanity, or worse, slang.

WICKETT: And here she showed her true worth, that brilliant Mistress Pickles, with a hit of cunning that would do a Parliamentary strategist proud!

PICKLES: Captain Wickett—

WICKETT: Yes?

PICKLES: *(Thinking it through.)* Would you be satisfied in relinquishing control of the money if you knew I had no control over it? I have a strongbox. You could put in it, before you leave, a bank note, and then lock it up—

WICKETT: And you could unlock it on the first!

PICKLES: Yes!

WICKETT: By Jove! That's an answer worthy of Minerva.

PICKLES: I'll go find that old strongbox this instant!

WICKETT: Except—

PICKLES: Yes?

WICKETT: Now, please don't take offense, but as an old Army man, I think of every angle.

PICKLES: Of course.

WICKETT: But theoretically, you have access to the money from the moment I leave, for you would have the key.

PICKLES: Oh. Indeed I would. I hadn't thought of that.

(They think.)

PICKLES: I could give the key to you, to take to Bath!

(He smiles, then frowns.)

PICKLES: Yes, of course, then we'd be right where we started.

(He smiles.)

WICKETT: I'll hide it! I will take the key from you and I'll hide it somewhere in the house, where you cannot hope to find it, and on the first I'll send a letter from Bath to tell you where it is! Even better! I'll place an advertisement in the free notices of the Army Supplement. It comes out on the first, and my copy will arrive with the morning post!

PICKLES: He appeared before me with laurel leaves in his hair. I stifled an urge to embrace him.

WICKETT: She was a kindred spirit. A soul-mate. And here began one of the most blissful periods I have known in my life. I recall one evening in my first month of residency, one detail of which will serve to indicate the depth and breadth of this amazing woman's intuition of what is correct and comfortable. We were both seated in the parlour.

(They are both seated in the parlour.)

WICKETT: I was reading; she was sewing. Together, as it were, in the same room, respectful, considerate, but separate, distinct entities, under no obligation one to the other, secure and content. Those who know only hot passion and its opposite, loneliness, cannot dream of the satisfaction in a cool and distant intimacy, for intimacy it is, made more intimate by the coolness and distance. Then, on that night: *(He coughs. After a moment he steals a glance at Pickles.)* Nine landladies out of ten, nay, nine-hundred-and-ninety-nine landladies out of a thousand would have remarked that cough, asked how I felt, was I cold, was I warm, was I catching something; reasonable inquiries, all, but requiring a reply which would lead to conversation, and which would have required a feigned interest in the other's health from that moment forward, irrevocably. All silence and comfort is lost forever. Miss Pickles, however, said nothing. I felt for her in that moment a cool and distant regard that I believe is as truly and deeply felt as the hottest passion ever imagined by a lady novelist.

PICKLES: I have begun a new novel. To be entitled *Hearth and Dagger*, its heroine is a girl of say five and twenty who inherits a fine mansion, but is forced to take in boarders in order to pay for the upkeep. One night, a mysterious stranger collapses on her doorstep. He begs of her a room, but requires complete secrecy. Despite the air of danger and stealth surrounding this tall and broad-shouldered figure, Lilly—for that is our heroine's name—agrees to his conditions, which will bring her to the brink of ruin, until, in the final chapter, she discovers his secret, which will involve some invaluable service to the Crown and which will result in his elevation to a peerage just before he proposes—no, she must marry him first, then he is made a peer; to show she has no concern for such things—no, no, he's already a peer, a duke in disguise, but she doesn't know it, and marries him anyway, and then he tells her—and finally, she is beautifully condescending to all her snobby relations. All of this came to me in a flash one evening, as Captain Wickett sat in my parlour and coughed in a most mysterious manner.

(He coughs.)

WICKETT: I say, Miss Wickett, do you think there's any more hot water?

PICKLES: I beg your pardon?

WICKETT: Hot water. Is there any more?

PICKLES: You said Miss Wickett.

WICKETT: Did I? So sorry. Miss Pickles. Is there?

PICKLES: Yes. A drop.

(He coughs. She looks significantly out.)

WICKETT: By the way, my nephew will be coming to visit me on Tuesday.

PICKLES: You have a nephew?

WICKETT: Yes, in the Cavalry.

PICKLES: I didn't realize! And in the Calvary!

WICKETT: Cavalry.

PICKLES: Do you think he would like to meet my niece?

WICKETT: I didn't know you had a niece.

PICKLES: Yes, she's been one of the most sought after beauties for, oh, it must be eleven or twelve seasons now.

WICKETT: Really?

PICKLES: Her father, my sister's husband, is cousin to the wife of the Earl of Shrowsbury. I'll just dash off a line to her.

(Miss Alexandrina Crosbie enters, letter in hand. She is quite extraordinarily fashionable. She is followed by Philip Arbuthnot.)

ALEXANDRINA: My dear funny Aunt Amelia has invited me to tea, to meet her tenant's nephew.

ARBUTHNOT: How rapturous.

ALEXANDRINA: I've half a mind to go.

ARBUTHNOT: Careful. He'll fall in love with you.

ALEXANDRINA: Exactly. I need a lover. Henry has been so very slow in offering marriage, and a doting love slave following me around is just the impetus he needs.

(Darlington enters, letter in hand. Arbuthnot exits.)

DARLINGTON: Tea with Miss Pickles' niece, the daughter of the cousin of the wife of an earl. Well, well, well…

(They arrange themselves in the parlour.)

WICKETT: Wishing for the sake of my nephew to impress upon Miss Crosbie that the Wicketts and Darlingtons are not without those attractions for which the Cavalry is renowned, I determined to indulge those reckless impulses which still flow in my more hot-blooded moments.

DARLINGTON: Determined to show that I was not unacquainted with the world of fashion in which Miss Crosbie certainly traveled, I was mindful to be as well-mannered and refined as possible.

ALEXANDRINA: Knowing full well that men of the Cavalry find the frivolities of London Society insufferable, I armed myself in advance with three-quarters of an hour of the most brutally realistic conversation.

PICKLES: Being vaguely cognizant that Alexandrina considered me something of an elderly fuddy-duddy, I thought to erase that impression with an exhibition of my most youthful gaiety.

(They are all standing.)

PICKLES: 'Drina! It seems like a positive age since I saw you last! Oh, do come in and tell me just every little detail; you make me want to dance, just looking at you!

ALEXANDRINA: Good afternoon, Aunt.

PICKLES: Aunt?! How severe you sound! Call me Amy! Captain Wickett, Mr. Darlington: Miss Crosbie.

WICKETT: Ah, damn me, Miss Crosbie, we're just two Cavalry men, hardly fit to be let indoors! Don't know what to do with ourselves off a horse. But we're Cavalry men, not city dandies, right, John?

DARLINGTON: Mith Crothbie. *(He bows low and kisses her hand with a flourish of his lace handkerchief.)*

ALEXANDRINA: Captain Wickett, Mr. Darlington. Please forgive me if I seem distracted, but I've just been contemplating a system of bridges to relieve traffic congestion around Billingsgate.

(A silence. They all sit. Darlington sits with elaborate refinement, crossing his legs and fondling a crystal topped cane. Wickett puts his booted feet on the table. Pickles stifles a scream, turning it into a girlish laugh.)

PICKLES: Oh, Mr. Darlington, Captain Wickett tells us you have a commission in the calvary?

DARLINGTON: In the Cavalry, yes. The 8th Light. But I have not yet received my orders.

WICKETT: Ah, the Cavalry! That's the life! Astride a fiery steed, charging down a slope, leaping and galloping like a madman, like as not have to kill some blackies in the valley.

DARLINGTON: My goodness, Uncle, you make it sound so dangerous. Have you ladies seen the uniform of the 8th Light? White breeches of angelic purity, scarlet coats to shame a Pope, and enough gold braid to hang a regiment. I shall be very pretty, don't you think?

PICKLES: Scarlet? Truly scarlet?! I will die if I don't get to see it. I will drop dead on the floor.

DARLINGTON: Pray, Miss Pickles, don't do that.

ALEXANDRINA: I read recently that the children employed in dying wool to such a color are quite poisoned by the dye, and fully one quarter of them do not live to see their twelfth birthday.

(A silence.)

ALEXANDRINA: I took a guinea subscription for their relief.

PICKLES: Under a pretext, Alexandrina and I left the room.

ALEXANDRINA: Do you think I have made it sufficiently plain that I am a serious thinker? I thought the bit about the bridges around Billingsgate was quite good.

PICKLES: Yes, indeed, my dear, but men don't marry thinkers.

ALEXANDRINA: I don't want to marry him, merely attract him. Men are attracted to girls who are intelligent and also high-spirited. I shall now be high-spirited.

PICKLES: Oh, good.

ALEXANDRINA: Though, I will say, Aunt, you might be a little more circumspect in your enthusiasm, as befits a woman of your years. And position. I'm thinking of your position foremost, of course.

PICKLES: Of course.

WICKETT: While they were gone, John and I discussed the morning thus far.

DARLINGTON: I wonder, Uncle, if I'm not being perhaps a trifle too elegant.

WICKETT: Perhaps.

DARLINGTON: I don't want her to think I'm a bloodless fop. I think it's time to show her my brooding, passionate side. I have a touch of the Young Werther about me.

WICKETT: I shall lock up the pistols.

DARLINGTON: Besides, she seems a rather serious girl.

PICKLES: Soon we were all reunited in the parlour.

    (Darlington suddenly writhes in some private torment.)

PICKLES: Mr. Darlington! Are you all right? Are you ill?

DARLINGTON: No, Miss Pickles; that is, yes, but mine is a sickness no doctor can cure.

PICKLES: Is it fatal?

DARLINGTON: Alas, yes, but it is not what you think. It is a soul sickness, and we all must die, must we not, Miss Pickles?

PICKLES: I'm sure I don't know. I've heard it said we all must die, but as it's what I call a losing proposition, I sha'n't put money on it.

ALEXANDRINA: Shall we play a game? I have one! See if you can guess: it's not drawing, but it is room. It's not orange, but it is apple. It's not gown, but it is dress. Can you guess?

PICKLES: It's not drawing, but it is room? Is it a drawing room?

ALEXANDRINA: I said very clearly that it is not drawing, so it can't be drawing room.

WICKETT: It's not an orange but it is an apple. Is it a pear?

ALEXANDRINA: No, it is not pear! Captain Wickett, have I stumped you? I shall give you a hint, the answer is not a thing at all.

PICKLES: Then what is it?

ALEXANDRINA: It's an idea.

PICKLES: Oh, dear, I'm sure it's too difficult for me.

ALEXANDRINA: Not at all, Aunt, it's quite simple. Now listen. It's not window, but it is wall. It's not hearth, but it is door. It's not mirror, but it is—Oh, I'm sorry. It is mirror, after all. What is it not? Well, it's not anything, hardly. Not is much simpler than is: it's not rug, or grate, or lamp, or picture, or—

WICKETT: Is it a book?

ALEXANDRINA: Yes, it is, Captain! Very good! Have you figured it out?

WICKETT: Book!

ALEXANDRINA: Yes, but have you divined the answer to the puzzle?

WICKETT: The answer isn't book?

ALEXANDRINA: Well, no, the answer is an idea, but book fits the idea. It is book, but it is not, say, newspaper.

PICKLES: Dear 'Drina, won't you just tell us?

ALEXANDRINA: It's terribly easy, if you'd only think about it. What is it about "book" that makes it different from "newspaper?"

DARLINGTON: They're both made of paper.

PICKLES: They both have words written on them—

ALEXANDRINA: Those are things that make them the same! What makes them different?

WICKETT: You know, this reminds me of the Sphinx asking that chap all those questions, or she'll eat him up. What was that chap's name?

DARLINGTON: Oedipus.

WICKETT: That's right. Oedipus. What goes on four legs, then two legs, then three legs?

PICKLES: Oh, a dog for the first one, then a bird, then, hmmm, three legs…what goes on three legs?

WICKETT: I can't remember; perhaps three legs was a lame dog, like that one down on the corner by the coach stand?

DARLINGTON: It is Man. Man goes on four legs, as an infant crawling, then on two legs in his youth, then on three legs when he is old and walks with a cane. The Sphinx might have added no legs, for when we are dead in our coffins.

(A silence.)

ALEXANDRINA: Double letters. Room, o-o, but not drawing. Apple, p-p, but not orange. Book. It is words with double letters.

PICKLES: Shortly after that, our two visitors took their leave.

ALEXANDRINA: Mr. Darlington, it's been a pleasure.

DARLINGTON: The pleasure was mine. *(He turns to Wickett.)* Uncle. *(He exits.)*

ALEXANDRINA: Aunt.

(Alexandrina moves downstage. Arbuthnot enters.)

ARBUTHNOT: How was tea with your aunt? Have you successfully captured your love slave?

ALEXANDRINA: Mr. Darlington was a crashing bore. One of those who think only of themselves, and put on bizarre airs, and pretend to be that which they are not. Too dreadful.

ARBUTHNOT: Too bad.

ALEXANDRINA: It's nothing. At any rate, Henry must propose soon, whether he is goaded by the presence of a love-slave or not.

ARBUTHNOT: I was pleased to hear of your aunt's tenant, as I recall with what tones of outrage you decried her decision to take in boarders. Perhaps now she will become a Mrs. and besmirch your good name no longer.

ALEXANDRINA: Philip! What a grand notion! I shall begin working on it at once!

(Arbuthnot exits. She produces pen and paper.)

ALEXANDRINA: Dear Aunt Amy—

WICKETT: And thus began that fateful correspondence!

ALEXANDRINA: I had a lovely time at tea yesterday. How is the delightful Captain Wickett? You never told me he was so very handsome.

PICKLES: The Captain is well, to the best of my knowledge. I'm sure I never noticed whether he was handsome or not.

ALEXANDRINA: Never noticed? Are you made of flesh and blood? Surely you have noticed, at the very least, his clear infatuation with you.

PICKLES: I will admit, I have been aware recently of Captain Wickett's, shall we say, especial solicitousness.

(Darlington enters.)

DARLINGTON: Dear Uncle, Well, what do you think? Should I ask the Crosbie girl to marry me? I think she can be had. She's at least thirty, wouldn't you say?

WICKETT: You could do worse, my boy.

DARLINGTON: Practically the cousin of an earl, and unmarried. Why do you suppose?

WICKETT: I couldn't say, my boy, but *cave canem,* as the saying goes.

DARLINGTON: "Beware the dog?"

WICKETT: No, no, the other one, what is it?

DARLINGTON: "Let the buyer beware."

WICKETT: That's it.

ALEXANDRINA: Dear Aunt Amy, Please do not be shocked by what I am about to ask you, but have you ever considered matrimony?

PICKLES: Why should I be shocked, my precious girl? Of course I have considered matrimony, often, and with great care and questioning, but until He Who Can Be At One With My Soul appears, and asks, there is nothing I can do.

ALEXANDRINA: Have you never thought, dear Aunt, that he may be at hand? Under your own roof?

PICKLES: Whatever can you mean, you strange child?

ALEXANDRINA: I mean, dear innocent one, Captain Wickett!

PICKLES: Oh!

DARLINGTON: Dear Uncle, I would hate to make an offer and be rejected.

Could you find out if the girl is amenable? It would save me a lot of time.

WICKETT: Dear Miss Crosbie, I hope you do not consider this letter an impertinence. If you feel it is improper, and your feminine intuition gives you no foreknowledge of its intent, I will cease this correspondence at once.

ALEXANDRINA: I believe, Captain Wickett, I do have an idea of the intent of your correspondence.

WICKETT: I will be encouraged that you allow me to write, and will ask that question which so closely concerns us all, would you object to a potential alliance between our families?

ALEXANDRINA: Let me say, Captain Wickett, that not only would I not object, but I would, on the contrary, rejoice.

WICKETT: Dear John, She has all but accepted you. I suggest you find your way over here as soon as possible to deliver your proposal in person. *(Darlington exits.)*

ALEXANDRINA: Dear Aunt, I have news for you that cannot be delivered in a letter, so I will see you tomorrow morning before noon to deliver what I am sure you will find most agreeable news, indeed, that most happy of news for an unmarried woman. PS: Let me only add that the unmarried woman to be made so happy is not myself. PPS: You should not be too surprised if Captain Wickett asks you a certain question this very evening, the nature of which I cannot disclose in so impersonal a way as in a letter, but which would alter both your *life,* and your *name.* I can say no more. *(Pickles swoons. Alexandrina exits.)*

WICKETT: I say, Miss Pickles! *(He rushes to assist her.)*

PICKLES: Oh, Captain Wickett, I believe I fainted.

WICKETT: Are you quite all right?

PICKLES: Yes, I believe so, just help me— *(She indicates the sofa. She reclines gracefully.)*

WICKETT: Would you prefer to be left alone?

PICKLES: Oh, no, Captain, please, sit with me a minute. My head is spinning.

WICKETT: Can I get you anything?

PICKLES: No, I'll be fine. I just wanted to know, Captain, are you happy? Here at Number Fifteen, I mean?

WICKETT: I think I can say, Miss Pickles, that not since I was in India, trekking through the snowcapped Himalayas, have I been so happy as I have been at Number Fifteen.

PICKLES: I'm so glad to hear it. It is what I want, to see you happy, you know.

WICKETT: Yes, I can read that in your every action, Miss Pickles.

PICKLES: The high Himalayas. What a sight that must have been.

WICKETT: You've no idea, Miss Pickles. The human imagination could in no way invent such a sight.

PICKLES: Heavens.

WICKETT: What's more, it isn't big enough to hold it. I know I can't remember one quarter of what I saw, and what I do remember is puny compared to the real thing, and grows punier with each passing year.

PICKLES: Dear me.

WICKETT: But I shall see it again. I plan to return, and hike at the feet of the Himalayas once more.

PICKLES: Captain, will you really?

WICKETT: Yes, I will. I promised myself the first time that I'd go again, and one day soon, I'll buy a pair of hiking boots, and set sail for India.

PICKLES: Shall I tell you, Captain Wickett, what my plan is?

WICKETT: I wish you would.

PICKLES: To tour Italy, from the heel to the Alps, to see all the great masterworks of the Quatrocento.

WICKETT: An admirable plan, Miss Pickles.

PICKLES: I have a request of you, Captain.

WICKETT: Yes?

PICKLES: Will you call me Amelia?

WICKETT: If you will call me Josiah.

(They sit.)

WICKETT: I immediately regretted it. I could feel my Christian name hanging over me like the sword of Damocles. My tongue positively rebelled at the prospect of addressing Miss Pickles as Amelia. A "Miss Pickles" one could ask for another biscuit, an open window shut, or a little less flour in the gravy. An "Amelia," though—One closed windows oneself for an "Amelia." One put out cigars for an "Amelia." For an "Amelia," one put down one's book and ran upstairs to fetch a shawl. In my easy chair I was anything but.

PICKLES: Josiah—

(He reflexively flinches.)

PICKLES: Good night

WICKETT: Good night—

(She leans in.)

WICKETT: Amelia.

(A knocking at the door.)

PICKLES: The next morning, quite early, there was a knock at the door. /
Excuse me.

(She exits. Darlington enters.)

DARLINGTON: You think she'll accept me? Are you sure?

WICKETT: I have it in writing. *(He brandishes a letter.)* "…not only would I
not object, but would, on the contrary, rejoice."

DARLINGTON: Well, that's a weight off my mind.

WICKETT: But look here, John. Do me a favour. The mattress in my room is
on its last legs, and I've been meaning to ask Miss Pickles to replace it at
her expense. Let me get her to agree to that before she finds out we are
to be relations.

DARLINGTON: But I planned to propose this morning.

(The doorbell rings.)

PICKLES: *(Off.)* Alexandrina!

WICKETT: At the very least, give me few minutes alone with Miss Pickles.

DARLINGTON: All right.

(Alexandrina and Pickles enter.)

ALEXANDRINA: Good morning, gentlemen.

WICKETT: Good morning, ladies.

(Long pause.)

ALEXANDRINA: OH! My eye! I have something in my eye. Aunt please, accompany me to the window.

WICKETT: An obvious, but necessary, ruse.

PICKLES: What is it? Which eye?

ALEXANDRINA: *(Stage whisper.)* Did you get my letter?

PICKLES: *(Stage whisper.)* Yes, I did.

ALEXANDRINA: *(Stage whisper.)* And can you guess what my news is?

PICKLES: *(Stage whisper.)* I have an idea.

ALEXANDRINA: *(Stage whisper.)* That the Captain is intending to propose marriage?

DARLINGTON: How is your eye, Miss Crosbie?

ALEXANDRINA: Agonizing, but thank you for asking.

DARLINGTON: *(Stage whisper.)* I don't believe there's anything wrong with her eye.

WICKETT: *(Stage whisper.)* They are conferring. Now you must find a way to
take Miss Crosbie into the back parlour. When I have obtained a new
mattress from Miss Pickles, then you may propose.

DARLINGTON: *(Stage whisper.)* How shall I get her into the back parlour?

WICKETT: *(Stage whisper.)* Get something in your eye.

ALEXANDRINA: *(Stage whisper.)* You must get him into the back parlour.

PICKLES: *(Stage whisper.)* How shall I do that?

ALEXANDRINA: *(Stage whisper.)* I shall help you. *(Normal voice.)* Ah! That is much better. What a relief to be able to see again. And speaking of vision, have you noticed, Captain Wickett, how lovely are the prints on the wall of the back parlour?

WICKETT: Yes, quite charming.

DARLINGTON: I've never seen them. Would you show them to me?

ALEXANDRINA: I especially wanted Captain Wickett to see them. Have you never pointed them out to the Captain, Aunt?

PICKLES: What?

ALEXANDRINA: The prints. In the back parlour. Have you never shown them to Captain Wickett?

WICKETT: I've seen them a hundred times, but John has never seen them.

ALEXANDRINA: I'm sure you've never given them the attention they deserve. Won't you let Miss Pickles show you their marvelous detail?

DARLINGTON: They sound enchanting. Won't you show them to me, Miss Crosbie?

ALEXANDRINA: I am terribly ignorant in such matters. But my Aunt is an encyclopedia of knowledge, Captain.

WICKETT: Perhaps some other time. But won't you please show them to my nephew?

ALEXANDRINA: Some day, of course, but now is your turn, Captain.

WICKETT: Ladies first.

ALEXANDRINA: Auntie?

PICKLES: Hmm?

ALEXANDRINA: The Captain wishes you to show him the prints.

WICKETT: You, Miss Crosbie, were the lady to whom I referred. Won't you be a docent for my nephew?

ALEXANDRINA: I couldn't possibly. But won't you allow my Aunt to be your guide?

WICKETT: Some day soon.

(Pause.)

DARLINGTON: OH! Miss Crosbie! I've gotten something in my eye!

(Pickles rushes to him.)

PICKLES: Let me, Mr. Darlington!

DARLINGTON: It's gone.

(Pause.)

ALEXANDRINA: I do think you are passing up a rare opportunity, Captain. The prints, I mean.

DARLINGTON: I should like to see them very much, Miss Crosbie.

ALEXANDRINA: But I so wanted the Captain to see these, as they are of horses, and he was in Cavalry.

DARLINGTON: But I am also in the Cavalry!

ALEXANDRINA: Are you? How nice. *(Pause.)* OH!

PICKLES: Your eye again?

ALEXANDRINA: No, how stupid of me. Would you like to see the prints in the back parlour, Mr. Darlington?

DARLINGTON: Oh, very much, Miss Crosbie.

ALEXANDRINA: Then, please follow me.

DARLINGTON: With pleasure.

(They move toward the back parlour. Pickles follows them.)

ALEXANDRINA: No, Aunt, you must stay here.

PICKLES: But don't you want me to go to the back parlour?

ALEXANDRINA: Not at all. We'll be fine.

PICKLES: But didn't you say I should go to the back parlour?

ALEXANDRINA: No, Aunt. I did not.

PICKLES: I thought you did.

ALEXANDRINA: I did not. You must stay here and keep Captain Wickett company. For Captain Wickett will be here in the front parlour. Alone.

PICKLES: Oh. I see. Yes, of course.

(Alexandrina and Darlington move into the back parlour.)

DARLINGTON: These must be they.

ALEXANDRINA: Yes. I admire them so.

(He examines them very carefully.)

DARLINGTON: Where exactly are the, um, horses?

ALEXANDRINA: Hmmm? Let me see. Well. I suppose there aren't any actual horses per se. But one does get such a horsy feeling, does one not?

DARLINGTON: Oh, yes. They are quite extraordinary.

ALEXANDRINA: Aren't they? I often wonder if my aunt might not get a better than expected price for them.

DARLINGTON: Oh, Miss Crosbie, surely you know by now that I have followed you in here under a pretext.

ALEXANDRINA: Yes, I understand quite well.

DARLINGTON: And have you formed an answer to my question?

ALEXANDRINA: What question is that?

DARLINGTON: If you say "No," I shall end my life. It's as simple as that.

ALEXANDRINA: Well, in that case, Yes.

DARLINGTON: Do you mean it? Are you in earnest?

ALEXANDRINA: Perhaps I am. What is the question?

DARLINGTON: Will you be my wife?

ALEXANDRINA: Oh. Is that the question? In that case, No.

DARLINGTON: Really?

ALEXANDRINA: Yes.

DARLINGTON: Well. I'm embarrassed. You must think me a perfect fool.

ALEXANDRINA: Not at all. I have a certain fundamental respect for all the men who propose marriage to me, no matter how inappropriate they may be.

DARLINGTON: It's just, you see, I had been given certain information that you might look favourably on my proposal.

ALEXANDRINA: Whence this erroneous information?

DARLINGTON: My uncle has a letter from you in which you said you would rejoice at such a proposal.

ALEXANDRINA: Oh, my dear Mr. Darlington! You are quite muddled. That question concerned an entirely different proposal.

DARLINGTON: I believe it did not. He wrote it at my request.

ALEXANDRINA: The letter I received concerned Captain Wickett's proposal to my aunt.

DARLINGTON: Not at all. He has never contemplated such a proposal that I know of.

ALEXANDRINA: Hasn't he? His letter stated quite plainly—

DARLINGTON: What?

ALEXANDRINA: But at this very minute he's—With my aunt—

DARLINGTON: To discuss the purchase of a new mattress.

ALEXANDRINA: Oh dear.

(She moves to return to the front parlour. Pickles suddenly shrieks and faints into Wickett's arms. Tableaux. A barrister, Edward Cagebee, in a white wig and black robes, enters. The curtains close on the parlour.)

CAGEBEE: Dear Aspasia, How are things in Bonn? I have undertaken a most extraordinary case lately, a breach of promise suit that a landlady has filed against her tenant. Through a highly unusual legal anomaly, I find that I am to represent both parties at the same time. I am sorry that you will not be here to witness the spectacle of my arguing both for and against my two clients. There was some talk of a conflict of interest, but I have made it quite clear that, in the finest tradition of English jurisprudence, I don't give a damn who wins or loses.

(They arrange themselves. Darlington and Wickett step behind a bar to the right, Cagebee steps in front of a bar center, Alexandrina enters and stands behind a bar to the left, and finally, Pickles enters, and clutches Alexandrina.)

CAGEBEE: Pickles vs. Wickett, My Lord. Breach of Promise. I shall be representing both parties. Let me begin by introducing Miss Amelia Pickles—

(She shrinks from the attention.)

CAGEBEE: —proprietress of the boarding house at Number Fifteen Telfair Circle, who has maintained a sterling reputation for propriety and virtue for many, many, many, many, many years.

(Pickles gives him a look.)

CAGEBEE: She is unused to the ways of men of the world, and when that gentleman there—dare I even use that word to describe this rogue, this abuser of women's hearts?—entered her house under the premise of being merely a tenant, how could she have known what spell he was weaving for her ruin? He wooed her, turned her head, flattered, cajoled, pressed, demanded—and when she expected him to behave as a gentleman should, he pushed her aside, shattering her illusions, and dashing her dreams of married life. *(He steps over to Wickett. Pause as he collects his thoughts.)* Everything I just said is poppy cock. Captain Wickett is a retired veteran of foreign wars who has served his country with bravery and nobility, and who, when taking up residence at Number Fifteen Telfair Circle, expected only rest and comfort in his waning years. How could he have known what spider's web he was entering, what bewitching enticements of feminine wiles would be spread out before him? He is a simple Army man, unused to the company of women and the beguiling tricks of a desperate female. Let me call my first witness, Miss Alexandrina Crosbie.

(Alexandrina steps up to the center bar.)

CAGEBEE: What is your relation to the litigants?

ALEXANDRINA: I am Miss Pickles' niece.

CAGEBEE: And what was your first impression of Captain Wickett?

ALEXANDRINA: My first impression was most favourable, he seemed an upright and honest fellow. But—

CAGEBEE: But? Please do not hold back, Miss Crosbie.

ALEXANDRINA: But I also felt a chill, some unnamable distrust, so ineffable that I dared not speak of it to anyone.

CAGEBEE: And did Captain Wickett ever indicate to you his intention of asking your Aunt to marry him?

ALEXANDRINA: Yes, he did.

WICKETT: NONSENSE!

(Darlington restrains Wickett.)

CAGEBEE: Please, Sir! Do not attempt to silence this woman! What have the innocent to fear from honest testimony? *(To Alexandrina.)* And how did Captain Wickett indicate his intentions toward your Aunt?

ALEXANDRINA: By letter.

CAGEBEE: Have you the letter?

ALEXANDRINA: Yes, I do. *(She produces it from a small bag tied to her dress.)*

CAGEBEE: Would you please read it to the court?

ALEXANDRINA: "Dear Miss Crosbie, I will be encouraged that you allow me to write, and will ask that question which so closely concerns us all, would you object to a potential alliance between our families? Signed, Captain Josiah Wickett, retired."

CAGEBEE: And what did you take him to mean by an alliance between your families?

ALEXANDRINA: Why, a marriage between himself and my aunt.

CAGEBEE: Thank you very much, Miss Crosbie.

ALEXANDRINA: Am I done?

CAGEBEE: Not just yet, Miss Crosbie. I have finished the examination of the witness, My Lord, and would like to begin the cross-examination. Miss Crosbie, you are a woman of fashion, are you not?

ALEXANDRINA: If the cut of my dress is in keeping with the current fashion, it is a matter of indifference to me.

CAGEBEE: You move extensively in society, do you not?

ALEXANDRINA: I am acquainted with some of the better folk, it is true.

CAGEBEE: And you are on intimate terms with one Mrs. Henry Balfour? *(Alexandrina's guard goes up.)*

ALEXANDRINA: I have met her once or twice.

CAGEBEE: Did you not maintain your intimacy with her during the entirety of her highly publicized divorce from Henry Balfour, witnessing her every day of testimony, including those in which she detailed those celebrated infidelities that ended her marriage?

ALEXANDRINA: One cannot desert a friend, or acquaintance rather, in her hour of need.

CAGEBEE: I mention this only to indicate that you have a fair knowledge of what is known as "the world."

ALEXANDRINA: I'm sure I don't know what your point is.

CAGEBEE: Only this, that you knew very well that Captain Wickett's letter concerned not himself and Miss Pickles, but yourself and Mr. John Darlington!

ALEXANDRINA: I knew nothing of the sort.

CAGEBEE: What is your opinion of Mr. John Darlington?

ALEXANDRINA: I have no opinion.

CAGEBEE: Come now, Miss Crosbie. Have you never noticed that he is over six feet in height, broad shouldered, even featured, and with a head of thick, wavy hair?

ALEXANDRINA: These details all escaped my notice.

CAGEBEE: And there has been no talk of marriage between yourself and Mr. Darlington?

ALEXANDRINA: None whatsoever.

CAGEBEE: You would like to see your aunt married, would you not?

ALEXANDRINA: Naturally.

CAGEBEE: And would stop at nothing to attain your goal!

ALEXANDRINA: Of what exactly am I being accused?!

CAGEBEE: No more questions. You may step down.

ALEXANDRINA: I would like to ask a few questions of my own, if I may.

CAGEBEE: You may not address the bench. You must step down.

ALEXANDRINA: I mayn't?

CAGEBEE: Please, Miss Crosbie. Will you step down?

(She moves back to the left with Pickles.)

ALEXANDRINA: He apparently fancies himself Robespierre.

CAGEBEE: I would now call to the stand Mr. John Darlington.

DARLINGTON: Might I confer with my uncle?

CAGEBEE: The defense does not object if the plaintiff does not. And the plaintiff does not, either.

(Darlington leans over to whisper to Wickett.)

DARLINGTON: Uncle, you know my aspirations in regard to Miss Crosbie.

WICKETT: What? Still?

DARLINGTON: Of course. I just hope you don't expect me to say anything in my testimony that will upset her.

WICKETT: Just tell the truth. She can have no objection to that.

DARLINGTON: Can't she?

WICKETT: What do you mean?

CAGEBEE: How long must the court wait, Mr. Darlington?

(Darlington steps to the bar center.)

WICKETT: John! What do you mean?!

CAGEBEE: Mr. Darlington, what is your relation to the defendant?

DARLINGTON: He is my uncle.

CAGEBEE: Do you have any knowledge of the letter sent by your uncle and lately read by Miss Crosbie to the court?

DARLINGTON: Yes, I do.

CAGEBEE: And to the best of your knowledge, to whom did it refer?

DARLINGTON: Well, I do know that it was sent by my uncle.

CAGEBEE: Yes.

DARLINGTON: To Miss Crosbie.

CAGEBEE: That is correct.

DARLINGTON: Could you repeat the question?

CAGEBEE: To whom did the letter refer?

DARLINGTON: And what did Miss Crosbie say?

CAGEBEE: She said it referred to Miss Pickles and Captain Wickett.

DARLINGTON: Well, I'm sure whatever Miss Crosbie says is correct.

WICKETT: JOHN!

CAGEBEE: Please, Sir! Must I have you forcibly removed?! *(To Darlington.)* Now Mr. Darlington, I was under the impression, but correct me if I'm wrong, that you were going to say your uncle was writing about you and Miss Crosbie.

DARLINGTON: Was he? I'm sure I don't know.

CAGEBEE: And has there been any talk between you and Miss Crosbie on the subject of marriage? The marriage of the two of you, that is.

DARLINGTON: Umm, what did Miss Crosbie say?

CAGEBEE: She said No.

DARLINGTON: No, then.

CAGEBEE: May I remind you, Mr. Darlington, that you are under oath?

DARLINGTON: No, I'm not.

CAGEBEE: Oh, yes, you are, Sir.

DARLINGTON: No, I'm not. I took no oath. None was administered.

CAGEBEE: Is that true? Heavens, I forgot. Well, um, you're not lying, are you?

DARLINGTON: Umm, no.

(Wickett is about to speak, but Cagebee turns on him, pointing a finger. Wickett sputters and gesticulates in frustration.)

CAGEBEE: You may step down, Sir.

DARLINGTON: Aren't you going to cross examine?

CAGEBEE: Hardly seems necessary.

DARLINGTON: All right then.

(John returns to Wickett, who turns away from him.)

DARLINGTON: Come now, Uncle. Don't be that way.

CAGEBEE: I would now like to call to the stand—

(Wickett takes the center place.)

CAGEBEE: I was saving you for last, Captain Wickett.

WICKETT: I can remain silent no longer.

CAGEBEE: Very well. Do you swear on this Bible that the testimony you are
about to give is the truth?

WICKETT: Why must I be sworn in when he was not?

CAGEBEE: That was an oversight. Why? Do you plan to lie?

WICKETT: Certainly not.

CAGEBEE: Then if you would just oblige me.

WICKETT: I swear.

CAGEBEE: Now tell me, Captain Wickett, how long have you held the post of
dog catcher?

WICKETT: What?

CAGEBEE: Sorry, so sorry. A different case altogether. Let me see…Now tell
me, Captain Wickett, when you wrote that letter to Miss Crosbie—

WICKETT: Wait, wait, are you speaking as my representative, or my opponent's?

CAGEBEE: That's a good question, let me see…um, I've an idea. If it please the
court, to save time, perhaps I might examine and cross examine simul-
taneously. Have you any objection, Captain?

WICKETT: I suppose not.

CAGEBEE: All right then, hmm, hmm, hmm, Captain Wickett!

WICKETT: Yes?

CAGEBEE: You have spent how much of your life in the Army?

WICKETT: Thirty years.

CAGEBEE: And in that time, how would characterize your experience with the
fairer sex?

WICKETT: I may be a bachelor, but I know a thing or two about women.

CAGEBEE: Are you sure? Wouldn't you say that your bachelor-hood has left
you somewhat a stranger to the distaff mind?

WICKETT: Not at all.

CAGEBEE: Captain Wickett, I'm sure you will agree with me when I say—that
in your bachelor-hood you have had little experience with women's ideas
of romantic love?

WICKETT: Ah, yes, I see. Um, that is correct.

CAGEBEE: Is it safe, then, to say, that until you came to Number Fifteen Telfair
Square, you had little to guide you in the seductive ways of women?

WICKETT: Yes, it is.

CAGEBEE: HA! I put it to you, Captain, that like any soldier, you are accus-
tomed to taking women for your selfish pleasure, with no regard for the
laws of God or men!

WICKETT: That is absolutely not true, I must say in the strongest possible terms!

CAGEBEE: It is absurd, is it not, to imply that you would or could be so callous to your own landlady?

WICKETT: Absolutely.

CAGEBEE: And it would not be stretching the truth to say that you never entertained for the briefest moment the notion of asking your landlady to become your wife.

WICKETT: Absolutely not.

CAGEBEE: Of course you never intended to marry her! Just to take what you could get and abandon her to her fate!

WICKETT: Not true! I never took anything from her!

CAGEBEE: Have you not, at all times, behaved with perfect politeness and rectitude toward Miss Pickles?

WICKETT: I have.

CAGEBEE: And when you wrote that letter, you were writing with no intention other than to inquire on the behalf of your nephew?

WICKETT: That is correct.

CAGEBEE: But with wicked cunning, phrased the letter in such a way as to deliberately mislead both Miss Crosbie and Miss Pickles!

WICKETT: Never!

CAGEBEE: Of course not. In fact, it is you who are the injured party, are you not, Captain Wickett?

WICKETT: Yes, I am, Sir.

CAGEBEE: One final question, Captain. What is your opinion of Miss Pickles?

WICKETT: I beg your pardon?

CAGEBEE: What do you think of Miss Pickles as a woman?

WICKETT: I don't know what you mean.

CAGEBEE: Have you ever regarded her with feelings of romance or passion?

WICKETT: No.

CAGEBEE: Have you ever regarded her with affection?

WICKETT: No.

CAGEBEE: Did you ever have cause to complain of the service or conditions at Number Fifteen Telfair Circle?

WICKETT: No.

CAGEBEE: On the contrary, were you not delighted with the food, warmth, and general domestic comfort of your lodgings?

WICKETT: I was.

CAGEBEE: And did not your feelings of general beneficence and good will attach themselves to Miss Pickles herself?

WICKETT: Perhaps, in some abstract way.

CAGEBEE: Can we not say then, that you, Captain Wickett, like Miss Pickles?

WICKETT: At certain isolated moments.

CAGEBEE: Can we not say then, also, that, at certain isolated moments, you felt genuine affection for your landlady, Miss Amelia Pickles! And let me remind you again, Captain, that you are under oath!

(Pause.)

WICKETT: Yes.

CAGEBEE: No more questions. You may step down.

WICKETT: I say, Cagebee! Was all that last bit for my benefit or hers?

CAGEBEE: Why, for yours!

WICKETT: Oh. *(Wickett returns to the left.)*

CAGEBEE: I now call to the stand Miss Amelia Pickles.

(Pickles moves to the center.)

CAGEBEE: Miss Pickles, when Captain Wickett first—

WICKETT: Aren't you going to make her swear?

CAGEBEE: Quite right. Do you swear that the testimony you are about to give is the truth?

PICKLES: I do.

CAGEBEE: As I was saying, when Captain Wickett first appeared on your doorstep, what was your impression of him?

PICKLES: I thought he was a gentleman—foolish thing that I was.

CAGEBEE: Are you wiser now, Miss Pickles?

PICKLES: Yes, I am. Sadder and wiser.

CAGEBEE: Sadder? Are you saying that you were in love with Captain Wickett?

WICKETT: She never loved me!

CAGEBEE: Captain Wickett! Please return to the stand a moment, if you will.

WICKETT: Why?

CAGEBEE: I have a question for you, just one. If you please.

(Wickett returns center.)

CAGEBEE: Captain Wickett, are you unlovable?

(Wickett gesticulates the absurdity of this question.)

CAGEBEE: Yes or No, please. Are you unlovable?

WICKETT: No.

CAGEBEE: You may step down. Thank you. Miss Pickles, you may resume your…

(Pickles returns.)

CAGEBEE: Now. I apologize for the interruption. Would you please tell the court, did you love Captain Wickett?

PICKLES: I suppose, in the confusion and crush of emotions, I suppose I thought I did.

CAGEBEE: You thought you did? Are we all here today, at a considerable expense to the Crown, because you thought your heart was broken?

PICKLES: I did love him.

CAGEBEE: And he jilted you, did he not?

PICKLES: He did.

CAGEBEE: And you are suing for damages.

PICKLES: That is correct.

CAGEBEE: What exactly are those damages?

PICKLES: I beg your pardon?

CAGEBEE: What are the damages when a tenant breaks your heart? It is still beating, is it not?

PICKLES: Do you mock me, Sir?

CAGEBEE: Not at all.

PICKLES: Is a breach of promise suit such a rare thing that a woman must explain herself?

CAGEBEE: I merely wish to familiarize the court with the particulars of your suit. How shall I put this delicately: You say Captain Wickett broke your heart. Is that all that he broke?

PICKLES: What do you mean?

CAGEBEE: Did he ever behave to you as a husband might?

PICKLES: He fell asleep in the parlour.

CAGEBEE: *(Out front.)* If the observers in the gallery would please refrain from laughing! This is not a matinee. *(To Pickles.)* What I mean to say is, did your condition as a woman change after Captain Wickett took up residence in your house?

PICKLES: *(Dawning realization.)* I think I see what you mean, Mr. Cagebee. In reply, I can only say that Captain Wickett took my girlhood.

CAGEBEE: Now Miss Pickles, I know this is trying, but please bear with me. What, exactly, do you mean by "girlhood"?

PICKLES: My innocence.

CAGEBEE: Innocence?

PICKLES: He stole my virtue.

CAGEBEE: And by virtue you mean—?

PICKLES: My honour.

CAGEBEE: What kind of honour?

PICKLES: My maiden's pride.

CAGEBEE: Maiden's what?

PICKLES: How plain can I be? He ruined me!

CAGEBEE: Ruined in what way?

PICKLES: He plucked my flower.

CAGEBEE: Your flower?

PICKLES: My bloom. My rose. My purity.

CAGEBEE: Come, Miss Pickles, say it in plain English!

PICKLES: He taught me of worldly things.

CAGEBEE: Geography?

PICKLES: I *knew* him.

CAGEBEE: Knew what?

PICKLES: I've said it as plainly as I can!

CAGEBEE: Are you telling the court that there was, between you and Captain
Wickett, carnal sexual congress?

PICKLES: Am I to answer such a question in a public courtroom?!

CAGEBEE: May I remind you, Miss Pickles, that it was you yourself who
brought this dispute into a public courtroom!

PICKLES: I cannot answer such a question!

CAGEBEE: You must!

PICKLES: And still I cannot!

CAGEBEE: And still you must! Have you carnal sexual knowledge of Captain
Wickett?!

PICKLES: Do you think I have no shame?! How am I to answer?

CAGEBEE: Yes or No!

PICKLES: Have you no heart?

CAGEBEE: Yes or No!

PICKLES: I can't bear it! I shall faint!

CAGEBEE: Answer the question!

PICKLES: Am I to be twice ravaged?!

CAGEBEE: YES OR NO!!

PICKLES: No.

CAGEBEE: I thought not. And at any time did Captain Wickett ask you to be
his wife?

(She thinks and thinks, turning it over in her mind.)

PICKLES: Yes, he did!

CAGEBEE: At this, the gallery made such a declamation of varying opinions
both for and against the witness that all proceedings were effectively
stopped until order was somewhat restored.

DARLINGTON: When the judges retired to consider their verdict, I found myself with the opportunity to speak to Miss Crosbie. / Miss Crosbie.

ALEXANDRINA: Mr. Darlington.

DARLINGTON: I think often of that day, looking at the prints.

ALEXANDRINA: Then endeavor to turn your mind to something else.

DARLINGTON: My feelings have not changed, Miss Crosbie.

ALEXANDRINA: Nor have mine, Mr. Darlington.

DARLINGTON: Tell the truth, Miss Crosbie. Did you turn down my offer of marriage because I am poor?

ALEXANDRINA: Mr. Darlington. Do not think I would marry any man only because he had money. I am simply one who is forced to seek her heart's true love from among those with over three thousand a year.

DARLINGTON: I see.

ALEXANDRINA: As I turned from him, I considered for the first time what it was that made him an inappropriate suitor, and realized that the reasons I had given him were not far from the truth. Even if I had wanted to marry Mr. Darlington, his lack of fortune placed him as far from my reach as the Prince of Wales. It was then that I felt the first pang that comes with the consciousness of deprivation.

DARLINGTON: At this point, she turned on me with such a penetrating look that I was quite flustered. And then it was time for the verdict.
(They arrange themselves as at the beginning of the testimony. Their faces tell the verdict; Pickles beams, Wickett fumes.)

WICKETT: I won't pay! Not five-hundred pounds, not one farthing. I'll give everything I own to African missionaries sooner than let her touch one penny.

CAGEBEE: Please be reasonable.

WICKETT: She never wanted to marry me! All she wanted from the moment she met me was to get her hands on my money! Marriage would be the ruin of all her plans!

CAGEBEE: It was then a look came into his eye which made me fear for his sanity, and my safety.

WICKETT: I'll do it. Yes! Ha ha ha! That's the answer! That's the trick to do her in! Tell them! Tell the court!

CAGEBEE: With a force of will bordering on the demonic, he compelled me to address the Court with his mad proposal.

PICKLES: I knew when I saw Cagebee approach the bench that some mischief was afoot.

CAGEBEE: If it please the Court, Captain Wickett would like to propose an

alternative settlement. Rather than pay Miss Pickles five-hundred
pounds, he will instead rectify her original complaint, and does hearby
offer her his hand in marriage.

PICKLES: What?!

WICKETT: A hush fell on the court. The gallery was gripped by a quivering
shock that was drawn out until it snapped, and the room erupted into a
tumultuous pandemonium that swirled around me like a cyclone as I
stood in triumph and the curtain rang down!

(The curtain drops.)

END ACT I

ACT II
A MARRIAGE OF ATTRITION

The Wedding Party stands before the curtain. Pickles and Wickett stand before the Reverend. Solomon Pinkney. They are flanked by Alexandrina and Darlington. Pickles wears a dress appropriate for the wedding of a woman past forty.

REVEREND: Do you Josiah Wickett take this woman as your lawfully wedded wife, to have and to hold from this day forward, for better and for worse, for richer and for poorer, in sickness and in health, to love, honour, and cherish, till death do you part?

WICKETT: I could not but marvel at the state to which I had brought myself. I could either pay five-hundred pounds or vow to love, honour, and cherish Miss Pickles. That I would not pay the money was axiomatic, but the shredded remains of my personal integrity rebelled at the thought of making a false vow.

PICKLES: It was my belief that he thought my nerve would fail me, and, in default of my stated vow of marriage, he would refuse to pay me my £500. I was determined, though, that if he made his vow, I would make mine, let the consequences be what they might.

WICKETT: It was as I stared at Reverend Pinkney's spectacles that the solution to my dilemma came to me. Are we not admonished to love our enemies? Undoubtedly we are, and if I could not love Miss Pickles as a wife, surely I could love her as an enemy. *(He turns to the Reverend.)* I do.

PICKLES: He did it.

REVEREND: And do you Amelia Pickles take this man to be your lawfully wedded husband, to have and to hold from this day forward, for better and for worse, for richer and for poorer, in sickness and in health, to love, honour, and obey, till death do you part?

PICKLES: I had forgotten about obey.

WICKETT: I could see her hesitate.

PICKLES: The injustice of it made my head swim. Where the woman is enjoined to obey, the man is asked merely to cherish. What onus does it put on a man that he must cherish his wife? Who can even say if he cherishes or not? There is no symmetry between the two words whatsoever. Suppose I felt myself uncherished? Would I be free to disobey? Yes, that was it! I would obey. I would obey every whim down to the last syllable,

as long as I knew myself to be cherished. The very instant the cherish-
ing stopped, so too would my obedience. *(She turns to the Reverend.)* I
do.

REVEREND: What? Oh, um, And do you, Josiah Wickett…No, no…I now
pronounce you man and wife.

(No one moves; they eye each other.)

REVEREND: Dear Elspeth, How are things in South Africa? I presided over a
most unusual wedding this morning. Have you ever noticed, Elspeth,
how upon the completion of a marriage ceremony, there is a little exha-
lation, a slight release? It's as if there had been some chance the thing
might not come off, but now it's done, and all is safe. There was no such
release this morning. There was, rather, an increase of tension, as though
the expectation of dashed hopes and thwarted desires had only begun.
(The Reverend exits.)

*(Alexandrina embraces Pickles, then exits. Darlington shakes hands with
Wickett, then exits. The curtain parts and the discerning eye will perceive
that the parlour of Number Fifteen Telfair Circle has become somewhat
smaller than in Act I. Pickles removes her veil and sits; Wickett sits opposite
her.)*

WICKETT: Well, we've done this thing, haven't we?

PICKLES: I'm sure I don't know what you call a "thing," but if you mean we've
married, yes, we have.

WICKETT: Then I say, make the best of it, ay?

PICKLES: By all means.

    (Pause.)

WICKETT: Well, then, shall we bury the hatchet?

PICKLES: I am certainly in possession of no hatchet.

WICKETT: Well, I certainly am not.

PICKLES: Do you mean to imply that I am?

WICKETT: Not at all.

PICKLES: What a thing to say. As if I walked around with hatchets.

WICKETT: Well, I haven't got one!

PICKLES: I should hope not.

    (Pause.)

WICKETT: Good night then, Miss Pickles.

PICKLES: Excuse me?

WICKETT: I said "Good night."

PICKLES: You said "Miss Pickles."

WICKETT: Did I?

PICKLES: That is no longer my name.

WICKETT: No, it's not.

PICKLES: As you should be aware.

WICKETT: I am, I am.

PICKLES: I don't suppose it's too much to ask you to address me by my proper name.

WICKETT: Not at all. Um—Good night, Mrs. Wi— *(He cannot do it.)* Mrs. Wi— *(Still he cannot.)* Good night, Amelia. *(He exits.)*

PICKLES: Early the next morning, I received a visit from my friend, Nellie Thimble.

(A knock at the door, then the voice of Miss Nellie Thimble calls from the hall.)

NELLIE: *(Off.)* Woo-ooo?!

PICKLES: In here, Nellie.

(Nellie Thimble enters with a newspaper.)

NELLIE: Have you seen it?

PICKLES: Seen what?

NELLIE: You haven't seen the Parliamentary page of the Morning Sun?

PICKLES: I rarely see the penny press, Nellie. My husband takes the *Times.*

NELLIE: I daresay it's in the *Times,* too.

PICKLES: What is it?

(Nellie Thimble opens the paper and gives it to Pickles.)

PICKLES: "The unexpected coalition between the Tories and the Radicals to stop the passage of the Reform Bill strikes us as being as unlikely a partnership as the recent marriage which took place, we are told, in Chelsea, at which an unwilling groom took an unwilling bride as a way of avoiding paying damages in a lawsuit. This curious union may be expedient in the short term, but has no future, as the bride may soon learn her lover has wooed with an ulterior motive, and the groom will learn his helpmate is not as easily controlled as he thinks." I am not easily controlled?!

NELLIE: Not you; the Tories.

PICKLES: No! It's myself! "The groom will find his helpmate is not as easily controlled as he thinks!"

NELLIE: They aren't talking about you at the end.

PICKLES: The implication is clear. My marriage is like the other, and the other is like so: the groom had ulterior motives and the bride is uncontrollable.

NELLIE: They don't say your name.

PICKLES: They say Chelsea. They name distinguishing details of our history! It is unmistakable!

NELLIE: These men don't even know you, Amy.

PICKLES: Just so!

NELLIE: And you had to expect some of the story to get around.

PICKLES: In a flash, I realized this was of greater import than an allusion in the *Morning Sun.* The whole of Telfair Circle was talking about my marriage in the most scurrilous terms imaginable. I knew I must take a formal position vis-a-vis gossip. *(She suddenly laughs with a gay peal of girlish amusement.)* But you have to admit, this silly story in the paper is rather naughty—but so amusing!

NELLIE: Yes, I knew you'd enjoy it.

PICKLES: Yes, my heavens! If you run across any more like it, please bring them to me. I'll paste them in a book.

NELLIE: I knew there wasn't a word of truth in what people are saying.

PICKLES: And what are people saying?

NELLIE: Oh, well, I'm sure you can imagine what wagging tongues have come up with.

PICKLES: Not the faintest idea.

NELLIE: Perhaps I shouldn't repeat it. So common.

PICKLES: I insist.

NELLIE: That your marriage is a fiction—

> *(A giggle from Pickles.)*

NELLIE: That Captain Wickett only married you to save £500—

> *(Laughter.)*

NELLIE: That you loathe each other—

> *(A ringing peal.)*

NELLIE: That you only agreed to his proposal because you were so desperate for a husband—

PICKLES: Yes, that's enough. How delightful.

NELLIE: Of course, I knew it was all nonsense.

PICKLES: Nonsense, yes, but there is some truth mixed up in there.

NELLIE: How so?

PICKLES: You've known me too long and too well, Nellie dear, to think I could be one of those simpering, weak-willed little things like in novels. I admit the Captain and I, on our way to the altar, have had our share of lovers' battles, like Kate and Petruchio, or Beatrice and Benedick, or—

NELLIE: Jason and Medea.

PICKLES: I admit it. In matters of the heart I am fiery. Tempestuous. My blood boils like a Hindoostani Princess.

NELLIE: And the lawsuit?

PICKLES: A lover's spat.

WICKETT: *(Off.)* Miss Pickles! *(Wickett enters in a huff.)* Miss Pickles!

PICKLES: Oh, you silly, romantic thing! How you love to tease me, calling "Miss Pickles" like when we first met!

WICKETT: Oh, all right. Mrs. Wickett. There. Are you happy? Now about my boots. You have once again—

PICKLES: Aren't you going to say Hello to Miss Thimble?

WICKETT: Oh. Yes. Good afternoon, Miss Thimble.

NELLIE: Good afternoon, Captain.

WICKETT: *(To Pickles.)* My boots were again hanging from a nail out the window on the back stairs.

PICKLES: I've told you, Captain, why I do that.

WICKETT: Yes, and I have told you, that in the winter months, it is too cold and damp to let my boots hang out a window all night.

PICKLES: Then leave them in your room.

WICKETT: I have explained, very patiently on at least two previous occasions, why I do not wish to have them in my room.

PICKLES: And I have explained why I don't want them in the hall.

WICKETT: Well, look at them! They are soaked through and ice cold! How am I to wear them like this?

PICKLES: They reek, Captain, with an odor most disagreeable.

WICKETT: Yes, I am aware of that. That is why I leave them in the hall.

PICKLES: Well, I don't want them in my hall!

WICKETT: You can't smell them from your room! And if you do it again, I shall be forced to take steps!

PICKLES: And then I noticed with what a look of delight Nellie was watching this scene unfold. *(Baby-talk.)* Does Captain want to keep his booties in the hall? Hmm? Well, that's where we'll keep 'em. How's that? Is Captain happy?

WICKETT: What?

PICKLES: If you want to keep your boots in the hall, I don't see as it could make much difference. Do you, Nellie?

NELLIE: Well, how bad do they smell?

PICKLES: Not bad at all. I shall take them now and place them near the fire in the kitchen. *(She goes to take the boots from Wickett.)*

WICKETT: No, no, I'll do it. / There was something almost supernatural in seeing Miss Pickles give in like that. And in front of a witness! Had I been a Roman Catholic, I would have crossed myself. *(He exits.)*

PICKLES: What a dear old fuss-budget he is.

NELLIE: I must be off, Amy dear. I've got to stop in at Number Eleven.

PICKLES: *Au revoir.*

NELLIE: *Au revoir. (Nellie exits.)*

PICKLES: I knew I could count on Nellie, if not to believe me, then at least to repeat my version of things up and down the circle. Whatever else she repeated I would deal with later. In the meantime, I planned to re-read the story of Jason and Medea, as I had a suspicion Nellie meant that as a gibe. *(Pickles exits.)*

(Wickett enters, dressing himself in evening clothes.)

WICKETT: I entered this marriage in full battle array, ready to fight the good fight until one of us capitulated or died. I was unprepared for the insidious campaign of brinkmanship and nerves with which I was met: a steady barrage of kindness, an onslaught of meekness, and a fierce bombardment of solicitude. I was lulled into believing the enemy had taken her bit of land and retreated from the field. That my life was altered I knew; how greatly I did not know until that invitation came, an invitation to an annual function at which our single presences never before had been deemed necessary, but to which our plural selves were graciously summoned.

VOICE OF A FOOTMAN: Captain and Mrs. Josiah Wickett!

WICKETT: From the moment we walked in the door, we were greeted with smiles, very wide smiles, and, I thought, great good cheer. Had I my wits about me, had I not been blinded by a sun's worth of candles and jewels, I would have recognized the sound of giggles. I do not dance, but Mrs. Wickett did not want partners.

(Pickles dances across the stage in a ball gown, in good taste, but a bit young. Philip Arbuthnot enters.)

ARBUTHNOT: Captain Wickett?

WICKETT: Yes?

ARBUTHNOT: Allow me to introduce myself. Philip Arbuthnot. I'm acquainted with your niece.

WICKETT: I have no niece.

ARBUTHNOT: No? Are you not the uncle of a Miss Alexandrina Crosbie?

WICKETT: Ah yes. By marriage.

ARBUTHNOT: By marriage. I just wanted to congratulate you. You and your bride have made quite a sensation here tonight.

WICKETT: A sensation? And how have we accomplished this feat? For I must admit I had no such purpose in mind when I arrived.

(Pickles is dancing with Darlington and laughing—a belle.)

ARBUTHNOT: Well, it was in large part accomplished before you arrived. The story of your romance has enthralled those of us who follow such things, and, of course, we all follow such things.

WICKETT: Such things as what?

ARBUTHNOT: Captain Wickett, you can hardly be unaware that certain details of your, shall we say, *court*-ship have been made public.

WICKETT: This is where I heard the giggle for what it was.

ARBUTHNOT: Two lovers nearly torn apart by jealousy and passion, yet all comes right in the end. Terribly romantic.

WICKETT: My instinct was to hold my ground and let the blows fall where they might.

ARBUTHNOT: I hope you don't mind a little good-natured teasing. You're bound to get a touch: "What ho, Romeo" and "What d'you say, Lochinvar" and that sort of thing.

WICKETT: Lochinvar? Romeo?

ARBUTHNOT: Don't be modest, Captain. You've more than earned those titles, if one quarter of what your wife says is true.

WICKETT: My wife? What's she been saying?

ARBUTHNOT: A brilliant conversationalist. But I suppose she has many rare qualities.

WICKETT: I decided not to disabuse Mr. Arbuthnot. Later, though, I would open a counter-offensive against Mrs. Wickett. / Many rare qualities.

ARBUTHNOT: And you've made a name for yourself in the history books. The first man to sue for breach of promise.

WICKETT: No, no! She sued me.

ARBUTHNOT: Oh. Don't let that get around. Doesn't reflect so nicely on you from an ardent lover's point of view. Still, I suppose it doesn't matter, as long as true love has found its way. *(Arbuthnot exits.)*

PICKLES: I noticed, as we returned home that Captain Wickett's brow was more knitted, and of a darker aspect, than it had been before the ball, but little did I realize the danger it bespoke for me when we arrived home. *(She turns to Wickett.)* Do you want anything before you go to bed?

WICKETT: Oh, yes.

PICKLES: What?

WICKETT: Guess.

PICKLES: What?

WICKETT: Guess.

PICKLES: I don't know. What?

WICKETT: *(Lascivious.)* I want you to guess.

PICKLES: Well, I don't want to guess. Tell me or do without.

WICKETT: I think you know, madam.

PICKLES: Sir, I do not like your tone of voice. What do you mean to imply by it?

WICKETT: Nothing improper.

PICKLES: I should certainly hope not.

WICKETT: At least, nothing improper between a man and his wife.

PICKLES: And what is that supposed to mean?

WICKETT: Just that when we were landlady and tenant it would have been improper for me to speak of certain things before you, things like—the conjugal act.

PICKLES: Captain Wickett!

WICKETT: But now we are man and wife, one flesh, and we may speak of such things, may we not?

PICKLES: I am going to bed now, and I shall latch my door!

WICKETT: I shall break it down! You cannot lock your husband out of your bedchamber! The law is on my side!

PICKLES: Captain, you may have spent however many years in the Army, killing ever so many men, but believe me, you will find a formidable opponent in Amelia Pickles!

WICKETT: I only ask my rights.

PICKLES: They are not your rights.

WICKETT: I'll divorce you.

PICKLES: Do.

WICKETT: I'll publish the reason.

PICKLES: So will I.

WICKETT: Will you? Will you indeed? From what I've heard you've already published quite a different story.

PICKLES: What do you mean?

WICKETT: I've been told that ours is a love match; that I sued you for breach of promise; that we are prone to lover's quarrels, and that I am your devoted servant.

PICKLES: Is it my fault that people gossip? That they gossip with incorrect information?

WICKETT: I put it to you, Mrs. Wickett, that you are the source of these false-
hoods as Lake Victoria is the source of the Nile.

PICKLES: It is untrue.

WICKETT: I put it to you further, that you have let it be known that ours is a
real marriage. Therefore, I claim my rights as a real husband! *(He grasps
her in his arms.)* And with that I seized her in my arms, with a quite con-
vincingly demented glare in my eyes, and a low, throaty laugh, like a
beast—all of which effects I had been outlining in my mind since my
talk with Mr. Arbuthnot several hours before. She was quite clearly terrified, and my plan I counted a resounding success.

PICKLES: Very well then.

WICKETT: What the devil do you mean by that?

PICKLES: I acknowledge the validity of your claim. I shall not deny you your
spousal privileges.

WICKETT: Ah. No? *(He releases her from his embrace.)*

PICKLES: I made a vow, Captain. I shall not break it, however loathsome I find
my duty.

WICKETT: Well, one doesn't want to be thought of as loathsome by one's
bride.

PICKLES: I can promise you, Captain, that I will let no word or action betray
my feelings during…my duty.

WICKETT: Well then…That's more like it. Yes.
> *(There is a pause. She looks at him. He looks at her, then away. She sits on
> the edge of the sofa, then leans back, then slowly slides into a semi-recumbent
> position.)*

WICKETT: Not here…
> *(She jumps to her feet.)*

PICKLES: I shall require a few moments in my room. If you knock on the door
in fifteen minutes, you will find it unlatched.

WICKETT: Very well.

PICKLES: I betook myself to my private chamber and was paralyzed by the
overwhelming number of decisions to be made. I had always let it be
known that I had had, in my early youth, some experience of love-making of the pastoral kind, and in my novels I alluded to such activity with
what I thought was telling understatement. Now I was forced to admit
that, in the art of seduction, I knew nothing. What should I wear? What
should I not wear? Where in the room should I place myself? And most
urgently, what attitude should I assume at each stage of the—event?

Several more minutes were wasted in deploring the state of feminine education in this country.

WICKETT: I realized I had gravely miscalculated. I had anticipated having to go no further than showing her mercy when she begged for it, but far from spurning my advances, she was orchestrating them. She was, undoubtedly, upstairs perfuming herself and arranging her déshabille. After the threats I had just made, and the show of masculine forcefulness, to abandon the rape would be galling. However, it was impossible that I should mount those stairs for our rendezvous.

PICKLES: When I had at last completed my preparations, I realized more than fifteen minutes had elapsed. When thirty minutes had gone by, I thought he might be in the hallway. When forty-five minutes had gone by, I felt the room grow suddenly cold. I returned to the parlour. *(To Wickett.)* There is a draft.

WICKETT: Yes.

PICKLES: Do you know where it is coming from?

WICKETT: Ah, no.

PICKLES: Nor do I. *(Pause.)* Well, I shall be in my room.

WICKETT: Very well.

PICKLES: Had he abandoned his intention of visiting me? I thought it would be too final to say "Good night." I chose my words carefully: / Until later.

WICKETT: Good night.

(She is deflated, and exits. Alexandrina, in a dazzling ball-gown, enters with Philip Arbuthnot. She has a dark scowl on her face.)

ARBUTHNOT: Alexandrina, are you not enjoying yourself?

(She forces a melancholy smile.)

ALEXANDRINA: You see right through my facade, Philip.

ARBUTHNOT: That is not difficult when you make faces like a gargoyle.

ALEXANDRINA: I find the thrill of such occasions as these to be somewhat mollified lately. I feel an emptiness in my life, which I know will never be filled by the vainglory of coronets and carriages and landed estates.

ARBUTHNOT: You mean to say you are renouncing your ambition of so many years?

ALEXANDRINA: Of course not. But I know those things will never fill my heart.

ARBUTHNOT: And what will?

ALEXANDRINA: A great passion.

ARBUTHNOT: And are those easier to come by than landed estates?

ALEXANDRINA: Do not vex me, Philip.

ARBUTHNOT: Never that.

(Darlington enters.)

DARLINGTON: As the crowd began to thin, I caught sight of my new cousin, and I threaded my way through the crowd to greet her, having thoroughly dismissed any notion of marrying her.

ALEXANDRINA: You must leave me now, Philip—but go as though it were your idea, and let me beg you to stay.

DARLINGTON: Miss Crosbie. I heard you were here tonight, but I must have missed you in the crush.

ALEXANDRINA: Mr. Darlington, let me introduce Mr. Arbuthnot.

ARBUTHNOT: Mr. Darlington.

DARLINGTON: Mr. Arbuthnot.

ARBUTHNOT: I'm afraid I see someone I must speak to. Will you excuse me?

ALEXANDRINA: Oh, please, Philip, please do stay.

ARBUTHNOT: I'm sorry, I'll return shortly, but I must just have a word with this person.

ALEXANDRINA: You'll have all night to speak to him, won't you stay?

ARBUTHNOT: I'll return shortly, Mr. Darlington, Miss Crosbie. *(He exits.)*

ALEXANDRINA: I suppose you despise me, now.

DARLINGTON: Do you? Do I?

ALEXANDRINA: You try to spare my feelings, and I thank you, but how can it be otherwise, after the farce that just passed?

DARLINGTON: I beg your pardon?

ALEXANDRINA: Could you not see how desperately I tried to keep my friend by my side? Can you not guess why? Is it not as plain as the moon in the sky that I did not trust myself to be alone with you?

DARLINGTON: I began to see the part it was required of me to play. / And why is that, Miss Crosbie?

ALEXANDRINA: For it must end, Mr. Darlington, you know that as well as I.

DARLINGTON: Must it?

ALEXANDRINA: Without a doubt. If we were free to call our hearts our own, then, perhaps—Oh, but what's the use of "if" and "perhaps"? They are part of a game children play, and we are not children, are we, Mr. Darlington?

DARLINGTON: Aren't we? / My part was quite easy, as she needed only the slightest prompting.

ALEXANDRINA: I think you know we are not. Shall I make a confession? I am on the wrong side of twenty-five, Mr. Darlington.

DARLINGTON: She might just as well have said she was on the wrong side of thirty. *(He shrugs.)*

ALEXANDRINA: When a woman reaches my age, she can no longer think as a child who reaches for the prettiest bauble, no matter how dear.

DARLINGTON: Can't she?

ALEXANDRINA: No, she cannot.

DARLINGTON: She turned away from me and said nothing. I took this to be my cue to take up the baton. / Why can she not? Why cannot that little girl, be she five-and-twenty or five-and-sixty, take up whatever bauble she chooses, as long as she listens to her heart.

ALEXANDRINA: She does listen, but what a cacophony she hears: so many different themes and melodies.

DARLINGTON: The words were flowing with a beauty that would have been impossible had they been true. / Is there not some theme that pleases more than the rest?

ALEXANDRINA: Many please, but there is one, barely audible, that presents itself to my ear, then fades away, and returns, and yet I cannot pin it down, or even remember its notes.

DARLINGTON: Is that the theme of your happiness?

ALEXANDRINA: *(Sincerely moved.)* Yes, the theme of my happiness. *(She moves away.)*

DARLINGTON: And there the scene ended. I felt a surge of elation that lasted well into the night. The elegance, refinement, and sophistication with which the thing had been handled was the high point of my career, and yet I had committed myself to nothing. I had, in truth, not thought of Miss Crosbie since last I had seen her, yet she had a grace about her that made playing the part of her lover the easiest thing in the world. In addition, I was perfectly safe in playing this game, as she had already turned down my offer of marriage.

ALEXANDRINA: Here at last was a passion worthy of the name. The sincerity of it was intoxicating. No one would ever know the depth of feeling in my soul, the vivid emotion in my heart, the tragic stature of my life. It was a secret that must go with me to my eternal reward—unless, of course, my diaries should somehow be made public. *(She calculates the probability.)* And as the poor man had a rich uncle, I could even, if necessary, marry him. Of course, I was as surprised as anyone when the residents of Number Fifteen Telfair Circle were again engulfed in a great scandal.

(The Hierarchy of the British legal system appears.)

CLERK OF THE COURT: *(Off.)* Wickett vs. Wickett. A bill of divorcement.
   (The Judge enters. Pickles and Wickett enter from opposite sides.)

PICKLES: We were able to dispense with the services of a barrister by invoking a little known pre-Norman privilege of freeholders within the walls of London.

WICKETT: Would you like to begin?

PICKLES: No, no, you go right ahead.

WICKETT: I certainly don't mind. If you wish to go first—

PICKLES: Not at all. You go first.

WICKETT: I don't mind if you wish—

PICKLES: I am content—

JUDGE: One of you must begin.
   (She sits in the witness' chair.)

WICKETT: Very well. Um…Mrs. Amelia Pickles Wickett, would you please state your name for the court?

PICKLES: You just said it.

WICKETT: What?

PICKLES: You said my name. You're not supposed to say, "Mrs. Amelia Pickles Wickett, what is your name?" That's ridiculous.

WICKETT: Will you please just state your name, thank you?

PICKLES: Mrs. Amelia Pickles Wickett.

WICKETT: Mrs. Pickles Wickett. Are you married?

PICKLES: Well, that goes without saying, doesn't it?

WICKETT: I will decide what goes without saying and what does not, thank you. Please answer the question.

PICKLES: He is antagonizing me, My Lord.

WICKETT: I merely asked a simple question.

JUDGE: Please continue.

WICKETT: I will ask you again. Are you married?

PICKLES: Yes.

WICKETT: And do you see the man to whom you are married in this room?
   (She looks heavenward and shakes her head.)

WICKETT: Please just answer the question.

PICKLES: Yes.

WICKETT: Would you please point out this man for the court to see?
   (She points at Wickett.)

WICKETT: Thank you. *(He produces a heavy sheaf of papers.)* Now, to choose randomly from my very complete documentation— *(He pulls a sheet*

from the pile.) Ah. This is typical. Do you recall what you ordered for
supper on the evening of the twenty-third of September?

PICKLES: No, I do not.

WICKETT: Will it refresh your memory to hear that you made potato soup?

PICKLES: No, it will not.

WICKETT: Well, you did. Do you recall what your husband said about that
soup?

PICKLES: No, I do not.

WICKETT: Will it refresh your memory to hear that he said it was ever so
slightly too salty?

PICKLES: No, it will not.

WICKETT: Well, he did.

PICKLES: Well, if you say it, it must be true.

WICKETT: Would Your Honour please enjoin the witness from making sarcastic comments—?

JUDGE: Please continue.

WICKETT: Now when this comment concerning salt was made, the maker did
not intend for it to be in any way mean spirited. The potato soup on the
evening of the twenty-third of September was indeed, from a factual
standpoint, too saline in flavour.

PICKLES: It was just right.

WICKETT: Has your memory come back to you?

(She turns her head away.)

WICKETT: On the evening of the twenty-fifth, you made a chicken stew. Do
you recall anything special about that chicken stew?

PICKLES: No, I do not.

WICKETT: It was prepared without any salt of any kind. On the evening of the
twenty-seventh you made an oyster broth. Do you recall anything special about that?

PICKLES: No, I do not.

WICKETT: Also made without salt. On the evening of the twenty-eighth, a pea
soup. Also without salt, on the twenty-ninth, cabbage, no salt. And is it
not true that went on for some month and a half?

PICKLES: I don't like a lot of salt in my soup.

WICKETT: For a month and a half she wreaked her terrible vengeance on her
powerless husband, who, in one innocent and unguarded moment,
expressed a simple wish for less salt in his potato soup, and what does he
get? Six long weeks of not a grain of salt in one dish of soup!

PICKLES: There's salt on the table!

WICKETT: Well, it's not my job to salt the soup! That's the cook's job!

PICKLES: Well, if you're too lazy to lift your arm and reach for the salt—

WICKETT: You did it just to annoy me! Just because I said "There's too much salt"—

PICKLES: I'm sure I have more important things to worry about—

WICKETT: You left it out just to annoy me! *(To the Judge.)* Was ever man so deceived by woman? Has ever man endured such spiteful treatment at the hands of the so-called fairer sex? Has ever a man—

PICKLES: My Lord! Don't I get to speak? Must I sit here in silence and be abused by this beast, this fiend, this, this—

JUDGE: Mrs. Wickett?

PICKLES: My Lord?

JUDGE: On what grounds are you suing for divorce?

PICKLES: Physical abuse, My Lord.

JUDGE: He beat you?

PICKLES: Oh, yes, My Lord.

WICKETT: I did not.

PICKLES: He most certainly did. He rained blows upon me until I was black and blue.

WICKETT: Her dress was on fire.

PICKLES: It is true, My Lord, that a very small part of my dress was smoldering in a very insignificant way, but he took that opportunity to pummel me with a ferocity from which I have never recovered.

WICKETT: I saved your life.

JUDGE: Mr. Wickett—

WICKETT: Captain Wickett.

JUDGE: —You are counter-suing, are you not?

WICKETT: Yes, My Lord, I am.

JUDGE: On what grounds?

WICKETT: She attempted to poison me, My Lord, with blackberry jam—

PICKLES: Piffle.

WICKETT: —that she herself made and then put away until its natural toxins were at such a level that one spoonful nearly ended my life.

PICKLES: It was off, My Lord, and let the record show that I ate more of it than he did, and was quite a bit more sick than he was.

WICKETT: She is clever, My Lord, crafty and clever.

JUDGE: Mr. Wickett—

WICKETT: Captain.

JUDGE: —Are you aware of your wife having ever been unfaithful?

WICKETT: No, not that I am aware of.

JUDGE: Mrs. Wickett, has your husband ever been unfaithful to you?

PICKLES: No.

JUDGE: Was the marriage consummated? *(Pause.)* Well?

PICKLES: Yes.   WICKETT: No.

PICKLES: No.   WICKETT: Yes.

JUDGE: Are you in any doubt on this question?

WICKETT: She adamantly refused.

PICKLES: That is a bold-faced lie!

WICKETT: She fought me off with physical blows and a vituperative tongue.

PICKLES: I waited in my chamber with the door unlocked for one hour and
forty-five minutes.

JUDGE: So it was not consummated?

PICKLES AND WICKETT: No.

JUDGE: Court is adjourned while I consider the matter.

PICKLES: But when is it my turn? Don't I get a turn?

(Darlington and Alexandrina enter from opposite sides.)

ALEXANDRINA: Mr. Darlington. I didn't realize you were here.

DARLINGTON: Nor I you.

ALEXANDRINA: I knew I had to come to give moral support to my aunt.

DARLINGTON: A terrible business, this.

ALEXANDRINA: And yet, one saw it coming.

DARLINGTON: Yes, one did.

ALEXANDRINA: There was something in the way they glared at each other, and
muttered curses under their breath, that did not bode well for a happy union.

DARLINGTON: Very true.

ALEXANDRINA: These people who are so ignorant of their own hearts. I pity them.

DARLINGTON: Oh, Miss Crosbie. How I love you.

ALEXANDRINA: Don't.

DARLINGTON: But it's true.

ALEXANDRINA: Please, not now.

DARLINGTON: Then when?

ALEXANDRINA: Never. What will such love-making profit us if it cannot be
legalized?

DARLINGTON: Can't it?

(She turns to him with a rueful smile.)

ALEXANDRINA: I think you know it can't.

DARLINGTON: I know nothing of the kind.

ALEXANDRINA: Oh, stop, you fool, stop!

DARLINGTON: I will not stop! I will press forward!

ALEXANDRINA: To where?

DARLINGTON: Why, to here!

(He steps forward. There is a brief pause of confusion.)

ALEXANDRINA: It is folly! I forbid you to propose to me.

DARLINGTON: Miss Crosbie, will you be my wife?

ALEXANDRINA: I will pretend I didn't hear that.

DARLINGTON: Then I will repeat it: Will you be my wife?

ALEXANDRINA: Yes, yes, I succumb. You have won me. When shall it be? Soon?

DARLINGTON: This was not what I thought she was going to say.

ALEXANDRINA: How our friends will tease us, the penniless bachelor and an old maid of twenty-seven.

DARLINGTON: But my dear. Didn't you say it was impossible that we should be married?

ALEXANDRINA: It is, but I don't care. From now on I shall do as my heart prompts me. Where should we go on our wedding trip?

WICKETT: I suppose we should discuss the settlement.

PICKLES: Don't worry. I shan't ask you for a penny.

WICKETT: No?

PICKLES: Just an even split of our combined assets.

WICKETT: Ah. Not a penny. Just half.

PICKLES: Not a penny more than is my due.

WICKETT: How your due?

PICKLES: What God has joined let no man put asunder, unless he pays.

WICKETT: Well, if you think I'm paying you one hundred pounds a year merely for the privilege of divorcing you—

PICKLES: Oh, no, not one hundred pounds. Half. Not one penny less.

WICKETT: What do you mean?

PICKLES: The law is on my side.

WICKETT: One hundred pounds. Half. Yes.

PICKLES: Half. One hundred pounds? What?

WICKETT: How much do you think I have?

PICKLES: I don't know. You spoke of inheriting a fortune.

WICKETT: Yes.

PICKLES: How much?

WICKETT: Well…,a small fortune.

PICKLES: How small?

WICKETT: Not that small.

PICKLES: How big?

WICKETT: How much do you have?

PICKLES: How much do you have?!

WICKETT: Two hundred pounds a year.

PICKLES: Two hundred a year?!

WICKETT: Almost.

PICKLES: Almost?!

WICKETT: How much do you have?!

PICKLES: Two hundred pounds a year!

WICKETT: Answer me! How much do you have?

PICKLES: Two hundred pounds a year! That's how much I have. A little more.

WICKETT: More? You have more than two hundred a year?

PICKLES: A little.

WICKETT: You said you were poor!

PICKLES: You said you were rich!

    (Darlington and Alexandrina cross to them.)

ALEXANDRINA: We have news! Do you want to hear? Yes? No?

DARLINGTON: Perhaps it can wait.

ALEXANDRINA: Aunt? Uncle?

PICKLES: Come, yes, I have news, too. Please excuse us, gentlemen. *(Pickles takes Alexandrina aside.)*

ALEXANDRINA: Shall I tell you my news first?

PICKLES: I just found out how much money he has.

ALEXANDRINA: How much?

PICKLES: Two hundred pounds.

ALEXANDRINA: A quarter?

PICKLES: A year.

ALEXANDRINA: Well. That's a blow.

PICKLES: Two hundred.

ALEXANDRINA: Perhaps the Captain will increase his allowance.

PICKLES: What?

ALEXANDRINA: I'm sure when I tell him our news, the Captain will increase John's allowance to say, four hundred.

PICKLES: I'm talking about the Captain. It is the Captain who has two hundred.

ALEXANDRINA: How much does John have?

PICKLES: The nephew? Nothing. He's penniless.

ALEXANDRINA: He can't be. Nobody is penniless. Even the most absolutely desperately poor have a hundred or a hundred and fifty.

PICKLES: There is no money.

ALEXANDRINA: Perhaps it's entailed.

PICKLES: No.

ALEXANDRINA: Tied up in litigation?

(Pickles shakes her head, "No.")

ALEXANDRINA: Aunt. Don't say that.

PICKLES: Why not? What is your news?

ALEXANDRINA: It can wait.

JUDGE: This court is now in session. First let me say that the two of you have done more violence to the sacrament of matrimony than anyone since Henry the Eighth. Marriage is a Holy Institution, not a game to be tossed out when it no longer amuses. I am proud to say I am married. I treasure my wife, and if she ever comes back from Italy, I'll tell her so. Now it is quite clear that even by the most elastic standards, no proper marriage ever took place between the two parties before me. Divorce hardly seems necessary. How, therefore, can I make my displeasure felt in terms strong enough to express the outrage I feel as a Christian, as a Husband, and as a Jurist? I can think of only one way. And so, after careful consideration, I have decided to reject this petition you have put before me. The motion for divorce is denied. May you live happily ever after.

(Pickles swoons as the curtain falls.)

END ACT II

ACT III
BLEAK FLAT

With the curtain closed. Alexandrina enters in a dressing gown, her hair down. Darlington follows her on, yawning, dressed in Victorian underclothes which cover him from neck to ankle.

ALEXANDRINA: Good morning, Mr. Darlington.

DARLINGTON: Good morning, *Mrs.* Darlington.

ALEXANDRINA: Afterwards, I found it extremely difficult to explain how I stumbled into my disastrous marriage.

DARLINGTON: Venice has been a fiasco, don't you think? I mean, the smell.

ALEXANDRINA: Of course, all of my friends and relations tried to convince me to retreat from my engagement, and I admit the urgency of this consensus made me somewhat rebellious. It is my nature that when all the world tells me to do A, I perversely yearn to do B, the perverse option B in this case being—

(She gestures at Darlington, who yawns and scratches himself.)

ALEXANDRINA: But that is not a complete explanation of why I married Mr. Darlington. I do not believe I am more than moderately motivated by feelings of spite, and I openly confess I was sensible of those masculine charms he possessed independently of my desire to be contrary.

DARLINGTON: How do you say "three minute egg" in Italian?

ALEXANDRINA: But more than these reasons was another. I had for some time previous felt myself in danger of becoming what people call shallow. What better way to prove the existence of unsuspected profundity than by marrying a man with no possible attraction than his own person? And even though I knew the feeling in my heart was most likely not that felt by passionate, profound women, I hoped the deed would evoke in me the emotion. And so I married. The only excuse I can give for what I did next is that the emotion evoked was not what I expected.

DARLINGTON: You know, Latin is not the slightest help with Italian. I'm beginning to think the classics are a colossal waste of time.

ALEXANDRINA: I've been thinking, John…

DARLINGTON: Yes?

ALEXANDRINA: Bologna is not on our itinerary.

DARLINGTON: No? If it's not, it must be the only town in Italy that isn't.

ALEXANDRINA: But we haven't seen the Bolognese Giottos.

DARLINGTON: Well, hang the Bolognese Giottos.

ALEXANDRINA: I only mention it because Kitty McBride is taking a party Tuesday week to Bologna and San Marino and Rimini.

DARLINGTON: That American girl? The one who was throwing money around Monte Carlo like it was confetti?

ALEXANDRINA: She comes from one of the best families in Chicago.

DARLINGTON: What exactly does that mean, the best families in *Chicago?*

ALEXANDRINA: And I knew you wouldn't want to go, so this is what I'm proposing. You go back to London the day after tomorrow, on schedule, and I'll follow in two or three weeks. Doesn't that seem sensible? For when shall I get another chance to tour Italy, hmm?

DARLINGTON: And thus was solved the great mystery of how I had won the long pursued but ne'er captured Alexandrina Crosbie. I hadn't won her at all. At the same time was solved the even greater mystery of how I would hold on to her: I wouldn't. Mingled with the disappointment was a measure of relief.

(She kisses him on the cheek.)

ALEXANDRINA: I'm glad that's settled. I'll cable you the date and time of my arrival in London, and please try to meet the train, for I shall be missing you horribly by then. *(She exits.)*

DARLINGTON: I met the train, at the appointed hour. That evening I got the cable explaining the tiresome delay, and the following week I got the letter explaining irksome postponement. After that, I got mainly tradesman's bills, which I never paid, but which never came twice. I didn't mind getting those so much, because *somebody* was paying them, and because they were always addressed to Mrs. John Darlington.

(Cagebee enters.)

CAGEBEE: After their request for a divorce was denied, Captain and Mrs. Wickett determined to appeal the decision. I explained to them that appeals are far more expensive than trials, and take twice as long. As two appearances in court in quick succession had decimated their bank balances, and a third would be quite impossible at the moment, they determined to continue to cohabitate for the sake of economy, and as soon as their finances recovered, they would file an appeal. That was twenty-five years ago. *(Cagebee exits.)*

(The curtain rises, even the less observant members of the audience will notice that the parlour of Number Fifteen Telfair Circle has grown considerably smaller and shabbier since Act II. The furniture is crowded together and the chandelier hangs just a few feet above head level. Wickett sits in his

chair—or rather sits in a Bath chair where his chair used to be—a blanket over his legs and a stocking cap on his head. A churchbell rings: five o'clock. Pickles enters, dressed in full Victorian ladies' sleeping gear, looking like a cross between Lucia di Lammermoor and Lady Macbeth.)

PICKLES: I am writing a new novel. Unfortunately, I can no longer read my own handwriting. Should anyone ask, I shall tell them I am writing in Polish. Very few people read Polish, so my secret is safe. The heroine is a beautiful young English girl who impulsively marries a mysterious nobleman from the continent. She goes to live with him in a castle in the Carpathian mountains, and he begins a systematic program of torture to drive her mad. Right now, I have her bricked up behind a wall in the wine cellar—but I can think of no way to rescue her, and it is only chapter two. In the future, I must remember to leave holes in my plots.

WICKETT: Her eyesight is failing. Sometimes when I sit quietly, she doesn't know I'm in the room. For a few minutes, it's like the old days, twenty-five years ago, when we were happy.

(She sighs heavily.)

WICKETT: Looking for something?

PICKLES: Oh! I wish you wouldn't scare me like that. I had an aunt who once died of apoplexy upon finding a spider in the sugar bowl. She started to bleed from the ear and was dead in forty-five seconds.

(He produces a pencil and notebook and begins writing.)

PICKLES: What are you doing? *(She leans forward, trying to see.)* What is that?

WICKETT: I so value everything you say, I'm making a note so I don't forget. "Sugar Bowl. Spider. Don't Forget."

PICKLES: If I find a spider in the sugar bowl I shall sue you for attempted murder.

WICKETT: One doesn't sue for murder.

PICKLES: I shall go one day soon and file that appeal for a divorce.

WICKETT: I shall go with you.

PICKLES: As soon as the weather clears. Have you seen my spectacles?

WICKETT: No. Why are you dressed for bed? It's five o'clock.

PICKLES: I couldn't sleep, so I thought I'd get up early. Why are you up so late?

WICKETT: Five is late?

PICKLES: Most people like to get to bed before dawn.

WICKETT: It's five in the afternoon.

PICKLES: It is not. *(She peaks out the window.)* The sun isn't even up.

WICKETT: The sun is already down.

PICKLES: At five o'clock?

WICKETT: Typical for mid December.

PICKLES: Oh. I'm so confused…Who are you? Why are you always in my house? Why do I have to spend my life with you?

WICKETT: God give me strength.

PICKLES: WHERE IS YOUR RENT?! YOU OWE ME THE RENT ON THE FIRST! I DON'T CARE IF YOU'VE GONE TO BATH!

WICKETT: I don't pay rent. That was twenty-five years ago.

PICKLES: Oh.

WICKETT: She goes a little mad now and then.

PICKLES: I can hear you.

WICKETT: Was I talking out loud?

PICKLES: He's gone utterly mad.

WICKETT: I swear, I'm fit as a fiddle in mind and body! *(He attempts to move as he did before, but cannot.)*

PICKLES: Don't swear.

WICKETT: That's not swearing. Swearing is to say "Damn" or "By God."

PICKLES: Those are oaths. Swearing is to say "I swear."

WICKETT: You've got it backwards. Saying "I swear" is an oath.

PICKLES: How can you look me in the eye and say "I swear" is not swearing?

WICKETT: I'll look it up in the dictionary. *(He tries to get up but the pain stops him.)* Oof. There. It's right there. Will you get it for me?
(She sighs like a martyr and hands him a book.)

WICKETT: This is the Bible.

PICKLES: What? *(She examines it.)* Oh. *(She hands him another book.)*

WICKETT: Now, let's see here…swear, swear…Wait a minute. I have the strangest feeling…I've done this before. We've had this argument before. Word for word. I got the dictionary— *(He looks at the open dictionary on his lap.)* Look! It fell open to the exact page! And it's smudged and dirty from use! *(Dawning fear.)* How many times have we had this argument?!

PICKLES: I know! I'll put it in a strongbox, and hide the key, and you can tell me where it is when I get back!

WICKETT: There are times when the loneliness is almost more than I can bear.

PICKLES: I can't bear this aggravation. I need serenity.
(She picks up a book and begins reading. He watches as she appears to become engrossed. She titters in amusement.)

WICKETT: Good book?

PICKLES: Very much so. *(She reads and giggles.)*

WICKETT: You can't read a word, can you?

PICKLES: I pay you no mind.

WICKETT: You're pretending.

PICKLES: Honestly, if you're going to badger me like this, I'll read in my room.

WICKETT: Admit it. You can't make out a word.

PICKLES: It just so happens I have read this book many times before, and I have a perfect recollection of every line. I am reading it in my mind's eye. *(He looks away. She returns to the book. He mumbles something.)*

PICKLES: What did you say?

WICKETT: Nothing.

PICKLES: I heard you.

WICKETT: I said nothing.

PICKLES: I am *not* stubborn.

WICKETT: You are.

PICKLES: I am not.

WICKETT: YOU'VE BEEN SAYING THAT FOR TWENTY-FIVE YEARS! WHAT KIND OF WOMAN SPENDS TWENTY-FIVE YEARS SAY-ING SHE'S NOT STUBBORN?! EVERYTIME YOU DENY IT, YOU ONLY PROVE IT MORE!

PICKLES: I do deny it.

WICKETT: There. That proves it.

PICKLES: It proves nothing of the kind.

WICKETT: Look. That curtain is red. Go ahead. Deny it. This table is made of wood. Deny that, too. This is my head. No, it's not. It's a cabbage! These are my fingers. No, they are not. They're smoked herring! This is my body! No, it's not! I exist. No, I don't! You're sitting in a chair. No, you're not! No, you're not! No, you're not!

PICKLES: Captain. I'm in my nightgown.

WICKETT: So?!

PICKLES: So what do you mean by this?

WICKETT: By what?

PICKLES: I waited in my room. Do you feel a draft?

WICKETT: No…

PICKLES: Don't you try anything, Captain. If you attempt any little thing I will scream to wake the dead!

WICKETT: Come to your senses, please, Miss Pickles!!

PICKLES: My name is Mrs. Wickett. Who are you? What are you doing in my house?

WICKETT: I am Alaric, king of the Visigoths.

PICKLES: I suggest you apply a cold compress to your head, Captain. You are overheated.

PICKLES: It's been at least a minute.

WICKETT: Well, we don't know when it started.

PICKLES: I wish I were wearing my good black dress.

WICKETT: They'll put you in it, after.

PICKLES: I know, but, I'd rather avoid that, if at all possible. Strangers, dressing me. *(Pause.)* Perhaps I should go change.

WICKETT: But then…I might miss it.

PICKLES: And I wouldn't want to be alone, just then.

WICKETT: Oh, no.

PICKLES: Help me to the settee.

(They sit. She arranges herself posing for death, very stoic.)

PICKLES: How's this?

WICKETT: Very appropriate.

PICKLES: Good-bye.

WICKETT: Good-bye.

(Pause.)

PICKLES: How long has it been now?

WICKETT: A couple of minutes?

(The sharpness of her apprehension begins to dull, and is soon reduced to a sort of abstract melancholy.)

WICKETT: She had more than quadrupled her aunt's record. How long must I wait before I could in clear conscience excuse myself for bed?

PICKLES: Well, now I'm embarrassed.

WICKETT: No, no. You'll die soon enough. I mean, we all will, in time.

PICKLES: That's very true.

(Pause.)

WICKETT: And now the precipitous things we said when her death seemed imminent hovered in the air all around us. We are often cautioned against saying words of anger in haste. Why are we not likewise cautioned against saying words of love in haste?

PICKLES: Why had I taken upon myself the burden of full blame? I felt as those in heaven must feel when the realize they were better behaved on Earth than strictly necessary for admittance to Paradise.

(They sit a moment in awkward silence. They glance at each other, then away.)

WICKETT: Perhaps I shall go to bed now. *(He starts to roll his Bath chair, but stops.)*

PICKLES: Captain…

WICKETT: Yes?

PICKLES: Would you mind sitting with me? Just a while longer.

WICKETT: No, no, not at all. *(He sits. Pause.)* How do you feel? Are you cold? Are you warm?

PICKLES: Do you think we could…would you mind if we…sat in silence?

WICKETT: *(Greatly relieved.)* Oh, on the contrary, Madam, on the contrary.

PICKLES: I don't mean to be…

WICKETT: Say no more, Mrs. Wickett. We are in perfect agreement.

> *(Tableaux Vivant of Pickles and Wickett. Alexandrina and Darlington enter. They are dressed in the manner of the early Twentieth Century.)*

DARLINGTON: Excuse me.

ALEXANDRINA: Yes?

DARLINGTON: Are you by any chance a Mrs. Darlington?

ALEXANDRINA: Who is it that asks?

DARLINGTON: Mr. Darlington.

ALEXANDRINA: John?

DARLINGTON: Alexandrina.

ALEXANDRINA: How have you been?

DARLINGTON: Quite well. And yourself?

ALEXANDRINA: Very well, thank you.

DARLINGTON: Well…

ALEXANDRINA: Funny to think, isn't it, that we are still man and wife.

DARLINGTON: Ha-ha.

ALEXANDRINA: Do you ever think we made a great mistake, twenty-five years ago? Do you ever wake up in some great bed, under a gilt ceiling in some huge, drafty palace and think of what we gave up? Of what might have been?

DARLINGTON: No.

ALEXANDRINA: No? Really?

DARLINGTON: Why, do you?

ALEXANDRINA: What? Oh, no, not really…But sometimes…Sometimes I think of Aunt Amy and the Captain, still together after all those years, and I wonder what it would be like to go through life with a help-meet, a companion.

DARLINGTON: He's miserable, and she's half-mad.

ALEXANDRINA: But the story, John! To be a part of a great love story, like Aunt Amy and the Captain.

DARLINGTON: Is theirs a great love story?

ALEXANDRINA: Can you doubt it?

DARLINGTON: No, no…Um, would you care to dine with me?

ALEXANDRINA: I'd love to, but the Sultan and I sail for New York at nine.

DARLINGTON: Ah.

ALEXANDRINA: I just have time for a quick visit. Do you think they are up? The house looks dark.

DARLINGTON: Oh, they don't live here anymore. They've moved to the St. Thomas Parish house. Your Aunt suffered a mild stroke and the Captain is bed-ridden.

ALEXANDRINA: They haven't been separated, have they?

DARLINGTON: Oh, no. I wouldn't dream of separating them. They are in adjacent beds, and as neither of them can move very much, they are together constantly, all day and all night.

ALEXANDRINA: Ah...A love like that. What can one say?

DARLINGTON: What indeed.

(The lights fade on Darlington and Alexandrina, then lastly, on Pickles and Wickett.)

END OF PLAY

tries covered by the International Copyright Union (including the Dominion of Canada and the rest of the British Commonwealth), The Berne Convention, the Pan-American Copyright Convention and the Universal Copyright Convention as well as all countries with which the United States has reciprocal copyright relations. All rights, including professional/amateur stage rights, motion picture, recitation, lecturing, public reading, radio broadcasting, television, video or sound recording, all other forms of mechanical or electronic reproduction, such as CD-ROM, CD-I, information storage and retrieval systems and photocopying, and the rights of translation into foreign languages, are strictly reserved. Particular emphasis is laid upon the matter of readings, permission for which must be secured from the Author's agent in writing. Inquiries concerning rights should be addressed to: The Tantleff Office, Inc., 375 Greenwich Street, Suite 603, New York, NY 10013, Attn: Charmaine Ferenczi

Snakebit by David Marshall Grant. Copyright, 1999, by David Marshall Grant. Caution: *Snakebit*, being duly copyrighted, is subject to a royalty. The North American Stage Performance rights (other than first class rights) are controlled by Dramatists Play Service, Inc. No professional or non-professional performance of the plays (excluding first class professional performance) may be given without obtaining in advance the written permission of Dramatists Play Service Inc., and paying the requisite fee. Inquiries concerning all other rights should be addressed to Sarah Jane Leigh, C/O ICM, 40 W. 57th Street, New York, NY 10019

The Uneasy Chair by Evan Smith. Copyright, 1999, by Evan Smith. Caution: *The Uneasy Chair*, being duly copyrighted, is subject to a royalty. The North American Stage Performance rights (other than first class rights) are controlled by Dramatists Play Service, Inc. No professional or non-professional performance of the plays (excluding first class professional performance) may be given without obtaining in advance the written permission of Dramatists Play Service Inc., and paying the requisite fee. Inquiries concerning all other rights should be addressed to Sarah Jane Leigh, C/O ICM, 40 W. 57th Street, New York, NY 10019

Nobody Dies on Friday by Robert Brustein. Copyright 1998 by Robert Brustein. Reprinted by permission of the author. All inquiries should be addressed to Carolyn French, Fifi Oscard Agency, 24 West 40th Street, New York, NY 10018.